Shift Happens!
Critical Mass at 20

Edited by Chris Carlsson, LisaRuth Elliott, and Adriana Camarena

Full Enjoyment Books
2012

Full Enjoyment Books
2844 Folsom Street
San Francisco, CA 94110
USA

ISBN 978-0-926664-08-1

DESIGN AND TYPOGRAPHY: Hugh D'Andrade and Chris Carlsson
COVER ILLUSTRATION: Mona Caron
COVER DESIGN: Hugh D'Andrade
BACK COVER PHOTO: Chris Carlsson

TRANSLATORS:
Italian: Laura Fantone, Susanne Zago
Portuguese: Seth Schoen, Chris Carlsson
Spanish: Adriana Camarena, Chris Carlsson
Finnish: Eeva Luhtakallio

THANKS:
to the Seed Fund for their financial support, and to Patrick Marks, Brad Borevitz, Joe Clement, Aaron Norton, and Ozzie Zehner for their editing help.

PRINTING:
Oceanic Graphic Printing (USA), Inc.
Printed in China

Table of Contents

Dedicated to the hundreds of thousands of people who left the predictable, soul-killing routines of daily life to ride a bicycle in an "organized coincidence" somewhere on Earth during the past twenty years.

The world is different thanks to those small acts; moreover, we have tasted how much better our lives can be.

With our imaginations informed and our hearts inspired, we ride toward an uncertain—but certainly shared—future.

For full enjoyment, not full employment!

All links listed in this book, author biographies, and a gallery of images from the worldwide Critical Mass movement, can be found at http://www.sfcriticalmass.org.

Shift Happens!

Critical Mass at 20

Critical Mass San Francisco, July 2007

Ruminations of An Accidental Diplomat
by Chris Carlsson

Realizing that 20th anniversary of Critical Mass was less than a year away, late last year we put out an international call for thoughtful analyses. We wanted to go deeper and further than the 10th anniversary book had done. *Shift Happens!* is the result, and we are extremely happy with the quality and breadth of the writing we received. Several dozen contributors and a wide range of experiences across the Critical Mass world fill these pages, where the original concept is still recognizable but has also mutated and shifted over time and space in fascinating ways.

I've been very lucky. During the past twenty years I've ridden over 100 Critical Masses in San Francisco and been welcomed to similar rides in more than a dozen other cities around the world. In the first few years I wrote a number of essays that I distributed as "xerocracy" to San Francisco riders at the beginning of our rides. Many of these short essays have taken on a life of their own and have been translated and reprinted many times in many places. Perhaps because I was a frequent and visible contributor to shaping the ethics, etiquette, and culture of Critical Mass, I've been given far too much credit for being "the founder" or the guy who started it all. My identification with the movement was further solidified when I edited a global anthology called *Critical Mass: Bicycling's Defiant Celebration* to celebrate the 10th anniversary a decade ago. That book has been an important reference point for the horizontalist, anarchic, innovative and internationally self-replicating social movement often called "Critical Mass."

It has given me great joy and pride to travel the world and be welcomed as a global ambassador for Critical Mass, and by extension for the radically transformative politics of bicycling. But I want to clearly repudiate the false history that gives me personally so much credit. Critical Mass is a fantastic example of collective action that escapes the typical historical framing that credits "great men" or "brilliant individuals" as the source of social movements. Critical Mass was born 20 years ago among dozens of people in San Francisco and has reproduced itself in over 350 cities around the world thanks to the diligent efforts of countless thousands across the planet. Often just a few people start riding together and it attracts others to join, gaining momentum steadily until it bursts onto a city's political and social landscape. Moreover, the concept of riding together en masse is open-ended enough that people have adapted it in many ways during the past decades, from altering the structure of formal recreational riding to using "Critical Mass-style" rides to bring attention to a wide range of political campaigns and issues.

And as we learn from some of the essays in this new collection, mass bike rides weren't invented in 1992. They took place in different parts of the world years before we started in San Francisco, notably in Bilbao, Spain and Helsinki, Finland where our writers describe earlier rides. Chinese cities were full of bicycles as primary transportation for decades; observing traffic patterns in 1991 Shanghai from a hotel window, New Yorker George Bliss described how bicycles would pile up at the side of a flow of traffic until they reached "critical mass" and broke through to create their own traffic stream—this is where our name came from. Not far from where I lived as a boy in North Oakland, early ecological activists staged an annual mass bike ride called "Smog-Free Locomotion Day" on Berkeley's Telegraph Avenue from 1969-71. In the deep social genes of San Francisco itself, mass bike rides of 5,000-8,000 cyclists jammed muddy, rutted streets a century earlier, in 1896, to demand "Good Roads" and asphalt (unknowingly setting the stage for the next vehicle of speed, convenience, and personal freedom that soon followed: the automobile). My mother was born and raised in Copenhagen where I visited as a small boy and then again in 1977 as a young adult—the sensible organization of public streets with space dedicated to bicycle transit was self-evidently preferable to the freeways and rigid, car-dominated street grids of my California childhood.

Critical Mass was a new beginning, but it grew quite naturally from fertile ground where many different seeds were germinating. When it finally emerged 20 years ago it was a hybrid product of late capitalist urban design, long submerged anarchistic political ideas, a growing refusal to submit to the imposed necessity of embedded technologies, and an urgent reclaiming of cities as a lost public commons. The ease with which it replicated itself across the planet was eloquent testimony (and a creative rebuttal) to the creeping monoculture shaping city life everywhere.

As a self-designated and accidental Critical Mass diplomat I've had a unique view of the phenomenon as it has emerged, expanded, and sometimes, waned. In February 2012 while in Porto Alegre and Sao Paulo, Brazil, I realized I had been witnessing a kind of "life-cycle" of Critical Mass in different cities.

‧ In the summer of 2003 I visited New York for *Bikesummer* and rode in the final event, the July Critical Mass. We had a glorious ride, topping 1,000 riders for the first time there, winding through Manhattan before eventually slipping over the Queensborough Bridge to a sculpture park on the East River. The weather was perfect, the happiness and euphoria absolutely overwhelming. Just a few years earlier I had discussed the apparent demise of NYC's Critical Mass with TimesUp!'s Bill DiPaola at the convergence center in Seattle during the 1999 WTO protests. Partly inspired by our conversations, and certainly by the impressive events of those protests, Bill returned with renewed energy and along with dozens of other New Yorkers, Critical Mass began to grow. By 2003 it was taking off and that July ride was a climactic moment, galvanizing and extending that sense of hopeful optimism and growth. A year later the Republicans came to town and from then on the New York Police Department carried out an insane, violent, and illegal vendetta against Critical Mass, more or less destroying it in Manhattan (read Matthew Roth's piece for the detailed account of this).

+ In 2002 I visited Milan, Italy with copies of the first Critical Mass book which had just been published. Mona Caron and I rode in Milan's Critical Mass in June and were bowled over by the beauty of full immersion in an Italian culture that itself had warmly embraced the mass seizure of the streets on bikes. Of course the Italians understood perfectly about public space, conversation, and its political importance. Whatever long-term decline the Left was experiencing there, Critical Mass helped a whole new cohort of thoughtful, radical people find new ways of engaging with each other and their city. It was magical. At least a couple thousand riders took to the streets that night and rode a long, circuitous route through Milan's sprawling urbanity. A year later we heard about a CM that went from fountain to fountain for spontaneous dipping. In 2009, I was back in Milan again for a *Nowtopia* reading at a local bookshop. As the reading ended, I was called to the door where someone was urging me to come outside to meet the Milan Critical Mass who had come to say hello. Sure enough, 150 zany cyclists were in the street ringing their bells and giving me a rousing welcome. They put me on a bench seat on the front of a trike and gave me a ride around the block, briefly making me their Pied Piper even though I could only grin and wave, trying to disguise my embarrassment. Friends there reported that Milan's Critical Mass had shrunken considerably over the years, and most people were far less enthused about it than they had been a half decade earlier.

+ Meanwhile, in the same decade, Critical Mass in Rome, Italy had taken off, inspired by the big ride in Milan in the early 2000s. In 2008 I rode in their three-day extravaganza called *Ciemmona* (the Big CM), and once again got to enjoy that wild euphoria of multiple communities of hundreds of beautiful people joining together to seize the streets together on bikes. Rome's scene was exploding and has continued to thrive to this day (several articles in this book describe it in detail, and how Critical Mass has fed

Critical Mass Vancouver, B.C., Canada, 2008

Personal Mass
by Hugh D'Andrade

I was walking down the street one day in Berkeley in 1993 when a group of about a hundred cyclists rode by. It didn't appear to be a race of any kind, and since I recognized a few lefty organizer types I immediately knew it was a protest or rally of some sort. I called out to one of the riders that I knew. He stopped and told me this was a regular event, something that happened monthly, a political thing to raise awareness about cycling issues.

That sounded interesting, but I would have forgotten all about it if it hadn't been for a flyer I saw a few days later at the Berkeley Bowl market. At first glance, the flyer looked like a standard-issue advertisement for a punk show: a rough collage with high-contrast, xeroxed images and type pasted in at odd angles. Looking closer, I found that this flyer was not so easy to nail down.

It didn't seem to be for a band of any kind. There was an image of a kid on a bike, and bicycle imagery scattered about. But the type was all over the place, with strange rambling text that sounded like gibberish but made sense on some strange, poetic level. After studying it a moment I realized it was a flyer for the bike ride I had seen earlier: Critical Mass.

So that's how I was drawn into Critical Mass. I made a point of making it to the next ride, which met on the second Friday of every month in downtown Berkeley. There were a lot of young, scruffy anarchist types riding alongside the type of earnest, fleece-wearing Berkeley liberal you might have met at the Ecology Center. I liked that mix of people, since I felt an affinity to both tendencies while not really belonging to either.

I started riding with the Berkeley Critical Mass regularly. The energy of the rides was positive and upbeat, and at the start of each ride there was a trippy, energetic guy who would leap up onto one of the trash bins and and speak funny, random poetry to the crowd while constantly spinning and flailing about, always a step away from tripping over himself. A lot of what this guy said didn't really make sense—in fact, I thought he actually might be a little crazy—but he had an infectious energy that set things off on a great note and got the crowd going. (I also noticed that he never used any boring leftist rhetoric. How refreshing! Whatever he was saying, he meant it.)

Later I learned that this person was Jason Meggs, a local activist, permanent UC student and professional troublemaker. It was his flyer that I had found so intriguing. From Jason I learned that the idea for Critical Mass had originated in San Francisco, that their ride was much bigger, and that it took place on the last Friday of each month.

At that time I rarely came to the city. As a non-driver, San Francisco seemed a long way from the comforts of the East Bay, where cycling was easy and comfortable on traffic-calmed, tree-lined streets. On the few occasions when I had tried to bike in the city I had been terrified. The only place to ride was in the narrow gap between parked cars and moving cars, trucks and buses—the so-called "door zone" where car doors swung unpredictably into your path—an easy way to die on San Francisco's narrow, crowded and busy streets. Moreover, motorists and bus drivers made no secret of their hostility toward cyclists: if you were on a bike, you were a nuisance and were in the wrong place.

So I wasn't in a hurry to ride in the San Francisco Critical Mass. But I did come into the city—on the BART train, not by bike—on occasion to visit the offices of *Processed World*, a radical magazine that had run a few of my political cartoons. They were located in downtown San Francisco, in an old office building on Market Street where all the offices appeared straight out of a Dashiel Hammet novel: marble hallways, old-fashioned furnishings, mysterious doorways to offices that no one ever seemed to use.

Processed World was a collective, but as far as I could tell the two main participants were Chris Carlsson and his business partner, Jim Swanson. Chris organized the meetings, made sure stuff ran on time, and Jim was the solid, entertainingly cranky former bike messenger who brooked no nonsense and whose brilliant illustrations had gotten me interested in their magazine in the first place.

Chris was already a famous activist, and it was no secret why. He was almost manically friendly and outgoing, constantly talking and making new connections with everyone. He had the gift of taking ideas that were utopian and thus insane to many people and making them enticing, even reasonable-sounding. He managed to make subversive ideas irresistible. I was forever amazed by his ability to turn tepid liberals into raving revolutionaries (at least as long as they were in the same room with him—I noticed that the spell often lasted only so long as Chris was immediately present).

Their typesetting business was where the magazine happened, and their crowded, smoke-filled office functioned as a kind of hub for all sorts of radical projects and initiatives. So I wasn't really surprised when I learned that Chris and Jim and some other friends had hatched the idea for Critical Mass right there just about a year earlier. It seemed serendipitous.

When I rode the San Francisco Critical Mass for the first time, some time in 1993, I was amazed at how different it was from the Berkeley ride. In Berkeley we were a hundred, maybe two hundred riders at most. But in San Francisco, the ride was hundreds of riders that stretched for blocks through downtown, more than you could count, and it was growing every month. As upbeat as I felt the Berkeley Critical Mass was, this was a vastly more energetic and exhilarating experience.

It's hard to describe what a difference Critical Mass made, how dramatically it transformed your experience of the city streets at that time. You felt it in your body the first time you poured out into the busy streets surrounded by hundreds of other cyclists, all of them yelling, singing, cheering and ringing their bells, voices echoing off the walls of the tall buildings. The sound was deafening, and the pleasure was infectious. Motorists and passers by seemed stunned, curious rather than hostile, happy for once to offer us the right of way.

Where before we darted about threatened, isolated, insecure, at risk for our lives—suddenly we felt safe. We had the space and the time to ride at a leisurely stroll, talk to people, feel the change of sunlight and shadow on our faces as we moved through the canyons of high rises. We began to see the city in a whole new light, as a place to socialize, meet people, to explore and experience spatially.

Speaking of spatial experiences, the hills of San Francisco are quite different, as it turns out, when you ride them with a group of other cyclists. For one thing, hills miraculously are easier to climb when you're in a group. Maybe it's the encouragement of the other riders, or the fact that you can weave a bit without worrying about getting sideswiped by a car, but a hill that you would otherwise avoid at all costs on a bike will suddenly seem fun, a challenging adventure. And of course, once you get to the top you can turn around, admire the sea of people surrounding you on both sides, and then ready yourself for the downhill journey. Why else would anyone live in a city with this many hills?

I became a regular on both the San Francisco and Berkeley Critical Mass rides each month. I loved that feeling of transformation, the experience of using my own energy in collaboration with others to make such a dramatic and, to my way of thinking, positive change. It was a temporary change, to be sure, but it was real, and we accomplished it ourselves. As the flyers that were circulated before each ride pointed out, there was "no one in charge" on Critical Mass. No organizing committee, no corporate sponsors, no government entities or process from the city. It was our event, comprised of the people who showed up and no one else. We didn't require permission, and we weren't waiting for someone else to organize our lives.

In our present era of flash mobs and spontaneous collaborations among strangers, inspired and organized by online communities, the novelty of this spirit of cooperation might not be immediately apparent. But it really did feel different from everyday life, and also from the kind of political and social activities of the time. In the early '90s, every rally or event was organized in top down fashion by one group or another, each with its own agenda and each viewing the mass of people who showed up as more or less passive participants in a pre-planned event.

Critical Mass was different. When passersby or newbie participants would ask, "Who's in charge?" we would respond by saying, "You are!" And even though our critics in the media and the police seemed to think this was a clever subterfuge, it really was a successfully decentralized, uncontrolled event.

In part, this was accomplished by participants constantly insisting on this being the case, making sure everyone got the memo that this was an open event without official sponsorship. But it's worth remembering that a large factor was the elegant, simple concept of having a regular, recurring time and place to start. This meant that no one had to do *anything* to make Critical Mass happen. If there were no posters or flyers or organizing in advance, it still happened anyway, every month, like clockwork. Critical Mass organizes itself, and this is one reason why it has lasted so long and why it has spread so quickly and easily around the world.

It was true that there was no one in charge of Critical Mass. But that isn't to say there weren't people who contributed time and energy to making it great. Chris and Jim and others, among them Joel Pomerantz, Beth Verdekal, and myself, produced flyers and stickers that we circulated in the crowd before the ride. We called this "xerocracy," the idea that anyone could make a flyer with a plan or an idea or a route to take.

Our group of serious Critical Mass enthusiasts—a term I always used in place of activists—fluctuated over the years but probably could have expanded to include a hundred or so people. From 1992 to about 2007 people met every month before Critical Mass at the *Processed World* office, where we started the party early with gin & tonics and bounced ideas about the ride off each other. We called it the "radical media clubhouse," and it was a great way to build community *inside* of a larger community.

I don't think Critical Mass would have had the character of joyous rebelliousness, that sense of being a hybrid that was part social party and part subversive political rally, if it hadn't been for the brilliant self-publishing that was produced in the early years, most particularly by Chris and Jim. Each month there would be a flyer with a beautiful illustration by Jim along with a lengthy and insightful essay by Chris that put everything into context and, for many of us, voiced concerns that we never heard expressed elsewhere.

What I loved about those flyers was how quickly they departed from the obvious (and important) questions of traffic priorities that Critical Mass raised to the basic problems that our social movements face as they go about the business of changing the world. How do we deal with angry, divisive people in our ranks? How do we create a truly democratic culture that encourages passionate discussion without degenerating into hateful attacks or repetitive sloganeering? How do we move from temporary shifts in our means of transportation to more permanent changes in the way we live our lives? And exactly what kind of lives do we want to live anyway? If we could somehow create the city of our dreams, what would it look like?

From one of Chris's flyers:

> *Many of us attracted to radical politics are very impatient—with the larger society, but also with ourselves and especially with people who don't see how much better life could be if our radical visions were pursued. This impatience with the slow development of organic human communities, communities that might really be able to construct a different logic to our daily lives, often leads to childish and simplistic confrontational stances. These postures are much more about reassuring ourselves that we are truly radical and willing to face danger than they are about contesting the organization of modern life.*

> *If radical bicyclists are so hot to go on freeways, instead of blocking traffic lanes why not wait for rush hour gridlock and then overwhelm the already stopped cars with dozens or hundreds of bicycles streaming through the traffic, departing the freeway at the next exit after a convincing demonstration of the ease, superiority and pleasure of bicycling? Imagine the surprise and support one might generate if such an intervention was carried out with courtesy and friendliness?*

> *It is a terribly rash assumption that someone stuck in their car is necessarily a big supporter of the status quo. Consider instead the complexities of human choices and constraints and try to create openings in people's minds, rather than assuming that someone who hasn't adopted your choices about what to buy, how to get around, and lifestyles in general is your conscious enemy and deserves your moral condemnation, rage, or self-righteous taunting. It's not easy to proceed politically when we take seriously how difficult, deep and personal are the changes we seek. But pleasure, passion, and patience can bring real progress. Remember, the Americans you scorn today must be your allies tomorrow if you are serious about changing life!*

At the time, I was working a boring desk job at a publishing company. The work that Chris and Jim were doing inspired me to teach myself what was then called "desktop publishing," the novel use of computers to set type and put images and text together. When the boss wasn't around I would use the company machines to put flyers together using the then cutting-edge software called "Quark," and on the second and last Friday of each month I commandeered the copy machine in the service of our monthly rolling parties.

Here's one I produced on company time that I still appreciate for its simplicity and economy of language:

> **Critical Mass isn't BLOCKING traffic—We ARE Traffic!!!**
>
> *At the end of every workday, thousands of people pour into the streets, in what has become a central ritual of life in the late twentieth century -- the daily commute.*
>
> *For most people, however, getting off work is not cause for celebration, or even relief. The ride home promises frustrating gridlock, disgusting air, and for us bicyclists, **constant** threats to our safety and well-being.*
>
> *But one day a month, the ritual is transformed. Hundreds of us get together and ride through the streets on bicycles, providing motorists, as well as ourselves, with a vision of how things could be different.*
>
> *We know that you aren't responsible for the organization of our cities around motorized traffic, and if we've contributed to your delay, **WE'RE SORRY!** But maybe you can take this opportunity to reflect on what a world without cars would be like. Or better yet, join us next time!*

In addition to the rabble-rousing of the xerocracy's text and imagery, there was the awesome civic engagement of the routes that were produced each month. Nowadays, the San Francisco Critical Mass is a thoroughly unplanned affair, and the route is decided on the fly by whoever finds themselves at the front of the ride (usually loud, aggressive young men). But in the early '90s, the flyers produced by our loosely affiliated group included "Suggested Routes" that, though not always followed to the letter, took Critical Mass off the beaten path to a new destination each time. We'd explore a different part of the city and end in a park where we relaxed, drank, and smoked. I remember ending several times in Dolores Park, but we also made visits to Twin Peaks, the Palace of Fine Arts, Sutro Heights, or crossed the Golden Gate Bridge to end in Sausalito. Often the text of the flyer drew from Chris's encyclopedic knowledge of San Francisco to offer asides on the history of the particular location.

By 1994, we had more than just a local success story on our hands. Sure, our little ride was a big deal, and the newspapers and TV stations covered it on a regular basis (usually getting the details wrong or painting us as nefarious ne'er-do-wells). But something amazing was happening *out there*, beyond the insular boundaries of the Bay Area. Critical Mass was spreading.

Of course it had spread to Berkeley right away. But very soon after that it seemed to be everywhere: Santa Cruz, San Diego, Boston… Then it was overseas, in London, Paris, Barcelona, Melbourne, Sydney. It seemed that every time I stopped into Chris and Jim's office on Market Street there was a new fax—yes, faxes were still common—or an example of that brand new (to me) phenomenon of email, from someone in another city on the other side of the world. And they all wanted to know the same things: How did it start? How did you deal with the cops? With angry motorists? With business-as-usual activists?

It was obvious that what we needed was a sort of "how to" manual to share the ideas and methods we had accumulated: xerocracy, "corking" (our method of holding traffic back at intersections), "no one in charge," etc. I volunteered along with our friend Beth Verdekal to put this together, and I found a local printer who was willing to produce hundreds of them for cheap. For many years they were shipped out to every person anywhere who wrote the *Processed World* office looking for information about Critical Mass. (It's amusing to me now to think how paper-centric we were, even as the Internet blew up around us. Jim Dyer put together a website at criticalmass.org, and this seemed like a *big* undertaking to me—a *whole website!*)

But perhaps all that xerocracy was always a flaw as well as a strength. Though we pushed this idea of xerocratic communication and invited others to join us in self-publishing, in practice this rarely happened. It may be easy to write something up, make photocopies, and pass them out to strangers, but most people it seems don't have the skills or the inclination to do it. (And sometimes I think that the slickness of our production set the bar a bit too high.)

Over the years, those of us creating stuff for Critical Mass tired of the hard work of putting these flyers and newsletters together. Chris and Jim turned their focus towards Shaping San Francisco, an interactive history project. I got involved with my own new career as an illustrator. Others from that early crew of enthusiasts moved on to new vistas—or had gotten themselves paid positions in the burgeoning field of bicycle activism and transportation advocacy. In any case, fewer and fewer flyers were produced, and we stopped transmitting our version of what Critical Mass is about.

There were a few years, from about 1994 to 1997, where our little crew almost entirely disengaged with the mainstream of Critical Mass. Instead of meeting with the main ride at Justin Herman Plaza at the foot of Market, we would meet instead at South Park, a smaller, more intimate park in the South of Market neighborhood. After talking and drinking for an hour or so we'd finally venture out in what we called a "mini-mass"—a group of about a hundred of us, so small that we didn't register on the police radar.

Our loose group dispersed a bit further when Chris and Jim dissolved their business partnership in 2005 and the clubhouse became less visited and later stopped existing at all.

***

One of the points that we pushed hard with those early flyers we circulated was the idea that Critical Mass was celebratory in nature, and not, as the media constantly informed the public, a deliberate attempt to punish motorists and make their lives difficult. This certainly wasn't why we rode, and we believed most others on Critical Mass shared our desire to be part of something positive.

But there had always been a battle around that, in part because the media's narrative of Critical Mass as an antagonistic event could become a self-fulfilling prophecy, leading people attracted to conflict to show up at an event which they had been told was inherently about conflict. But it's also true that our country's political culture is such that dualistic thinking is the obvious assumption for many people. So whether we wanted our ride to be "pro-public," and not "anti-motorist," those elements were there. We had always jokingly called this tendency the "Testosterone Brigade," since so much of that bad energy seemed to be hormonal in nature and not the result of deep thinking or any political theory as such.

Well, one result of the disengagement of our group of founders and early enthusiasts was that these elements within Critical Mass that we had successfully battled in years past came back, rooting themselves firmly within the culture of Critical Mass. We would see or hear of people behaving badly at Critical Mass, apparently looking for fights, with small groups stopping to jeer at the rare occasional irate motorist. These folks never got the memo—the one where everyone agreed that this type of activity was self-defeating and anti-social.

If things seemed to get particularly bad, we would make a few hundred copies of a standard flyer we made for just this purpose. It very clearly lists a series of "Do's and Don'ts" for Critical Mass. It did seem to be effective.

One part of this process I found disturbing was the fact that I often heard second- or third-hand reports of people who found our flyers annoying, and interpreted them as a kind of authoritarianism. I found that pretty objectionable, and looked for ways to have a dialog with anyone who disagreed with me. But those elements, such as they were, simply weren't interested in any dialog or engagement.

In 2009, Chris and I and a few others finally began using 21st century tools to engage the public. In this age of social media and Internet saturation, there are so many efficient ways to get ideas to the public that don't involve wasting paper! So we started a blog that would concern itself with Critical Mass and bike culture generally, as a way of putting our ideas out there. It might also provide a forum for people with views different from our own to get involved, which would be difficult but might be useful.

We decided after some debate to call it "SF Critical Mass" and to park it at sfcriticalmass.org. We also started a Facebook page and a Twitter account under that name. We realized we ran a risk of being perceived as somehow being the "official" voice of Critical Mass, but we decided the value of being easy to find outweighed that, and we prominently featured text that said these forums were entirely "unofficial," while encouraging others to start their own pages. (At present there are several Facebook pages such as criticalmassSF, etc., which is as it should be!)

We amassed thousands of followers on Facebook and Twitter, which makes getting a message out vastly easier. And the blog has been successful in contributing to the ongoing dialog around Critical Mass and local transportation politics. Many times we have been able to influence the public debate on issues we ordinarily would not be able to affect. For instance, when local media began obsessively hyping a fake news story that the police were planning a crackdown on Critical Mass, we were able to deflate that narrative with some simple logic that got picked up by other news sources. More recently we had some pickup on a piece I wrote debunking hype around the danger to pedestrians posed by cyclists, a subject brought up by the tragic death of a pedestrian due to an apparently negligent cyclist. I argued that this accident is statistically insignificant from a traffic planning perspective, as this exceedingly rare event is dwarfed by the dozens of pedestrian deaths caused by negligent motorists in the Bay Area each year.

I also spent a lot of time between 2009 and 2011 arguing with commenters on our blog about Critical Mass. On the whole, I found people to be pretty open to my arguments, even when they didn't agree with me. And I often learned stuff I would never have thought about otherwise.

Case in point: one commenter wrote to complain about the habit on Critical Mass of riding, parade-style, right through red lights (a common criticism). He said that in San Jose there was a group ride called the Bike Party that stopped for red lights, and that we should do the same.

I brought a group of cyclists and Critical Mass enthusiasts down to San Jose to check it out. Though the San Jose ride had been going for more than a year, no one I knew had ridden on it, though by all reports their ride was huge and really fun. We were eager to check it out.

The San Jose Bike Party reminded me of how Critical Mass was in the early days. Though they had an official organizing committee and stopped for red lights (easy to do when the streets are wide and the blocks a mile long), their ride had a really well-designed route, and it was clear that the people involved really cared about their ride and were committed to the project of building community through cycling. Certainly the vibe was overwhelmingly positive and celebratory.

A while later someone asked me what I thought about a Bike Party in San Francisco. I thought it was a great idea, and said so, and several other Critical Massers agreed with me. There's room for all kinds of social movements, and some will function without organizers, as Critical Mass does, and some will function with organizers and other elements that work better for those people. I used a silly slogan for this approach: "Different spokes for different folks."

The San Francisco Bike Party began in early 2011, and I've been a supporter and collaborator with them. It's been interesting to see how having a core of organizers on a ride really does make a difference. SFBP remains much, much smaller than Critical Mass—perhaps two or three hundred people, as opposed to 1000-2000—but you never see SFBP riders getting involved in boring fights with motorists, or angering bus riders by circling pointlessly in intersections.

Sometimes I think that the insistence on not having an organizing committee for Critical Mass was not entirely positive. It was the right thing to do—it kept our ride from being taken down by officials who certainly would have pinned a lawsuit on someone if they could have found a victim, for one thing. And it also created a space where anyone could say whatever they wanted, a genuine public space not controlled or policed by any entity whatsoever. But it also hurt us by depriving us of structure and communication.

What it also did was make it so that there was no institutional memory for our ride, no way to continue to transmit values and culture from one generation to another. When our group of active non-organizers pulled away, no one stepped up to fill our shoes, because we had never asked anyone to. Maybe we thought that by demonstrating what we considered good civic engagement—creating these flyers, spreading this new model to other cities, starting a digital dialog—that others would use the space that we opened up for their own purposes. Sometimes they did, but mostly they chose not to, and this led Critical Mass to become sort of like an abandoned garden—wild and woolly, with wonderful elements, but with some annoying weeds and some waste products that are unhealthy.

* * *

One thing that many critics of Critical Mass never hear is how it has changed lives for the better. I am one such person.

My life improved immeasurably as a result of Critical Mass. I wasn't just drawn into Critical Mass. I was drawn into a whole network, a positive life-style based around bicycling with other likeminded people that made me healthier and stronger. I pedaled all over San Francisco in the '90s, became intimately connected to its many secret routes and treasures and finally realized I was in love with it. I moved here from the East Bay in 1997 and I have never looked back. That same year I started a book group with some Critical Mass friends using the "Critical Mass principle"—one regular day each month and a regular meeting place, so that it organizes itself—and we have been meeting monthly ever since. I have made literally hundreds of friends I would never have otherwise known: cyclists and activists, artists and subversives, city planners and brilliant, interesting people I've stayed close to for twenty years. And I've been involved in dozens of projects—political, artistic, and social—which originated in Critical Mass or took those communities as a building block.

I'm only one person! Imagine the hundreds, thousands of others for whom similar things are true. These social bonds are personal and sometimes invisible, but they are not trivial. They have real, enduring value. They are the stuff from which a good life, and a good society, are built!

I expect Critical Mass to be here twenty years from now, thanks to its elegant design, which requires no intervention whatsoever to continue on the last Friday of each month, forever. I personally am done contributing to this movement. I am tired of the same arguments, the same debates. But I hope others come along who see it for what it is: a truly open, ongoing social experiment to which anyone is free to contribute. There are so few of these spaces in existence! But these types of movements have always been around, and they are always moving and changing. One day, the world will be full of social movements made up of autonomous, self-organizing people that function without top-down decision making, and with the full engagement of all of their members. That is a future to which we can be proud of contributing.

The Great European Bike Love Link

By Giuso Ciclocuoco

My name is Giuso, I am 36 years old and I currently live in Paris, France, home of the *Velorution*. I am originally from Rome, the capital of Italy, and probably one of Europe's craziest Critical Mass cities. I have been a part of European bike movements now for almost ten years, and I have witnessed some interesting examples of "nowtopia" that I am proud to share.

Since my first participation in the Critical Mass movement, I saw the great potential hidden beneath the practices of self-organization, do-it-yourself, and most of all, free and non-commercial links between fellow people around the globe. This was to become my personal motivation throughout all these years: share love and knowledge, cook food for enormous numbers of cyclists, and most of all, recycle bikes.

When we started the Critical Mass movement in Rome in 2002, all of us were looking for something that could fuel and enhance our monthly gathering. At that time, most of the riders in Rome didn't have much knowledge of bikes, and only a few really knew how to fix their two-wheeled beauties (in Italian, bicycle is a female noun, *la bicicletta*). But the energy and typical Italian hot blood made us come out of the dark, and become one of the most creative groups of cyclists on the old continent.

After some months of Critical Mass happenings, we saw more cyclists coming more often. Still we thought it could be better organized, and that we needed powerful and creative tools to ensure that Critical Mass would grow steadily and create an alternative bike culture in Rome. After one year of Critical Mass, the collective decided to organize a big anniversary party that would rock our majestic city. We thought about it for weeks, and came up with an idea: we would celebrate the death of the car. Some artists made a cardboard car, and we held a procession in the city, applauded by pedestrians and other cyclists. The party finished with burning the car, while cyclists were dancing and cheering the new evolution of city streets. Of course, this was just a start in our creative strategy.

We witnessed more people than ever at that CM, xerocracy was flourishing, everyone was invited, and in the end, more than 300 people showed up. For us, it was a real triumph (the Roman Critical Mass never had more than 100 people before that). And so the collective gathered once more, after some months of varying numbers participating in the rides. We thought about what we would do with our next CM anniversary. Some of us came up with an idea: let's organize a huge ride. We decided to call it the Interplanetary Critical Mass (*Critical Mass Interplanetaria*). We called everyone around the world to come and give us a hand in creating positive mayhem in the streets of Rome. Our anniversary was in May and we decided it would be three days of Critical Mass rides, open air workshops, talks, movies about bikes, etc., all self-organized and with a very low budget. The social center I was working with helped by providing shelter for strangers coming to town for the event. I personally created the first interplanetary logo poster, and helped organize the event, coordinating the campsite with other people.

We never would have imagined it, but it turned out that more than a thousand people came that first year of *Ciemmona* (this is Roman slang for "Big CM"). For us, it was a real revolution. Romans were startled! During three days, we rode, we sang, we cheered one another, we cried tears of joy, we made friends with people from Spain, France, U.S., England—some of whom still show up every last weekend of May to enjoy Rome at its best. Since then, years have passed, and the Interplanetary CM has only gotten bigger and bigger. Last year, we were seven thousand or so. Two dozen cyclists double-checked the unbelievable data! I remember organizing the Friday night dinner at the social center. We cooked meals for more than a thousand people. It gives you goose bumps when hundreds of smiling faces thank you for the pasta and the chocolate mousse—it was overwhelming.

The most interesting part of this crazy huge CM gathering was the aftermath. After the party was over, standing on the beach 26 km south of Rome all together in peace and bike harmony, we were having a last chat with our friends from France and Spain. The people of Madrid were having the same problems with traffic, and especially with their stubborn and narrow-minded politicians. The French had more luck with politics, since they had big bike lobbies working for them, but the idea of mass participation in such an event made it clear to them, this idea had to be brought to France too.

In 2007 the Spanish organized *La Criticona*, the "Big Critical," in Madrid, where something like 2,000 people participated. Most of us from Rome went, to make our friendship grow. It was awesome, to see an idea emerge like that, everywhere, in so many different colorful variations. We had created Bike Love International Unlimited, and the results were more visible everyday. After the huge masses, I know of people from all over Europe staying in contact, writing letters, falling in love, sharing knowledge, starting up similar experiences, making babies, and even relocating themselves to be closer to each other.

The French *Velorution* (a word game, it is an anagram of revolution, and *velo* means bicycle in French,) was something that also needed a little boosting. As you might know, Paris has a great bike culture, and bike lanes are growing everywhere, but less than 100 people were riding together monthly. So in May 2009, in Rome for the *Ciemmona*, some Parisians told me we could and should do this in Paris, too. I thought it was a great idea. (Criminal minds always look for new activities!)

So in July 2010, we did it. We invited everyone to Paris, and held a four-day experience that was really marvelous and unexpected even for Parisians. Bike games, bike jousts, movie shows in an artistic squat, big masses around the Eiffel Tower, you name it, we were doing it. More than a thousand people showed up, and for the *Velorution*, that is quite impressive! The *Velorution* is somewhat more militant than other Critical Masses, because *Velorution*, according to French laws, must be an association. It lobbies and participates in talks with the Mayor's office. Asking to take the streets is compulsory, and so the *Velorution Universelle* had official authorization. This may seem awkward, but this is France, with its laws and its social liberties. If you ask for something, you will eventually get it. And that's precisely what we did. We asked for the right to occupy the streets. We asked for, and received, permission for a random route, with no predetermination of the starting and ending points. This is something of a rarity in France. The police officers were amazed and confused, but let us do it without interfering. Some police officers on bikes came with us, and were more than happy to.

Since then *Velorution* has grown bigger and stronger, we started a bike workshop in Bastille Square, and we are lobbying against the fake public bike system called *Velib'*. This may seem strange, but the truth is *Velib'* is a greenwashing operation by this huge multinational corporation called J.C. Decaux. In order to provide "public" bikes to everyone, they made an agreement with the Parisian administration. All of the advertisement spaces in Paris now belongs to them. Plus, the system is very hierarchical, with workers being overused, mechanics poorly paid, while the corporation itself makes enormous profits. We would like to implement a truly public system, with unemployed people getting decent salaries and running communal bike workshops, and get back the space that Decaux invasively occupies with ads of fast cars, naked girls, and all sorts of useless commodities. Not a world we want to live in, for sure.

But let's get back to our ideas, and our creative visions.

What all these huge Critical Masses around Europe made clear to me was that we had something in common, all of us, and that we had to share experiences, in order to create a European culture of Bike Utopia. And that's precisely my goal now. My involvement in Critical Mass led me to accept an even bigger challenge: The construction of community bike workshops.

While in Rome from 2003 to 2008, I participated in the creation of a series of bike workshops. The one I was most involved with was the Don Chisciotte (Don Quixote) bike workshop in the *ExSnia* social center, a rundown warehouse that was occupied and self-organized since 1995 in the eastern suburb of Pigneto, Rome. There, among the most crazy, colorful, utopian people I have met in my life, we started the most creative DIY bike workshop ever. We were all following Piero, this handsome, tall guy with an art degree, in love with mechanics and grease. At that time, I was more of a cook than a mechanic. Every time CM wanted to end somewhere cozy and familiar, *ExSnia* and the kitchen I managed offered decent meals, music, and a bit of human warmth for about 2.5 euros a meal—an offer almost no one ever refused. And there my surname *Ciclocuoco* was born: the bike cook, the guy who knows nothing about mechanics, but sure knows how to fill bellies for 500 people in a single night.

One day, Piero left, along with the Cyclown Circus (and if you don't know who they are, just google them, you'll love the idea). So the collective managing the workshop started questioning how to increase our mechanical knowledge. That's when I became more involved in grease, spanners, and welding equipment than in tomato sauce or fresh-made pasta. Hey, everyone's gotta follow their path, right?

The interesting thing I noticed in bike workshops is that it was fun, and pretty easy too—that is, if you didn't leave your bike under pouring rain for a year or so! Ideas were growing in my head. What if we could become something important for urban cyclists, actually representing a viable and decent alternative economy? By that, I was thinking about salaries, self-organized co-op bike workshops where anyone interested could become a bike mechanic—not only to repair bikes, but most importantly, to teach others how to do it by themselves. It is, after all, a pretty hard task. Every day, dozens of people came to our workshop with these typical self indulgent phrases: "Oh, but I can't do these things on my own," or "I'm really terrible with tools," and the best one, "How about you do it and next time I'll try?"

ExSnia was like a mom to me, a huge collective space. Energies were dense; you really don't mix utopia with pragmatism—but you sure can make them co-exist in peace! Along with other friends at *ExSnia*, we wanted to gather people from a whole bunch of European bike workshops during the Interplanetary CM in May 2006. For months, we flooded mailing lists both in and outside of Europe to organize the first European Forum of Self-Organized Bike Workshops. We collected addresses and contacts of more than 70 bike workshops around Europe, and 18 came to participate. The idea was alive, the friendship and brotherhood between the people of Madrid's CM, of France's *Velorution*, of Italy's autonomous movements, becoming a reality. And even though this forum didn't quite achieve what we expected, it nonetheless helped us gather valuable information, and share thoughts, ideas, and concepts with all the others. A precious three days I'll never forget...

In France in 2006, there were something like ten bike workshops—three came to participate, from Toulouse, Lille, and Marseille. Today in France, there are 50 self-organized workshops. Some are co-ops, some are associations, some are in squats. They have around 30,000 participants each year, and have created 35 full-time, self-organized jobs, and with more than minimal wages.

In Spain, I have seen bike workshops spring literally out of the ground! Almost every suburb of Madrid has a workshop, there are three in Barcelona, one in almost each major Spanish city. To open one, I personally went to Bilbao in Spain, riding a tall bike loaded with tools. Unfortunately, it was evicted six months later. So much for that effort!

In Italy too, bike workshops are alive and kicking, and if you ever travel there, make sure you check where the workshops are. You'll do yourself a huge favor, believe me.

As for me, I left Rome in search of some room to let my experience grow, and here in Paris I started a bike workshop with some friends called *cycloficine* (the bike pharmacy, an infection from Italian bike culture). We provide support to those *banlieues* (suburbs) you probably saw burning some years ago. We donate bikes, sell some in public auctions, and provide information on self-repair. We play games with kids, too, especially during hot summer weekends (because these kids do not have the luxury of choosing a vacation).

Lately, the French Foundation for Social Justice gave us funds to start a program of mechanical education for teenagers and young unemployed people. The idea is to kickstart a bike workshop in every district of Paris and its outer suburbs, and provide citizens with mechanical expertise, donated by people who really know their stuff and who enjoy sharing their pleasure and their knowledge with their fellow neighbours.

We have a phrase in the *cyclofficine*, and I leave you with it:

> give me a bike, i'll pedal some time,
> teach me to fix it, i'll never stop riding.

Peace, love, and grease on your hands people. Stay marvelous, the world needs you.

Links

http://www.ciclofficinepopolari.it/ — the Italian bike workshops
http://www.heureux-cyclage.org/ — the French ones
http://cyclocoop.org/ — the bike workshops I work in currently.

Paris, France

PHOTO BY PETER MEITZLER

We ARE Traffic

Daniel S. Libman

The power of the Chicago Critical Mass only becomes apparent once the ride is over. While it's happening it's all energy—electric and social and inclusive. People are kind to one another the way they are on vacation. Even most of the motorists seem to be at least experiencing the ride as novel, if not fun. "What's the cause?" a woman in a Volvo shouts out her window on a recent ride. "Friday!" I answer. She makes an incredulous face. "Seriously," she calls out, "Are you raising awareness for something?"

I've biked too far past her to continue the conversation, and my answer wouldn't have satisfied anyway. "Yes," I should have said, "We are raising awareness. For *something*."

But for what? It's too glib to assert that the answer is different for every rider, that each Critical Mass seems to have its own unspoken theme which only becomes apparent in hindsight. And it's too easy to solder our ride to a catchphrase about recycling or about renewable energy or—shudder—another debate about the righteousness of bicycles versus cars. Is it too obvious to suggest that when that woman leaned out of her car to have a conversation with guy on a bicycle—that *might* have been the whole point? Could it be just to experience the pure joy of taking to the streets to do nothing more radical than wishing passersby a "Happy Friday?"

But there is something subversive going on underneath the rolling party. It *is* a radical notion that the bicycles get to decide how quickly or slowly the traffic moves. When I try to explain the appeal of a Critical Mass ride I invariably begin with its polar opposite: me alone on my bike in the corn fields. I live in a rural part of Illinois and have to drive two hours just to get to the starting point of the Chicago rides. Aware as I am of the absurdity in this, there is simply nothing I can do about it. I work 90 miles west of Chicago and if I want to participate I have to get there. I can't be a one man Critical Mass in my farming community—that would be me just going out for a bike ride, and I do this with mind-numbing regularity as it is. I bike alone for miles and miles and hours and hours, long loops around the cooling towers of the Byron Nuclear power plant, from the Casey's General Store gas station in Oregon to the Casey's in Polo to the Casey's in Stillman Valley, my route a rural *via doloraso* on wheels.

And yet I don't think that Critical Mass should be only an urban movement. We need riders in the corn as much as we need them anywhere. But the terms are different. Alone, I'm just the guy in *that outfit*, the guy with the blinking lights on his jersey, tolerated if I'm lucky by the ag kids in their outfits: Carhartt overalls and ball caps with seed company logos. Very rarely am I afforded my lawful three foot leeway. If cars think about me at all after passing by, it's only to glance once in the rearview mirror to see if I'm still upright, checking to be sure they haven't committed a moving violation.

Critical Mass on the other hand, gives motorists an opportunity to think more about the guy on the bicycle. What we're really doing, regardless of how much fun we're having, is creating moments (long moments, perhaps) for drivers to think about the other. Little children love stuffed animals because the teddy bear they hold are cuddly, loveable versions of something which terrifies them. Critical Mass is the raging grizzly version of that defenseless dude on the bicycle you cut off on your way to work this morning. It only works if we do it together, which is why I make the drive to get there.

In Chicago our rides are imbued with an almost congenital sense of civic pride. Most of us enjoy our city—for me this is where I was born. (I moved into the farmlands reluctantly, with a bit of literal, not metaphorical, kicking and screaming. Mostly screaming.) And though we Chicagoans may have trouble with certain political structures—each rider his or her own private bugaboo—it still gladdens the heart to be biking past the Chagall mosaic, the Picasso, the Bean, historic neighborhoods like Pilsen and Bucktown, kinetic corridors like Michigan Avenue and Rush Street—the audacious landmarks of Chicago.

I can only imagine what it felt like 20 years ago. In 2012 there is no sense of danger in the enterprise. Indeed, several dozen of the hundreds (thousands?) who turn up to ride are uniformed police officers who pedal beside us, and who by proximity become part of the Critical Mass, regardless of their costuming for the evening. And the cars, lined up not going anywhere, they are also part of the Critical Mass for a night. These drivers didn't ask for it, but it is happening, and each one of them can choose to be charmed or angry or simply bemused—no response is going to get their cars moving one second sooner. Sometimes it feels—regardless of the fun we on our bicycles are having—that the Critical Mass is really for them, for the drivers. We ask: Can you rise to the challenge of equanimity? Can you stand to lose control, even for an hour? Will you allow yourself to be subsumed enough by what's happening around you to high-five the bicyclists going by, to smile and wave back, or are you going to keep your windows rolled up and simmer?

One night we massed up doing loops around the small cement island where Rush Street angles to meet Wabash, just between Delaware and Chestnut (known locally as the Viagra Triangle). We had big numbers that night and soon clogged the roads, bringing everything to a standstill—restaurant and club patrons filled windows waving, choruses of "Happy Friday" briefly replaced the sounds of motors and honking. A guy pedaling a sort of flatbed truck, on which a woman in a Hawaiian shirt plinked at a ukulele, parked himself in the intersection. The bars seemed to empty and the patrons joined with us for a impromptu Don Ho tribute. More than anything you want *everyone* to be having fun, bicyclists and the bar patrons and the motorists too. Your heart goes out to the motorists who become angered, who refuse to let Critical Mass work on them. But one frustrated guy sitting on the hood of his SUV had resorted to shouting.

"All you're doing is blocking traffic!"

A woman beside me on an old, blue Schwinn looked at him long enough to sweetly deliver the perfect answer. "We're not blocking traffic. We *are* traffic."

My favorite rides are the ones that end up by Buckingham Fountain. The bikes circle triumphantly, the clipped-in riders de-clip and drag their shoes on the new cobblestones, their cleats throwing sparks which shoot like geysers from their soles. You can stay back with the evening tourists and just watch the display, amazed at the sight like it's a giant, living Fourth of July pinwheel. And when this spectacle is finished, the bicyclists all disappear from the main arteries and are absorbed back into the bloodstream of the city, going off their separate ways.

I however, sheepishly make my way back to a car—often parked scores of miles from where the Mass has petered out, (miles even from where the Mass began since I can't afford to park in the city). And that's when you feel the real impact of what you've held in your hands for one evening, and what you won't have again until the next month. It's dark when the ride is over and the cars are no longer cowed. They no longer see you as a movement, or as an impediment to getting to the bar or the movie theaters or home, they no longer see you as a threat to their plans for the evening.

In truth, once the ride is over and you're alone again on your bicycle, they no longer see you at all.

ΣΥΝΑΝΤΗΣΗ ΠΟΔΗΛΑΤΙΚΗΣ ΟΜΑΔΑΣ

CRITICAL MASS

28/3

ΣΑΒΒΑΤΟ, 12.00 • ΛΙΟΝΤΑΡΙΑ

CRITICAL MASS είναι η ιδέα δημιουργίας αυθόρμητων ομάδων ποδηλατιστών ανά τον κόσμο, με σκοπό την εξάπλωση της χρήσης του ποδηλάτου!
Η **Critical Mass Ηρακλείου** είναι μια τέτοια ομάδα στην πόλη μας!

http://**cmheraklion.blogspot.com**
Facebook: **criticalmassheraklion**
e-mail: **criticalmassheraklion@googlegroups.com**

Original art by Mona Caron, used here by Critical Mass Crete, Greece

LET'S
BIKE!

Artwork by ©MONA CARON

How Critical Mass Built the LA Bike Movement
By Adonia E. Lugo

L os Angeles may seem like the last place you'd find bikey innovation, but because of its history of social action on bicycles it is home to an exciting bike movement. While researching my dissertation project about bikes, bodies, and public space in LA, I found that the informal networks formed through bringing Critical Mass to Los Angeles continue to shape the bike movement there to this day. Participating in bike activism in LA as an ethnographer helped me to understand the theoretical concept of "human infrastructure," the networks of support that make social change possible or impossible. Bike advocates tend to focus on physical infrastructure like bike lanes instead of on the social life that makes urban transport cycling possible. But, the relationships advocates cultivate through their shared social lives should be considered just as significant to a movement as the actions they take through official channels. This is a story about human infrastructure in LA, where Critical Mass sparked politically-oriented bike advocacy and, through networks, fostered a movement that enabled the large-scale public event, CicLAvia, that I helped start during my fieldwork.

Critical Mass showed up in Los Angeles in 1997. Eden Wurmfeld had moved to town to work on an MFA in film at UCLA. Like many other people who knew bicycling before trying it in Los Angeles, Eden found herself, "amazed by how bike unfriendly Los Angeles was, considering the climate was so perfect for biking." She biked to campus from 3rd and Crescent Heights, avoiding busy thoroughfares as much as possible. Eden said she preferred riding on residential streets because on large streets, "the manmade elements seemed to make it so treacherous."

Eden and her brother, Charles Herman-Wurmfeld, had ridden in Critical Mass, or "Massed," in San Francisco. Charlie also moved to LA in 1997, riding his bike down Route 1. As soon as he rolled into town, he unwittingly chose a nasty route, riding along congested Wilshire Boulevard. He quickly learned that in LA, "the streets were highways." Four lane roads cut through residential blocks, and the social faux pas of traveling outside of a car short circuits the physical possibility of enjoying the wide lanes on a bike.

Elsewhere in LA, Ron Milam was working at the Surface Transportation Policy Project to increase public spending on bike and pedestrian infrastructure projects. A native Angelino, Ron had been riding a bike here from a young age, but, "fell in deeper love with bicycling" when he transferred to the University of Oregon. Ron had Massed while studying abroad in Copenhagen, and he had interned at the Bicycle Transportation Alliance in Portland. On a trip to UCLA, he heard the idea of having a Critical Mass in LA and met Eden and Charlie. In April 1997, they distributed flyers, and, "the last Friday of the month came, and we met at UCLA, and handed out whistles, and said, ok, we're gonna go to the beach, and this is Critical Mass in Los Angeles, here we are, and we rode off, you know, with whistles, bells, like righteously proud...all five of us." In the early days, another group started at the beach and met up with them partway, totaling about 30-50 people, Charlie recalled.

Eden said that these early rides, "got together some like-minded people who wanted to be biking in Los Angeles, and we quickly figured out that we needed something different from the traditional Critical Mass." Because of the lack of a strong bike movement in LA at that time, the rides became a breeding ground for bike advocacy. Critical Mass brought together people who had experience working in other kinds of movements, and the rides would soon lead to more official advocacy work.

There was already a network of environmental groups in LA from which the bike movement could grow, observed Joe Linton, who embodies this crossover between political advocacy and grassroots organizing. Joe had grown up biking in Orange County, discovering that he could bike from Tustin to the coast along the Santa Ana River trail. Living and working in Long Beach, he went carfree in 1991 to protest the Gulf War, and became involved with a broadminded education group called Long Beach Area Citizens Involved (LBACI). Joe learned about the conservation and restoration group Friends of the LA River (FoLAR) through LBACI, and joined because he used the river path to bike commute in Long Beach. Discovering that Joe was a bicyclist, the head of FoLAR asked him to become their bike person. He drew on his experience as a political and environmental organizer to become a bike advocate, and he subscribed to newsletters from the San Francisco Bike Coalition and Transportation Alternatives in New York.

LBACI also introduced Joe to the Los Angeles Eco-Village at 1st and Bimini in Koreatown, where Lois Arkin and others had been experimenting with intentional community and urban sustainability since 1994. Joe moved onto the block in 1996. The next year, through volunteering with Food Not Bombs he heard that a Critical Mass had started. He quickly became a regular, helping start an eastside ride that would meet up with the UCLA group.

The first political action from the early rides came when a local activist in West Hollywood called on Critical Mass to leverage support for bike lanes on Santa Monica Boulevard. Joe described the landscape of bike advocacy in LA at that point as populated by "lone wolves" who championed individual issues, but without a shared agenda. After a statewide bike summit in 1998, Chris Morphus of the California Bicycle Coalition approached Ron and told him that LA could use a bike coalition. So he tossed the idea around to a few folks, and he hashed it out with Joe after the next Critical Mass. Sitting at sandwich shop, Doughboys on 3rd Street, "we just sketched out on the back of a napkin a set of next steps, so a month later we brought all the existing bike advocates in the room," Ron recalled. With the Santa Monica Boulevard success fresh in their minds, and a whole county of issues to address, the Los Angeles County Bicycle Coalition (LACBC) was born.

As you can imagine, very little money or political support went to bike projects at that time. Joe had insight into regional transportation and engineering projects, while Ron's work had trained him in federal transportation funding. By starting a countywide bicycle coalition, they would be taking bike advocacy in Los Angeles to a whole new level. Ron became a 22 year old executive director, backed by a board that included Joe, Eden, Charlie, and others. Eden framed LACBC as building on the potential and energy of the early rides, commenting that, "Critical Mass was great, I think it raised some awareness, and was fun, but my concern was that it was going to piss off drivers and not get us what we needed, which was safe biking conditions." Those rides had created the conditions of possibility where these disparate folks, with their various experiences, could come together and form a bike movement in what many people consider to be the United States' most car-addicted city. If the poor conditions for biking in LA were the powder keg, Critical Mass was the spark that made the bike scene there explode.

LACBC won some early victories by holding the city accountable for maintaining and installing promised bike lanes. At the same time, the network created organically through Critical Mass built important social institutions that worked outside of political channels. Jimmy Lizama, an early participant in Critical Mass and a founding board member of LACBC, also moved to the Eco-Village and started helping friends repair bikes in the kitchen of an uninhabited unit. This grew into the Bicycle Kitchen/ *Bicicocina* repair cooperative, which eventually moved to its own storefront and started what is now known as the Hel-Mel Bicycle District at Heliotrope and Melrose in East Hollywood. As told in an interview with the ride founders on LA Streetsblog in July 2009, the camaraderie felt by folks at the Kitchen led to small group rides, eventually becoming the Midnight Ridazz in 2004. Today the Midnight Ridazz are a loosely federated network of people who post ride announcements to an online forum. Their biggest ride of the year, the All-City Toy Ride, before Christmas, attracts thousands of participants from all over the county.

A whooping of a pack of Midnight Ridazz rolling through the city at 1 AM may seem like a far cry from the political lobbying and research campaigns carried out by LACBC, but both contribute to a more bike-friendly city. Reflecting on his time in the LA bike movement, Ron commented that, "you need to have formal organizations and you need to have more informal networks to play on each other." A movement is a network of action that does not depend on one or two individuals to keep its momentum. Charlie and Eden went on to become filmmakers rather than bike advocates. By the time I arrived in LA in 2008, Joe and Ron had also moved on to other projects. The formal work of LACBC continued in other hands. They both still lived at the Eco-Village, though, and that's where I met them.

My partner at the time, Bobby Gadda, and I had spent a year learning about the woes of LA biking while living in nearby Long Beach. One of the most significant things I noticed was the low status of people using bikes. Many of us in the bike movement forget that for the uninitiated, bicycling not only seems scary due to aggressive drivers, but can also be a symbol of poverty and other forms of disempowerment. When he lived carfree as a filmmaker, Charlie knew that industry people thought of him as an eccentric because, "bicyclists are part of that myth in LA...only people without means and going nowhere are on bicycles." Because I was an anthropology student concerned with diversity and social justice, I was interested in promoting bicycling as a social good for all of LA's communities, not just for a particular subculture or recreational elite. It seemed like this could be accomplished by making bicycling a sanctioned activity.

We had first visited the Eco-Village in June 2008, chatting enthusiastically with Lois about Bogotá, Colombia's *Ciclovía*, which opens over 70 miles of city streets to bicyclists and pedestrians every Sunday. We traveled there in August 2008, and through Lois' contacts, Bobby and I met Jaime Ortíz-Mariño, the visionary behind the event. We returned to LA that September ready to preach the *Ciclovía* gospel, and at our first Eco-Village potluck we met Ron, Joe, Jimmy, and Aurisha Smolarski-Waters, who had been an LACBC board member and was currently on staff. We gushed about ciclovías enough that Aurisha invited us to a board meeting the following week. There, the topic of an ad-hoc *Ciclovía* committee came up. We signed on, as did another newcomer, traffic engineer Stephen Villavaso.

Allison Mannos, then an environmental justice intern at LACBC and later their first Urban Programs Coordinator, hosted the first *Ciclovía* committee meeting at her apartment in East Hollywood. Again crossing over between movements, prominent environmental activist Jonathan Parfrey had also been interested in the potential of a *Ciclovía*, and he attended the meeting along with conservationist Sandra Hamlat. We started meeting once a month to strategize what groups and individuals might help support the idea, and experimenting with routes through the city. Villavaso's partner, graphic designer Colleen Corcoran, designed our logo and we settled on a name: CicLAvia (see-kluh-VEE-ya). Others joined the effort, including Joe.

Later in 2009, Aaron Paley, an event organizer who ran a production company called Community Arts Resources (CARS-LA), published a piece in Los Angeles Magazine encouraging Mayor Antonio Villaraigosa to consider the benefits of a *Ciclovía*. Lois saw the piece, sent it to me, and I emailed Aaron and invited him to join our committee. CicLAvia benefited tremendously from Aaron's expertise as a community event organizer. Political and philanthropic connections got our committee members into meetings with the mayor's office and CARS-LA led the development of a funding strategy.

CicLAvia would close streets through official channels, rather than being a mobile, embodied closure like Critical Mass. This would lower the barriers to participation to a more diverse group than self-identified cyclists and political dissidents, but it would raise the barriers to facilitation because closing streets in Los Angeles is very expensive. We quickly figured out that it would take more than a few enthusiastic newcomers to convince the city to support CicLAvia, and the experience of established figures like Jonathan, Joe, and Aaron proved invaluable.

On October 10, 2010 (10-10-10), the first CicLAvia closed 7.5 miles of streets and connected Boyle Heights and East Hollywood. An estimated 40,000 people came out and enjoyed the streets. I rode and walked the route, filming the day like many others. I have never seen so many happy faces on any city streets, let alone those in traffic-choked LA. On the 4th Street Bridge over the Los Angeles River, many people stopped to take pictures, experiencing the city in a way they never had. Perhaps they had known the river only from chase scenes in action movies. More CicLAvias followed in 2011, and at the fourth event on April 15, 2012, an estimated 100,000 people walked and rode along the route.

Things like *Ciclovías* bring urban transport cycling to a wider population. Giving people a chance to ride through places they usually avoid by driving on highways gives them the opportunity to imagine themselves as bicyclists, to imagine a city where biking makes more sense than sitting in traffic. When I spoke with him this summer, Charlie commented that, "CicLAvia is a brilliant 2.0, an institutionalization, much less rebellious, a more sanctioned model, but it's the same thing: We're here, we're queer, get used to it. You have to be seen in order to be in play." CicLAvia brings Critical Mass to the masses by making something socially transgressive—riding a bike in a street—normal for a few hours.

Critical Mass opened the door to engaging creatively with public space and social life on bicycles. This shaped the future of bike advocacy in LA. Honestly, I never rode a Critical Mass in LA, but the networks built during those early rides influenced my development as an advocate. As a democratic event that makes no individual's participation more significant than any other, Critical Mass puts the emphasis on the whole while showing how each individual fits into the larger picture. Social change starts with individual actions: this is the message that Critical Mass spread in LA, and this is the message that I hope continues to get passed on with CicLAvia.

San Francisco Critical Mass on Potrero Hill, August, 1999   PHOTO BY CHRIS CARLSSON

Critical Mass Porto Alegre

By Marcelo Kalil

The Brazilian government found a brilliant solution to lessen the impacts of the world's financial crisis: reduce taxes on car production and make it possible for almost everyone to buy one through long-term payments. This made it easier for people to buy a new car. It was a dream come true, more precisely, Brazil's president's (Lula at that time) dream—he dreamed of the day that every single Brazilian citizen would own a car.

The outcome of that was quite predictable. São Paulo set new records for traffic jams every year. The current record is over 200 km of simultaneous traffic jams. In the city where I live, Porto Alegre, they attempt to keep cars flowing by doubling street widths, taking away public park spaces, green areas, reducing sidewalks, building monstrous bypasses, and things like that. And even that has not been enough to diminish traffic jams. Everyday they're bigger and more common. Even though Porto Alegre is considered the state capital with the most trees per citizen, the air (and noise) pollution is ever increasing. It is now considered the second most polluted city in Brazil—80% of that pollution comes from car emissions.

Porto Alegre's Critical Mass had been growing steadily for a whole year. From six waterproof, inexperienced cyclists on a rainy Friday on January 2010, we turned to seventy by the coldest days of winter, and when summer came back, in December, we were almost two hundred. Porto Alegre is a very car-centered city and whenever you talk about using a bicycle as transportation the answer is quick: "I'd love to ride my bike to work if only the traffic wasn't so aggressive," or "I'd rather use a bike than my car, but this city has too many steep hills," and so on. So no one ever imagined Critical Mass would get so big we would actually need corking.

We could feel the changes we were making. Every time you looked at the streets you saw more and more cyclists while more people came to CM on the last Friday of the month. Everybody was thrilled and filled with joy. A friend said to me after her first time in Critical Mass: "I've never felt so free!" Indeed. I believe I can speak for many people when I say that Critical Mass made me feel for the first time that the city is mine, too, and it is what we make of it. For a few moments, the streets that scared us were the streets that made us smile. And our joy was contagious, it made more people want to ride bikes. We were changing the city through joy.

That first year bore many fruits: Critical Mass generated another bike ride, the Guerrilla Gardening Bike Ride; PedalExpress, a bike courier cooperative, started; and we were organizing a bicycle community center called *Cidade da Bicicleta* (City of the Bicycle).

In February 2011, when the last Friday of the month came, the weather forecast was predicting rain. But it was summer, and a good subtropical rain doesn't hurt anyone. It was a special evening, there was going to be a party to celebrate the official inauguration of *Cidade da Bicicleta* after Critical Mass.

Over 150 people defied the predicted rain and showed up for that Critical Mass. As soon as we left Zumbi dos Palmares Square, where CM gathers, I saw an angry driver who was trying to force his way through the bicycles with his black VW Golf arguing with some cyclists. Some people stopped riding to check on the confrontation, but it seemed under control. There were already a few cyclists asking for the driver to calm down, assuring him that the ride would pass in a couple of minutes. So the ride went on.

My girlfriend and I were three blocks further when I heard a crashing noise. The scariest thing about that noise is that it didn't stop, it continued on and on, as I turned my head in its direction, then it passed right by my side. It kept moving forward at increasing speed, a black blur throwing friends of mine, acquaintances, and a lot of other people off to every side, leaving behind a trail of wrecked bikes, helmets, shoes, and screams. I still can hear the crashing noise and the screams when I talk about it.

At first I was paralyzed. I saw a friend of mine, who was a bike courier, lying on the ground, bleeding, with someone holding his head and crying. I didn't have the guts to see who else was hurt. Seeing all those wrecked bikes and chaos I couldn't imagine the possibility of no one being dead or permanently injured. My first thought was protective. I figured out we had to stop the cars before another one could endanger us even further and hurt more people, just to realize a few moments later that we needed to make the traffic flow so the ambulances could get to us.

The ambulances came and took our friends to the hospital, and we stayed, deciding not to leave the area until the police arrested the madman who hurt us. That didn't happen. Someone shouted that we should arrange an open meeting to decide what to do. The meeting was set for Sunday at *Cidade da Bicicleta*. Everybody was to announce that meeting through their blogs, e-mails, and social networks.

I thought it was the end of Porto Alegre's Critical Mass.

I didn't sleep that night. That crashing sound and the bad feelings that it brought looped in my head all night and morning.

The next days were a marathon of interviews for the local and international media, and reading the news, browsing the web, to check if the driver was found, talking to friends to get news of the injured. I couldn't hear the sound of a speeding car without my heart trying to jump through my mouth. Distressing, tiresome, frustrating.

I was afraid to ride my bike. Who would be brave enough to ride a bike in Porto Alegre after what had just happened? I fought with that feeling, and with my stomach unsettled I decided I should do it then or I thought I'd never do it again. I did it. And the unimaginable happened: the city was full of bikes. I still don't know if I was delusional, but in the following days I noticed even more bikes in the streets than before the attack. Maybe people were showing their solidarity, maybe they were trying to make a statement... Who knows?

And then there was the meeting. There wasn't enough space for everyone in *Cidade da Bicicleta*. There were over 200 people in there—many of them hadn't been on Critical Mass but wanted to do something about it—so we had to hold the meeting in the backyard. And there were so many bicycles you barely had room to even get to the backyard. Everybody spoke in turn and after many hours we reached a decision: we would march on the following Tuesday asking for more humane cities and for the end of impunity for traffic crimes—because homicides where the car is used as a weapon are not treated as seriously as when other weapons are used. The protesters would meet at the same place CM gathered, would continue to the exact site of the incident to perform a die-in, then they would go to City Hall. People were also invited to show up at Cidade da Bicicleta on Monday afternoon, to paint banners, posters, create stencils and other art to express our feelings during the march.

Monday afternoon at *Cidade da Bicicleta* there were dozens of people sitting on the floor, painting posters, spraying banners, cutting stencils. People had brought ink, fabric, paper, and other materials. The atmosphere was filled with *solidarity and cooperation*, everyone was doing their part without being asked to.

On Tuesday, when we got to Zumbi dos Palmares Square, there were already a couple hundred people. Besides all the material we had produced the day before, there were a lot of different banners, posters and even stickers going around. Someone printed 200 posters with, "It was not an accident" written on it, and below a drawing of a half black car, half pistol. There was a samba group playing Carnaval marches with thematic lyrics. And the crowd was growing and growing. There were dozens of reporters and police officers, but mostly it was ordinary people, by foot, by bike, skateboards, with their faces painted, holding signs. Someone had built a cage with PVC pipes around his bike and a girl built a cardboard shield for hers.

The march started and we filled the streets. People stood watching on the sidewalks shouting words of support. Some of them joined us and the march kept growing. Soon we got to the site where Critical Mass was hit, we laid down on the asphalt, we screamed, we cried. It was a magic moment, we were back in that place full of awful memories but we had brought in reinforcements: thousands of people who came to show us solidarity and support. We got up, we kept on. About 4,000 people were marching in the streets, singing along with the samba band who improvised the lyrics and created new songs every few minutes. After all the suffering, I was over-flowing with joy once again.

There was a rumor circulating that the mayor was going to meet with representatives of the protesters at the City Hall, but when we got there we learned that he had gone away. So we kept chanting and singing, we did another die-in and stayed there until someone came out of the City Hall to announce that the Secretary of Local Governance would talk to us.

There was a meeting with the Secretary where representatives of the pro-testers demanded that the government should immediately implement poli-cies that would guarantee more security for bicyclists such as traffic calming, bike paths and bike lanes, educational campaigns aimed at drivers, and more space for pedestrians, among others. The Secretary proposed regular meet-ings between cyclists, City Hall, and the EPTC (Porto Alegre's Department of Transportation, responsible for planning and implementing changes in traffic). The idea seemed good, a permanent forum where cyclists' demands would be heard and where we could decide along with City Hall changes that would make the city more pleasant for *people* to live.

That night my soul was cleansed and I slept for the first time in days, smiling. It seemed things were for the best. Everybody had left the hospital in good enough shape, some broken bones, but nothing permanent, and it seemed that things were going to start changing for the better in Porto Alegre.

But the next day, the nightmare came back.

One of our friends who was most seriously injured had to go back to the emergency hospital with suspicion of brain hemorrhage. He had to stay in the hospital for a few extra days of observation. We were distressed again. So much for our peace of mind.

Days passed slowly, our friend was eventually discharged from the hos-pital, the driver was found and charged with seventeen attempted murder charges (the number of people who reported injuries)—he had his driver's license suspended, but he remains free until the trial.

On the following days and weeks we received solidarity from all over the world. We received the cutest card from Manchester's Critical Mass, there were bike rides in support of Porto Alegre's CM all over the world, from Buenos Aires to Barcelona. It seemed that most of the city's drivers were sympathetic as well, showing more respect to cyclists and even stopping for pedestrians at zebra crossings (something unusual in Porto Alegre)—with a few extroverted exceptions: such as aggressive drivers screaming "Strike!" (in English, in reference to bowling) when passing by cyclists. But as the episode faded in the citizens' memory, things were slowly returning to normal.

The following Critical Mass was one of a kind: there were people coming from different parts of Brazil, such as São Paulo and Curitiba, to ride with Porto Alegre's CM. It was a huge ride by our standards. I believe there were more than 500 bicyclists, almost all of them people who had heard of Critical Mass for the first time in the news after the murder attempt. And it was beautiful, there were people in windows of buildings and sidewalks showing their support. Whenever we stopped at a red light everybody started clapping their hands in synchrony. The Mass was more alive and stronger than ever!

Eventually life got back to normal. The meetings with the City Hall and EPTC were a fiasco— almost all of our demands and suggestions were completely ignored. The ones that were initially accepted were later dismissed—like the cycle path in a four-lane avenue where the cyclists' demands for an extra 30cm to the path's width to guarantee safety was denied because it would, in the words of the Secretary of Transport, "completely stop car traffic."

I believe our strength is *in the streets*, not in politicians and their meetings. *We do our politics in the streets.*

It's been now almost a year since the attack on Critical Mass. The homicidal driver is still at large, waiting for his trial. The local government didn't spend a single dollar to turn Porto Alegre into a bicycle friendly city, on the contrary, it's still spending *our money* to build useless and ugly bypasses.

Nevertheless, the number of bicycles in the streets of Porto Alegre is rising exponentially. I'm surprised every time I take my bike for a ride with the ever growing number of cyclists in the streets, using bicycles for transportation, though there's no official incentive to it. And the streets are safer! The number of cyclists might have risen, but the number of people injured in accidents involving bikes in 2011—even considering the 17 injured on the attack on Critical Mass—dropped 20%. The more bikes in the street, the safer it is to use them!

And the good outcomes don't stop there, there are other movements in town that were influenced by Critical Mass, such as *Largo Vivo*—when a group of citizens decided to occupy the square in front of the Public Market every Tuesday as a protest against its conversion to a parking lot and to repudiate the affirmation of a government representative that the parking lot would bring "more qualified customers" to the Public Market. Since then you can join a lot of people there every Tuesday evening, with music, street artists, picnics, etc.

The city is changing, its citizens waking up to the fact that our actions make the city what it is. And a lot of that is due to Critical Mass.

Postscript:

Since I finished writing this article, a few things have changed.

City Hall went from being a supposed ally to a hostile opponent: the EPTC asked for a public investigation of Critical Mass, alleging that it threatens public order. Supposedly some of CM's riders were "aggressive" and "threatened to throw their bikes on cars" (they drew that bizarre conclusion by watching footage of cyclists raising their bikes over their heads). This began a public inquiry to evaluate if Critical Mass is really a threat.

But some pro-bike activists managed to turn the situation against City Hall itself. The Public Prosecutor proved to be a great ally. Besides not finding any threat coming from Critical Mass' participants, he is now investigating City Hall for not obeying a municipal law that demands that 20% of all money obtained through traffic fines be used for bicycle infrastructure: bike lanes and cyclepaths. City Hall is having a hard time explaining why they didn't use the money as the law requires.

It's been over one year since the attack on Critical Mass, and we decided to transform that negative date into something positive. We hosted the 1st World Bicycle Forum from February 22-26, 2012, and it turned out to be a great success. Most people that showed up were from Brazil, but we had participants from Venezuela, Chile, Netherlands, Scotland, the U.S., and Belgium. During the four days there were over 40 workshops and six bicycle rides. Porto Alegre's Critical Mass set a new record of almost 2,000 participants.

On February 25, 2012, there was to be a protest to mark the one-year anniversary of the attack on Critical Mass. We left the *Gasômetro* (the old power plant turned into a cultural center) where the World Bicycle Forum was taking place, to Zumbi dos Palmares Square. From there we would follow the same route as the previous year's ride and stop on the exact spot where we were hit. Once again it was raining and the rain kept many people away. Nevertheless there were about two hundred people standing in the rain, waiting for something to happen. With an amplifier plugged in to a 12-volt car battery, a singer that came from another state sang a song that he wrote about the attack on Porto Alegre's Critical Mass. When he finished singing, people who were on last year's ride gave speeches and testimonies. But there was still something missing.

And then someone screamed a suggestion: "Naked bike ride!" People looked at each other, uncertain of what would happen, if anything at all. Porto Alegre had never before had a naked bike ride. Then someone started to undress, and then another, and yet another... and soon there was a critical mass of bicyclists and the ride started. Since this ride wasn't planned nor announced on the internet, the authorities weren't aware of it and for the first time in the last year we had neither police nor traffic guards escorting us.

It was too cold to be riding naked in the rain, but nobody cared. We had a superb ride and once again we managed to make a bad thing good.

As the Forum ended we were filled with a feeling of "mission accomplished," but we were already missing all the new friends we made and all the talk about bicycles and changing the world through our actions. We didn't just talk, we were actually changing it. Never in the history of Porto Alegre and Brazil have people and media talked so much about bikes. Since then the bicycle as a means of transportation has become an prominent issue addressed by local and national media. Bike culture is here to stay. Bikes came to Porto Alegre to return the city to the people, to make it a more humane, a cleaner and safer city for all of us.

I'm glad to be a part of this.

Pedaling with Ghosts of the Industrial Revolution in Manchester, England

By Vanessa Bear

It's where the industrial revolution began, where the computer was invented, where people first danced to house music in the UK. Zooming past chrome and glass modern buildings that sit next to crumbling mills, riding over cobblestones that lead to highways, it's clear that Manchester is a city that embraces change. One of the main changes that's occurred over the past 10 years being the huge increase in bicycles used as transportation. Many would say that's mostly due to Critical Mass.

The first Critical Mass bike ride in Manchester was inspired by reports in the radical press of those happening in San Francisco. It was organised as part of an anti-roads and G8 protest. However, this was only a one-off event and it wasn't until 2004 that Critical Mass in Manchester became a regular monthly sight on our city's roads. At first the rides were very small with only around 10 people attending. In order to increase the numbers and to build a wider and more supportive cycling community I founded *I Bike MCR* in 2006.

I Bike MCR provides a variety of cycling events, with Critical Mass being the main event of each month. As a way to make the ride more of an event, activities following the ride were planned such as punk gigs, film screenings, and alleycat races. People coming to the gigs would only know the location if they came on the ride first, and with one ride people were hooked and came month after month even when their favourite bands weren't playing afterwards!

In 2005 a group of cyclists rode around the UK to spread news and information about the upcoming G8 protests taking place in Scotland. There were around 70 people riding together, stopping off at cities to do workshops and to meet like-minded people around the country. The workshops were inspiring but the most inspiring thing of all was that this was when Critical Mass in Manchester started to be noticed. The G8 bike ride came along on our Critical Mass increasing our numbers to over 150 people that month and creating such an incredible spectacle that everyone wanted to know what it was and when the next one would be. To get more people cycling, we just need more people cycling!

Seven years later Manchester Critical Mass is still taking place every month. Our numbers are growing and growing. We are a very friendly ride, with people decorating bikes and choosing fancy dress themes. People are very keen to promote the idea that everyone in a car is a potential cyclist and Critical Masser and with that in mind we are more of a carnival celebration than—as we are often misinterpreted (by those who haven't been on a ride)—as an angry mob.

We're lucky not to have had problems that have been encountered by London and New York in that we have very little interaction with the police. We sometimes get followed by a car but have never (yet) been asked to stop a ride. In fact the only real interaction with cops that I can remember was a policeman arresting a driver for dangerous driving when attempting to speed past the whole ride on the wrong side of the road.

Before Critical Mass there was no real bike culture in our city, no place where we could meet. In 2004 our city was a very different place for a cyclist. Hardly anyone used a bike for transport and it was alienating to do so. Now, with the increased fashion to ride we have countless bikes on the roads. However, Critical Mass has definitely helped that process here as well as creating a place for us to meet and share our experiences. Many people riding a bike have said they were inspired to do so when they saw the monthly throng of cheerful, carnival-like riders going past them whilst they were standing at a bus stop. It has also inspired amazing community bike projects such as *Pedal MCR*, a community bike co-op that recycles bikes, has a drop-in tool club for the community, provides Earn-A-Bike programmes, and much more.

A strong radical wimmin's bike community has also emerged called Bloomers. We organise maintenance classes, rides, cycle training, and holidays for wimmin and even our own "Clitical Masses." The group was started after wimmin met at Critical Mass and shared experiences of how cycling is a male-dominated arena and wimmin are often made to feel inadequate on training rides and in bike shops. So we created something of our own where we can build our skills together, which has given many wimmin confidence and knowledge to make their cycling sustainable and enjoyable.

It's not just bike projects that have grown from the roots of Critical Mass. A plethora of other projects have been created and helped to grow through CM. Our Critical Mass rides often end or stop off at community projects, protests and occupations to show solidarity and to lend a hand. So many Critical Massers going along to help, or to show solidarity, have an incredible effect.

Students recently occupying Manchester University received a Critical Mass solidarity visit this winter, which inspired many students to get involved who had not heard about the occupation. Squatted community social centres often host our after-Critical-Mass parties. This is where many people first have been introduced to the concept of squatting, which has helped to overcome negative stereotypes by opening people's eyes to a creative and inspiring community.

Our rides have also helped community projects, with stops at city parks such as Platt Fields Park, to get people involved with the group by painting railings, gardening, and painting murals. We painted a huge mural on an off-road cycle route where there was a creepy tunnel. The mural really helped to brighten it up and made it feel less unwelcoming. The whole neighbourhood got involved—people from Critical Mass, community members and families all helped to turn a dark spooky place into a bright and user-friendly path.

A regular Manchester Critical Masser, Brian, has even used the rides to gain essential conservation data by attaching bat detectors to bikes to gather information about the various species in the area, as well as providing information on how we can all help.

An annual ride connected with Manchester Critical Mass is our annual Santcat—like an Alleycat Race and Critical Mass mixed together. Everyone has a vague shopping list with five potential present ideas (something to cuddle, something to draw with) and has to choose items in each local community store we stop at. Then, together we wrap everything collected and take the presents down to the Children Refugee and Asylum Seekers Christmas Party! It's a great way to raise awareness and to help, even in a small way.

For many people on the Mass these links with other activities also provide a life-changing initial exposure to the many people in the city who are creating new ways of living, and enable them to get involved and strengthen the community to help make real change.

With more and more people cycling maybe one day there will be no need for Critical Mass here (we can dream!). But now more than ever in these hard times, it is so essential for us to have that sense of community, the feeling that we're in it together. Together we can create real change and we see proof of it every month and in the community projects it inspires and helps to sustain, and as our numbers increase, at every Critical Mass.

Bicicritica, Madrid, Spain, 2010

"Alegria Entre Tus Piernas": To Conquer Madrid's Streets[1]

by Elisabeth Lorenzi

I ride around the city and I ride regularly in *Bicicrítica* (this is the name of Critical Mass in Madrid) so I am in tune with the movement for sustainable mobility focused on the bicycle. I am also keenly aware of the intense relationship that has been formed between *Bicicrítica* and the social centers of *el movimiento de okupación* (the squatting or Okupation Movement[2]) for their mutual expansion.

Bicicrítica encompasses a great many perspectives, motivations, practices and influences, and affinity with the Okupation Movement is one of them. One of the greatest strengths of the Okupation Movement has been its role as an integrator of different citizen movements and initiatives, including unique activist practices that were pioneered by *Bicicrítica*. Based on Critical Mass practices, do-it-yourself (DIY) bicycle workshops have emerged in autonomous and okupied spaces.

The workshops in autonomous spaces offer bicycle repair and mechanical knowledge, and have become focal points of *Bicicrítica* expansion. Currently, there are nine DIY workshops distributed in different autonomous spaces of different styles (*CS Seco, EPA Patio Maravillas, CSA La Tabacalera, CSOA Casablanca, CSOA La Enredadera, CSOA El Dragón, Escuela Popular de La Prospe*). And new connections keep emerging. In the Summer of 2011, the People's Assembly of the Mortalaz neighborhood, related to the 15M[3] movement, began pedaling their own monthly Critical Mass around the neighborhood and also guided the *Bicicrítica* over to their location to embrace it on their home turf.

As the problem of mobility in cities, and the bicycle as a tool for improving this situation, becomes more important in the discourse and practices of many *centros sociales okupados*, they help sustain the growth and maintenance of bicycle-related actions. These DIY workshops, which are connected to each other through common initiatives related to bicycling in Madrid, in turn open a window on connections among social centers, other movements, and the general citizenry.

The okupied social centers mean much more than the space they occupy. They are directly influencing the broader political moment. The activities they host give rise to countless social links and initiatives.

In a mutually beneficial process, *Bicicrítica* has brought a broader public in contact with okupied spaces, people who had never imagined participating in these type of spaces. This article focuses on the connections between the rise of the alternative bicycle culture surrounding *Bicicrítica* and the multiple realities that constitute the Okupation Movement.

On Bike Around Madrid—Brave, Crazy, and Athletic

The bicycle culture is well established in Madrid with specialized stores, racing infrastructure, and exclusive facilities. But there is little interest in the bicycle as everyday transportation. Bicycling is sport, in the gyms and on the highways, and is well loved. Bicycling is recreational, a way for couples or families to spend a Sunday together on rides and excursions. It is the first vehicle of freedom for children. And it is the device by which the sedentary middle-aged person can try to get on the road back to youth. As a means of transportation it faces an uphill battle.

The bicycle in the city is actually nothing new, having been a popular means of transportation at the end of the 19th century. By contrast, the car was the last system of transportation adopted in cities. It filled streets in the USA in the 1930s and in the 1970s in Europe, and has only been widening its domination during the last 50 years. Since Critical Mass started in San Francisco 20 years ago, many efforts have emerged to reclaim space for more sustainable means of transport. Also, more and more people are questioning the use of petroleum and the consequences that it brings: wars, pollution, and the high cost of energy used in relation to energy extracted. Bicycling is a way of pointing to those facts.

Until now the saying, "Madrid is not made for bikes,"[4] has reinforced the idea that the bicycle is best used to escape the city, rather than as a transportation alternative. In fact, Spain has many elite cycling athletes and this has contributed to bicycling becoming a popular sport and recreational activity. This paradoxical relationship matches perfectly the design of the city's cycling paths which shunt the bicycle into parks, assuming bikes are more for athletic training than for commuting (the most important cycle path in Madrid, *el Anillo Verde* encircles the entire city, for the most part through the best green areas). The new Madrid Cycling Plan proposes by 2016 an ample network of separated bicycle lanes mostly passing through parks. Although a notable increase in bicycle routes may be planned, it is based on a recreational, not transit role.

Diverse cities in Spain are responding to the new bicycling movement. Some cities like Barcelona, Sevilla, and Vitoria are embracing the bicycle as a symbol to distinguish themselves as places with a good quality of life and modern urban sensibilities. Most of them have been surprised by the rapid increase in the bicycling once infrastructure has been provided, whether public bikes or bike lanes. While Madrid's bicyclists catalyze a range of citizen initiatives and new daily life dynamics, the daily experience of a bicyclist remains relatively solitary in the gray breath of traffic. That isolation is heightened by the incomprehension of friends or colleagues who pat you on the back condescendingly and call you "brave," "crazy," or "athletic."

Madrid is a hilly city and many of these hills dot the peripheral neighborhoods, but we also have good weather (although it is not advised to pedal under a blazing summer afternoon sun). The traffic is noisy, congested, dirty… but not everywhere. Madrid is almost the geographical center of the peninsula and like many Mediterranean cities, has a center, the Puerta del Sol. Everything flows to the center through an urban design that combines radial compartmentalization with two concentric traffic rings to channel traffic. Long commutes inevitably pass through disagreeable bottlenecks.

Madrid, in comparison to other cities, has an ample and affordable urban transport network, which most people use. In peak hours it is badly overcrowded. The system tends to leave the peripheral areas without good connections amongst each other. This tendency of the transit system to converge towards the center has helped the bicycle become an alternative means of public transportation. As a form of transport it also knits together the "small homeland" of Madrid, unifying different neighborhoods, while allowing riders to cover greater distances in less time. In a city divided by concentric boundaries, it is common to use the bicycle for trips within the zones marked by these asphalt borders, the districts, the neighborhoods, the "central almond."[5] Meanwhile, the car has become less popular for short trips within the city, whether because of congestion or the lack of available parking. Ironically, increased bicycling in Madrid actually meets social desires for greater efficiency in commuting, quality of life, and social opportunities.

Urban cycling in Madrid is an emerging movement based on riders who experience its difficulties and benefits. But, local government has largely ignored the growing embrace of cycling, which has emerged from below at the initiative of the citizenry itself. This genuine grassroots mobilization has seized public imagination, but even more, the bicycle as a battlehorse of social mobilization has captured broad attention in Madrid. Pedestrians and car drivers have finally noticed, and statistics confirm what has been well known to those who frequently steer their pedaled mounts over Madrileñan asphalt: bicycle traffic is multiplying. The 2009 Report on the State of Mobility in the City of Madrid declared the number of bicycling citizens has doubled in one year, reaching 45,000 daily trips (0.6% of total trips). That is not such a great proportion of cyclists among city residents, but something is happening.

What provoked this growth? Was it the pro-bike initiatives of the municipality? Clearly not, since these are nearly nonexistent. Urban cycling is the result of citizen efforts, the mobilization of mobility.

Bicicrítica, the Citizen Mobilization of Mobility

Bicicrítica is the best example of citizen mobilization. The last Thursday of each month at 8 pm, hundreds (or thousands!) of bicyclists gather at the central Plaza of the Cibeles to ride together. From the window of City Hall, the Mayor can see the Mass. Everyone knows where it begins, but not everyone knows what the route will be, nor where it will end. This information circulates on virtual forums and is carried out by whomever decides to lead it. The global spread of this movement coincides with the extension of the Internet, the virtual space that allows information, opinions, events, and goals of *Bicicrítica* to be dynamically debated. The Madrileñan Critical Mass is so successful and popular that we joke it will "die of its own success." The global motto, "Ride Daily, Celebrate Monthly," had special resonance in Madrid and complemented perfectly the other catchphrase, "Put the fun between your legs," which is flaunted with particular brilliance on the back of t-shirts and identifies the Madrileñan Critical Massers.

Bicicrítica, like Critical Mass elsewhere, embodies two distinct characteristics, simultaneously making political demands while also holding an open celebration. As a leaderless, critical, and playful mass, it presents a challenge to that which is normally considered "critical" in the city. "Is it a demonstration? What are you demanding?" often ask the pedestrians who watch the mass go by. "We want bicycles on the street!" we answer. But we aren't just asking for it, we are effectively making it happen then and there. *Bicicrítica* is obviously a collective bike ride that only exists when it happens. But it is also a social movement that is articulated three different ways: the *Bicicrítica* on its own, the web and email lists where it is discussed (along with many other topics), and the DIY bicycle workshops located in social and autonomous spaces.

Critical Mass is not an isolated movement. It is a discourse and praxis connected to other movements and broader discourses, which has led to its rapid growth, since often the activists of related movements take the initiative to promote *Bicicrítica*. But Critical Mass also embodies the desire for immediate and sustainable access to a better quality of life.

As a celebration, it fills the streets accompanied by music blaring from sound systems carried by bicycles. The music bikes are also a reference point and guide for the ride. Sometimes rides have ironic and humorous themes, appealing to riders to come in costume. "Carnaval" and "Elegant" are repeated every year, but other themes have been "Beach," "Pirate," "Back to School," "Olympics 2016 towards Tokyo," and so on.

Riding in *Bicicrítica* puts one into a slow rhythm, sprinkled with conversations among cyclists and occasional disputes with impatient car drivers or pedestrians facing the endless river of cyclists. Combine this with the lack of consensus about stopping or not stopping at red lights, and the mass can be seen as disorganized. But underneath the apparent disorganization is a different kind of social self-management oriented to the shared pleasure of the moment. Invisibly, the monthly ride is activating imaginations and expanding the repertoire of local collective action in an urban context while informing what it means to be Madrileños.

Madrid's *Bicicrítica* has been heavily merchandised by its own participants, offering t-shirts and stickers with the popular symbol of *Bicicrítica*, as well as the website. It is an interesting way of both disseminating and self-financing, usually initiated by DIY shop workers. The sale of these products during the *Bicicrítica* also offers the occasional participant tangible evidence that the movement exists, helping reinforce the social cohesion around the bike and its re-establishment as urban transport.

On many occasions *Bicicrítica* ends at party where food and drink are offered for nominal prices, usually organized by activists belonging to the DIY workshop where we arrived. Activists have the greatest access to the opportunities offered by autonomous spaces, and the greatest need to find cash to cover the needs of the workshop. At a pragmatic level the party is a form of financing the workshops and the social centers or other collectives. And the *fiesta* is always a special occasion to reinforce social bonds while also connecting to a new tradition of how the *Bicicrítica* ends.

Bicicrítica has steadily grown month after month over the last six years. On the first one in October 2004, there were only four cyclists in the rain. They never even started to ride. By October 2010 there were 3,000 riders. As a monthly gathering, Madrid shares the forms that have been made globally recognizable by Critical Mass in more than 200 cities around the world: organized spontaneity, no acknowledged single leadership, xerocracy, DIY, and above all, occupation of the street and flow of traffic by a mass of cyclists. Riders assume personal and collective responsibility for the development and diffusion of *Bicicrítica*. Madrid is the Spanish city where the monthly ride gathers the greatest number of people, but others are also notable, such as the ones in Barcelona, Bilbao, Valencia, Sevilla, A Coruña, and Valladolid. *Bicicríticas* have also proliferated in neighborhoods and towns on Madrid's periphery: La Latina, Moratalez, Ciudad

Lineal, Alcalá de Henares, Getafe, Alcobendas, Pinto...

Bicicrítica offers an exceptional environment for socializing and empowerment around the bicycle, but it only happens once a month. The monthly gathering becomes a cultural stew where new initiatives and social opportunities emerge, whether for activism, pragmatic organizing, or pleasure. In Madrid, for example, there are different associations that have been working for years to make this city a more rideable place and have built the foundation for bicycling as a legitimate transportation choice. But it has been the DIY workshop activists who have done the most to diffuse bicycling broadly and promote *Bicicrítica*, as they now offer weekly and daily activities related to the bicycle. The DIY bike workshops are housed in autonomous spaces, and when participating in them, visitors and activists merge urbanism, transit, political mobilization, and technological skill-sharing.

The workshops' development depends on the initiative of the most consistent participants. Unity has been established among the workshops because they have spread virally like an expansive wave by the same people who started the first workshops. Each workshop is self-managed, openly inviting all to participate in its decisions and initiatives. A principle has been established to share in the economic management of funds obtained through activities related to *Bicicrítica*. This practice has become a conduit between the different autonomous spaces that house the workshops, that otherwise do not have formal communication.

History and Expansion of DIY Bicycle Repair Workshops

In 2009 I witnessed the emergence and development of eight DIY bicycle workshops. In general terms, these places offer support to bicyclists to fix or reinvent some aspect of their bike, construct a new one from loose parts and facilitate the lending of rebuilt bicycles. Tools, recycled parts, and people with a passion for mechanics are the basic infrastructure of these workshops, where not only is it important to know about mechanics, but also to have personal initiative, creativity, and a cooperative spirit.

Besides offering mechanical education, these workshops are the principle centers for gathering and articulating ideas and initiatives related to *Bicicrítica*. They are an important resource, not only because of the mechanical support, but because they are in spaces that offer important infrastructure for cycling events (space for parties, silk screen t-shirt printing, virtual support, guest housing). They are places that favor conviviality and open discussion, the foundation for new initiatives. All the spaces share similar values: autonomy, an anti-authoritarian political vision, support for social movements, and open participation and use of these informal spaces.

The location of these workshops in these spaces is not accidental. There are not many spaces that freely offer space to projects without formal structure, a certain malleability of space, and that support improvised and immediate initiatives. "Do It Yourself" is the inspiring motto of Critical Masses since the beginning. It is a guiding principle that perfectly coincides with the philosophy of the social centers.

The first *Bicicrítica* started in October 2004, followed by the first workshop in Spring 2005 in the old Centro Social Seco,[6] an initiative embodied by the pioneers of the *Bicicrítica* who requested space from the Assembly there. Knowing about this type of place in other cities, and the desire to have a proper space to manage tools and experiment, motivated contact with the Assembly. The DIY bike workshop relates to the social center as a hosted project, participating in some other initiatives, but without fully integrating into the internal debates or decision-making processes of the center. To get the word out and gather some funds, the early *Bicicríticas* ended in parties there, with drinks and dinner. Its development was parallel to it.

The *Centro Social Seco*, after two years of pressuring the municipality to grant them relocation, got a new place! After the move, the bike workshop was larger, had more participants, was more visibile, and took on more responsibilities over space management. The new social center, no longer an okupa, must pay rent and therefore the projects that are housed there must contribute. The same summer of the move, the "*EPA Patio Maravillas*"[7] (EPA Patio of Marvels) was inaugurated, a *centro okupado* in the central neighborhood of Malasaña. Users of the *Seco* bike workshop proposed to establish a new one in that space and started by adding new people. More people come to *Bicicrítica* in the summer, increasing our forces, but also our needs. Meanwhile, visitors and participants at the new central location, attracted by its initiatives, embraced the workshop as a regular meeting place, many later joining *Bicicrítica*.

In Summer 2008, another workshop was born at the *Palacio Okupado Malaya*, which was called *Cicloficina* (Cycle-Office). The open communications between the activists of *Patio Maravillas* and the founders of *Palacio Okupado Malaya* helped inaugurate another bike workshop in that center. As soon as the new social center opened, people on the *Bicicrítica* email lists were encouraged to help recondition and use the space. The location, near the Lavapiés neighborhoods (low income, central *barrios*), and the condition of the space, facilitated outreach to local residents. Days after the inauguration of the workshop, the space was evicted. Despite its short duration, the expectations established by the workshop, the call for parallel activities, and an end-party of the *Bicicrítica* at this site raised visibility for the social center.

Similarly, this process has reacquainted many cyclists with the movement and its surrounding diversity. People who actively participated in its rehabilitation began germinating other future new workshops.

Until this moment all the DIY workshops were tightly connected to *Bicicrítica*. As more workshops were started it became more diversified. These newer places came into contact with other processes, developed their own motivations, and the number of activists increased to the point that *Bicicrítica* became less central. New means of communications have developed beyond the *Bicicrítica* email list, allowing matters concerning the DIY workshops and social centers to migrate out of the communication flow that originally generated them. The reproductive trajectory of some workshops has tended to unify experiences and reference points, generating a sense of shared purpose among most workshops, even if the structure or gestation of the space itself is different.

On other occasions the activists in DIY workshops are usually intermediaries between the larger spaces and the needs of cycling events. In 2009, animated by the success of the *Bicicrítica*, a group called for an international event (intergalactic, in fact!): the *Críticona*. For this occasion, social centers housed most of the related activities and provided a lot of the lodging for people who arrived from other cities to participate. The Social Bicycle Forum was celebrated in November 2009 with activists from different cycling organizations at the *EPA Patio Maravaillas*.

80% of the different activists that I interviewed had no prior contact or experience with social centers before participating in a bike workshop. Some activists, after taking part in a workshop, joined anti-eviction struggles, and the okupation of new workshops. Over time, some *Bicicrítica* activists have become activists of the Okupation Movement.

In Spring 2009, new workshops were inaugurated. One is in the "Solar" okupation of Lavapiés, a small cleared and fenced space, boxed in by buildings and the narrow streets of this barrio. In time, the space was fixed up to be more viable in winter, with infrastructure to house projects that require materials and tools. Bicycles inspired a self-managed repair project, including plans to be open every day. Other new bike workshops opened too: *La República Independiente de la Grasa* (Independent Republik of Grease), located in the peripheral *barrio* of Carabanchel, the *Bicilab* at the *Punto de Encuentro La Enredadera* ("The Creeping Vine" Meeting Point), an okupied social center located in the *barrio* of Tetuán, the *CSO Casablanca*, the *CS el Dragón*, and the *CSO La Tabakalera*, and others that now constitute a labyrinth of workshops that open and close according to the luck of the social centers that host them.

In the Summer of 2011, another workshop burst on the scene. This time a critical vision of gender identities and relationships helped found a trans-lesbian-feminist workshop and bicycle school. From this space, the participants want to show that the world of the bicycle, like any other, has much to do with gender: men, women, dykes, trans… and that the repair shops in particular are heavily masculinized. They call themselves *Cicliátrico*. Here is an excerpt from their founding manifesto:

> *A few months ago, a* compañera *(female colleague) who's been around the workshops for awhile, started the idea of taking a day or two a month to gather women, dykes, and transpeople to learn about bicycle mechanics. This proposal reached us through the* Bicicrítica *forum and from there we began inviting colleagues who had a trans/feminist past and are passionate about the bike! We met while preparing the bikeporn (movie festival) that we enjoy during September [...] We gathered daily cyclists (bike activists and not) who are interested in topics of gender and sexuality to plan the* CICLIATRICO *project, a space for those of us who stand outside the obligatory HETERONORMATIVITY and those of us who resist and struggle again the HETEROPATRIARCHY and its violence.*
> —*Tino Mutante,* Cicliátrico *workshop*

They created a space for empowerment, autonomy, and self-management where the relationships would be horizontal, given that in other workshops women, lesbians, and transfolk did not always feel comfortable. In this space, there is no fear of making mistakes and learning is a collective experience. The bicycle is understood as a potent tool to break gender, sexist, and *machirulos* roles that have been encountered also in the world of bicycles.

The bicycle is a means of transportation that has a very intense relationship to the body (it intensifies the body's inherent potential), but also makes the body visible in the city, especially in a city like Madrid where bicycle riders are not so abundant. Therefore, it is not a coincidence that initiatives arise where the bicycle, body, and gender identity are related.

Elsewhere in Europe, queer theory is already involved with reconquering sidewalks and interacting with okupied space. A good example is Schwarzercanal[8] in Berlin, a queer community project around a *Wagenplatz* (caravan settlement) in a forest east of the city. As such, it is a networked project, a point of confluence for homosexuals and friends and part of a broader network of autonomous spaces, *okupas*, and other *Wagenplätze* in Berlin, Europe, and beyond.

Bicicrítica and DIY Workshops: Chickens and Eggs

At a pragmatic level, the strong activism of many workshopists within

Bicicrítica has been an animating force behind the rides, even though *Bicicrítica* on its own does not require much maintenance, nor resources. It is passed on by word of mouth, and it has plenty of people attending. By contrast, the workshops need resources, more regular involvement, management help, and therefore a more or less permanent social structure.

The first workshop was inaugurated with certain expectations, but these have changed with the proliferation of new workshops. In practice, new needs have been generated and new ideas to meet them, while the okupation of spaces has transformed imaginations of okupiers AND cyclists.

Social centers are one of the local forms that embody and express the politics and practices born in the global prototype that is Critical Mass. The presence of social centers in Critical Mass initiatives does not happen only in Madrid, but is important to the existence of Critical Mass in other European cities too (e.g. London, Rome, Paris). Is the Okupation Movement a structural form to use specific values of Critical Mass in the European context? Or is it the structural and political characteristics of these cities that make these movements converge?

These social centers are not isolated because connected channels of communication live through the activists, participants, and the movements that use these spaces. The social centers constitute an important support for *Bicicrítica*, but at the same time *Bicicrítica* also provides support and an important means of communication, while also mediating the relationship between the larger society (as traffic) and the social centers (as outposts of cultural and political transformation).

Notes

1 This article is a summary of a more extensive article published in Spanish. Lorenzi, Elisabeth (2010) "Centro social en movimiento. Los talleres de autoreparación de bicicletas en espacios autogestionados" en *Okupaciones en Movimiento. derivas, estrategias y prácticas* (ISBN: 978-84-935476-6-0). *http://tierradenadieediciones.com/tierradenadie/?p=215*

2 *El movimiento de okpuación* ("Squatting movement") is a widespread practice in Spain, as in all of Europe, that consists of taking abandoned lots and buildings to use as gardens, urban farms, places to live, social and cultural centers, and meeting halls. The okupa movement brings together a wide variety of ideologies that usually justify their actions as acts of political and social protest against speculation and to defend the right to housing facing economic or social hardships. The squatter movement also often defends the use of solar, buildings, and abandoned spaces and its use by the public as social or cultural centers. The initial experiences of occupation in Spain can be found in the late 1970s as part of a citizens movement as well as a tactic of the anarchist union, CNT. The squatters' movement started to develop in Madrid in the mid and late 1980s, but the main expansion occurred in the 1990s, essentially as one of the main actions promoted by the autonomist movement and groups of social anarchists. A heavy wave of criminalization and the instability of most of the squats provoked a fierce crisis in the squatters' movement during the first part of the 2000s, with the exception of few remarkable cases. Recently, at the end of the last decade a new explosion of squats in Madrid took place simultaneously with a greater diversity of experiences, actors, ideologies and cultural references. As a novelty, three squats were even legalized. After the May15 Movement 2011, a new wave of squats, both social centres and houses, placed squatting again on the public agenda of Madrid.

3   Since the People's Assemblies started at the occupation of the Plaza del Sol in May 2011, the extensión of the 15M movement was extended to spread direct participatory democracy in the local context, the assembly method, the recovery of public space and critical thinking. For this reason, since June there are weekly People's Assembles in every neighborhood and locality, that create their own commissions and work groups to work out of reflection and direct action. One of the most well known actions is aimed at halting the eviction of people unable to pay their mortgage to the bank.

4   On occasions this saying has turned into a public declaration made by high ranking officials. For example, here is one of the declarations given to the press by the previous Mayor of Madrid, Jose María Álvarez del Manzano, with respect to the unauguration of the *Anillo Verde Ciclista* that surrounds the city of Madrid. "José María Alvarez del Manzano indicated that 'the bicycle in Madrid' is not a means of transportation, because the orography of the city does not allow for it, therefore this lane is an opportunity to carry out sport on it." In addition, the mayor insisted that security is one of the primary aspects of the plan. (*El Mundo* June 5, 2001)

5   Common name given to the downtown zone encircled by the first traffic ring.

6   The social center with the longest history in Madrid (20 years), similar to so many other social centers that were born in the early '90s in Madrid, the *CS Seco* began with an autonomous initiative and with the *barrio* (or neighborhood) collectives of the late '80s. Situated in a marginal zone where it was abandoned, the road taken by the social center is modest. It is known for the consistency and durability of some of the projects that inhabit the space: a library, an alternative distributor, a rehearsal space, alongside a large number of activities (talks, workshops, parties, and concerts). For years, the activities and discussions evolved through a clear strategy of establishing a neighborly climate and combating the urban redevelopment plan that proposed to raze the center. Years of negotiation and constant work succeeded when the district council offered them a permanent space in exchange for rent in 2007. *http://www.cs-seco.org/*

7   The *Patio Maravillas* is an old school that was okupied in 2007 and described by its promoters as an Autonomous Multivalent Space. The school had been closed for 7 years when it was okupied and the work of reconditioning and organizing the different activities that integrate the neighborhood began. Its philosophy of revindication, while remaining respectful, allows a great number of collectives and people to be embraced, who little by little incorporate themselves, and take this space as a point of reference. In January 2010, after an intense campaign of defense and with much support, it was evicted. The same night, after a demonstration, another building was okupied in the same *barrio* and the activities continued. *http://defiendelo.patiomaravillas.net/*

8   *http://www.schwarzerkanal.squat.net/*

Maravillosa Ciclococina DIY bike workshop in EPA Patio Maravillas, Madrid, Spain

Masa Crítica Buenos Aires

By Julieta Cal

On the first Sunday of December 2010, one thousand riders congregated for *Masa Crítica* Buenos Aires; as many people as on its Second Anniversary a few months earlier. We knew we had increased in numbers each time. But, this time, for the first time, we decided to ride on the highway that traverses the city, and transform it into a sea of bikes. So many of us madpeople on *ciclas* (bicycles) rolled triumphantly with hands to the wind, sun on our faces, towards a broken toll gate that was finally and beautifully breached by the *cletas* (also bicycles).[1] There is no way to adequately describe our righteous revenge against the lifted barriers, and the surprised and gloomy faces of the fellows in the tollbooths. It was the paradigm of *la Masa (Crítica)*: a free will concept lacking hierarchy, where an individual desire becomes collectively expressed. Entering the highway on a bike, a skateboard, or even on foot became the ultimate (re)appropriation of a public space forbidden to the minorities that commit the outrageous crime of self-propulsion. Because we are slow, we are told, "Don't stop the future, hippies!" Nevertheless, *Masa Crítica* is coherent with the contemporary course of Argentine history and the current creation of its future.

Questions about leadership, about citizen empowerment , about rejection of the abuse of power by the authorities have been asked many times in the history of Argentina, but most recently in the beginning of this century. One thing is certain, street assemblies, neighborhood community centers, trade fairs, food sharing, *piquetes*, *cacerolazos*, carnavals, benefits, and marches— to mention only a few instances of popular organization in the streets— should be celebrated in the face of the open wound of the deprivation of freedom and use of public space suffered in past years. Through the transition away from dictatorship, and towards democratically elected governments (for better or worse), public space in Buenos Aires such as streets, parks, plazas, public universities, public schools, public hospitals stand as both arenas for the struggle of the oppressed, and places of celebration of community life.

After the big crisis of 2001, when people lost most of their lifetime savings due to the steep and fast devaluation of the Argentine peso and banks held the money, a new concept in the public emerged: *horizontalidad* (horizontality).[2] The middle and lower class realized that their claims were not so different from each other's after all (in the words of today, we are the 99%), and it was realized (not for the first time, but in a different way than ever before in the history of the country) that the power belongs to the people and that the current "leaders" can be pushed aside by the people. "*Que se vayan todos, que no quede ni uno solo,*" (Let them all go away, let not one of them stay) was the #1 chant on the 2001 charts of protest songs.

Still, the appearance of Critical Mass in the land of tango almost four years ago raised a challenging question: Would a city that talks about the Revolution in every café understand the revolutionary potential of the human powered machine?

Masa Crítica Buenos Aires had two beginnings. The first was in 2005 when a Uruguayan and two Argentinians created a forum[3] to pull forces together and establish CM in the capital city of Argentina. After three attempts the ride froze up, but the idea was kept on standby. Three years later, on August 29th, 2008, the impulse was renewed with the help of Nadine, an Austrian recently arrived in Buenos Aires. An avid Critical Mass rider in Vienna, she sent a message to the still existing Yahoo! group encouraging cyclists to try again, offering to help organize. Her message put the metaphorical foot on the bike pedal once again, and this time the ride gained momentum.[4]

Since its first edition, *Masa Crítica* Buenos Aires has started every first Sunday of the month in the Plaza de la República, (a neural center of the city, at the crossroad of Corrientes and 9 de Julio Avenues), where the *Obelisco* stands tall.

In this highly symbolic spot of Buenos Aires (the *Obelisco* is probably the most used image as an icon of the city), we have seen all sorts of gatherings. The protest tents stood for months of the indigenous people of Argentina and from other parts of South America clamoring for recovery of their lands; soccer fans have celebrated local and national teams' victories; stages have been set up for free musical concerts; and sadly also car races have also started and ended here. Every year the Malvinas War Veterans gather around the *Obelisco* to remind us of that nonsensical war.[5] Choosing such an appealing spot was part of the success of the second beginning of *Masa Crítica*.

A good percentage of the participants of Critical Mass are there because it is so much fun to ride around the city with so many other people, with such a variety of personalities, nationalities, stories, talents. Dogs, runners, skaters, and rollerbladers have joined the party as have very original custom and tall bikes, choppers, modified or newly created frames, wireless stereo systems (where two different bikes can each carry a speaker and play the same music), people in costumes, live music. Creativity is a strong feature in every ride. Some bikers even carry a plant on their heads; "Think Green!" says the plant. If we tune in a little deeper, we can sense that underneath our rolling wheels, beneath the streets of Buenos Aires there is a pounding of many heartbeats, sounding the reunion of people struggling for a better world. In a city whose people have held myriad political banners and flags, the pacifistic and peaceful (except for a few altercations that happen now and then) rolling of wheels with no political slogan but *un auto menos* (one less car), *revolución en bicicleta* (revolution on the bike) or *más amor, menos motor* (more love, less engines) speaks to a different kind of politics—that of direct action, of building community, of bringing people together to prove that the whole is more than the sum of its parts.

Talking to bicyclists who have attended Critical Mass in San Jose de Costa Rica, Santiago de Chile, Paris (France) or La Plata (Argentina), and exchanging experiences with them about CM in the different cities, it is clear that certain doubts and questions are shared beyond the specificity of each city. We've even found many similarities around initial organization and communication, but each city develops a certain personality and impulse to its CM. In Buenos Aires there is stable and healthy disorganization as people gather for the *pedaleada* (ride), which tastes like the chaos of the new millennium struggling in full attention of the neurotic traffic on the street. For example, except for some massive returns to the *Obelisco*, the majority of the routes have finished in different public places with a slight leaning toward the northern area of the city.[6]

The first two years were also ones when *Masa Crítica* was intensely spread through word of mouth and xerocracy. The goal was to invite random cyclists anyone would run into on their daily rides to join the next Mass, as well as to educate them as to the general functioning of CM during the event, that is to say, to build a sense of mass-community. Communication during the ride was efficient. With less than 300 people on bikes in a space of fewer than 200 meters, a good shout would be enough to arrange taking a right or a left, or maybe a tall-biker would hold up a sign with an arrow indicating the direction the mass was flowing.

Certain "unruled" rules would be sacred: the whole *Masa* would stop if anybody had an accident, or the role of corking (its function being to stop car traffic at green lights) would rotate eventually among all the *maseros*, many of whom would hold friendly, "Thanks for waiting" signs. Before the Second Anniversary though, and thanks to voluntarily spreading the word that many *maseros* took on, *Masa Crítica* reached the newspapers and massive audience TV channels and radio stations, and so: BOOM! The second anniversary celebration exceeded 800 bicyclists. Since then, the average has been more than 1000 bicycles every month, and some months the crowd adds up to 2000. That number was even surpassed on the Third Anniversary (October 2011); some estimations put the number closer to 3000.

If you were to join the head of the *la Masa*, the same questions would be often heard: "Where are we headed now?" or "Should we turn here?" We believe that the observations made in the original Critical Mass manifesto are quite clear, and that it is up to each individual to align with that philosophy or not. Many, though, seem to not want to be oriented by others, but at the same time seem to want a fixed solution to their questions. The increase of bicyclists has introduced new debates, such as if there are or should be any leaders in the group. Some have begun to say—including worried parents — that *Masa Crítica*, which gathers children, youth, and adults, is not the best setting for the development of this kind of "anarco-cleteras" (anarcho-cyclist) work.

Within the "unorganized coincidence" of Critical Mass, its growth seems inevitably to lead to a diversity of preferences within the ride, and even the founding of new ideas and forms of organization. So, we've stepped away from the physical concept of holding on to the "mass." The *pedaleada* now branches out at a critical moment of choice, and the group divides on the go between those who want to climb a highway or enter an airport, and those who consider this unnecessary. Thus, the free and leaderless spirit inside each *masero* is not sacrificed.

The transformative process of CM points out that we are doubtlessly moving forward. The split in route that is seen on the ride now is simply a manifestation of the split in the structure of *Masa Crítica* Buenos Aires as it grew, which was accelerated first by the rise of participants between October 2010 and April 2011, but also by the change in virtual forums. The creation of a Facebook group was a turning point, not only in the number of members (it was 15 times bigger than that of the first Yahoo! group), but also in the quality of debates around solutions. The proportion between the number of members in the forum and the actual action taken to advertise the mass decreased. Roughly, if 2 of every 10 online panelists photocopied a few flyers and handed them out, that would result in a bigger gain in number of participating cyclists than the sometimes superficial exchange of comments in the virtual world.

Yet, this dissolution of the original core of *maseros* into a bigger mass heralded a widening of the political movement for use of public space and other social movements in the spirit of the original tenants of *la Masa*. On the one hand, bicycling became more mainstream. On the other, new forms of self-managed organizations were started by *maseros*, and pre-existing organizations gained a sympathetic affiliation to the ride.

The recently reelected Mayor of Buenos Aires, Mauricio Macri, who saw the rise of *Masa Crítica* during his government, used bicycle promotion as one of the banners of his campaign. Under his administration bike lanes were added to the city map as never before in the history of the city, some of them in better conditions than others (no thorough studies have been made to detect benefits to different neighborhoods). Also the citywide public bike sharing system was implemented, where any person can borrow a bike in the many stands distributed along downtown and surroundings, and return it to any other stand in the network. This system has helped to get white-collar workers into bicycling in the city. Big credit for these actions should be granted to the local activists that gained a space and voice at City Hall.[7] Critical Massers in general, however, maintain a critical eye toward bike events that the city government wishes to link to the ride, so as to avoid "infiltrations" of the ride itself, or cooptation of the movement.

In any case, the reach of *Masa Crítica* in Buenos Aires goes way beyond any kind of political cooptation. There is no doubt that upon years to come CM will be a resounding referent of a deep change and a massive return to human-powered vehicles as the axis of an elemental need: that of easing the congestion of motorized vehicles in the big cities. The change has already started, because so far the ride has encouraged families, elders, handicapped, travelers, clerks, and more to grab their bikes and try riding through the city of wretched traffic for themselves. Thus, many more brave hearts on two (non-motorized) wheels have appeared showing those who travel in packed buses or subways that self-propulsion is a beautiful thing. Critical Mass in Buenos Aires, with its message of coexistence, helps transcend with extra doses of tolerance towards the impatience, and sometimes violence, of car and motorbike drivers.

Equally important are the *Masa Crítica* acquaintances that have bonded into friendships, which in turn have propelled dreams into coming true. From small leisure projects, such as groups that organize weekend rides out of the city, and more institutionalized projects, like the urban cyclist association focusing on promotion of bicycle safety, have emerged, as well as self-managed spaces linked to Critical Mass (or at least to its spirit) in many different ways.

Consider the *Fabricicleta*,[8] a DIY bike repair workshop (but also a space of teaching, learning, and socializing to promote knowledge about bicycles) which was created by the original *maseros*. Interest rose among those who wanted to share knowledge and exchange information with other bicyclists. This longing became a reality with the establishment of a self-managed workshop in a space recovered, occupied, and maintained by the "Villa Urquiza Popular Assembly" since the years of the *horizontalidad*.

La Cocovilla[9] is another project birthed by a die-hard *masero*, Sergio. It is a village made of clay, with educational programs about recycling, permaculture, and all sorts of projects based on recovered materials.

Then there are the pre-existing projects that found synergy with Critical Mass. The best example is probably the *Oniriciclos*.[10] Their name comes from the union of two words *Onírico* + *Ciclos* (Oneiric, or, dreaming + Cycles); a pet name applied to bicycles with a double meaning as both dream bicycles and cycles of dreams. The collective *Delironautas en Oniriciclos* was formed months before the first *Masa Crítica* Buenos Aires, and Juan Manuel tells of the first encounter and fusion of the two movements:

> We had decided to take a ride around the city and when we were passing by the Obelisco *we saw a few crazies on bikes that were calling us over. There were 26 riders on the first edition of Masa, October 2008. It was by coincidence that we arrived there and connected to a bunch of people from different sectors, who beyond their formal occupations, developed individually creative projects. In this manner, we began forming a group, with diverse projects that pushed the same way: to explore the creativity that blooms with the beautiful riding of a bicycle.*

So what is the next dream-cycle of the Delironauts? They are planning a ride to begin on December 21, 2012 (mind you, it is the date of the end of a world cycle on the Mayan calendar), starting from Montevideo, Uruguay to arrive finally in San Francisco, U.S.[11] The project aims to document the cultural plurality of the continent, while challenging the standing centralization of cultural production (which is just another way of social marginalization), and unequal access to aesthetic education and exchange.

Velatropa[12] is another project that has been going on for two decades now, but has become strongly linked with *Masa Crítica*. Located on the campus of the Ciudad Universitaria in Capital Federal, *Velatropa* is a natural park and interdisciplinary experimental and educational center that explores questions of sustainability. Their objective is to exemplify forms of bridging the gaps between global, local, urban, and rural ways of life, where humans reclaim their role as stewards of nature. *Velatropa* has a seed bank, educational programs on urban farming, natural forms of construction, constructing with recycled materials, and rationalizing the use of natural resources, and they integrate school kids to their programs.

A final mention goes to the *Gratiferia* (Free Fair), which shares in the economic freedom of the Critical Mass movement, by promoting a sociopolitical-economic cultural movement for peace and well being for all. The *Gratiferia* functions successfully without attendants, and nobody gets rich on exchange with another. We seed the economy of the new era by sticking to our slogan: "*Traé lo que quieras (o nada) y llevate lo que quieras (o nada)*."

("Bring what you want (even nothing) and take what you want (even nothing)!") The *Gratiferia* is a public space that aims to address the illusion of scarcity.

In conclusion, we venture to say that the peaceful irruption of Critical Mass in a city with an intense history of social movements raises the potential for a new revolution, the only one we believe in. This is a community of awareness and nonviolent self-organization, but most of all, returns us to a pace of life that two feet on two pedals can handle.

Notes

1   Youtube video of that ride at *http://www.youtube.com/watch?v=y6j01vYCkx0*
2   For reference, see Sitrin, Marina (ed.). *Horizontalism: Voices of Popular Power in Argentina.* AK Press, 2006
3   Yahoo group MCBSAS *http://ar.groups.yahoo.com/group/mcbsas*
4   Recently, Nadine wrote an email remembering those days:
    " […] even though I had participated in CM in Vienna, Austria (…) I never imagined how much effort it required to organize it nor that it would work out so well! […] When I read for the first time that it had surpassed 1000 participants, when you were on the newspaper or the TV, when you overtook the freeway, or when the Fabricicleta opened I was (…) super excited and proud of you guys,(…) I went back to Austria knowing that it is worth it to believe in such a thing as "urban cyclism" (…), that things that can seem impossible at the beginning can actually become possible
5   The Malvinas Islands, called Falkland Islands by their controlling country, the U.K., have been longly claimed by Argentina; to make long story short, this claim led to a two month war in 1982, in which the British reasserted their power over the islands.
6   Sometimes in the beginnings the *tombola*, or lottery system, would be used to decide a final destination: each rider would write down their preferred arriving spot, then stick it to the spokes of a wheel chosen for the game, then the wheel was turned. A child would grab a paper and so the end was set, and even though it was seldom followed, it served the purpose of calming anxieties before the ride.
7   Specifically Javier Salas, who is an ophtalmologist by profession with the soul of a bicyclist, having done his first long bike trip when he was 9. He gave up his career to work in the transportation area of the government of the city, assuming the mission of insisting, from his low hierarchy spot, in the creation of a large network of bike lanes. He formalized the "bicyclist round tables" where any citizen or visitor could attend and participate in the discussions related to the vehicular chaos that reigns in BA. Javier, like many other of us, understand that more pedestrians, bikes, skates, and rollerblades can help in decongesting the otherwise slow traffic of the busiest areas of the city.
8   *www.lafabricicleta.com.ar*
9   *http://lacocovilla.com.ar/*
10 *http://oniriciclos.blogspot.com/*
11 With Argentina at one of the earth's poles, the idea of a longitudinal continental ride uniting Ushuaia (Argentina) and Alaska (USA) also became the obsession of another group. Gigi and Javier, who met during a *Masa Crítica porteña*, will begin their ride on July 1, 2012, with technical support from original *maseros*. *http://viajerosdelosvientos.bligoo.com.ar/*
12 *www.velatropa.com.ar*

Rome, Italy, Ciemmona 2008

Let's take back Rome!
Critical Mass, Ciemmona and CiclOfficine Popolari (People's Bike Kitchens) in Rome
By some members of the Network of People's Bike Kitchens of Rome

Critical Mass Rome started in May 2002, thanks to a few daring cyclists (20 to 50 people) who started meeting on the last Friday of every month in Ostiense Square, renamed the Critical Masses Square. The first few Critical Mass rides were generally euphoric, with some moments of tension, because the average driver in Rome is not used to seeing adults riding bikes in the city. Most people abandon the bike at age 14, get a scooter, and immediately buy a car when they come of age. Before 2002, bicycles in Rome were found only in basements and garages, and as decorative objects. Urban cyclists were rare animals: poor, unlucky, unimaginable relatives of the sport cyclists, the kind only normally seen on Sundays on Roman boulevards.

In this urban landscape, with an average of one car per inhabitant, Critical Mass Rome reclaimed the right to be part of traffic and to go beyond that. To be effective in pushing people to use the bike everyday, it was necessary to create support centers aimed at giving information on the use and maintainance of the bicycle in a unfriendly city like Rome. This meant also creating a social space where people could teach each other how to repair bikes used as means of transportation, by sharing mechanical knowledge.

In 2003 to fulfill this need, two "bike kitchens" were created inside two squatted social centers: the *Macchia Rossa* (*Red Spot*) in the Magliana neighborhood, and the other *Don Quixote* in the Prenestino area—in separate parts of the city. The bike kitchens immediately produced a new political voice in Rome, critiquing transportation models based on the dictatorship of automobiles. These groups used the bike on a daily basis as a form of direct action. A new political subject appeared in Roman demonstrations and social movement spaces: the biker activist—always with one pant leg rolled up and one down, and black grease on her/his hands.

Social centers started organizing events with the bicycle as a lifestyle theme. The bike kitchens became places where everyone could learn and contribute her/his capabilities, whether using the welder or becoming metal parts fetishists. The first monster bikes were created including two-story bikes, recumbents, long johns, rickshaws, and carts. The explosion of creativity took place on a foundation of everyday bicycling, leading to the formation of a community of cyclists and mechanics. It started to spread like wildfire, shaping a new kind of political awareness. The community centered around this daily struggle—but also with a monthly celebration in the Critical Mass ride—became more participatory, fun, and effective. Soon two bike kitchens were insufficient to satisfy the growing demand to learn to fix, disassemble, grease, polish, and improve bikes (e.g. by attaching a cart for pet transportation or for kids). In 2004, some *Don Quixote* mechanics opened another kitchen in the social center *Angelo Mai* next to the Coliseum. Rome, by then, had bike kitchens covering all the main areas, providing a self-made infrastructure for urban bikers' safety and service, making cyclists more aware of their presence and strength in numbers.

A crucial step before 2004 was the national Critical Mass in Milan during the Climate Change Conference (COP9), opposing the conference's inadequate politics with concrete action: pedaling! A freight train car was rented in Rome to transport all kinds of human powered vehicles and forty participants. Milan was overrun with 2,000 bicycles and the whole demo ended with a memorable drunken evening, where the idea of a huge Critical Mass in Rome developed. We had a vision of a great international, interplanetary day to celebrate the birthday of Critical Mass in Rome. We would call it the BIG CM (*Ciemmona*).[1] It began in May 2004 and we hoped it would become an annual event.

In May 2004, the first Interplanetary Critical Mass started, with people shouting, *"Rome, Start Pedaling!"* Car drivers stared in total disbelief. Motorists were swamped in a sea of bicycles, and they got the first hint that Roman traffic had inevitably changed. Gradually the attitude of the people locked in their cars started to shift, along with the urban image of the Eternal City. Many drivers faced the facts: it's quicker to go to work on a bike, you avoid traffic jams, you are not responsible for pollution, you keep fit and save money. From the windows of cars threats of physical assaults and aggressive verbal insults gave way to words of solidarity and participation: "When is this ride again? I want to come too!".

Apparently many started to appreciate that moving around Rome by bike means seeing the Roman ruins, the Renaissance art, the churches by Bernini, and appreciating the baroque architecture directly. Who could deny that it is much better than being stuck in a metal box looking at the bumper of the car in front of you? Critical Massers and bike kitchenistas realized they were working on a larger project of urban environmental and social education of the Roman people. The most utopian among us started posing key questions across various neighborhoods: who said that technology has to be expensive, fed by oil extracted from the earth in distant lands and then arrogantly and militarily subsidized by our State? Who said that the way to move around our city has to support a *doomed and violent* economic system?

Why should we be responsible for the destruction of our cities and the entire planet? What if chains and pedals could change a city symbolic of late capitalism, based on consumption and fake democracy? Perhaps a bike kitchen is the political place where people can reconnect with their city and their neighbors, creating a democratic vision beyond electoral democracy? Can bikes be a path toward egalitarian democracy? Are simple activities like repairing bicycles revolutionary?

So far the city administration has only thrown away money on 100-foot-long bike lanes, while dividing the sidewalks into bike and pedestrian lanes, something everyone was already doing on their own. No euros have been spent to increase awareness and promote the use of bicycles.

Rome is becoming an increasingly neo-fascist city in which individualism and pollution are rampant, and nobody cares. Critical Mass, bike kitchens, and daily bicycling are a pure novel countercultural movement in the third millennium. The era of illegal rave parties has passed, and the *Notti bianche*[2] events—costing millions of euros—became mainstream. In this context, *Ciemmona* became *the* self-organized and self-publicized event: the largest and freest event in Italy.

In the last eight years, *Ciemmona* has expanded into three days of activities: the last Friday of May birthday celebration in the usual place, same time, same predictable belatedness. The special Interplanetary Critical Mass ride is on Saturday—the climax of the three days—growing over the years from 1,000 people to almost 10,000 in the last couple of years. On Sunday, the *gran finale* is the out-of-town ride to Ostia—a beach town 15 miles from Rome—where the bikers can enjoy bathing in the polluted sea. During these three days of Critical Cycling many people from abroad are hosted in a free campsite in the meadow of the *ExSnia Viscosa* squat, across from the *Don Quixote* bike-kitchen headquarters.

If the wrench is the symbol of this new *velorution*, Rome is a key place for it, as the capital of one of the rich European countries, where the dissemination and promotion of cycling "from below" is pushed both by Critical Mass rides and bike kitchens. The will and determination of few urban cyclists, who worked on a common project in their free time, have brought the everyday acceptance of bikes into daily life.

Bike kitchens are among the few autonomist spaces uniting utopia and concrete service, turning upside down the contradictions of urban everyday life. In Rome, the bike kitchens keep developing: In 2006 the most central social center near the Coliseum was evicted, but the same people founded

Ciclonauti and re-opened a permanent bike kitchen with the consent of the city government. Some other former members of the bike kitchen created an occupied space called *Ciclosoccorso* (Cycleaid), in a different neighborhood, formerly an area with a natural gas tank. The least "politically militant" parts of the Critical Mass crowd continue holding a weekly cycling picnic, ongoing since 2006, and very successful in recruiting new bike fans.

In 2007 a new bike kitchen was founded by the *Associazione Ex-lavanderia* in a former insane asylum. *La Strada* social center also opened a bike repair place in 2007; and in 2008 the historical squat *Forte Prenestino* also started a bike kitchen. In 2009, even in the ghettoized periphery of eastern Rome in Torbellamonaca, the bike kitchen *la Gabbia* (the Cage) opened. The name hints at the concrete and toxic wasteland surrounding the place, and how the bike can be a tool of resistance against this urban landscape. There was also an experiment that lasted two years from 2007 to 2009, which saw a *CiclOfficina* (bike kitchen) within a space occupied by undocumented migrants called *Sans papiers*. When the place closed, its bike tools were used to open the bike kitchen *Pirata* in 2009 in the Quadraro area. Even at the University of Rome, Sapienza, an autonomous bike kitchen space opened, also with some bike-sharing on campus, offering free bikes, know-how and bike tools to students. In 2010 another bike kitchen opened called *Luigi Masetti*, dedicated to the anarchist cyclist, in the Centocelle neighborhood. In 2008 the "Network of People's Bike Kitchens" started in Rome to hold together and coordinate the increasingly vast and heterogeneous movement.

At the end of 2009, a sad episode hit the community of Critical Mass Rome: Eva Bohdalova, a loyal CM rider, was run over and killed by a car near via dei Fori Imperiali. Since then, Critical Mass memorialized her by moving the gathering point for the CM to the place where the accident happened: via dei Fori Imperiali Square, Pole 27. Eva's death shook many participants in Critical Mass Rome and bounced all over the media. In order to politically express our pain over this violent death, which happened right in the center of Rome near the Coliseum, some of the Critical Mass Rome founders created a committee called "Traffic kills you." This new committee tied together many Italian cycling organizations with the goal of pressuring institutions to recognize the rights of cyclists and pedestrians, and enforce European-wide regulations. We continue demanding 20 miles per hour speed limit in the city, pedestrian-only zones, bicycle lanes, protecting 'light' traffic, and increasing intermodal transport (bus+ bike, train+ bike, etc). These keywords have become part of the institutional language, infiltrating the urban planning committees of our capital.

Although so far Roman and Italian politics have not made any significant improvement, some of us continue to struggle on the difficult path of dialogue with the institutions. But most importantly, once a month we continue to meet all together in that place where action becomes horizontal and direct, where our life is subtracted from the daily routine and becomes artistic—a lively and gentle rebellion. That place is Critical Mass, and it is only possible because of all the people who believe in the subversive use of the bicycle, in Rome and everywhere else.

So, let's meet on the last weekend of May for the Interplanetary *Ciemmona!*

A few links:

http://www.tmcrew.org/cm website of Critical Mass Rome
http://www.ciemmona.org— interplanetary Critical Mass
http://www.ciclofficinepopolari.it network of Roman bike kitchens, addresses and links to many Italian bike kitchens

Notes

1   In Italian the letter C is pronounced "chee," the letter M is pronounced "emme," if you add the suffix -ONA at the end of the word it means big: CI-EMM-ONA is big CM, i.e. Big Critical Mass.

2   In English "white nights," *Notte bianca* is the title of an event that took place in Rome between 2003 and 2008, based on opening cultural venues all night—museums, theaters, concert halls, special performances in the squares. They were very successful, with 1.5 million participants. The city sponsored them and received good publicity and monetary returns.

Sao Paulo, Brazil 2008

Critical Mass is Dead.
Long Live Critical Mass!
By Thiago Benicchio

Critical Mass, called *Bicicletada* in Brazil, has been going for a decade, but was never that big in São Paulo, except for on annual World Carfree Days. In São Paulo, Critical Mass was the "Big Bang" for all the public and private initiatives concerning urban cycling, and also a significant inspiration to many other cities in Brazil. From the idea that regular people do use bicycles to move around, to the recent public spaces opened by the city, it's undeniable that this small and creative crowd was responsible for starting real changes in a car-centric city with 12 million inhabitants. On the other hand, São Paulo's *Bicicletada* wasted a lot of its power as a social movement, and in recent years suffered from the boredom of becoming just another bicycle ride without any deeper political, cultural, or artistic expression (even those related strictly to bicycles).

After the first period of 2002-2004, the years of 2005 and 2006 experienced a slow but constant growth: during summer, 30 to 50 or sometimes around 100 people attended; in the winter, 10 to 30 people. The monthly rides never got any significant media coverage. Instead, a small network of blogs and websites were responsible for its propaganda and coverage, starting with the Independent Media Center (Indymedia). No media usually means no police interference either. The only two big police confrontations that ever happened in mass bike rides took place during the World Naked Bike Rides in 2008 and 2009 in São Paulo, ending with people arrested and police using pepper spray, and a lot of media coverage.

The first time I went to a *Bicicletada* in São Paulo was on September 22, 2004, a "World Carfree Day" ride. I was shooting a video documentary about transportation and was interviewing one of the participants. Until that day, I had not ridden a bike in about 10 years. The historical association of bicycles and sports in Brazil made me think that the 10-kilometer ride proposed by Carfree Day Critical Mass was something that only an athlete was able to do. The ride went well, with around 50 people leaving Paulista Avenue towards the old downtown. I was not only able to complete the route, but also discovered that a bohemian journalism student could use a bicycle to move around. I kept the bike that I borrowed from my sister for three more months, bought a new one after that period, and joined that fun crowd of cyclists in their rides, while also becoming a regular commuter cyclist.

The second step after meeting *Bicicletada* people was joining the email group created to discuss and plan the rides. There I discovered that the first time the name *Bicicletada* was used in Brazil was during the early anti-globalization protests of the 2000s. A poster published in 2001 calling for a July 20 anti-G8 meeting is the first historical record of a Critical Mass ride in Brazil. During the inspiring anti-globalization "Global Day of Action" against the G8, IMF, FTAA, WTO, and other institutions, people (re)discovered reclaiming the streets as a nontraditional way of protest. Trucks with union or party leaders making speeches in loud voices, or marches with people holding flags and repeating chants, was replaced by soccer games or parties on main avenues, individuals distributing DIY pamphlets, black blocs, or even people dancing and riding bicycles to block roads and contest the capitalist order.

Many of the groups and individuals participating in antiglobalization protests didn't ride bicycles in their daily commute, so there's a small winter between the first time a *Bicicletada* happened in São Paulo and the origin of the monthly movement. On a Saturday morning, June 29, 2002, a small group gathered on Paulista Avenue and rode downtown in the first monthly *Bicicletada* in São Paulo. At first, the Saturday rides didn't have more than 15 people and happened irregularly. Attendees were mostly antiglobalization activists and students until the end of 2004, when the decreasing number of participants almost killed the idea of a Critical Mass in São Paulo. After some online discussions and a couple of meetings, the group decided to give up the Saturday rides and (re)start it on Friday nights. In April 2005, the first Friday night *Bicicletada* happened in São Paulo with 7 people. The ride ended above São Paulo Art Museum (MASP), where Indymedia activists were exhibiting documentaries about media oligopoly and the domain of the Globo television network in Brazil.

The change to Friday nights—along with the rapid increase of traffic due to Brazil's economic "development," some very creative actions, the diversity of political views inside the Mass, and a growing network of individuals using the Internet to publish content, pictures and ideas—all were crucial for making *Bicicletada* an important event in São Paulo. It was also indirectly responsible for the recent small changes in city policies concerning bicycles.

From The Streets To The Internet (And Vice-Versa)

In the early days, when Critical Mass was happening on Saturdays, the Internet was not so popular in Brazil and the propaganda was based mostly on xerocracy and pamphlets left on parked bikes. The first enthusiasts were anarchists and university students. In January 2002 an email group connected people from all over Brazil trying to organize rides in cities like São Paulo, Camboriu, Rio de Janeiro, Brasilia, and Florianopolis. In 2003 a specific listserv for the São Paulo Critical Mass started.

The Internet was a very important tool for the growth of Bicicletada in a huge city that's also short of public spaces. Articles, photos, and videos published first on the Indymedia website, and later on corporate social media sites (like Blogspot, Geocities, Youtube, and Flickr), helped to spread the idea. A few enthusiasts, amateur journalists, photographers, and videomakers kept up a continuous flow of new media. When I joined *Bicicletada*, I started a blog called *Apocalipse Motorizado*,[1] with a monthly report advertising the ride, and following up with multimedia coverage of the rides. The blog title was inspired by a book of homonyms published a few years before by one of the first CM participants. The book gathered articles written by a few radical ecologists and thinkers like Ivan Illich and André Gorz. The book's appendix was called "Some anti-car ideas," with Carbusters magazine texts, information on "how to organize a bike parade," an explanation about CM principles, and cartoons by Andy Singer.

Between 2006 and 2009 *Apocalipse Motorizado* reached around a thousand unique visitors daily and is still a good archive for all the photos, videos, articles, and links to the CM rides between 2005 and 2009.[2] Along with the *Bicicletada* website,[3] posts on Indymedia,[4] and sporadic reports on other blogs, *Apocalipse Motorizado* helped to spread Critical Mass ideas and images. Curitiba, Aracaju, Porto Alegre, Brasilia, and dozens of other cities started to replicate the actions, pamphlets, posters, and signs made by São Paulo riders (in the same way São Paulo people got inspired by San Francisco's, or New York City's ideas about CM). At the same time, other blogs[5] started to focus on urban cycling, helping to grow the "critical mass" of knowledge about riding bikes in the city—a very "unknown" (or abandoned) subject in São Paulo.

The Internet, of course, is just a media used to spread ideas; the noted websites were in fact supported by dozens of citizens taking pictures, shooting videos, or writing articles about the monthly rides on social networks and in email groups. The street actions and the strong group of people willing to participate and promote *Bicicletada* every month were the main reasons for its growth and importance in São Paulo and Brazil. The creativity of some provocative urban art actions, and the constant search of peaceful ways to share the roads between bicycles and motorized vehicles, also promoted the movement's growth. *Bicicletada* cyclists in São Paulo have worked to avoid conflicts with drivers probably because of the intrinsic survival needs of a small group (a few hundred—or even a thousand—cyclists are miniscule compared to São Paulo's population or to its six million motorized vehicles). Even though we challenged the status quo by replacing automobiles with bicycles every last Friday of the month, we were well aware of our weakness in case of physical confrontation with drivers or police. São Paulo CM always occupied a street space compatible with its size: when the group was small, only one or two lanes were taken on four-lane avenues. When we had larger crowds, the group usually took three lanes, leaving the bus lane free for motorized traffic.

In the early years, São Paulo *Bicicletada* was also an informal educational group, distributing hundreds of pamphlets to drivers with information about cyclist's rights, inspiring cartoons, and words about how to share the road safely. Those pamphlets were produced by individual participants, sometimes in a collaborative way with others, and then replicated via xerocracy. That was the first time in history that many drivers in São Paulo received any kind of information about the bicycle as a means of transportation, cyclists' rights, or the benefits of cycling. The chaotic situation of urban mobility in São Paulo, with its huge and always growing traffic jams, made it easier for drivers to understand that cyclists were not enemies of drivers or "road thieves" stealing lanes, but that the increased use of bicycles helps everyone by reducing traffic jams. The image of hundreds of cyclists in a space where just a few cars fit is very self-explanatory and can be easily understood in a city clogged by automobiles. Still, some episodes of road rage and psychopathic drivers happened over the years. But there's no record of seriously injured people or significant fights involving CM riders and drivers. [Until the infamous incident in Porto Alegre in February 2011.]

The "educational disobedience" of São Paulo's *Bicicletada* also tried to maintain good relations with transit passengers and pedestrians. Riders consciously left the bus lane free to demonstrate that the big "space thief" is the private automobile. It's not an exaggeration to say that many cyclists in São Paulo learned to yield to pedestrians in Critical Mass. Those two issues were urgently discussed among *Bicicletada* participants, since the free bus lanes were also used by eager car drivers, and stopping at crosswalks sometimes was dangerous due to splitting the group and allowing cars and motorcycles to get inside the mass. Anyway, the positive balance between transgression and respect during CM history in São Paulo not only made *Bicicletada* grow, but also attracted sympathy, respect, or at least tolerance from the majority of the population.

Cyclist Education and Urban Art

Bicicletada also had a great role as a cyclist "street school," especially concerning tips and hints on how to survive daily traffic. The free and direct exchange of information and experiences between strangers every month is, in fact, one of the most impressive characteristics of Critical Mass itself. The non-commercial and non-mediated space in this monthly Temporary Autonomous Zone makes every participant a teacher-student with the full and equal capacity to learn, explain, and dialogue with others. In a very hostile city, the exchange of information and knowledge about the best routes or the best way to "fight" traffic has generated strong solidarity among participants and resulted in a very active cycling community. Before *Bicicletada* there was almost no one providing information and help for the urban cyclist. In the early 2000s, the local government was still considering the bicycle only as a weekend toy, with some bike lanes inside city parks. Except for rare exceptions, like the zine *Bike na Rua*, or the Night Bikers, cycling entities and groups were only focused on leisure or sports.

The defiant and new activity represented by *Bicicletada* extended also to urban interventions and art. From the beginning to mid-2009, participants were able to take unified actions during or outside the rides to promote cycling or contest the car-centric culture that still dominates São Paulo. The unity never meant an automatic alignment of political or ideological views, but only a chain of trust and debate that allowed even the most conservative cyclists to support small civil disobedience acts such as painting bike lanes in a DIY way, or even "blocking" traffic during a few hours every month. Brazil lived 35 years (1964-1989) without full democratic rights (even formal ones), most of this period under a military dictatorship (1964-1985). The social destruction caused by this historic period goes far beyond the dead, disappeared, or exiled political prisoners. Less visible, but as severely damaging, is the legacy of a citizenry with very limited political experience. The first elected president in 1989 replaced the military dictatorship with a "consumer dictatorship," implementing strong and violent neoliberal changes. This political background makes the monthly Critical Mass much more important, with people gathered in the city's public Agora for direct action towards a new social and political reality.

While Critical Mass rides can be considered on the left of the political spectrum, the greatest "revolutionary" aspect of *Bicicletada* São Paulo was the opening of space for citizens to practice their right to meet in public and act directly without fearing political repression. During its history, CM participants protested against G8 meetings, contested a car company event in a university, visited students occupying the dean's offices at another university, and "disturbed" the opening of a multi-million dollar bridge made only for cars—with a picnic! The exercise of direct democracy inspired a real and deep political evolution for many participants, as the last Friday of every month was the first political experience in their lives.

São Paulo *Bicicletada* also dared to interfere directly in urban space. The actions taken by Critical Massers went far beyond the monthly ride, causing significant social repercussions reproduced in other cities around Brazil. In 2005 some participants decided to place signs to make drivers aware of bicycles on the road. São Paulo did not have any such signage and still had very limited bicycle infrastructure on its 16,000 kilometers of paved roads. But now there are some "official" signs on a small network of "bike routes" built in 2011. In 2007, some of the participants started to paint bicycles on the ground, creating an unofficial network of bike lanes that also became part of the City's initiatives four years later. The "people-made bike lanes" happened both during Critical Mass rides and also by small groups on separate actions. As the "Urban Repair Squad" network was growing, the quality improved, and the bicycles painted on the ground spread to many important streets, making regular citizens start to believe that the new bike lanes were actually painted by the city. For a few months, riding on streets covered by the "pirate" bike lanes became much safer, as cyclists just needed to show drivers the bike signs and paintings on the ground. That was all done with a few spray cans and just a few hours of work. The concrete effect of those actions cannot be scientifically measured in terms of how many drivers started to be more respectful of cyclists, but the symbolic effect brought not only by the paintings and signs themselves, but also by the social buzz generated by photos, videos, and articles about the "new bike lanes" made many people realize that something was missing in our urban planning.

Reclaiming the Streets and Bicyclist Square

In February 2006 the opening of *Praça do Ciclista* (Bicyclist Square) during a CM ride also helped to open society's eyes about bicycles. The *Bicicletada* meeting point was always an empty space at the end of Paulista Avenue, one of the most important in São Paulo. For a long time, the spot was called "the corner of Paulista and Consolação". But it was never a real corner. It was a small plaza in the center median with a small garden and a statue in the middle. Most importantly, it didn't have an official name. Rediscovering and reclaiming public spaces was always an important issue for São Paulo Critical Mass. "Get out of the car and take the streets," is imperative for the survival of a city deeply affected by the absence and low quality of public spaces. Cyclists immersing themselves in their urban habitat allow for new perspectives about the nature of reality, and consequently help to shape imaginations about new ways to transform it.

On the last Friday of February 2006, a small group decided to name the *Bicicletada* meeting point as *Praça do Ciclista*. Since it was not exactly a square, the fine irony of naming that space as a square was celebrated with a carnival street party. Handmade signs were installed, some videos were shown, an opening ceremony happened, and music was played. One of the videos shown, "Still We Ride" (about NYC CM) had just been translated and subtitled in a collaborative way by CM participants. In the following months, Bicyclist Square continued being maintained by people: the signs were replaced as soon as the city removed them, trees were planted, graffiti art started to decorate its walls and garbage was collected at every Critical Mass. *Bicicletada* finally had a name for its meeting point, written in all the pamphlets and posters calling for the monthly rides. In October 2007, *Praça do Ciclista* finally became an official landmark in São Paulo thanks to one of the city councilor's support. In November of that year, San Francisco-based artist Mona Caron visited São Paulo, rode with CM and painted a small mural at Bicyclist Square.

All the actions in Critical Mass were made on a DIY basis, without asking for permission or seeking any "sponsors" beyond the participants themselves. The pacific, creative, diverse, festive, and educational behavior of *Bicicletada* participants gained informal support from many government employees and different social groups, including the police. *Bicicletada* was the first social movement to "disturb traffic" in Paulista Avenue since a judicial agreement settled by the city prohibited any kind of protest in 2002. The prohibition was then justified due to Paulista Avenue's location in a district full of hospitals. But many speculate that the real reason for the ban can be explained as an effort to demobilize the massive anti-globalization protests in early 2000. The slow reopening of Paulista Avenue to protest starting with Critical Mass can be explained by the fact that the ever-growing number of cars were creating huge traffic disturbances in the region—making the argument that moving bicycles cause traffic jams more obviously silly. Besides, Critical Mass never fully blocked the Avenue. Critical Mass participants always played very well with the idea that Critical Mass can be a protest or just a "coincidence" of cyclists that decided to ride together in the same direction at the same time. The non-hierarchical nature of Critical Mass, without formal organizers that could be fined or punished by the government was also well explored by participants. The same "social and political marginality" that resulted in a city very hostile for bicycles—without any infrastructure, planning, or law enforcement benefiting cycling—resulted also in a complete absence of ways to enforce traffic laws against cyclists.

The Mainstream

Whether in New York City or San Francisco, the moment when Critical Mass lost its early aura perhaps was due to police repression. In São Paulo the moment in which the *Bicicletada* substantially lost its transformative potential perhaps took place in 2007, and has very different roots. As traffic congestion continuously worsened, especially in the expanded center of the city, the little ant-like work done by some dozens of individuals during Critical Mass and on our blogs and social networks caused the number of bicycle riders to grow substantially, at least among middle-class people.

Residents of the richest neighborhoods closest to the city center find themselves spending up to an hour just to drive 5-7 kilometers across town. If it used to be difficult and time-consuming to come and go from work, that was the predicament of the poor who lived in the peripheral slums of São Paulo (and since it was only the poor, it was not newsworthy in the mass media). The "success" of the development model based on the automobile brought the dire effects of motorized urban life to all social classes. It's no wonder that São Paulo posseses the largest fleet of helicopters in the world! But helicopters are not middle-class vehicles, and are used only by the wealthy. The absurd growth of car ownership combined with the paralysis of local government, either incapable or lacking interest in creating a quality network of public transit, rapidly became the "transit problem" at the top of the social agenda, but now also affecting the middle class.

The spread of news about the use of the bicycle on the internet and permanent street actions of the *Bicicletada* led many people to discover the bike as an excellent way to escape traffic jams. At the same time the experience of biking in São Paulo was not very friendly, making the *Bicicletada* an excellent place to meet other cyclists ready to act in favor of change. Thus, the number of participants grew each month.

Even in a city so explicitly committed to the automobile, it became impossible to continue betting on the highway model as a solution for the problem or, at least to sustain a discourse so explicitly in favor of investments and public policies subsidizing the car. Public works destined to support car infrastructure are still pursued on an industrial scale, moving fortunes and feeding political campaigns, while wide layers of society have realized that something *was* very wrong in the organization of urban mobility.

In 2007 World CarFree Day finally made it to the mainstream, with the participation of formal organizations, businesses, politicians, and media. The lack of understanding about the horizontal quality of Critical Mass, without leaders or representatives, led to the rapid increase of harrassment by NGOs, politicians, consultants, or reporters seeking responsible leaders or organizers in order to make partnerships or to conduct interviews. Still, at the 2007 World CarFree Day, on a beautiful sunny Saturday in September, over 500 people showed up for the first time and maintained the horizontal structure without representation or formal organization among the cyclists. One small scuffle between the police who tried to get traffic moving and some participants, among them the Secretary of Environment, helped to feed filmmakers' and photographers' cameras, multiplying the quantity of news covering the cycling transgressions in São Paulo. In the following months, the *Bicicletada* became a real critical mass, attended by at least 300 people every month.

During 2008, with a network of blogs, websites and small groups emerging in the *Bicicletada* or inspired by it to become more and more active, other efforts to contest the society of the car began to gain strength. The inauguration of the Estaida Bridge exclusively for private cars, quickly pictured on a new postcard for the city, was invaded by a small mass of cyclists who decided to have a picnic in the middle of the road. In the same year, the first massive World Naked Bike Ride in São Paulo challenged a false sense of Brazilian moralism and police repression as the streets were filled with painted bodies enjoying themselves.

Various reoccupations of public space began to happen in various places in the central city. In that year, the World CarFree Day ride again attracted over 500 autonomous riders in the middle of a Monday, without massive support from social organizations or media like there had been the year before, when the 22nd of September fell on a Saturday. Dozens of small actions happened, as much in real spaces of the city as they did through mobilizations activated on the Internet. The bicycle, as a rebuke to the model based on the car, has grown steadily in the imagination of São Paulo. Civil society was definitely winning, creating new non-institutional mechanisms to transform reality.

1968 and Forty Years Later

In the months of December and January, a large number of Paulistanos leave the city in search of beaches to alleviate the difficult conditions of life in a city known as the "Locomotive of Brazil." Imagine living inside a locomotive! The job opportunities and the possibility of rich material abundance, added to the absolute domination by the car, and to the abandonment of public space, transformed the city into a habitat inconvenient to everything but work. So everyone wanted to leave at the first opportunity, and this opportunity generally happens soon after the consumer hysteria and interminable congestion that happens around Christmas.

One part of the growing cycling community involved with *Bicicletada* decided to challenge the logic of escape, transforming the last months of 2008 into one of the most enjoyable and awesome periods of my life. A small group of madmen decided to stay in São Paulo and enjoy the beach days engaged in various urban interventions, holding picnics in parks and squares, small "happenings" in Bicyclist Square, countless wandering rides through the city, and putting in practice the idea to hold a Critical Mass every week during December. In that month I heard for the first time in life the phrase, "Congratulations for bicycling," coming from a group of people in a car. My New Year's champagne for 2009 was guzzled in the middle of an empty avenue, together with a half dozen cyclists that enjoyed an almost childlike moment of belonging to a city that everyone had wanted to escape. In that night, we visited three parties, travellers of space and time with our bicycles, enjoying the dawn of the 1st of January in an ecstasy of a special new year.

Thirteen days later, on a very rainy 14th of January morning, I took off for Belém do Pará to work. While this was going on, the same Avenida Paulista that hosted Critical Mass on the last Friday of every month became the scene of the greatest moment of media exposure for *Bicicletada*. Unhappily, and perhaps as usual, the media spotlight came because of a tragedy.

News of, "A cyclist hit on Paulista" was published on a website the same morning and rapidly hit the email lists of *Bicicletada*. The main city TV news broadcast the incident on its morning breakfast news, with images shot from a helicopter. Even though they didn't have any information about the identity of the victim, some listserv participants decided to go the site of the accident. Márcia Prado, 40 years old, born in 1968, was cycling on the Avenue when she was hit by a bus and died on the spot. She had participated regularly in *Bicicletada* since 2007 and was one of the people with whom I had just passed the end of the previous year, having such an intense and wonderful time. Around 50 cyclists a year die in São Paulo, but this was the first time that one of us fell to the transit challenge of trying to move through the city.

I received the news at the beginning of the morning, 2500 kilometers from São Paulo. On the phone a friend told me what happened while he cried. I cried and continued crying every time I had to deal with it. It was confirmed on the *Bicicletada* listserv and the mobilization began soon after. Dozens of emails were exchanged and a protest and homage was set for the end of the same day. Still nobody had a clear idea about what had happened, but everyone reasoned that something had to be done and that the street would be the only place for it. Like Critical Mass, the only certain thing we could predict was the hour and location of the meeting.

At the beginning of the night it rained heavily in São Paulo and dozens of cyclists arrived at Avenida Paulista, some dressed in white, others carrying flowers, and still others, with only their tears and a feeling mixed of fragility and indignation. That night, nothing would be able to stop a more pure and unspoken synthesis of Critical Mass: the cyclists took to the streets, blocked traffic, cried, lit candles, and hugged each other. The police quickly arrived with guns in hand, ready to stop the interference in service to the supreme logic of daily traffic flow. Flowers, candles, tears, and conversations made the agents of law and order understand what had happened there. A traffic lane was opened. Motorists, buses, and motorcycles passed slowly by and were notified by the cyclists that a life had been take in that spot by a society that puts the "healthy" movement of transit above respect for the life of cyclists and pedestrians.

A ghost bike was installed, the asphalt was painted with a white bike, and a plank was decorated with flowers. In the following days, various demonstrations took place along Avenida Paulista. The ghost bike remains there today. And as of this writing (February 2012) the only punishment recieved by the bus driver who killed the cyclist was suspension from his job while the case dragged on through the courts. One cyclist, commenting about the ghost bike homage to Márcia, said that it was the "best way to communicate and reach public conscience," better than they had ever hoped to see. A white bike installed in one of the most important boulevards of São Paulo, passed by tens of thousands of pedestrians every day, broadened significantly the social vision of urban cyclists. The mobilization that occured that 14th of January brought wide media attention and repercussions, and contributed significantly to the extension of discussions of the bicycle as a means of transport. Márcia was one of the signatories of a text called "Manifesto of the Invisible," produced by many hands among the participants of *Bicicletada* in September 2008, denouncing exactly the invisibility of cyclists in daily traffic, and demanding that the right to ride with safety be fully respected by all city motorists and guaranteed through actions of local government.

The Hype

Appearing in the mainstream media in 2009 had two opposite effects for the *Bicicletada* and its participants. On one hand, it notoriously strengthened the public discussion about traffic and mobility by bicycle. At the same time, Critical Mass noticeably weakened as a movement of contestation, and as an inspiration for new realities. Capitalism is incredibly efficient at coopting and assimilating rebellion and transgression to turn them into products, perhaps more so in societies with a low level of political conscience like that of Brazil. Exactly when the liberatory potential of *Bicicletada* appeared to be starting to subside, there emerged a true bicycling community in São Paulo, based on real solidarity, a profusion of blogs, groups, collectives, and entities linked to cycling. The response of the status quo was still timid, but the insistent push of civil society began to provoke some reactions by the government and businesses.

The number of blogs, websites, groups, collectives, and cycling subcultures multiplied themselves for better or worse. On one side, the diversity created new horizons for the fight over urban transportation, helping bicycle culture reach many more people. On the other side, an excessive fragmentation began to generate disputes of the type typically seen in countries with relatively recent capitalist democracies. Thus, both veterans and Critical Mass "newbies" began to see possibilities for individual success, or even for collective efforts that pursued other horizons of action. The lack of political maturity caused banal disputes and small acts of sabotage inside our own group, which soon could no longer be called a group after having grown too much without trying to maintain the solidarity that characterized our earlier days.

At the same time, public power, reacting to all this social activity, finally began to see the bicycle as a means of transportation and also as an instrument to capture political dividends. This new public face, however, was used more as publicity than for medium- or long-term planning on behalf of urban cycling. The appropriation of ideas born in Critical Mass made by business and government brought to the middle-class imagination some values until then unknown, but maybe in doing so, restricted that same imagination to the bourgeois limits of middle-class values. There weren't any reliable studies on the number of cyclists in São Paulo, but probably there are fewer today than in 2005. When the middle class finds the bicycle to be an individual solution for the collective problem of urban immobility, it reverberates in the media and governmental action.

It's interesting to note that the beginning of lower class "motorization" has the same roots as the discovery of the bicycle by the middle class: bankruptcy and the ensuing devastation of systems of collective transport, along with public policies of planning and urban management. If a middle-class youth starts to use a bicycle to avoid spending an hour to go seven kilometers, the poor population (that always depended more on bicycles than higher spenders) begins to have access to motorcycles, and with this, avoids spending two hours or more to travel 20 or 30 kilometers.

Brazil is a country where the media is heavily concentrated in a few communications corporations, and inspite of recent advances in the distribution of wealth, continues to be tied to a profound social inequality: the rich remain very rich and the poor remain very poor. *Bicicletada* was always a movement made up mostly of middle-class participants (with rare exceptions). The hype about bicycles occasioned by the absolute gridlock across the city inspired everyone to think about using this vehicle in cities, and certainly, resulted in a greater focus on pro-bicycle public policies, still nascent and fragile. These policies are transforming the urban imagination and can have positive results in the medium and long term. In any event, beyond creating a cycling community in the city, the *Bicicletada* also gave rise to a powerful social mobilization around the issue. It might lack maturity, but this is an historic process, inexorably and unavoidably slow in a society as complex as São Paulo.

After 2009 many *Bicicletada* participants began to follow other paths, perhaps because they were discouraged by the creative weakening of the oppositional movement, or because they felt attracted by other work opportunities and individual success in new marketing sectors, or because they believed that these choices could be allied to the desire to create structures more solid and lasting than the radical transformation of the previous two years. It's a fact that the *Bicicletada* was the source of an historic transformation that is still beginning, but was also the "big tent" for all the initiatives realized afterwards across society. *Bicicletada* continues to exist and can count on the spontaneous appearance of around 150 cyclists every month, still enjoying moments of great creativity, contestation, and joy. Diverse initiatives that emerged from the cycling Big Bang of Critical Mass are also increasingly active, even if they lack a sense of historical memory (another Brazilian characteristic), which makes it difficult to understand where we came from, and where we're going. Thinking radically, perhaps the concrete result of this fragmentation and subsequent assimiliation by the status quo, will not last and could be superceded by a radical evolution of the original movement. But history is not made of possibilities in the past, but by learning how it is happening now, and how it will shape daily life in the future.

An open epilogue

During 2010 and 2011, many of the old-time participants were not attending *Bicicletada* monthly, or they stayed in *Praça do Ciclista* when the ride departed. The "playful-educative" open space had become a space for childish disputes and conflicts, whether against drivers or even among cyclists.

On the morning of Friday, March 2, 2012, Paulista Avenue was once again the venue of a sad event that *might* change the future of *Bicicletada* and the cyclist's movement in São Paulo yet again. Three years after the death of Márcia Prado, the biologist Juliana Dias was hit and killed by a bus while riding to work. Eyewitnesses and CCTV cameras show a bus crossing in front of Julie and knocking her to the ground before she got hit by the bus that killed her. The news of another fatal crash on Paulista Avenue quickly spread on the Internet, and within the hour, a dozen cyclists were already there. Even before confirmation of the cyclist's identity, people were mobilizing on the *Bicicletada* listserv and on social networks.

Some lanes were closed for police and traffic authorities to investigate. The traffic jam started to increase—nothing much different from its usual routine congestion. Police gently pushed cyclists to the sidewalk so traffic could move "faster." Julie's identity was confirmed by a friend who worked at a police station. Around noon, a group of around ten cyclists crossed the police line and staged a "die in" on Paulista Avenue, lying down on the ground with their bikes beside them. They were removed by police officers some minutes later.

That long Friday afternoon repeated the same sad plot described above that many of us experienced in 2009. Electronic messages flew around, scheduling a protest-homage for the same day. Mass media once more pointed their lights and cameras at the sad event in Sao Paulo—and also towards four other cyclists killed in four other cities in Brazil on the same day! Around 6 pm, the first cycling protesters were already at Bicyclist Square. Juliana was a *Bicicletada* participant and also part of a collective called *Pedal Verde* (Green Pedal), that meets once a month to ride and plant trees around the city.

Around 8 pm, a strong wind started to blow in *Praça do Ciclista* and then the first raindrops began falling. The rain intensified and 700 cyclists occupied the full four lanes of Paulista Avenue. We headed towards the site of the "accident" to place another ghost bike, with cyclists walking and pushing their bikes. The rain suddenly became a thunderstorm and followed the huge group all along the walk. The mixture of water, tears, and chants asking for "Mais amor, menos motor" (more love, less engines), made that march one of the most sad and intense moments of my life. When we reached the site, another massive "die in" was made in the four now-flooded lanes. In a magical moment, a few minutes after the ghost bike was placed, the huge thunderstorm suddenly stopped.

The ghost bike for Juliana Dias is still installed where we put it, a few meters from the one placed in memory of Márcia Prado. Paulista Avenue is a common route for many São Paulo cyclists as it's a flat and direct connection between the south and west zones of the city. Beyond one of us being dead on the ground that morning, the huge and powerful protests related to the venue where it happened, a road that many of us commonly ride on our daily commute. A nationwide protest was called during the weekend and happened simultaneously the following Tuesday, March 6, in more than 15 Brazilian cities. In São Paulo, around a thousand people attended to protest against traffic crimes and demand better conditions for cyclists in our cities.

The death of someone always has the potential to bring those who are still alive closer together. In the following weeks, the several groups and individuals that had left São Paulo *Bicicletada* in the previous years to follow other paths increased their dialogue. A meeting of entities and collectives was called for March 24, 2012 which gathered dozens of activists to talk about their perspectives and the possibilities for improving and coordinating their actions. Besides talking about the origins and goals of each group, the discussion raised the idea of being more active in Critical Mass.

Many old-timers returned to *Bicicletada* on March 30, 2012, joining some 400 riders on the monthly ride. It's impossible to say this soon how effective "getting back to origins" will be to fix the fragmentation and diminishment of *Bicicletada* I described above. "Bike hype" is still a reality in São Paulo and politicians and corporations are still trying—often successfully—to co-opt activists. This dynamic is aggravated by the imminent October 2012 municipal elections, which capture all too much political energy, even from cyclists. It is still a slow process to face the huge challenge of transforming a city. Gaining the political maturity that would allow people to take history into their own hands will still take a while, and may not happen on bicycles in any case. Nevertheless, March 2012 *Bicicletada* was the most pleasant ride that I've attended in the past two years, reinvigorating—at least temporarily—the potential of this movement that will celebrate its 10th anniversary in June 2012. *Bicicletada* is dead, long live *Bicicletada*!

Notes

[1]   *http://www.apocalipsemotorizado.net*

[2]   *http://www.apocalipsemotorizado.net/bicicletada*

3   *http://www.bicicletada.org*

4   *http://www.midiaindependente.org*

5   Some websites that also supported Critical Mass and contributed to urban cycling ideas in the early times are: CicloBR (*www.ciclobr.com.br*), Falanstério (*http://falansterios.blogspot.com/*), Transporte Ativo (*http://blog.ta.org.br/*), Vá de Bike (*www.vadebike.org*), gira-me (*http://girame. wordpress.com*), Pedalante (*http://pedalante.wordpress.com*) and Escola da Bicicleta (*http://www. escoladebicicleta.com.br/*).

Many others came in the following years: Quintal (*http://nossoquintal.org/*), Coletivo Ecologia Urbana (*http://ecourbana.wordpress.com*), Igual Você (*http://igualvoce.wordpress.com*) and Panóptico (*http://panoptico.wordpress.com/*), among others.

Bicicletada
de fevereiro

Praca
do
Ciclista
3anos

sexta-feira (27/02)
encontro festivo: 18h / massa crítica: 20h
av. Paulista, entre Bela Cintra e Consolação

San Francisco in A Coruña:
Masa Crítica as a Prototype of Global Action
By Carlos Diz Reboredo and Moncho Vázquez

Mass media often covers the monthly presence of bicycles on the street. But we participate in a mediated culture of spectacle dominated by Hollywood language. The imagination of many spectators—and even our own—becomes populated by references to large cities and big statistics. But what function does *Masa Crítica* serve in a small city? How does it develop and survive far from the screens and the great metropolis?

We start from something well known: *Masa Crítica* is a global movement in a time when "global" has been instituted as a fundamental category that contributes not only towards redefining the dimensions of space and time, but also political action itself—the recent plaza occupations in the North of Africa and its later translations to camps in Madrid, New York, and London, are real examples of this phenomenon. Nevertheless, the challenge for us is to trace the singularities that the movement encompasses and modulates from our local geography, in the context of the small city in which we pedal and from which we write: A Coruña (Galicia, Spain).

We could talk about the *Masa Crítica* as a leisure ride, encounter, or monthly celebration, but here by contrast, we'll present it as a "prototype," that is, as a permanently open process, work-in-progress, creative and capable of maximizing links, networks, and relationships.[1] A prototype appears as something unfinished, subject to multiple interventions and reconfigurations by anyone, and ready to redefine, in action, its sense and reach. Take for example one of the forms of expression and distribution for which Critical Mass is best known: xerocracy. It allows us to design, implement, and distribute flyers, posters, and leaflets with our ideas, drawings, proposed schedules, and themes. At the same time, the Internet globally distributes said images and messages that are then locally translated in a multitude of cities across the world, to which cyclists apply changes and variations, adjusting the original model to their own features and particularities, incorporating their own twists and perspectives. In this manner, *Masa Crítica* appears before us as a polimorphing and multivocal global prototype that renegotiates with the stroke of the pedal its global meaning through multiple local accents that imbue it with life, narrating it and practicing it in workshops, routes, festivals, encounters, and protests across the planet.

With our vision and wheels framed to the specifics of the Coruñan case, we will not disavow—it would make no sense to do so—the local, regional, national, and international flows that pierce, nourish, and recompose it. We look at the city as a political stage for citizen action, and public space as negotiable discourse through tales, practices, and embodiments. We will take a brief look at the alternative networks that emerge and are woven between *Masa Crítica* and other projects and collectives, generated at time by a politics of proximity that connect to global trends—economic, political, ecological, and cultural. We focus on developing a policy/politics centered in places, understood as specific localizations of global networks; a policy for and by a specific place, but with global reach.[2]

Metropolitan Landscapes—Where Does the City End?

From physics we know that "critical mass" refers to the minimal amount of material required to provide a chain reaction. In the same way that reaction expands in the realm of bicycling, cities and urban planning have been moving towards metropolitanization of urban areas and corporate privatization of public spaces. They follow chain reactions dictated by markets, shaped by the politics of spectacle and production of brands, reproducing on a global scale the same patterns of construction, segregation, supervision and relationship to surroundings—a creeping monoculture. In this manner, "becoming metropolitan" signifies the contemporary, and it is in this unfolding where zones of production and territories of struggle arise.

By the end of the seventies, social revolts in alliance with students and minorities ruptured the Fordist production paradigm—the factory as the central axis of work and life. The urban crisis was connected to the end of the post-war economic boom, and it provoked a "spatial twist" and a reformulation of ways of understanding the city. At the end of the Second World War, the process of suburbanization launched in the U.S. by Robert Moses—that would later influence all European cities—introduced changes in ways of life: new infrastructures and products, emptying out of the urban centers, and maximization of individualism and defense of property. New forms of socialization and behavior related to leisure and tourism transformed public spaces into places of consumerism, while the car redefined distances and urban time, sustaining an oil culture, and with it, legitimizing the geopolitics of its extraction.

The surging fetishism surrounding the car and its promotion provoked its gradual colonization of space, that would break what had until then been the principal function of the city—a meeting point. Cities were transformed into places of transit (places of passersby). This spatial colonization expelled citizens from the places where their public lives had previously taken place, pushing them toward the private sphere, first in their homes and then towards malls/shopping centers, that in time would become the "Main Street" of any city.

However, the protests of the seventies clamored for another lifestyle and another experience of the city, at the same time that a model of global urban geography was consolidating itself.

In Spain, the effects of the Franco dictatorship (1939-1975) and the slow transition process afterwards, related not only to institutional transformation, but also to adapting to the new European economic zone. This slowed the remodeling of the Spanish urban landscape. Towards the mid-20th century, the lack of concrete and steel, the growth of population, inflation, the increase of real estate prices, rural poverty and rural exodus all provoked the appearance of settlements and slums at the edges of cities. In A Coruña, the population baptized this displacement in a beautiful metaphoric exercise with names such as "Korea" or "Katanga," precisely two contemporaneous locations of the Cold War with a strong presence of communist guerrillas.[3]

In the seventies, a movement of neighborhood associations in Spanish cities attacked urban planning processes.[4] These associations, organized into assemblies, protested against the American downtown model and public policies that attempted to popularize car use, highway networks, and expressways, while poor quality public services and lack of housing continued. A decade later, the fever for malls would invade urban public space, while shifting economic power to the service sectors. Industrial displacement and the decentralization of productive activities outside of cities accelerated, which only served to increase the duration of the displacements.

The new metropolitan model has been eroding the distinction between city and country. If the previous city constituted a geographic, economic, political, and social unit, today with the information technology revolution and mass media, "towns and cities are transformed into intersection points, stations, and crossings within an intense metropolitan network."[5] When we talk, then, about "the metropolitan area" or metropolitanization, we do not refer so much to the size of the city or to the number of inhabitants, but to the roaming tendency of a form directly affecting modes of living. We understand the city in its circuits of connection with larger or smaller points of population, explain its particularities by detecting the networks of production and consumption that cross it. We pay attention to the transborder exchanges and flows of merchandise, peoples, technologies, messages, and images that are established between a local and international space, turning every space into an intersection of roads on the global map.

In this panorama, *Masa Crítica* works as a useful vector for reformulating concepts related to urban public space and its relationship to citizens, environment, health, economy, culture, technology, body and politics.It also helps to reconsider the concept of mobility not only from a spatial but also temporal perspective: "To conceive of mobility in space, but to be incapable of conceiving it in time, is the characteristic that defines contemporary thinking, trapped in an acceleration that surprises and paralyzes it."[6]

Seven Years Pedaling in a Postcard

Since November 2005, *Masa Crítica* has been celebrated without interruption in A Coruña. Each first Friday of the month, at peak rush hour (8 pm), cyclists gather at the City Hall plaza—where official architecture and the movement are juxtaposed for the moment—and after ringing their bells and occasionally raising their signs, they start a collective ride in which festive, joyful, and co-opting elements are combined. Its history does not vary much with respect to other cities: street occupations, chants and demands, amicable chats, flyering, costumes and carnavalesque moments, event promotion, corking, smiles directed towards upset drivers, music all with an inclusive, decentralized, and horizontal character.

A Coruña shows on its skin, despite its reduced size, the clawing of the transnational dynamics previously summarized. Its population nears 250,000 inhabitants, though it nearly doubles if we consider the surrounding area. Situated on the extreme Northwestern Atlantic of Spain, far away from the postcards of sun and beach, its climate is cold and rainy, with a wind that blows hard through its alleyways. The dense circulation of up to 100,000 cars a day[7]—and the attendant risks and architecture of security, overwhelms those who have not yet incorporated the bicycle into their daily practices. They are confronted by cyclists who deny that the wind, cold, or rain are sufficient to impede cycling —"It is not a matter of bad weather, but of wearing the right clothes!"—taking example from cities of northern Europe (e.g. Amsterdam or Copenhagen) with more adverse atmospheric conditions, and yet with established urban cycling traditions.

The destruction of public spaces has been ongoing in this city. The paradigmatic example of aggressive privatization are the 12 shopping centers built in a radius of less than five kilometers. The most recent—Marineda City—has a surface area of half a million square meters, and claims to be Spain's biggest mall—and third largest in Europe! It is connected from the periphery into the metropolitan network through a recently inaugurated roadway. In this manner the city is defined by its capacity to turn towards the outside.

*On one hand, it wishes to seduce foreign tourists. On the other, urbaniza-
tion is governed by the need to facilitate access to airports, bus terminals,
and great transit axes. The facility of entry and exit is the number one imperative, as is the equilibrium of the city rested in its external counterparts.
[. . .] It is possible that the bicycle has a definite role: help human beings
recover conscience of themselves and the places they inhabit, inverting the
movement that projects cities outside themselves.[8]*

A Coruña makes an effort to produce a branded image that could grant
it a certain distinction and gain an attractive and seductive position in
tourist markets, projecting towards the exterior its historic legacy—the
roman lighthouse of the Tower of Hercules was catalogued by UNESCO
in 2009 as the patrimony of humanity—and reproducing on a thousand
postcards its most acclaimed attribute, such as the longest coastal boardwalk of Europe. It is precisely on the length of the boardwalk where there
is an accompanying bike lane, which in a jovial tone, some local bicycle
activists call the *"carril-guiri"* ("tourist-lane").[9]

Nevertheless it is important to highlight that in recent years, as an effect of transnational community strategies, the European Commission has
been encouraging development of "a new culture of mobility" among the
countries of the Union, defined by criteria of accessibility, sustainability,
and co-modality, that is, the capacity to integrate multi-mode transport
into the urban network.[10]

These international policies have led to municipal rental bike services
where "users" can take and return a bicycle from many stations. In general,
these stalls are automated: the user identifies herself through a code or
chip card, or even by way of cellphone, in such a way that the human-
machine interface is accentuated in the space-time embodiment of the
technological city, whose pores are nourished by new surveillance infrastructure, and provide a certain "liberty" under control. In Galicia these
services have been installed since 2007 with support of INEGA (Instituto
Enerxético de Galicia): the rental *Bicicoruña* public service possesses 200
bikes and total of ten stations or pick-up points, a percentage of 0.81 bikes
for every 1,000 inhabitant and 0.04 stations for every 1,000 inhabitants. [11]

Masa Crítica and Its Politics of Networks

A Coruña does not exactly have a big urban cycling culture, nor does *Masa
Crítica* gather great multitudes. Its historic maximum is around 103 participants and on average about 30 people gather every month. There are
regulars who always come, and new faces have been joining over time.

Perhaps it is no coincidence that in the last two or three years we have seen more cyclists in the streets. However, we should be cautious to attribute this success to *Masa Crítica*. Even so, it is reasonable to think it has played an important role. Alongside terrible crises—environmental, political, economic, and social—which shape the possibilities of consumption and common transit habits are ridiculously tepid public policies directed at favoring "sustainable mobility." *Masa Crítica* envisions another form of urban life. The different use of public space performed monthly by the ride has set a foundation for increased urban cycling at a local level.

As we mentioned at the start, we think of *Masa Crítica* beyond its monthly occurrence, in the interstices of the networks that, directly or indirectly, are woven or helped to unfold by it. In this city, the cycling movement does not start or end each first Friday of the month. Between each ride, cyclists pedal daily and various collectives organize and put into place lifestyles that speak to us of the possibility of constructing other types of relationships and other experiences with our surroundings.

Some of these projects have been born in the midst of the *Masa*, such as *ReCiclos*, a self-managed recycling and DIY repair bicycle workshop (to be further discussed). Others are catalyzed by *Masa Crítica*, or use it as a platform inserted within a cultural promotion circuit, attending to rides or information exchanges on Internet forums or email lists. Critical Mass, which appeared in 1992 as a happy prolegomenon of a worldwide wave of mobilizations, unfolds today on a global horizontal axis. Thanks to the efficacy of its unorganized self-organization, its hospitality and aggregating character, and its unquestionable success in public re-presentation, it acts as a gathering net, an inclusive and contagious movement that opens the possibilities of social and political forms of action. In some ways it generates other "critical masses"—cyclists or not—that integrate the convoluted multiplicity of contemporary movements. The concept itself of "critical mass," and this is important, has become generalized in citizens and activist discourses, turning into a recurring trope, to the extent that in the 15M movement, for example, it appears in a multitude of assemblies, tweets, and forums.[12]

In A Coruña, *Masa Crítica* organizes another annual event, the *12 horas en bici* ("12 hours on bike"). It is a day in which different people, alternatively, pedal uninterrupted. On occasions, this celebration accompanies Park(ing) Day, when people occupy a parking spot by filling it with grass, plants, or bicycles for the whole day. Also organized is an annual naked bike ride, with which we demonstrate that cyclists "ride unprotected (naked) among traffic." Also, the different *Masa Crítica*s of Galicia—present in eight cities of the region—celebrate Galega Mass each summer, which gathers a significant number of *maseros* (Critical Mass riders). Weekend rides are also organized, Critical Mass night rides, bike-polo matches, and even comparative mobility studies between different types of transport have been developed by the environmental department of the university in response to activists' requests. Alongside these initiatives, in a combination of centrifugal and centripetal impulses, *Masa Crítica* becomes hybrid. It infiltrates different projects and initiatives, producing knowledge and experiences, functioning as a network. Creatively acting in the logic of a swarm, *Masa Crítica* produces a form of intelligence, headless and decentralized. The swarm is an intelligent system that does not require central control, whose intelligence is fundamentally based on communication.[13]

To cite a few examples of that intercommunication, various cycle activists participate in *Zocamiñoca*, a project self-defined as a "cooperative of conscious and responsible consumption." In recent times, inspired by other projects at a state level, various *maseros* collaborated with the cooperative as bike messengers, distributing products in cargo bikes and giving this vehicle a different type of presence in a city not used to such scenes. Also various activists of *Masa Crítica* have collaborated on occasion with the self-managed social centers and *okupa* homes, giving talks about the history of the movement or its local activities, organizing workshops about mechanics, or taking the *ReCiclos* workshop to plazas. Many have participated in the 15M encampment and joined with Food Not Bombs, combining in this manner recycling and public space, two of the major points of recovery/reclaiming of the movement.

In another example of contagion and feedback, cycle activists of A Coruña have been collaborating on a platform *Salva o tren* (Save the Train), in defense of the short distance train that runs the risk of being eliminated with the arrival of the AVE (Alta Velocidad Española—high velocity train in Spain). In February 2010, they participated in the mobilizations that took place in the city during the celebration of the European Transport Summit. Finally, in the bundle of itineraries and lines that run through the multiple and multi-situated practices of cycle-activists, various participants of *Masa Crítica* also joined global events such as *la Criticona*—the largest Critical Mass in Europe, next to *la Ciemmona* of Rome, or *Vèlorution Universelle* of Paris—celebrated in Madrid and Bilbao, or the Cyclocamp, a festival thought up as a convergence point or interconnection for projects based on DIY culture, celebrated during the Summer of 2011 in Ottensheim, Austria.

Prototype, Trajectory and Public Space

Often we think of the city as something finished, immutable, a structure incapable of being perturbed or bending even just a bit; some even thought of capitalism in the same way, and before then, others thought so of social-ism. We know it is not true. By definition, "urban" is what happens, what is always happening; and the city is the framework par excellence of the changes, crossings, borders, flows, and contagions, the place of encounter of the unexpected, the unknown, the foreign. To be precise about the con-cept of prototype, we want to think of *Masa Crítica* in the same manner. If she transforms and constructs relational spaces as she passes through the city, she also operates on herself every time that she moves through, every time she narrates herself through the Internet or when she conju-gates verbs with the speech of other movements, when she joins with other projects, and with the body of the city herself. And she doesn't act alone, but with others, in others and through others, and in many paths; this is why we define *Masa Crítica* as a global prototype.

Prototypes only acquire value and meaning, they can only be defined, to the extent that they are generated, constructed by way of an iterative process: step by step, piece by piece, idea by idea. Its fragility is at the same time its potency; they are not stable because they have not been closed, and they have not been closed because their value is in their openness, in the movement, in the cracks that are gateways to other forms and possibilities. In their analysis of prototyping within the *Medialab Prado*, Corsín and Estalella fix its origin in the language of open source code, open by definition and produced among all. But what interests us most is not the object itself, but the prototyping action. In their recent application of the concept to the encampment and the *barrio* (neighborhood) assemblies prompted in Madrid by the 15M move-ment—where by the way *Masa Crítica* has also been very present[14]—they've employed the pertinent expression: "prototype of political action." We are no longer simply prototyping objects, but relationships and societal forms.

Masa Crítica would, then, be an open source code prototype. It is not only the openness of the process of production but also that the documentation of production is open and, therefore, shared. Forming DIY repair bicycle shops by consulting on the Internet what others have done, designing street theater and tactical celebrations according to what is seen in other cities, con-structing bike trailers with used inner tubes documented on YouTube, or learning to weld and assemble the pieces of a cargo bike from notes taken during *Cyclocamp*,[15] are examples of these forms of prototyping. But, in the same way that at *ReCiclos* we "fabricate" a bicycle by recycling pieces and technologies that redefine its symbolic meaning and value—taking parts from old bikes and incorporating them in new models—*Masa Crítica* at a global and metaphorical level functions like that bicycle to which changes and grafts are applied.

The city can only be understood in motion, because it is itself movement, a landscape seen and lived as physical space in constant change. "*Critical Mass,*" in its original definition by George Bliss,[16] is born in a static moment, a waiting in tension until the group of cyclists grows larger, but takes on visibility and power as soon as it starts rolling, being many but moving as one body.[17] When *Masa Crítica* occupies the street and inverts the habitual order of the urban roadways, slowing the rhythm of cars and accentuating the corporal and direct practice of physical space, it unfolds a new cartography that speaks of another city, of other topographies, embodied in the experience of cyclists. It unfolds a type of symbolic architecture that goes beyond concrete and asphalt, that prioritizes relationship space over transactional space, the anthropological experience over the geography of geometric space.[18]

While pedaling, the sense of "urban" is renegotiated through subjective experience. To go to where a body can, to stop at any spot to chat with a friend or a neighbor, to take on more city and more territory on your own, to not stop at gas stations, to not depend or wait anymore for another vehicle, to feel the light, the smoke, the bell ring and horn, the rain, and the even the flying stones. When cycling, the rider is in direct contact with the rise and fall of the land, and connects directly to an *ecology of the living*. On the street and in the plazas, but also in workshop, festivals, assemblies, and in cyberspace *Masa Crítica* can be interpreted as a roaming creation, anonymous, an *opera aperta*, an invitation to "make the most," an *oeuvre* in movement characterized by "the possibility of a multiplicity of personal interventions."[19]

When rolling through the streets, the movement of bicyclists act as trajectories, as forms of writing or acts of speech. These trajectories are not coherent with respect to constructed space, written and invented in spite of a pre-fabricated environment. "It is about unforeseeable phrases in a place ordered by the organizing techniques of systems."[20] Through this phraseology, different wishes are drafted, and fundamental dilemmas are proposed. "Grammar supervises the propriety of terms,"[21] as the grammar of urban plans and cemented institutions confronts *Masa Crítica*. *Masa Crítica* is a form of enunciation, a manner of speech, and play on words, transforming the rhetorical alterations conjugated in public space into political and antidisciplinary acts. This repurposing of public space is constant within a movement that understands what is "public" as a place of relationships, encounter, information, play, learning, and politics.

In A Coruña, the fad for shopping centers is only one example of the process of metropolitan privatization. The car is granted unrestrained privileges with respect to other vehicles, and public space is sanitized by mass media and the political class it serves, while among activists it becomes ideology.

What does it mean when we say public space? For urbanists, architects, and designers, it means an emptiness between constructions to be filled according to the objectives of marketers/promoters and authorities, who tend to be the same. In this case, we are dealing with zonesto be altered over and over again, an environment to be organized in order to guarantee good fluidity between points, adequate uses, desirable meanings, a clean space, so that the business constructions or official buildings in front of those spaces have their security guaranteed [. . .] To speak of space, in a context defined by capitalist organization of territory and real estate production, always ends up as a euphemism: in reality it is meant as land.[22]

In a global landscape overwhelmed by flows and velocity, a small city like A Coruña does not remain at the margins of such dynamics, but to the contrary, it is soaked in them until numbed. In this late phase of modernity, public space is conceived at the highest spheres as a derivative of commerce: it must allow circulation, traffic, and thus streets turn into simple communication channels, accelerated by the rhythm of the city. The car, still today, continues to represent that image of progress linked to freedom of movement and speed: "Its effect on public space, especially over space on streets, is that space becomes insignificant or irritating unless it can be subordinated to freedom of movement [. . .] To the extent that one can use an automobile to gain freedom of movement, one stops believing that the medium could have any significance, except as a way of achieving the objective of one's own movement."[23]

Capable of entering and exiting from official institutions—integrating itself into the cultural programming of the city government through classes in riding and basic bicycle maintenance, or conducting mobility studies for the university—the intelligence of *Masa Crítica* radicalizes in the interstices, in tracing ephemeral itineraries throughout the metropolitan area, through which to weave, step by step, a prototype of citizen action that, despite knowing that its success will not be measured in terms of "complete" or "closed," it could come close to, in its openness, new forms of public living.

ReCiclos Workshop: Recycling as a Political Practice

Directly connected to *Masa Crítica* appears *ReCiclos*. The fact that many people refer to it as the "workshop of *la Masa*," tugging at metonymy, shows the close relationship between both projects. The experience began in December 2008, in the basement of an old bookstore, managed then by the assembly of the social center *Própolis*. The workshop was born in the del Agra neighborhood, the zone of greatest population density and with most migrants in the city. It is a run-down *barrio*, with narrow sidewalks and without a single park in an impoverished zone.

The workshop is self-organized on the basis of DIY culture, occupying two floors that for years have been freely ceded by the tenant to artist and activist collectives. These various underground collectives have been defending alternative forms of citizenry, as well as migrants who—even today—make use of the space to gather, organize, pray, and dance.

ReCiclos works in a relatively simple way, based on three "Rs": recover, repair, and *regalar* (to gift). Initiated by local *maseros*, its opening was inspired by experiences in other Spanish cities, such as that of *Patio Maravillas* or the *Centro Social Seco* in Madrid.(The phenomenon of self-repair workshops extends all across Europe: the *cicloofficina* in Rome, the bike-kitchen in Austria, and the *ateliers* in France are examples of its continental ramifications.)

Opening one afternoon a week, the workshop works as a place of encounter, where knowledge and projects are exchanged. Tools are made available, which have been donated or bought with a common fund. There are old abandoned bicycles or bikes that people have gifted, available as fixer-uppers. But there are also hundreds of loose parts, some defective, and others in perfect condition, gathered as donations from bike stores or recovered from old machines: handlebars, wheels, seats, derailleurs, chains, mixed into the smell of grease and rubber.

Self-repair denotes the will to make the workshop into a place of empowerment where people use tools and share mechanical knowledge with people present. Each person must repair and on their own create the bicycle that they will later take home free of price, with the condition to use it, or return it, if not, to the workshop, so that others may use it.

Mounting or assembling parts, the action of bricollage is carried out, curiously, using parts which the newer they are, the more hermetic and less malleable they are. Nevertheless, the prototyping action carries out constant twists and reconfigurations of objects. Acting as an escape valve from the market system, the workshop works as a political laboratory where recycling is conceived as a tactic of resistance. The discourse of sustainability, so often publicized in recent years by the government, is for some cycle-activists a discourse articulated by the means of power, through which sustainable development is defined as the achievement of western modernity, seen uncritically and taking as a given the economization and commodification of nature.[24]

From within *ReCiclos*, the bicycle is understood as a symbol capable of sustaining various struggles. Ecology goes beyond the environment, the same way *Masa Crítica* goes beyond mobility. Recycling as a political tool speaks of other forms of relation, production, and consumption:"The question of what type of city we want cannot be divorced from that which asks what type of social links, relationship to nature, lifestyles, technologies, and aesthetic values we want. The *right to the city* is much more than the individual freedom to access urban resources: it is about the right to change ourselves by changing the city."[25]

Invisible Cyclists and Ways of Envisioning

Just before the dawn sun delivers its first rays, Miguel is ready to leave. When he walks outside the gate, with the cold of first hours, he takes his bicycle and rolls downstream towards the longshoremen's dock. This helps him avoid the exaggerated price of the bus that he could only take back home, in any case, because service does not start until later. Miguel is one among many in the battalion of "invisible cyclists"[26] that make use of *Re-Ciclos* and pedal about A Coruña. From the Californian docks of Long Beach to the port of our city on the extreme European west, the image is reproduced every morning. The "migrants"[27] go down to the port on their bicycles to load and unload, if they are lucky, materials arriving—like them—from other ports, fated to enter into circulation through the local circuits of distribution and consumerism. A globalized market stimulates among our local actors daily creative micro-tactics of vital engineering.

It is common among the movement and within its aggregating nodes—social centers, cooperatives, Internet forums, workshops, zines, etc.—to repeat a discourse that, based on categories of risk and security, critiques the lack of protection and visibility of urban cyclists. Therein lies one of the greatest gambles and successes of the movement: to make them visible, present in everyday life. Now, what of those others which we make invisible in our own tales? The problem of invisibility supposes a complex grid of crossings and power relationships, difficult to cover, but at times it is cyclists themselves—and among them, elites and mainstream currents—that marginalize from their myths and histories the migrant bicyclist or impoverished cyclists. Very briefly, we counterpose mainstream cycle activism—see the case of *Cycle Chic*—with lifestyles of an invisible current that—living on the border—makes the bicycle an indispensable means of life and a tool for carving out territories within the city.

We will not deny that differences exist among migrants. Among the community of Senegalese and Peruvians—the two with greatest presence at the workshop—we could even distinguish two generations, differentiated by their position towards the bicycle, justified at the same time by age differences. The first of them, represented by the parents of the children who come to *ReCiclos*, is most focused on the utilitarian aspects: with the bicycle they move easily, arrive at the port, and above all, save some money at month's end. For the younger ones, however, who may fight over who gets to take a

BMX or some old 20-inch tires home, the priority in some cases is aesthetics as a sense of distinction,[28] or said in a less academic form and in their own words: *"¡una bici guapa para hacer el tanto!"* ("a handsome bike to fool around on!") . . . Nothing that differentiates them from the rest of the non-foreigner youth that come around every Monday. But, when they go out on the street on their bicycles? What makes them invisible? Invisibility is a function of the way one sees, or as Dan Koeppel put it: "Are they invisible, or are we blind?"[29]

Many of these cyclists are invisible to power and institutions, to ministries or police, because some find themselves in irregular situations, without work permits or resident visas, or without other legal papers. They are also invisible to the Left due to the above—unattended and forgotten. But, let us not fool ourselves, invisibility can be employed as a protective mask. The expression "to be present" is used by Sassen to speak of "countergeographies of globalization."[30] Once the urban space has been denationalized by the effect of multinationals, the focus should be direted at specific places where those who do not have power, but do have the power to produce, use their presence in the city to establish themselves as informal political subjects. However, when you feel observed and when you know that a police check can change your life, to be present becomes a risk and, on occasion, to move about unperceived can become a true art.

Once the old institutions of imprisonment—schools, jails, or barracks—are in crisis and the functions of control are delocalized, the migrant begins to develop out in the open. This is when the same city acts as a means of surveillance, under a logic of urban prevention and segregation, imposing categories such as "dangerous class," clandestine, risk subject, etc.[33] These "invisible cyclists" are categorized sometimes by our own contaminated sight, within the network of separatist cleansing. From that optic the invisible will be those who do not play any role in the new metropolis, those who are inserted into other discourses, "floating populations of urban nomads who occupy local pockets of extreme hardship, porters of poverty, decadence, sickness, drugs, crime, and violence."[32]

The city merges with the skin of cyclists. But it also does not let itself be seen, hiding in secret corners and intimacies invisible under the footprints of passersby. The migrant body on bicycle is ignored, but by making one body with the city as a migrant settles in, it is then the same city that does not tell all, that stays silent, and helps the migrant new resident escape from the great eye.

In their itineraries, migrants redraw a completely different map of the city. They enter and exit from the public and the private, from official institutions and autonomous zones, using the bicycle to trace routes between their populated barrios and the poles of wealth. The irregularity and insta-bility of these itineraries speak to the fragility of urban life. As for the poor and sick of Johannesburg, the maps of life are traced in movement between the workshop and work, between the wheel and the docks: "Mobility is not a temporary state, but a basic condition for survival in the city."[33]

The invisible social opposition alluded to by Chris Carlsson continues to grow, making the bicycle into a symbol, not only of "desertion from the hy-per-exploitation of the car/oil nexus"[34] but of an entire contaminated moral ecology. In these times, *Masa Crítica* and *ReCiclos*, in their small daily ges-tures, gamble on another way of seeing the city, and in doing so, of looking at ourselves. The processes of metropolitization accentuate the modern values that regulate the behavior of bodies in space, by ordering, distributing, track-ing, and punishing them, separating them to avoid contagion and infections. Public space is lived increasingly more as *spaciousness*, or as Isaac Joseph says, "as social space ruled by distance."[35] If only for the sake of stopping our igno-rance of what is right in front of us, stopping our talk of invisibles, we must make an effort—just like the global prototype has been doing for the last twenty years—to merge our bodies and our spaces. And pedal.

Notes

1   The notion of "prototype" from which we take inspiration is being developed, among others, by the an-thropologist Adolfo Estabella and Alberto Corsín, who carry out an interesting ethnography in rela-tion to the Medialab-Prado (Madrid), a space oriented to the production, investigation and distribution of digital culture. For an understanding of said concept and what they themselves define as "work in progress" see among others: "Prototyping: A Sociology in Abeyance" and "Prototyping Relationships: On Techno-Political Hospitality," both contributions to *Anthropological Research on the Contemporary Studio* http://anthropos-lab.net/studio/episode/03/, or visit the website *http://www.prototyping.es/*.

2   S. Sassen, 2003. Countergeographies of Globalization. Gender and Citizenry in Transborder Circuits. Madrid, Traficantes de Sueños, p. 38.

3   J. M. Cardesin, 2011. "'Spain is Different': Economy, Politics, and Urban Growth (1940-2000)," in Lars Nilsson (editor), *The Coming of the Post-Industrial City. Challenges and Responses in Western European Development since 1950*. Stockholm, *Studies in Urban History*, No. 38.

4   For a detailed analysis, see M. Castells, 1986, *The City and the Masses: Sociology of Social Urban Move-ments* (Madrid, Alianza). This movement had great repercussions on the Spanish state, and its capacity to transform the urban structure.

5   E. Soja, 2008, *Postmetrópolis*. Madrid, Traficantes de Sueños, p. 220.

6   M. Augé, 2007. *Por una antropología de la movilidad*. Barcelona, Gedisa, p.89.

7   See Plan Director de Mobilidade Alternativa de Galicia, de la Consellería de Medio Ambiente, Ter-ritorio e infraestructuras de la Xunta de Galicia, de septiembre de 2011. [Master Plan of Alternative Mobility of Galicia, the Environmental, Land and Infrastucture Council of the Xunta of Galicia, September 2011].

8   M. Augé, 2009. *Elogio de la bicicleta*. Barcelona, Gedisa, p. 63.

9   Guiri is the name of with which, in joking tone, the Spanish refer to tourists. With this name, there is an underlying critique of the urban model that offers scarce preference for cycling mobility. The bike lane that runs along the coast is not useful to daily commuting cyclists through the inner city or neigh-borhoods, to go to work or to the university, all far from the tourist points that are strategically placed on that route.

10 For more information about an institutional concept of mobility, see "Green Book towards a new cul-ture of urban mobility," published by the Commission of European Communities, *http://ec.europa.eu/transport/clean/green_paper_urban_transport/doc/2007_09_25_gp_urban_mobility_es.pdf*.

11 Data taken from *Master Plan of Alternative Mobility of Galicia, op.cit.*

12 In speaking about the 15M movement, we refer to the social mobilizations that, in plazas or in cyberspace, have been unfolding in Spain since May 2011, with the "Arab Springs" of North Africa as antecedent and followed by Occupy Wall Street. Often, outside Spain, activists and media refer to this movement as *#spanishrevolution*.

13 For a reading of the intelligence of the swarm, read M. Hardt and T. Negri, *Multitude: War and Democracy in the Time of Empire*. Barcelona, Debate, pp. 120-122.

14 At the Puerto del Sol in Madrid, symbolic meeting point of the 15M, a sign was present at the camp: "The wheels will move the world." During the final months, frequent joint action between *Masa Crítica* and 15M, converging in demonstrations and shared organizing routes. Within Galicia, the *Masa Crítica* at the city of Pontevedra (80,000 residents) was born as a result of the 15M.

15 As a consequence of this flow of knowledge and routes, the *Ciclofactería* was recently inaugurated at the *Okupado Social Center* in Palavea (A Coruña) where a good part of the knowledge acquired in the *Cyclocamp* is put to practice. The starting point of this project was born in the midst of Hackmeeting in October 2011, a transnational encounter of "hacker culture" narrowly linked to the prototype and logic of open source code.

16 See. T. White, 1992. *Return of the Scorcher*. Green Planet Films.

17 Precisely the reading of social movements made by authors Michael Hardt and Toni Negri, who analyze the logic of networked movements as a multitude composed of the sum of multiple singularities, that are not reduced but conserve their particularities at the same time that they join a common cause, coincides in this case, at least in Spain, with the official transit code which considers cyclists riding in group as a sole mobile unit in order to determine right of way priority. See Article 23, point 5, section C of the Ley Sobre Trafico, Ciculacion de Vehiculos a Motor y Seguidad vial, at *http://www.dgt.es*.

18 For a distinction between anthropological space and geometric space, see M. Merlaw-Ponty, 1997. *Fenomenología de la percepción*. Barcelona, Peninsula, where anthropological space consists in discerning as many spaces as different spatial experiences.

19 U. Eco, 1984. *Obra abierta*. Barcelona, Ariel., p. 96.

20 M. de Certeau, 2000. *La invención de lo cotidiano. Vol. 1*. México, Universidad Iberoamericana, p. 41.

21 *Ibid*. p. 46.

22 M. Delgado, 2011. *El espacio público como ideologia*. Madrid, Catarata. Pp: 9-10.

23 R. Sennet, 1978. *The Decline of Public Man*. Barcelona, Paidós, p. 24.

24 See B. Santamarina, 2006. "Anthropology and environment. Review of a tradition and new perspectives of analysis in the ecological problematic," in *AIBR*, No. 002, pp. 144-184.

25 D. Harvey, 2009. "The right to the city," in *Carajillo de la ciudad*. Barcelona, Universitat Oberta, p. 23.

26 We take the concept of "Invisible Riders," article by Dan Koeppel, published in *Bicycling* magazine, August 2006.

27 We use the category "migrant" to question the classic dichotomy "emigrant/immigrant." An image copied on to that of the city, the migrant is someone who moves, but whose movement is always active, not reduceable to a punctual journey. His life takes place "in between." Every immigrant is at the same time an emigrant from the other point of view, from the home he leaves or the family he abandons. Given the uncertainty of what will come, the migrant—especially the one that suffers the quasi-generalized precarity in our sphere—lives disposed to leave again.

28 See P. Bourdieu, 1991. *La distinction. Criterios y bases sociales del gusto*. Madrid, Taurus.

29 D. Koeppel, op.cit.

30 S. Sassen, op. cit.

31 A. de Giorgi, 2006. *The government of excessiveness. Post-Fordism and control of the multitude*. Madrid, Traficantes de Sueños, p. 146.

32 E. Soja, op.cit., p. 223.

33 F. Le Marcis, 2004. "The Suffering Body of the City," in *Public Culture* 16 (3): 453-477, Duke University Press.

34 C. Carlsson, 2002. "Cycling Under the Radar: Assertive Desertion" in C. Carlsson (editor), 2002. *Critical Mass: Bicycling's Defiant Celebration*. Edinburgh, AK Press.

35 M. Delgado, 1999. *El animal público*. Barcelona, Anagrama, p. 33.

Ambato, Ecuador, 2011

The Blind Spot
Subcultural Exclusivity in Critical Mass
By Adriana Camarena

The farmer pedaling on a dirt road, whether in Durango, Mexico, or the outskirts of Pretoria, South Africa, or a low-income or migrant worker riding through a tangled and polluted urban environment, is a well known world figure. These bicyclists, however, remain considerably outside the cultural margins of Critical Mass. In the context of movements for sustainable cities, reclamation of public space, and high-quality urban environments, the bicycle has reappeared in the last twenty years as a vehicle of progressive thinking, and even fashion. But long ago, it became and still remains the transport vehicle *par excellence* of the vast majority of the world's impoverished population.

Critical Massers like to think of ourselves as an open-ended group, welcoming to all, irrespective of race, ethnicity, gender, income status, or politics. The panoptic nature of the ride seems to have kept it going through the years, riders preferring inclusiveness and a reclamation of public space over political divisions. Yet, for all its free-wheeling nature, the culture of Critical Mass is simply not as inclusive as it thinks itself to be. In fact, Critical Mass San Francisco has been criticized as a movement of the "white middle class."

A quick survey of attendees at a Critical Mass in SF does reveal an over-representation of white Americans, but even within that racial group, riders seem to span the wide range of affluent middle class, working "middle class," *déclassé*, and straight out poor whites. For many, though, class diversity does not change the analysis. In the U.S., or in San Francisco at least, to label a movement *white middle class* is code for something other than just race or class. It is a claim that the movement is culturally close to the dominant political and economic class.[1] More explicitly, from my observation, it is code for a movement that has lost its radical edge as it expands through incorporation of numbers of *left liberals* of any class.[2] This is sometimes referred to as *co-optation* or *cultural assimilation*, meaning that a movement is absorbed by pre-existing political and market institutions. Sometimes co-optation is a way to neutralize the threat posed by a movement. Co-optation does not need to be seen as only negative, since it is the way that a radical movement also succeeds in changing the preferences of mainstream culture. Bicycling, sustainability, urban redesign, enjoyable public space have all become policy choices in our cities as a result of tenacious direct action. However, a movement that never grows through incorporation of numbers of poor or disenfranchised people is a movement that will never succeed in challenging existing hierarchies and injustices.

San Francisco is not the only place where Critical Massers seem more politically empowered vis-à-vis poor or disenfranchised members of society. In Mexico, Peru, and Ecuador, where I have been privy to observe other bicycling movements and participate in mass rides, the personal culture of participants seems—like my own—distant from that of impoverished and disenfranchised peoples. For those among us who wish to change not only the preferences of society, but its political and economic structures, I propose that *we* Critical Massers turn a critical eye onto ourselves to understand our own connections to dominant culture, as well as our vast cultural separation from low-income, migrant, working-class, and other marginal or disenfranchised people, who are the majority of cyclists in the world.

A Ride Towards Co-Optation in Three Gears: From Radical Movement To Hip Trend To Mainstream Bicycling Policy

Most origin stories of Critical Mass start with a core group of lefty-thinking activists, often self-described radicals, who kick off a movement to take public space back from car-crowded streets in a celebratory fashion. These lefties and radicals have often spent a great deal of time already thinking about or working on opposing capitalist democracies in one way or another. Critical Mass emerges as an exercise in organizing horizontally by recovering public space and power on bicycles.

Radical activists tend to be young—in the contemporary sense of young—ages 20 to 40. They often look hip and edgy too. They've made their own outfits, their own bikes, their own language, squatted a space, dumpster dived, cut their own hair, got pierced and tatted, edited a zine or journal, rocked a band, gardened their own food, and otherwise transformed themselves into a walking-talking message of revolt against mainstream culture. They appear creatively new vis-à-vis commodified versions of urban people.

This visible message of revolt is often picked up by other young people, who are neither radical nor political, and at best, rebellious in the traditional sense of youthful contention, or progressive in a left-liberal kind of way. In current slang, these trendy and politically fashionable people are called "hipsters." Like the dreaded tag phrase white middle class, the label hipster implies political hypocrisy or a kind of street-cred bankruptcy.[3]

Critical Mass grows when large numbers of people outside core organizers spontaneously join; for the most part these include leisure cyclists, hipsters, and liberals. As the ride expands, the core group of organizers also expands and splinters. If Critical Mass survives this phase, the ride becomes truly headless, without specific leaders or political bearing. Most Critical Mass rides I've been to stabilize into this type of organized coincidence.

Meanwhile, some riders with radical ideas go on to create bike kitchens in low-income neighborhoods, or facilitate bike co-ops for migrant bicycle riders. Perhaps they move on to new projects like urban gardening, or an occupation movement. Other riders with more moderate political views take up office in City Hall as transport and urban redesign experts, or establish a nonprofit organization to lobby for bicycle rights. Others have kids, and nostalgically keep going on the ride, while holding office jobs and a mortgage. Some are just goofballs loving the opportunity to dress-up in costume and ride. Still others become cycling merchandisers of fixies, messenger bags, and chic fashion.

Following some years of Critical Mass (or similar rides) and a proliferation of bicycle culture, bicycling and walking "suddenly" appear as real transportation choices, or at the very least, natural leisurely things to do in a city, leaving behind any radical roots. Before you know it, you have Sunday Streets[4] in your city, and public bike rentals. A nonprofit organization in Quito, Ecuador called *Ciclópolis* —a spin-off from an original group of bicycle activists—exists with the primary activity of managing Sunday Streets with government funds. Quito's 28-kilometer Sunday Streets event, is so long that for one day riders from economically polarized neighborhoods on opposite ends of the city mingle. In Mexico City, Marcelo Ebrard, the Left-party mayor of Mexico, invested heavily in creating public bike rentals that are widely used in the center of the city. Ebrard also declared First Mondays as *Lunes de Bicifuncionarios* (Bike To Work) day for city officials, and began Sunday Streets in the Mexican capital. These initiatives were shepherded by bicycle activists who began the city's first mass night ride. In San Francisco, the less consistent Sunday Streets are likewise an enormous gregarious success, with people filling in every gap in the street with music, food, art, interaction, and movement. The event is supported through a mélange of government, large corporate, small business sponsors, nonprofit organizations, and an armada of volunteers.

The concept of group rides has also been taken up creatively by people that Critical Mass never reached. New rides have appeared. In the Bay Area, Bike Party monthly group rides have sprung up in San José, Richmond, Oakland, Hayward, San Francisco, and many other cities, where contrary to the norms of Critical Mass, riders carefully follow the rules of the road. Moreover, these rides are often initiated in neighborhoods of heavily-policed racial minorities, such as Latinos and African Americans. People from these neighborhoods, who were never attracted to the celebratory-confrontational nature of Critical Mass, create their own group ride, and often actively reject association with Critical Mass, distancing themselves from police face-offs and emphasizing a safe space for leisure and exercise.

Expansion of the bicycling culture in this way is a good thing, since it shows that we can make a better world through engaging with existing institutions. But without a doubt, the appropriation of ideas and techniques born out of Critical Mass turns the original movement into an oddity *untrendy, passé*. The barking, howling, and singing against the hierarchies of capitalism, and any rider-police conflicts appear outdated or no longer necessary in the face of the mainstreaming of bicycle rides.

Except for places such as Madrid where the ride is deeply connected to the variety of radical occupations taking place right now, Critical Mass in most places stabilizes as a fun ride, a good monthly exercise in collective self-organization, and a good moment for collective re-imagination of streets. From a radical point of view, that's still good, and still merits showing up to guard the occupied space as ground gained, but as far as revolutions go, it's not. More distressing from a radical point of view, despite minor infrastructural improvements, the co-optation of mass bike rides leads down the slippery slope towards top-down public policy decisions that limit citizen participation.

The Bizarre Case of Critical Mass Shanghai

I recently learned that a Critical Mass took place in Shanghai in 2011 in the context of Earth Week. A You Tube video of the ride shows a variety of cyclists, some on expensive looking bikes and fixies, riding in a small *pelotón*.[5] I was intrigued by the imagery of this Shanghai ride. Following one link and googling another, I ended up at the website of a group called People's Bike: Shanghai Urban Cycling, whose stated goal is to "fuel the love of riding as something more than a means of transportation in China."[6] Their website is *very* hip. Their message is clear: bicycles should be seen as a form of leisure in China.

I mentioned the video to Michael Rauner, a San Francisco photographer who was invited in 2011 on an artist exchange to Shanghai. The entire trip was carefully supervised by Chinese government officials who herded the artists towards areas and aspects of the city that symbolized its progress. Michael has ridden in Critical Mass San Francisco since 1993, and when I asked him about the bicycling masses in China, his quick response was, "There is nothing glorious about masses of bicycling workers in China."[7] His comment was reflective of that fact that today large numbers of cyclists were only to be found in low-income neighborhoods, at the edge of Shanghai, with only a few random cyclists skirting through the horrendous car traffic jams downtown.

Another photographer from Sweden (who will not be named) was once hired by a Chinese municipal agency to make a tourism video of Amsterdam. Upon review of his work, he was asked to remove the images of mass cycling —a large part of Dutch culture —because in the eyes of his clients they portrayed Amsterdam as a backwards place which Chinese wouldn't want to visit. By odd contrast, images of cool and hip young Chinese fixie riders are officially promoted online as "what it means to be young in China."[8] In plain terms, these riders exemplify the assimilation of global market monoculture in China.

From across the wide Pacific Ocean, sitting in front of my "Made in China" computer in San Francisco, I pondered this mixed message. Images of bicycling masses of workers are disappeared, while trendy riders are lauded. China was the country where urban mass bicycle rides were the norm; where one person's observation of riders amassing on an intersection until they tipped over into the street, inspired the name for Critical Mass rides in the Western world.

Where, then, in the future of China and the subculture of Critical Mass, does this leave the masses of Chinese cyclists for whom riding is *primarily* "a form of transportation" to and from hard work? Moreover, why wouldn't China take advantage of this fact, and play up its critical masses of bicyclists in daily life, if it really wants to be leading the trend of bicycling? I find an answer in Mexico, my home country, where like in China, the bicycle is still a vehicle of the poor, and a symbol of underdevelopment.

Pueblo Bicicletero: The Daily Masses of Bicycling Workers

In Mexico, when a town is called a *pueblo bicicletero* (a bicycling town) it is a derisive phrase meant to indicate the backwardness of a place. For decades, particularly through the Golden Age of Mexican Cinema, the bicycle was heavily portrayed as the vehicle for the working poor: postman, newspaper deliverer, water carrier, messenger, knife sharpener, flower vendor, baker, among many other iconic Mexican workers for whom the bicycle is not only a means of transportation to work, but an implement of work. This image of the bicycle established its reputation as a charismatic vehicle of poverty, and a retrograde technology vis-à-vis the car.

Remarkably, the postman, the newspaper deliverer, the water carrier, the messenger, the knife sharpener, the flower vendor, and the baker still use pedal power delivering their services within the megalopolis of Mexico City. On Saturdays, I would wake-up to the flower vendor at my door. When I am home for a visit, I still find him to say hello. He has four children, and every day he takes a two-hour bus ride from the next state with buckets of new flowers for his tricycle that he parks in someone else's garage. He is one of many tricycle service riders in the city.

In September 2009, Chris Carlsson and I attended the Second Annual [Mexican] National Cycling Conference in Guadalajara, Jalisco. On a lunch break, Chris and I took a walk around the historic downtown. We had not advanced more than a few blocks, when we came upon an old school Mexican bike messenger named Don Francisco Gonzalez Estrada. He was 66 years old, and riding a 1957 Turismo *bicicleta*; the kind you *only* see in Mexican Gold Cinema movies. He accepted our invitation to attend the bike messenger panel that afternoon. On the panel was a bike messenger from Los Angeles, California; another from Ciudad Guzman, Jalisco; and a pair of fixie aficionados from Guadalajara. During the Q&A, I introduced Don Francisco to everyone, and he told a bit of his story.

> I bought my first Turismo bicycle in 1957, the same day the singer Pedro Infante died in a plane crash. Before the 1980s, people respected cyclists on the roads of Guadalajara. Our bicycles had license plates, and we had to carry registration papers. We had to have a front light, and red back light. We were treated like another vehicle on the road by city regulations. (...)

He also gave some advice to the new generation of urban cyclists:

> I always take my extreme right on every road; even when I cycle against traffic. If I see someone hurtling towards me, I step off the road, on to the sidewalk. I have never had an accident.

The crowd reacted to Don Francisco as if David Byrne had entered the room. Cameras flashed, recorders appeared under his lips, people wanted a piece of him, there was awe and respect. Some people approached him but didn't know what to say: a living legend—an iconic Mexican bicyclist— was in their midst. Don Francisco took it all in stride with a smile, enjoying the recognition.

In March 2011, I travelled by bus through Juliaca, Peru, an amazing highland desert town that made me feel like I was passing through Burningman. It was Carnaval week, and as the bus rolled non-stop through the border town, I caught a glimpse of a Peruvian couple glittering in gold and dust in the sunset light, and everywhere we looked, there were roofed tricycles, bicycles, and moto-taxis billowing dust behind them—an unexpected dreamscape.[9]

Almost a year later, in January 2012, I went to Oxkutzcab, Yucatán where once again I found myself in a fantasy-town of bicycles, tricycles, and moto-taxis. Trying to get out of the town in our rental car, I stopped a baker-bicyclist for directions, and bought the most outstanding cheese danishes I've ever had. Like in Juliaca, people in Oxkutzcab are poor. Most of its population migrates to the U.S. for work, many to San Francisco. While I may revel in the imagery of bicycle masses in Juliaca and Oxkutzcab as an urban cyclist's dream come true, for people there, bicycling is simply cheap and pragmatic. In these towns, bicycle lanes are irrelevant, plazas are still central to shared life, and people's priorities are set on earning enough to sustain their family with dignity.

I met Silvano on the corner of Cesar Chavez Street and South Van Ness in San Francisco, while he stood there waiting for work. He has worked 25 years as a migrant day laborer; eight years at a car wash. One day, he paid a compliment to my bicycle, and told me how in one good year of work, he bought himself a titanium frame bike which he took back to Durango, Mexico. Silvano said that all his friends made fun of him because he liked to ride his bike and cared little for big trucks. Silvano was unusual. He dreamt of going back home, and being able to afford enough to set up a bike shop and make a modest living out of that. Most migrants dream bigger, like Hugo, who I also met on Cesar Chavez Street. Born and raised in a farming culture in Puebla, over the past eight years, he has been sending back money to support the growing family agricultural business by buying tractors and large trucks that can haul weight, and show finally and definitively that the struggle to escape from the *pueblo bicicletero* was successful.

Around the 12th of December there are always mass bicycle rides in Mexico City, when townsfolk from every niche of the country, as well as migrant laborers from abroad arrive for the annual pilgrimage to the Basilica of the Virgin of Guadalupe. Pilgrims from far away towns overtake the highways and main city avenues in caravans, taking turns riding bicycles or walking next to support vehicles.[10]

In the past years, I've made a point of talking to people who have grown up experiencing poverty and its circumstances. I've learned from my unsuspecting *maestros* that unlike many of them, I feel entitled to "happiness" (in a way that verges on petulance, by contrast to their expectations). I also feel entitled to make big demands upon established institutions, and to get a response. As lefty or radical activists like to chant, "What do we want, and when do we want it?"

On the Outer Rims of Cities and Poverty

Critical Mass is said to be a response to the culture that accepts the car as a symbol of development under the Fordist industrial model. (For the moment, ignore the irony that most bicycles are produced under a Fordist industrial model.) In the so-called developing, underdeveloped, and Third World countries (and now increasingly, developed nations) economic subordination weighs heavy. On a global scale, severely impoverished populations represent from 40% to 90% of a such countries. These poor populations are increasingly urban, but have also been pushed out from inner cities to the outer rim suburbs and slums of metropolitan areas. In addition, the car has become more accessible with cheap credit. Lower middle class families and even poor families can now get an automobile by indebting themselves. And they often do so, because the option is between a two-to-three hour round-trip car commute versus a four-to-eight hour round-trip commute on several legs of slow, often decrepit, public transport.

While people with higher incomes are moving back into the inner city and picking up the bike for a short to medium work commute to the office, for the majority of city dwellers, the "cheap" car still presents itself as the best alternative to move to and from work. In spite of this, most working class people must use public transportation. In the context of days spent commuting between a city center and its outer rim, the notion that a Critical Mass ride through the city is going to attract or politicize the people most affected by terrible urban design and atrocious public transport policy decisions is a bit ludicrous. In addition, Critical Mass has come to be associated with a political message of hip, radical, cool bicycling, most likely to draw in the young and trendy who are already willing to consume and reproduce the image of what it means to be politically progressive in the city. For poor and working class people struggling to make ends meet, our new bicycling culture may seem politically alien.

In Magritte's sense of saying a pipe is not a pipe, the bicycle has stopped being merely a two-wheeled vehicle. It has become a conceptual symbol for a whole swath of movements around sustainability, urban redesign, anti-oil wars, environmentalism, horizontalism, poetry, gender freedom, etc., and barely recognizable anymore as simply a vehicle. Among those of us who see ourselves as "urban cyclists," the bicycle is a vehicle of our political propaganda, as much as it is a means of transportation.

Perhaps this is why a government-sponsored Sunday Streets may have more radical effects on the broader population than a Critical Mass ride. Public space is opened up and embraced by working-class folk on their own terms. Once in use by a broader number of people, whether for leisure or small commerce, that space will likely be defended, and maybe extended. I still remember the Bike Angel who appeared soon after the Mexico-Cuernavaca cyclepath was inaugurated in 2004. He was a scruffy and sweet *chaparrito* (shorty) who sat or walked alongside the cyclepath until a spandex-clad yuppie got a flat tire, or someone fell off their bike. He would then patch it (or them) up, hopefully for a tip. The presence of the Bike Angel also made another point: Better transport infrastructure and policies may alleviate some of the hardship for the poor and working class, but it won't break any existing hierarchies.

If it's a revolution with bicycles that we seek, we have to look elsewhere. Another 2011 video from across the world shows a mass of bicycles (with a sprinkling of motorcycles) in Damascus, Syria.[11] The video is titled "دوما مظاهرة جميلة علي الدراجات الهوائية -" or "Always—A beautiful demonstration of the bicycle". The riders chant defiantly against President Bashar Hafez al-Assad and the army of the ruling regime. A French news outlet reported that Syrian authorities routinely confiscate and destroy bikes and scooters after an insurgent action, as two-wheeled vehicles are the most effective means of escape for rebels.[12] I watch and rewatch this "critical mass" ride through Damascus streets. It befriends the motorcycle, reminding us that the bicycle is a vehicle, and that in many parts of the world, there are more pressing concerns than bicycle lanes. Sometimes a bicycle is just a bicycle, and that can be enough to support a revolution; and Critical Mass is not a mass revolution, even as its wheels turn month after month, year after year.

Revolt or Reevaluate?

My analysis of Critical Mass is not so different from the narrative of co-optation of any other social movement with a radical component. My objective here has been to turn the eye back onto ourselves, and ask an existentialist question. After reading this, left liberals in the Critical Mass movement may continue feeling empowered knowing that their front-door connections to dominant culture can affect policy. For radicals seeking to topple capitalism and its consequences, the problem is different. How can radical organizing, or in the case of Critical Mass, radical activity, expand not towards the center of political dominance but towards the people already marginalized and left out?

One model for new engagement is found in aforementioned bike kitchens, often established in low-income neighborhoods. The success of these bike kitchens has less to do with bikes, and more to do with the creation of a meeting place, where not only does a kid or worker find a way to create or fix a vehicle according to his or her priorities, but organizers find themselves affected by new relationships with people who are *not* in proximity to their politics, class, or culture. In these meeting places, you may suddenly find yourself negotiating ideas of race, ethnicity, class, gender roles, sexual preferences, labor unions, religion, politics, and conservative beliefs with people who do not share your subcultural preferences. Conservative or reserved cultures of working class and migrant populations may be much more challenging to radicals and left liberals, than differences radicals and left liberals find among themselves! Without overcoming this cultural chasm, we're bound to learn little about how to build a social movement in dialogue with poor and disenfranchised people.

The key seems to be in creating space—many multiple spaces—conducive to a practice of direct democracy among marginal, disenfranchised, and radical people. Given the current lack of diversity, Critical Mass may not be the ideal space to begin that practice, but nothing stops us from bringing new relationships created outside the ride, and lessons learned from establishing those new relationships, to transform how we behave and engage in Critical Mass.

Notes

1   The rest of the world doesn't necessarily frame social and economic inequality in racial terms. Sometimes power inequalities may circle around a question of a dominant ethnicity, or a dominant mestizo or mulato pigmentocracy, but other times established networks of power are harder to define on the basis of skin tone; instead class strata (and its cultural representations) becomes a distinguishing characteristic.

2   Left liberals are generally citizens who uphold concepts of social justice, human rights, free and fair elections, fair trade, environmental sustainability, international solidarity, race and gender equality, multiparty elections, the free market, even if with notable insistence on implementing top-down policies for the bottom social rung. My point is that left liberals don't challenge capitalism, and despite good intentions, and irrespective of race, gender, ethnicity or class, are carriers of the cultural boundaries that recreate an impoverished and working class people. Left liberals are also often connectors to state and societal institutions that transform city policies around social movement demands. They are not necessarily the "middle class" but they do provide a stabilizing or co-opting link between social movements and existing market and government institutions.

3   Mark Grief writes,
    "I think the reason the attribution of hipsterness is always pejorative is that the "hipster" is actually identifying today a *subculture* of people who are already *dominant*. The hipster is that person, overlapping with declassing or disaffiliating groupings—the starving artist, the starving graduate student, the neo-bohemian, the vegan or bicyclist or skate punk, the would-be blue-collar or post-racial individual—who in fact aligns himself *both* with rebel subculture *and* with the dominant class, and opens up a poisonous conduit between the two." "What *was* the Hipster?," *n+1*, p. 9.

4   The original Sunday Streets is attributed to an initiative known as the weekly Ciclovía in Bogotá, Colombia.

5   Critical Mass Shanghai—2011 *http://www.youtube.com/watch?v=1lSg4C82ykw*

6   People's Bike: Shanghai Urban Cycling at *http://peoplesbike.com/pplsen/?page_id=1316*; A similar message is projected by a video that defines "what it is like to be young in China."

7   My friend, LisaRuth Elliott, who once rode in the China bike masses, says the experience is pragmatic.

8   Based on image alone, it is acceptable to be young while cycling through the city on a fixie, or DJing, skateboarding, using social media, rocking the music scene, watching new cinema, and digging Michael Jackson, the Beijing Olympics, and global brands such as Coca Cola, Adidas, and more. See "We All Want To Be Young in China," *http://vimeo.com/21426600*

9   A few months later in May, mass riots exploded in Juliaca over new mining and oil projects in the region of Puno that would displace thousands. Hundreds of striking miners and activists arrived in Juliaca and occupied the airport to have their demands heard; several died in police confrontations. The government was forced to rescind the mining license granted to the Canadian firm Bear Creek.

10 Migrants who dare return to Mexico for the holidays will later have to face the daunting task of reaching the North border of Mexico to cross the deadly Arizona desert. The route up North is lined with organized crime running border-crossing businesses. In June of this year, 49 decapitated bodies were found in the city of Monterrey. City officials calmed the urban population down by saying there was nothing to worry about, since they were only migrants.

11 امود - ةرهاظم ةليمج ىلع تاجاردلا تاوهاوئة or "Always – A beautiful demonstration of the bicycle" *http://www.youtube.com/watch?feature=player_embedded&v=Xv0EZx_W-g8*

12 Bikes on the frontline of Syria's deadly crackdown, France 24/4 International News, 16/08/2011, at *http://observers.france24.com/content/20110815-syria-security-forces-destroy-motorcycles-scooters-bikes-anti-government-protests*

Bicycling in the Public Sphere

By Lusi Morhayim

The freedom to make and remake our cities and ourselves is ... one of the most precious yet most neglected of our human rights.
—David Harvey, 2008[1]

As the automobile became a priority for urban planners, in many cities pedestrians and bicyclists became marginalized users of the streets. Today, we live in cities that are primarily built for transporting ourselves from one place to another in motor vehicles. Bicycling is thwarted by dangers of getting doored and being run over by automobiles. Critical Mass first started on the premise of riding safely together in the public spaces of the city. But it did more than that to the bicycle community. Critical Mass also opened up a space for bicyclists in the public sphere of transportation and urban planning.

Freedom of assembly and speech are first amendment rights that give people the opportunity to voice their demands publicly. Yet these are contested rights as, "social production of and control over public spaces in practice define to what extent citizens have rights to the city."[2] Critical Mass rides are one of a kind amalgamations of protest, appropriation, occupation, and festival-like events. With this unique quality, the rides attract a large crowd and simply the sheer number of bicyclists grants them access to the roads. Instead of presenting opinions in city meetings, organizing campaigns, or going into long bureaucratic processes, Critical Mass bicyclists demand their urban rights by appropriating the streets.

During one of the rides in 2010 in San Francisco, I approached a bicyclist (female, in her early 20s) wearing a shiny silver cable around her helmet and metallic blue tights.[3] She said that her outfit shows that she does not care what motorists think about her, and she continued:

> No one asked us if it [the city] should be organized that way ... People who were coming from a petroleum-centric mentality organized the city ... to move people as if they were goods to create money ... There are so many lines of buses going into the financial district ... but there is only one MUNI to get to Golden Gate Park. It's really [about] where the city is placing its resources and what it's emphasizing. So, we are saying that ... we don't need to participate in that necessarily ... although it's the built environment and the built reality, we can ... forge our own path through that and ... we don't need to listen to your signals and to your stop signs and to your one-way traffic.

Critical Mass rides are an apparent statement of bicyclists' urban needs and their frustration of feeling marginalized in the realm of urban planning and transportation. Of the 69 bicyclists who responded to an online survey[4] about Critical Mass distributed in 2012, 49% strongly agreed, and 29% agreed, with the following statement: "I participate in Critical Mass because I want to make a statement regarding the lack of bicycling infrastructure." Additionally, 48% of the respondents strongly agreed and 30% of them agreed that they "want to show the automobile drivers that bicyclists are traffic too." By demonstrating their ideal use of the streets, bicyclists communicate their needs to the rest of the public.

Nancy Fraser states that the ideal democratic society depends on free communication between mainstream publics and counterpublics that co-constitute the public sphere.[5] Bicyclists' counter position on the mainstream transportation model and automobile-dependent urban form unites them as a counterpublic. Their shared interest in urban form stems from their shared worldviews, values, lifestyles, and identity traits. Most of them highly praise global environmental and social responsibility. For instance, in the survey, a total of 77% of the respondents agreed and strongly agreed with the statement that they participate because they do not want to contribute to oil consumption. In total, 81% agreed and strongly agreed that they participate because they do not want to contribute to environmental pollution. Bicycling is one of the ways in which their values and worldviews are manifested in their everyday lives. According to the survey, despite the fact that 54% of them own an automobile, 46% of the Critical Mass bicyclists reported that bicycling is the transportation mode they use most often when they commute and that was followed by a combination of bicycling and other modes at 23.5%. Only a total of 18% reported that they drive and carpool when commuting.

Withal, there are even stronger motivations than pro-environmental worldviews that motivate people to participate in Critical Mass. "It is simply fun to ride together with other bicyclists" (78%) and "I enjoy the city in a way I cannot enjoy otherwise" (65%) were the two most strongly agreed with statements in the survey. In the interviews too, Critical Mass bicyclists overwhelmingly used the word "fun." One bicyclist said that "streets are our playground." Collective experience plays a significant role in enjoying bicycling in the city. Being in direct contact with the people on the street and the surroundings, and sharing a fun experience together are essential in eliminating sense of social isolation that many of the bicyclists reported that stem from living in an urban setting.

Even though today San Francisco is much more bicycle friendly compared to 20 years ago, interviews with the bicyclists in the city demonstrate that participating in the rides is still significant for many bicyclists in order to connect with other like-minded people and support them. A bicyclist in her late 20s says:

I like to be surrounded by like-minded people ... I would love to not ever have to buy a car. If there are other people out there who are working to make cities more bikeable, then I like to be around them, and I like to feel like I am working with them ... Biking is a total good for me ... When I hear about things like the recent [BP] oil spill it strengthens my resolve to not want to contribute to anything it has to do with that ... I just want to remain in the bike community and bike around town with people.

Bicyclists find in the rides both a sense of comradeship and also political solidarity. A quote from another bicyclist in his 50s indicates that bicyclists recognize political benefits of being part of a like-minded community:

Bikers are really part of a community; it is just like politics, you are part of a party ... I think those are certainly some of the real benefits of riding a bike. You are in a community, a lot of like-minded people, you know they tend to be environmentalist; they tend to be some way very political too, supporting various measures good for bikes... political part of it ... is keeping the breath of the progress, keeping the breath of obstructions that we still deal with.

Critical Mass rides foster and strengthen bicyclists' sense of community and collective identity. Streets are the places in which the bicyclist counterpublic and its discourses are being formed and also sustained. For instance, flyers are often passed around at the beginning of the CM rides about upcoming environmental talks, movie screenings, and other issues that would appeal to bicyclists. Critical Mass also gathers an ideal crowd to collect signatures for political campaigns on environmental issues. "Stop Texas Oil. No on Prop 23" organizers' visit to one of the CM rides in San Francisco to collect signatures for their campaign—a campaign that eventually stopped oil companies from suspending California's efforts to create green jobs—is a case in point. Examples from other countries also demonstrate parallel practices. A Critical Mass ride in Tel Aviv, Israel in 2011 ended in a park where bicyclists met with the city's nonprofit urban gleaners organization called "City Tree." The urban gleaners prepared bowls of salads for the bicyclists made of greens collected from the gardens and parks in the city. They gave information about the organization and where to collect such edible greens within the city limits. These are some of the ways in which Critical Mass rides unite like-minded publics and foster a community that may be mobilized to demonstrate its voting power when needed and support each other in different ways.

During the rides, Critical Mass bicyclists subvert everyday experiences and temporarily create spatial experiences that correspond with their counterdiscourses. The efficiency of the automobile, a symbol of modernity, becomes greatly reduced. Instead of automobiles, people—with no barriers between them—fill the streets. Seeming like street theater, CM rides dramatically demonstrate what the streets might be like with fewer automobiles and more bicycles. The experiences generated by the Critical Mass rides are counter to what streets today typically have to offer. With this counter experiences, it introduces new cultural codes, challenges existing ones, and culminates in social and cultural change.

Compared to twenty years ago, today the city is more supportive of Critical Mass and similar events and other grassroots bicycling organizations have been flourishing in the Bay Area. The East Bay Bike Party (a ride modeled after one started in San Jose and which attracts thousands of people), the Berkeley moonlight bike ride, community rides in Richmond, the San Francisco Midnight Mystery Ride, and the San Francisco Butterlap Ride are some examples of the growing urban grassroots bike rides. An increase in the amount and variety of such rides demonstrate that demand to have safer access to the streets is only growing and being accommodated.

The transformation is not only in the social realm, but also in the physical landscape of the city. San Francisco, in 2010, announced a plan to increase the existing 48 miles of bike lane infrastructure by 64%, and several other projects to make the city more bicycle-friendly. The city is also working on making streets more livable for pedestrians. "Sunday Streets" traffic closures since 2006, and more than a dozen "Parklets" (permanently extended public spaces where curb parking existed before) are some of the examples.

There is no quantifiable way to know how much of San Francisco's social and physical transformation may be attributed to Critical Mass alone. Nevertheless, CM played a pivotal role in challenging automobile culture in San Francisco and around the world. Today, San Francisco is becoming a more bicycle and pedestrian-friendly city. This was achieved by giving more space to people, and taking away space occupied by private automobiles—similar to how bicyclists in Critical Mass rides have been doing for the last 20 years.

Notes

1 Harvey David, "*The Right to the City*," New Left Review, vol. 53, September-October 2008.
2 Mitchell Don, The Right to the City. Social Justice and the Fight for Public Space, New York: The Guilford Press, 2003.
3 Interviews about Critical Mass were conducted with bicyclists who participated in San Francisco Bay Area Critical Mass rides, and Bike to Work Day between May and September of 2010, and in Tel Aviv, Israel in 2011.
4 An online survey about San Francisco Critical Mass was conducted.*in* early 2012. Information about the survey was distributed online, and through flyers in the January 2012 Critical Mass ride.
5 Fraser Nancy, "Rethinking the public sphere: A contribution to the critique of actually existing democracy" in Habermas and the Public Sphere, edited by Craig J Calhoun, 109–42. Cambridge: MIT Press, 1992.

This article is adapted from an article titled "From Counterpublics to Counterspaces: Bicyclists' Efforts to Reshape Cities" that has been accepted for publication in the "*Justice Spatiale | spatial justice*" Journal.

Putting the 'Critical' in Critical Mass:
Patriarchy, Radical Feminism, and Radical Inclusiveness
By Mario Bruzzone

From the beginning, Critical Massers have tolerated a certain *dudeliness* among us. (That's a technical term, *dudely*.) One early and persistent example is the "Testosterone Brigade." Since the early years of the ride, the Testosterone Brigade has been generally identified as those particularly aggressive cyclists who confront cars and drivers by pounding on the windows of stopped cars, riding at and around oncoming traffic, and generally causing a ruckus.[1] Those were the early years. Twenty years later, they're still around.

But Critical Mass also perpetuates another sort of dudeliness, less about explicit acts of violence and aggression and more about patriarchy.[2] Male privilege is produced and supported institutionally through bodies and bodily aspects of communication, including mentality, decision-making structure,[3] speaking and listening, and gender performance.

This dudeliness, in many ways, reflects wider bike culture. When I worked at the San Francisco Bike Kitchen (2005–08), internal statistics put female shop usage somewhere between 25-33%. Likewise, racing bike clubs show an approximate 9:1 male to female ratio. Increasingly, throughout the decade of the 2000s, as "urban cyclists" became a legible community (and market) for capitalism, it became normal to see the slogan—on stickers, patches, or just scrawled on a table at a bar—"Bike jocks are still jocks." The stickers were potent reminders that even while cyclists identified ourselves as alternative, as outsiders, we still reproduced patriarchy. We were, often, just jocks.

People have been recognizing the patriarchy in Critical Mass for a long time, whether pointing to the Testosterone Brigade, or to whom those at the front of the ride listen to. Among radical direct action communities, the problem of patriarchy needs to be addressed critically. It's one thing to be tired of fixing the same problem, and it's another entirely to forget, to ignore, to attach our own blinders to the rest of the problems that we ourselves have had a hand in constructing. This essay is meant, then, to be a reflection on the ways that patriarchy exists in Critical Mass, in order to move towards a more feminist Critical Mass.

What's it *For?:* Epistemology and the Performance of Patriarchy

The notion of performance is an important one.[4] Early feminism tended to "essentialize" male and female as categories—that is, first, to presume that the categories exist and that there are two of them, and second, that there is something fundamental to these male and female categories prior to socialization. Performance suggests something different—that gender is not about what you are, or what parts you have, but about what you do. You aren't a gender; instead, you perform gender. Performances are how things in the world become inflected with power along gendered lines. Performance is both how we perpetuate gender norms for ourselves ("I can't wear a pink shirt. I'm a boy!") and how we enforce gender norms on others ("You can't wear a pink shirt. You're a boy!"). These performances are repeated, which is how they come to have meaning and importance.[5] Even if gender is performed, it is still lived, especially in everyday situations.

Critical Mass is, similarly, an event and a performance. We ride our bikes around, we cork intersections, sometimes we dress up in costume, and we perform gender.[6] We perform patriarchy, not just as the Testosterone Brigade, but as a group that often, to outsiders and insiders, looks rather masculinist and can make decisions in masculinist ways. The situation is both a problem and, in its own way, an opportunity: there's nothing "natural" or "essential" about dudeliness, about machismo, in Critical Mass. We have the possibility of doing Critical Mass differently.

We gender our performances based on objectives. Our performances of Critical Mass are related to what we think Mass is "for." Even when Critical Mass is scorned, the underlying political question is always about social change. At the same time, the change that Critical Mass brings about, or tries to bring about, is contested.

A first view is that San Francisco Critical Mass is a type of political protest, albeit one with tactics distinctive from more everyday protests. It is typically articulated as against car culture, and when formed as a demand, it tends to be for bike "amenities" such as bike lanes, sharrows, or traffic calming. Some further subsume it into being a general protest related to environmental issues.[7] To the extent that demands are left vague, this is a strategic vagueness: Critical Mass continually pressures local officials to enact better conditions for cycling without sacrificing a freedom to adapt demands based on changing conditions and ideas. This is unlike formal political processes and negotiations. Because car culture is so concretized and pervasive, any actual list of demands—as in, "We'll be here till you do these things!"—is also a poor tactical decision.

There is a similar view that demands are what you make to a state, and Critical Mass, while a protest, is not a protest directed at the state. This is why it's so hard for agents of the state—bureaucrats, police officers, politicians, and so forth—to figure out what to do with it. Instead, Critical Mass is a protest directed at a culture and at cultural practices that are instantiated by the apparatuses of the state but not reducible to them. It's not because of the state that the city lacks easy bicycle access; that there's no bike lane on 5th Street is an example but not the reason. The reason is cultural. In the same way you don't make demands of capitalism or patriarchy, you don't make demands of car culture: because you can't. But you *can* challenge capitalism, patriarchy, and car culture.

Then there is a view deeply distinct from these. This account is the T.A.Z. account, after Hakim Bey's *Temporary Autonomous Zones*, a touchstone for radical organizing for the past two decades.[8] Rather than waiting for a revolution to come, Bey and the T.A.Z. account emphasize the here-and-now. "The T.A.Z. must be the scene of our present autonomy," he writes. "But, it can only exist on the condition that we already know ourselves as free beings."

In terms of Critical Mass, this view argues for an understanding in which Critical Mass is not a protest of the existing social order but the enactment of a desired new order. T.A.Z.s, argues Bey, are always ephemeral, and it is in this spirit that activists should understand their own projects: a spirit in which invisibility to the state (or state practices) is the desired condition. What Critical Mass does is liberate a space from state control and hierarchies to make a celebratory space not built in response or resistance to car-centric society, but free from it. This is *direct* action, not state-directed, not an appeal to government, but instead a physical intervention—a performance—in a form that both anticipates and enacts the future we want.

Feminism and the Temporary Autonomous Zone

From a feminist perspective, it matters whether Critical Mass is a protest or a T.A.Z. To see Critical Mass as a protest is to rely on visions of the state and legal frameworks that have a long history of patriarchy. This includes social democratic notions of protest.[9] I will mention only two feminist criticisms of this picture of the state, but there are many. First, the reality is that women—and those who don't perform mainstream white maleness enough—have been systematically excluded both from formal politics and from market exchanges. The historical exclusion of women in particular from political community has meant that "consent" to governments has nearly never included them—women have only been voting in the U.S. for less than a hundred years. Women's exclusion from markets has also devalued women's labor. Consequently, to take on power, women have had to assume "male" ways of interacting—you can think here of Hillary Clinton or, more locally, Dianne Feinstein. [10] A patriarchal state requires patriarchal demands; a patriarchal culture only hears patriarchal ultimatums.

Second, and more conceptually, notions of the social democratic state make implicit claims about a separation of some activities from public life. Some areas—like the family—seem to be removed from public life, in that the state only claims sovereignty over them in very rare cases, like spousal abuse. The public sphere is imagined as a *rational* domain in which we discuss resource distribution; the private is the domain of *emotional* life. This cultural segregation has meant a segregation of home life from the rest of social life—and home life has been gendered female.[11] One can trace a line in Western cultures in which men have been considered rational and women irrational since Aristotle,[12] and this finds instantiation today in all sorts of areas, not least of which are the often drastic absences of women in math and science.

That classic '60s aphorism that "the personal is political" contests exactly this separation between domains. The aphorism suggests two things: first, that the body itself is a site where politics is enacted; and that an individual's identity and individual practices are not separated from power. The consequence, then, is to both reinforce behaviors gendered masculine as the political and the powerful, and to reinforce that bodies gendered feminine are not powerful or political.[13]

So, to sum up: First, the historical circumstances of the liberal state demand stereotypically masculine ways of acting in order to effect change. Women who want to create change within a state are likewise required to act masculine but are punished for doing so.[14] For Critical Mass, advocacy, or "effectiveness," requires taking up ways of thinking inflected by patriarchy precisely because we live in a patriarchal society. When we ask about Critical Mass's larger effects, it tends to be in a way deeply riven by masculinism: we look at ways we can leverage politicians; we look at aggregated, statistical changes; we assume that we can quantify Mass. The state we look to leverage is itself contradictory as well; it either ought to be paternalistic and manage the home, or it ought to practice rational management of the public and leave the private, the emotional, alone. Either Critical Mass is an aggregation of private desires outside state management and moral authority, or Critical Mass is a rational response to car culture and can be evaluated through clever use of metrics.

Given the feminist criticisms of the state, then, it seems like the T.A.Z. notion should be a better conception of embodied praxis. Consider Gustav Landauer's notion that the state is less as an existing entity than a description of certain types of hierarchical interactions between people. If so, the state is not so much a permanent thing but a relationship that constantly pops in and out of existence. T.A.Z.s occupy the interstices where state is not present, where it is not performed. Bey puts it this way: "The T.A.Z. is in some sense a tactic of disappearance."

Even if they are strategic absences, for Bey, the T.A.Z. is absolutely lived. He envisions them as "whole mini-societies living consciously outside the law and determined to keep it up, even if only for a short but merry life." He writes, "The T.A.Z. is like an uprising which does not engage directly with the State, a guerrilla operation which liberates an area (of land, of time, of imagination) and then dissolves itself to re-form elsewhere/elsewhen, before the State can crush it." T.A.Z.s are "a bit of land ruled only by freedom." Simultaneously, Bey envisions the T.A.Z. as quiet and domestic, belieing what the initial imagination of guerrilla operations as life "outside the law." He compares the T.A.Z. to a dinner party, then asks how the T.A.Z. can be "everyday life." He lists a litany of already liberated or readymade T.A.Z.s— picnics, conferences, forest conclaves, and gay faery circles. The T.A.Z., Bey says, is "wild but gentle—a seducer not a rapist, a smuggler rather than a bloody pirate, a dancer not an eschatologist."

So, is Critical Mass a T.A.Z.? Critical Mass is in some sense part of everyday life in San Francisco, and certainly very fun at times, but in no way is Critical Mass autonomous in the sense that Bey meant. Indeed, Critical Mass is the complete opposite of a tactic of disappearance. The whole event is surrounded by police, for one thing; whenever the officers' (and the state's) limits are tested, whenever an offshoot tries to bike onto the Bay Bridge at the Harrison Street ramp or tries to get on 101 South at Cesar Chavez or make the merge onto the deck of the Golden Gate Bridge from 19th Avenue, the motorcycles (and occasionally the Highway Patrol) make a line and block the group. Critical Mass is always toying with the state, and the state is toying with Mass right back.

Thus, for the T.A.Z. argument, there tends be the unspoken assumption of *selective* autonomy at Critical Mass, the idea that we can choose what to make ourselves autonomous from. We liberate ourselves from state identities—which are largely based on personal histories—but not from our knowledge of how to ride bicycles. Critical Mass explicitly assumes itself to be a "leaderless" movement, and as such expects itself to somehow, by fiat of its leaderlessness, be freed from power regimes. It's not that free.

T.A.Z.s, Voluntarism, Power

While the T.A.Z. is imagined to be the opposite of dudely confrontation like riding your bike at oncoming cars and so forth, it's also the very opposite of deciding which way Mass turns by the loudest or most charismatic voice. The latter is, in my experience, the actual way that such decisions get made. While the leaders are temporary and rotating, it's a specific masculine form of leadership—one that looks a lot like the deeply gendered values of strength and independence and assertiveness—that is consistent. Such forms both exclude people who don't fit within the proper boundaries, and they discipline anyone who wants to have a say into male-gendered ways of acting.

Voluntarism tends to reproduce unequal power relationships when those relationships are not intentionally and deliberately addressed. The T.A.Z. account of Critical Mass ought to be a feminist account, or at least compatible with one. The account wants badly to see Critical Mass as a sort of validation of unalienated community life—and yet the issue is that we re-enact the very practices we want to make autonomous from. Critical Mass *has* leaders. It's exactly the issue with the T.A.Z. account—the account's conceit, in the literary sense—that it tends to pretend that independence from the social constructions we've brought with us is possible.

The T.A.Z. myth is that Critical Mass is a neutral plane of power, or a level field of power distributed horizontally.[15] The myth is that power is negative, that power is something we fight. Better to understand power as what makes things go.[16] There is no Critical Mass without power, on this account, and anyway that's not the point. The issue is what kind of things we do with our power.

In the past 20 years, one of the biggest shifts in thinking throughout the broadly leftist direct action community has been a rejection of instrumentalism. We no longer accept reducing people to "masses," pawns in a political game, nor can we accept that the ends justifies the means. We've realized that the *process* of production is just as productive as the things we produce, that the protests and guerrilla gardens are just as transformative in how they work as are the policy responses or food grown. Instead of formulaic utopian visions or specific ideological regimes, the mass of movements from the Zapatistas to Ya Basta! to Occupy Everywhere to Critical Mass has focused on practicing its own, transformational, direct democracy.

A Caring Mass

Feminist philosophers have developed an ethics centered on care over the past 30 years. The ethic of care takes as a starting point an explicitly relational world view—as opposed to a view where the atomic unit is the person, here the atomic unit is the *relationship*. The conceptual change is that, simply put, there are no things in the world without relationships, so relationships constitute all social phenomena.

This means that "autonomy," that central term of the T.A.Z., is relational—an achievement of a group, not the achievement of a single person.
Autonomy as independence is, in the words of Eva Feder Kittay, "a fiction,
regardless of our abilities or disabilities, and the pernicious effects of this
fiction are encouraged when we hide the ways in which our needs are met
in relations of dependencies."[17] We are dependent nearly all the time, for
our food, for our shelter, for our jobs, for companionship. Even capitalist
business is dependent on personal relationships, on suppliers, on (gasp!)
governments and legal codices.

In consequence, if autonomy is a group achievement, one person's
freedom is inseparable from another's freedom.[18] Critical Mass provides
a readymade example of this: we are only free together. Yet we are also
always related back to the world we are trying to remake. Care for others
and care for the self are not separable, just as you are not alienable from
your relationships with other people on the whole. Even more, care makes
us; care is productive.[19]

Relationships are continually in process. To the extent—in the T.A.Z.
account—that we are liberating ourselves from the state, we seem to be doing a pretty good job of maintaining white and male and class and hetero-
normative privilege, even by those who do not identify as those categories.
Where the T.A.Z. account is about autonomy and freedom, and demands
that we look to those things, the ethic of care looks to our relationships,
and considers relationships deeply relevant to producing autonomy and
freedom: Who is here and who is not? What does it do to those we care
about when we go down a narrow, steep, and curvy street (like Lombard
Street) three at a time instead of as a group? "This made me feel..." is perhaps the most important phrase we can use, and hear.

The Rolling Escort: Revisiting Staleness and Inclusivity

For the past few years, there's been a sense that Critical Mass has become
stale, at least in San Francisco. Sometimes this has been a statement—of
the, "Eh, Mass," variety—and sometimes a question—something like, "Are
we all tired of Mass?" This collective sentiment arises not only among bike
advocates, but among more casual Massers as well. Activists have given a
series of rationalizations for the continuing relevance of Mass,[20] but I have
seen little evidence that these rationalizations match what we actually feel.

The rolling police escort has stabilized Critical Mass in San Francisco to
a large extent. The last major incident occured around 2007. The regular-
ization of the escort makes it feel traditional, since in some sense Critical
Mass is transformed into something that government can respond to. In *A*

Thousand Plateaus, one of the touchstones for Bey (and radical philosophy in general), Gilles Deleuze and Felix Guattari referred to this as "capture,"[21] both by a particular political mentality and by a political apparatus, in this case, policing and the police. The latter, the political apparatus, is clear. The mentality, though, impacts both how we conceive of Mass and also what we think of as appropriate behavior in it.

Critical Mass in San Francisco looks very little like San Francisco. Alongside the questions of gender performance I've brought up here, it behooves us to ask what else we are doing, and who else we don't see, when we act in masculinist ways—all of us, myself included. Where is the Queer Brigade at Critical Mass? The Bike Anti-Jock Liberation Front? I mean, where are the groups that actually already exist: The Positive Pedalers, the Bike Kitchens, the Scraper Bikes? These relationships are important. Even, and especially, in their absence, we are in relationship with any of these groups, because we have a relationship of power—one way or another—when we are and are not riding in Critical Mass.

The persistence of dudeliness is not separate from the staleness, even if dudeliness doesn't completely drive the feeling of staleness. As organizers and allies, there's huge potential—and an ethical obligation—for a stronger Critical Mass. The alternative is to admit to ourselves that this community we collectively enact at Critical Mass is fine as it is, that it shouldn't try to include everyone who's not there. We need to ask where the people who we don't see actually are. We look towards a Critical Mass that does look more like San Francisco, or the San Francisco we want to make.

Radical Inclusivity: Or, Doing the Work of Feminism

We are—all of us—doing things that mean that others are not part of Critical Mass. Rather than try to confront the endless supply of dudes arguing that the absence of a formal leader is the absence of power and hierarchy, we have ample opportunity to alter the structural conditions that allow male privilege to retain its power as it is enacted during Critical Mass. The possibility is opening our community; that is, doing the work of opening it.

These epistemological issues of Critical Mass—how we think about what it is, and what we're doing there—have deep effects. They matter in what we do. Every time we recognize that it's always a dude who yells, "Let's go!" at Pee-wee Herman Plaza, it's a feminist issue. Every time Critical Mass goes down a narrow road that resultingly splits the ride into 50 tiny groups, it's a feminist issue. Every time Critical Mass starts to thin but *does not* circle up, it's a feminist issue. Every time we look around and see people who mostly look like us—dudes—it's a feminist issue. Every time we fail to have a discussion about these situations, it's a feminist issue.

As far as this sounds like a simple call, undoubtedly what will unfold is complexity, difficulty, and work. It will never be as simple as an invitation. But it's this work, and the potential for work, that keeps renewing community projects and happenings like Critical Mass. To Critical Mass, I say out of love: there's so much work we have to do, even (and especially!) after 20 years, that I can't wait.

Notes

1   The contemporary definition of the word *dude* is actually found in the dictionary, as a "regular guy or fellow". This usage of the word is associated with the edgy culture of skaters or surfers, but has expanded to other uses. I use the word *dudely* or *dudeliness* to refer to qualities of traditional heterosexual masculinity in an urban setting.

2   The "How to Make a Critical Mass" booklet of 1994 talks about what to do with the Testosterone Brigade; and for the 10th anniversary anthology of Critical Mass, Joel Pomerantz mentions them again. "How to Make a Critical Mass" is available at *www.scorcher.org/cmhistory/howto.html*. Pomerantz's essay is "A Critical Mass Cultural Glossary" in *Critical Mass: Cycling's Defiant Celebration*, ed. Chris Carlsson, (Oakland: AK Press) pp. 231-34. Steven Bodzin's essay in the same anthology also mentions the Testosterone Brigade; Bodzin memorably calls them "a pack of spiteful dogs" (p. 103).

3   The introductory chapter to Allan Johnson's 1997 *The Gender Knot* (Phildelphia: Temple University Press) is a readable primer—but definitely a primer—to what patriarchy is, and has the benefit of being available (as of this writing) on Google Books. A few theoretical touchstones include Simone de Beauvoir's *Second Sex* (1949); Kate Millet's *Sexual Politics* (1969); Cynthia MacKinnon's *Sexual Harassment of Working Women: A Case of Sex Discrimination* (1978) and her two-part article "Feminism, Marxism, Method, and the State" in the journal *Signs* (1982/83); bell hooks's *Feminist Theory: From Margin to Center* (1984) and *Outlaw Culture* (1994); and Judith Butler's *Gender Trouble* (1990), among many others. Since Critical Mass makes decisions, it therefore has a structure to do so.

4   Performativity is best known through the work of Judith Butler, including her 1988 article "Performative acts and gender constitution: An essay in phenomenology and feminist theory" in *Theater Journal* 40(4) pp. 519–531, her 1990 book *Gender Trouble* (New York: Routledge) and her 1993 book *Bodies that Matter: On the Discursive Limits of Sex* (New York: Routledge). But use of the concept is widespread, including by scholars like Eve Kofosky Sedgwick and, in feminist science studies, Karen Barad. Some material in this paragraph is paraphrased from Moya Lloyd's 1999 "Performativity, Parody, Politics" in *Theory, Culture, Society* 16(2), pp. 195–213.

5   Judith Butler calls performativity "the stylized repetition of acts through time". Butler, *Gender Trouble*, p. 179.

6   We also perform all sorts of other things, like race and class.

7   Susan Blickstein and Susan Hanson write, "Those active in Critical Mass may participate for any number of political reasons—to support global environmental policy change, to protest local and national transportation priorities or to politicize public spaces—but most participants also noted that Critical Mass is simply a good time." The paper is "Critical mass: forging a politics of sustainable mobility in the information age," *Transportation* 28, 347–362; (page 361).

8   Bey, Hakim. 1991 [1985]. *T.A.Z.: the Temporary Autonomous Zone, Ontological Anarchy, Poetic Terrorism*. New York: Autonomedia. I first came across Bey while reading about the Reclaim the Streets movement in England in the '90s. The T.A.Z. idea has been taken up in all sorts of ways, from rave culture and Burningman to Critical Mass to squatting and co-op housing to the Occupy movement. It has also been debated and contended with, so none of these are uncritical, naive uptakes. The point is simply that it's been important historically.

9   Liberal views of protest are essentially social democratic notions of the relationship between the state, the market, and people. The fundamental assumption is that the state exists to take care of its people. The base unit of this view is the individual, and though individuals can be aggregated for policy purposes, it's individual needs or goals or desires that are primary. For this state, its foremost tool is the law, and "the market" (a.k.a. capitalism) is a rather inventive technology for resource distribution, but still subservient to questions of general welfare. "Democracy"—nearly always electoral republicanism—tends to be seen as the most efficient technology for people to make their needs

known. This view's main argumentative strength is that actual state repression and oppression do not count as arguments against the state itself, but as arguments that some government is a bad version of the state. (Think here of Jim Crow laws.) In recent decades, as statistical thinking has become increasingly valued, real states have become seen as deviations from the mean of the proper state—a odd recasting of Plato's theory of forms. This view is also broadly compatible with positivist and teleological framings of history, in which Progress perpetually drives us forward.

10 How many times did the U.S. national media say something horrifyingly sexist about Hillary Clinton during her 2008 presidential campaign? Let me answer: tons. All. the. time. See Amanda Fortini's "The Feminist Reawakening: Hillary Clinton and the Fourth Wave" in *New York* magazine, April 28, 2008, for just a few of the gruesome quotes from Tucker Carlson and Chris Matthews.

11 Women continue to do the vast majority of housework and childcare in heterosexual nuclear families; and the practice of "mothering"—which, as Virginia Held has pointed out, has only the events of birth and nursing to do with sex—remains intimately connected to the home.

12 On men as "rational," the history is actually worse than you probably are aware of. See Virginia Held's *The Ethics of Care: Personal, Political and Global* (Oxford, 2005: Oxford University Press), p. 59.

13 For the point about the personal and the political, I am indebted to The Institute for Experimental Freedom's "The Dictatorship of Postfeminist Imagination" found at *www.politicsisnotabanana.com*, though I adapt the relevant passage to my own purposes here.

14 Again, similar critiques exist for the raced and classed nature of advocating for social change.

15 As Jai Sen has written: "We must accept that open space is not inherently open, neutral, or equal, let alone progressive; it can only be so if we struggle for it to be so. Open space is not a 'level playing field.' It is subject to all the same forces as exist in the society within which it is created or practiced, of segmentation, marginalisation, and exclusion, and of resource concentration, power play, and privilege." From 2010's "On Open Space: Explorations Towards a Vocabulary of a More Open Politics," *Antipode* 42 (4): 994–1018.

16 Marxists have long pointed out that one of the techniques of capitalism, and especially industrial capitalism, is to alienate us from the work that we do. Marxist feminists have pointed out that such alienation is, historically speaking, strongly gendered; in other words, that it takes place in masculine conditions and on masculine terms. But further, feminists have argued that inalienable work—what Marx called the work of social reproduction like feeding, cleaning, and so forth—has been likewise gendered, but female. This is not to say that any of these are essentially female, but rather that empirically we can recognize what the gendering has been, *and* that the gendering has been produced. Likewise this production is the precursor and the precondition for the actual practices becoming part of the performance of femininity. But the division between production and reproduction in the world is often not so simple. The "social reproductive" work of caring can in fact be productive, can be transformative, as with caring for a child. Child care doesn't just reproduce a workforce for a disembodied capitalism; the actual practice actually helps produce a person. This shift in thinking is in many ways a denial of a separation of instrumentalism, between means and ends. Held, *The Ethics of Care*, pg. 32.

17 Kittay. 2001. "When Caring is Just and Justice is Caring," *Public Culture* 13(3), p. 570. See also Kittay, 1999. Love's *Labor: Essays on Women, Equality and Dependency*, New York: Routledge.

18 Heckert, Jamie and Richard Cleminson. 2011. "Ethics, relationships and power: an Introduction," in R. Cleminson and J. Heckert (eds.) *Anarchism & Sexuality: Ethics, Relationships and Power*, New York: Routledge, p. 4.

19 Marxists have long pointed out that one of the techniques of capitalism, and especially industrial capitalism, is to alienate us from the work that we do. Marxist feminists have pointed out that such alienation is, historically speaking, strongly gendered, that it takes place in masculine conditions and on masculine terms. But further, feminists have argued that inalienable work—what Marx called the work of social reproduction like feeding, cleaning, and so forth—has been likewise gendered,. This is not to say that any of these are essentially—i.e., inherently—female, but rather that empirically we can recognize what the gendering has been, and that the gendering has been produced. This production is the precursor and the precondition for the actual practices becoming part of the performance of femininity. But the division between production and reproduction in the world is often not so simple. The "social reproductive" work of caring can in fact be productive, can be transformative, as with caring for a child. Child care doesn't just reproduce a workforce for a disembodied capitalism; the actual practice actually helps produce a person. This shift in thinking is in many ways a denial of a separation of instrumentalism, of between means and ends.

20 See, for instance, the conversation in May 2010 hosted on sfcriticalmass.org—not the official organ for SF Critical Mass, which has no such thing—which asked whether Critical Mass had "outlived its usefulness." Included in that conversation were three longtime San Francisco bike advocates, including Dave Snyder, the former director of the San Francisco Bike Coalition. *www.sfcriticalmass.*

org/2010/05/25/is-critical-mass-bad-or-good/

21 Deleuze and Guattari. 1994. *A Thousand Plateaus*. Minneapolis: University of Minnesota Press, transl. Brian Massumi.

Critical Mass San Francisco on Market and 3rd Streets, July 2005.

Paris, France, Velorutión Universelle, 2011

Political Critical Mass in Rome

by Rotafixa *(Bike welder, bike painter, bike writer, bike dreamer, daily biker: biker)*

Critical Mass in Rome, Italy created a new way of acting politically. In less than a decade, it taught us to resist the hegemonic politics that have dominated Italy for decades. With Critical Mass we (re)discovered a way to relate to the world around us, and rediscovered the point of connection among all human beings. We even became reacquainted with the key to what makes us human, things like the opposable thumb, nomadism, communication, and an ability to connect the individual and the collective. Our species has these qualities, which are especially effective if used together.

During the last few decades we haven't been living well. We depend too much on cars, and those who want to move by other means are struggling, especially bicyclists. Critical Mass emerged out of this need, establishing that roads are not just for motorists, but are actually much better without cars.

Not knowing where the Critical Mass rides go has a deeper resonance; humans don't know where our species is going either! Supporting each other, sharing an intention, joining something we have only heard of, perhaps going because your beloved mentioned the idea to you. This "thing" called Critical Mass embodies many different motivations. It is so refreshing to become part of a community of people you don't know, and find that group acting together effectively. In Critical Mass we share an intention to engage in the simple act of riding bicycles through the city streets, once a month. These meetings nourish a dream some of us cultivate in solitude: What if we were a really huge mass of bikers? The dream comes true in Critical Mass.

However, the most important aspect of Critical Mass is the absence of a recognized leader. We learned to act without a leader and still be totally effective, while the media bombards us with the idea that we needed a leader. This suddenly and obviously appears wrong.

How does Critical Mass work? Nobody knows where the "brain" of the ride is, how it is directed. Nobody is the leader, the big boss, the insider. Of course there are point-persons who help with stability and continuity in Rome as elsewhere. They are informal and creative leaders in the moment, not because they took power or were elected in any way. This is the common experience in Critical Mass rides across the world. In Rome we are trying to change the way we experience streets collectively, and not only by organizing Critical Mass, but also by working with other leaderless initiatives. We are trying to change the way we relate with media, institutions and political leaders. I am part of one of these organizations, and thanks to the media, we now meet people who are not bicyclists but listen to us. We have a voice in promoting the collective good while also increasing Rome's cyclability. The recent initiatives of the city administrators to improve spaces for cycling show how effective we are, despite them.

For example, in February 2011 we were summoned by a city councilor to discuss our demands that had been presented publicly in the media. We participated as an anonymous organization, under the name "Traffic Kills," and we also invited other more "traditional" associations which advocate for cyclability. The councilor listened only to the presidents of those associations, but he listened to ALL the members of our anonymous group, which contributed to a more complete understanding of the issues. Many of the changes we advocated for were later implemented. The councilor instinctively understood the legitimacy of the people speaking and this was amplified by the knowledge that we were not only speaking for ourselves but also for other bicyclists—without a popular mandate—which added responsibility. Similar results coming out of other meetings have confirmed that this approach really works.

Who makes up "Traffic Kills"? We are a group ranging from six to eleven people, interested in organizing cyclists in Rome; we have a support network, but it isn't really quantifiable. We don't represent anybody. We sign our proclamations and manifestos with a collective name, or we use multiple names, depending on who we are addressing. We can speak to the Mayor or the district representative as needed, but we try to discuss ahead of time what we will say to them. Anybody can issue press-releases or statements. We trust each other deeply.

Over time, the media started to trust us. They appreciated events we organized, but also the journalists themselves experience traffic congestion and can see that using a bike in the city is a smart choice. The media knows very well that moving across Rome is total chaos, and so they also want to propagate our message. Our view has gained such traction in the mass media that those in power, reading the daily news, started worrying: Who are these bikers? Where is their leader? Can we talk to him? But the leader does not exist, just like in Critical Mass. When we have been invited to speak to the politicians in power (the Power, as I prefer to put it), we try to show up each time with different people. We also like to enter the discussion by playing different roles each time—staying silent, writing a statement, quarreling, speaking—depending on the occasion. This is a helpful confusion that prevents the Power from knowing exactly know who to speak to. Their goal, of course, is to cut a deal with "the leader" behind closed doors, in order to undercut or co-opt the movement. We want a real change, which can only happen collectively, not by way of a traditional leader and the institutional structure that implies. We communicate with the Power, but as interlocutors we are horizontal, only playing that part temporarily, casually, in continuity with the collective stance.

Today, in 2012, in Rome, ten years after our first Critical Mass and 20 years after the first in the world, we are creating a Critical Mass politics. It may not always work but we are just at the beginning, and no one can stop us.

P.S.

Since I wrote this contribution in February 2012, Italy has witnessed a kind of bicycle revolution, with the same characteristics I described before it happened. A new group of about 30 bloggers (including me), organized on horizontal principles, has given life to a spontaneous movement with the name of *#salvaciclisti* (literal translation: ' save the cyclists', but it is also a play on the word *salvagente* or life jacket). In less than two months the movement has gained 15,000 adherents and has been able to reach the ears of the media and politicians. In less than ten days we drafted and presented a bill to Parliament, signed by dozens of parliamentarians, which articulated all our demands. We organized a demonstration in Rome on April 28, in conjunction with a similar demonstration in London, to demand that finally bike riding be respected and given support in Italy to promote smooth and zero-impact transportation. As I am writing now, in early April, I have no idea how large the demonstration will be, but based on the notoriety of the movement and the many discussions that are happening everywhere, I suspect that we will be in the thousands.

In the true style of "political critical mass," (especially in this case) there are no leaders. The coordination of the group's actions (flashmobs, blitzes, newspaper articles, radio and tv appearances, delegations to interact with politicians and administrators) is done by an anonymous collective formed by the original bloggers and based on principles of self-determination and mutual trust. Everything we do has two fundamental characteristics: consensus process and paying attention to all opinions The best and most efficacious idea wins. Until now we have not missed a beat.

More and more people (from politicians to the people on the street) were asking us, "Who is the leader?" so we decided to provide them with a fake one, *Pio La Bici* (Kip The Bike), which in Italian sounds like a legitimate name. We sent this with an accompanying photograph of a sleeping child with his hand resting on a bike. Everybody finally stopped wondering who the leader is and we can now continue our work in our own style, the style of the future. And this gives us enormous strength.

GRAPHIC BY CYCO

Guadalajara (Mexico):
A Critical Mass of Associated Citizens
by Jesús Carlos Soto Morfín, Ciudad para Todos

Here is the story of a movement that started five years ago in Guadalajara, Mexico, my city. Let's compare it to the wheel of a bicycle, where the hub ties the spokes together and allows the rim to hold its shape. The hub also stands for a deep desire, difficult to express, because it cannot be interpreted nor represented in a sole idea. At first glance it is the desire to live in a better world, one more just, equal, environmentally responsible, and amenable to human conviviality.

Yet we are critical. We do not succumb to nostalgia fora lost past. We commit to social happiness and hope for a better future. Active citizens are not waiting for the ideal conditions to take the street. They take it despite the circumstances, despite the barriers, despite the danger.

Like the hub—the critical piece of a bicycle—people gather and organize at the heart of efforts to change things. There are many spokes of the wheel. I will concentrate only on some to explain what is happening here:

1) Instead of the authoritarianism of our Mexican political system, the critical mass of active people in this movement demands discussion, dialogue, and democracy.[1] We all want to participate in the design and construction of the city we desire.

2) Confronted by the violence in Mexico, another important spoke is the construction of pleasant physical spaces. Even the poorest people should be able to enjoy a bench, a park, a sidewalk, an opportunity to move without being crushed. In sum, we oppose violence with solidarity, empathy, quality space, integration of neighborhoods, neighborly links, friendship, and trust.

3) Confronted by relentless pressure from the market, the mechanization of work, and the lack of economic alternatives to enjoy life, this movement proposes "the free" (generosity and doing things freely): easily replicated low or no cost actions which are fun and free to all, innovative strategies to improve economic life, the right to enjoy a free city that offers ample public life (e.g. free outdoor film screenings, neighborhood tours to explore our shared life, bike rides of hundreds of thousands).

4) This collective movement proposes the joy of living, protesting, speaking, and organizing against a leaden discourse imposed by the intermittently repressive and indifferent authorities. Instead of typical demands, this movement engages in ludic forms of protest through art, music, painting, wandering, and pursuing a bohemian lifestyle. This also addresses an

apathetic society that fails to resist the surrounding reality. Enjoyment and shared pleasure is a much stronger foundation for oppositional political movements than bitterness and resentment.

5) Repudiating the assumption that things which are public are the exclusive responsibility of politicians, this movement—at times unconsciously, sometimes fully aware—proposes to understand "the political" as that which affects us all. Every part of this country is our shared patrimony, something that has been forgotten by the collective imagination. Each street, park, metro, bus, sidewalk, streetlight, plaza, school, hospital, or day care center is public. That is to say, it belongs to all of us.

There are many more spokes to this wheel, but I will focus on these in terms of the diversity of actions that take place here. The movement does not have a precise origin. There have been urban movements demanding better services and quality spaces for decades. Groups of university students spoke about public space in the 1990s. Since the '90s, early collectives in favor of protecting the environment have been pointing out the bad air quality due to car saturation in cities. Since the '70s and '80s urbanists warned about the invasion of the automobile and proposed pulling the emergency brake, at least within downtown city zones. But these voices were rarely heard. Today my city is a dispersed low density city, covering a very extensive territory, and cannot ever aspire to be the pleasant self-contained Mexican city it used to be. Cities like Amsterdam, Madrid, or Paris have managed to remain compact, but they did not have to face the challenges of urban fragmentation and social segregation in the same way that Latin American and other post-colonial nations did.

Guadalajara once imagined itself as an athletic city, but now it is a city on wheelchairs, even if it wants to give its competitive best. Metropolitan Guadalajara tripled its vehicular fleet, reaching two million cars for a little over four million inhabitants. A powerful automobile industry has flourished here: it is said that we have more car dealerships than Chicago, New York, Los Angeles, or Houston. In Mexico, there is a great deal of money concentrated in the hands of a few, but there is unrestrained purchasing of automobiles by many. There are easy credit lines to buy cars, subsidies for gas, cheap imported automobiles that benefit no one locally, while there are few or nonexistent car taxes. The government at all levels delegated city design and planning to the invisible hand of the market. Supposedly the real estate sector would be naturally wise in shaping the development of the city.

Our government also stopped investing in public transportation almost 30 years ago. In this vacuum a mafia of bus companies has bloomed, which is not strictly public. These private interests menace each electoral period by blocking streets, forcing politicians to raise fares, to grant subsidies, or to impede route changes, without offering a quality service in exchange. For the state it has been easier to bet everything on the automobile rather than to confront this problem. During the last six-year presidential term, the Mexican government invested slightly over five billion pesos (approx. $500 million) in infrastructure for cars: bridges, underpasses, widening of avenues, new streets. Not surprisingly the invisible hand of the real estate market has built everywhere, without order or planning, and only to profit. This unplanned, unregulated madness has destroyed enormous forest areas and created a disjointed territory. The State of Jalisco in which Guadalajara is the largest city has, after Mexico City, the longest average commute in Latin America at one and a half hours. We have the municipality with the highest growth in the country: Tlajomulco. Hundreds of thousands of residences have been built on a protected natural reserve, dozens of kilometers away from the urban nucleus.

Here are the actual histories that make up the spokes of our wheel in Guadalajara:

In 2004 the "Via RecreActiva" was established, taking example from Bogotá, Colombia's Ciclovía, in which some principal arteries of the city are closed off to cars on Sundays to allow only for skateboards, rollerskates, bicycles, pedestrians, dogs, and recreational workshops. This proved it was possible to create another kind of public space, one that weaves different social classes together through the whole city, like the two hemispheres of the brain, between rich and poor.

Birth of the Critical Mass of Citizens, 2007[2]

In 2007, a second generation of urbanist civil society organizations was born protest against another new highway infrastructure project. Previously that year, some people began promoting World Carfree Day, celebrated worldwide every September 22nd. Already, the first nocturnal bicycle rides were taking place, started by a few underground characters from alternative sectors and cafés. Every week, on Wednesday nights between 100 to 300 cyclists managed to gather. When September 22nd arrived, the government, rather than join in the celebration, decided to open one of the most important avenues of the city. World Carfree Day promoters came into the streets to protest, creating a human barrier against cars and allowing pedestrians to cross the street.

The new civil society groups have been essential actors in the debate about transit in the last five years. Their initial demand was the total halt to the López Mateos viaduct and an Integral Urban Mobility Plan with a short-, medium-, and long-term vision. The goal was to reverse the harm done to the city and direct all efforts towards a sustainable city that gives priority to pedestrians, cyclists, and public transit as the foundation of functional mobility.

The 2007 protest against the construction of the viaduct began with the attempt to dialogue with the city government. We wanted to show why their plan was toxic for city life, and seek a consensus on a city plan that would not be solely dedicated to cars. It was a frustrating experience. City Hall not only showed itself resistant to dialogue, but once we did begin talking, the politicians did not have the slightest idea of what we were demanding. Our proposals sounded to them like fantasies so they simply responded:

> *A city for people? That is exactly what we are doing. Our plans will ensure that everyone may move by car, or however they wish. Progress has arrived and there is nothing we can do to stop it.*

After a couple of attempts, our movement gave up the pointless dialogue with City Hall (without completely closing the door). There was a radical strategy shift. Now we would talk to the citizenry in general to form a critical mass to generate sufficient pressure to make the government shift its public policy.

"Festivals of mobility" that first confronted governmental institutions migrated to parks to find families, artists, musicians, professionals—children and adults, men and women. There were lots of activities in the festival which were extremely fun. Panels explained our proposals and the problems of the city. In workshops, children learned to use bicycles, repair them, and travel safely. There were also workshops for designing the ideal city. As a first stage, it was full of dreams and illusions, very refreshing and enthusiastic.

The protests, festivals, and intervention into public spaces resulted in 2008 in a State contract for an Urban Non Motorized Mobility Plan (*Plan de Movilidad Urbana No Motorizada* [PMUNM]). During a trip to Portland, U.S., we participated in our first international Conference of Towards Carfree Cities. We ran into public officials from our own city at the same event! We knew that they would meet in a luxurious building with Gil Peñalosa from Colombia and the Portland consultants Alta Planning. We crashed the meeting with a pair of radical Americans who wanted to find out about the Mexican situation.

The consultants and our State government were meeting to plan the PMUNM, but without any participation of Guadalajara's civil society groups. This would be an invisible plan, concocted by specialists behind closed doors. As we say in Spanish, "we put a cry in the sky," and forced the project to gestate through a different model. Foreign consultants were welcome, but the project had to be led by urbanists based on Guadalajara who would guarantee civic participation in the plan's design. This is how the foundation of the Guadalajara cyclist movement was born.[3] The *PMUNM* was completed in 2009, promising 1,500 km of cycling paths and various pedestrian corridors around the metropolis. This was a clear example of how important it is to be in the right place at the right time, and take advantage of it.

Making a Critical Mass, with Pleasure, 2008

In 2008 the First Thursdays bike rides started up.[4] These rides attracted a greater number of cyclists than other nocturnal rides. In a few months we reached five thousand cyclists. This was unprecedented for any citizen mobilization in our city. Those rides are ongoing and represent the clearest example of Critical Mass in the city. There have been other days, too, on which rides have been held to protest one specific issue or another.

In September we were invited by Dan Raven, a British citizen who established the Urban Earth initiative, to cross Mexico City on foot from end to end. Sixty-four kilometers over three days.[5] Dan carried out the project to draw attention to the fact that in 2008, 51% of humanity lived in cities and we had to think of cities as the future of humanity. Returning from that experience we had to repeat the same walk through Guadalajara, an action which is repeated every year with different routes and purposes, visiting famous architectural sights in the city.[6]

That same year we initiated 8m^2, a tropical version of Park(ing) Day in which the name refers to the average space (in square meters) that a car occupies in the city. We took over several blocks where we replaced cars with chairs, umbrellas, rugs, board games, *aguas frescas* (traditional fruit flavored drinks), guitars, hammocks and even camping tents. This later turned into the "nomadic park,"[7] a more ambitious version that took entire lanes from cars and transformed them into temporary cycle paths, or widened sidewalks, where we celebrated the King of the City: the pedestrian. Nomadic parks were staged in low-income neighborhoods, in parts of the city drastically lacking green areas. It also stimulated local businesses and facilitated links between neighbors.

From Performance to Civil Disobedience:
Bridges to Nowhere, 2009

By the end of 2008 we had already launched the design of the *PMUNM*, established a Cyclist and Pedestrian Council for the municipal government of Guadalajara,[8] and created our own Citizen Council for Sustainable Transport.[9] Public officials were excluded from the Citizens' Council in order to protect our autonomy and our ability to deliberate without interference from the agencies we wanted to pressure.

2009 was the year in which the movement suffered its first great disappointment. We began the year with the best of spirits, carrying out many street actions, educational discussions, and strong work on social networks. We dominated the digital environment, where we organized spontaneous actions, sustained fluid communications among organizations and were able to contact media and others directly. The bike rides continued to grow on first Thursdays with a different theme proposed each time. Participants were invited to put on appropriate costumes for Day of the Dead, the Anniversary of the Mexican Revolution, "Law of the Jungle," Labor Day, Social Activist Day, and so on.

In spite of the palpable energy and enthusiasm for another city model, the Jalisco state government announced in mid-2009 plans to build the "Matute Remus Suspension Bridge."[10] This proposed bridge took the Golden Gate of San Francisco as its model, but instead of crossing the ocean, a river, a cliff— or going to the moon— in Guadalajara it would pass over four lanes of the same avenue that in 2007 had seen the original protests.

We were flabbergasted by the announcement. We could not believe that despite all our effort this was the government's solution for the exponential increase of cars. The proposed bridge also threatened to destroy an urban park that served as a micro-lung in a city devoid of green spaces.[11] If that was not enough, the project would cost 450 million pesos (approx. $38 million), half of which could have covered the completion of the *PMUNM*. Not a single cent had yet been allocated to the promised alternative transit plan.

We organized a protest at the exact spot where the mega-VIP bridge would pass. Once again, enjoyable actions were the medium. We carried out field trips, open air movie nights, Critical Mass bike rides, and installed a symbolic cemetery representing threatened public space. This took place during months of media frenzy critiquing this "great work" as a monument to the car. The Governor's seal of approval was never in doubt.[12]

At the start of November the first tractors arrived and marked with red paint the trees that would die, close to 800 during the first stage. Our citizens' groups had already discussed legal strategies to stop the project, as well as stronger actions in case it went forward anyway. Legal action failed to stop the project so we transitioned from a spontaneous and improvisational approach to setting up an onsite camp on the night before groundbreaking. Three dozen tents greeted dawn on the median slated for destruction. We made front-page news every day that week. Reporters from television, radio, newspapers, and magazines besieged us. Even university students interviewed us as case studies. It was not the first time that a protest camp was set up in the city, but it was the first time that it was directed against a public construction project of this nature by a part of civil society that had never done this before.

The government launched a promotional campaign for the bridge called *"Pásala Mejor"* (translated as "have a better time," but with the double-meaning in Spanish of "make a better crossing"), which emphasized the time saved by motorists using the new bridge, allowing them more time with family. In response we launched the campaign "Have an Even Better Time" where we announced the benefits of a different kind of mobility, with dignified and efficient public transport, many cyclists and pedestrians on the streets, and many thousand fewer cars congesting the city. In addition, we explained the negative impact that the bridge would have on the area, seeking support from neighbors, something that never happened.

We filled our protest camp with yoga, theatre, movie projections, drawing workshops, and a 24-hour information center. Participants distributed themselves among the trees planned for removal.[13] The camp lasted throughout the month of November, as we tried to provoke a dialogue with authorities to think about different solutions. One message on a banner clearly stated: "We do not want asphalt bridges, but bridges of dialogue." Another announced the exasperation experienced at the time: "When will the citizenry be listened to?" The trees fell one by one, in spite of the temporary protection provided by the youths that climbed into them. We weren't able to cover them all, nor all the time. The place was cold and eyes were bloody from pollution, given that it was one of the most traffic-choked intersections in the city.

After a month of resistance, we gave up and broke camp. The State had refused to dialogue despite telling the media it would. The neighbors had surrendered before putting up a fight and only they had legal standing to sue to halt the work. Finally we realized that we were not really a critical mass of citizens, but a well-organized minority, a few lunatics and dreamers. Our hope was shattered and with it, the joy of fighting on. Days after breaking camp we returned to the site to climb the trees that would be felled. In that way we carried on for days, until suddenly, from night to morning, all the trees disappeared. We had lost and the bridge was completed one year later. But we weren't finished.

Snatching Victory from Defeat, 2010

In Summer 2009, several months after the camp against the suspension bridge, local elections took place in Mexico. A politicized citizen emerged across the country. In Guadalajara it was composed of many of us who had participated in the broader movement for a sustainable city, and we put together a broadly integrated program called "Platform 39."[14]

This was a mobilization against a closed political system based on a stifled creative abundance. Participation by civil society is not allowed in Mexico beyond voting for elected representatives—who barely, or badly, represent us in most cases. The political parties are riddled with vice and corruption, they do not manage public resources with transparency, nor do they have internal rules based on genuine democracy. Mexican parties don't build democracy, do not create political schools, and have not been capable of presenting solutions to the challenges that we face. They have merely been the facilitators of an insatiable market that seeks to privatize the country, generating exclusive zones accessible only to elites, while monopolizing industries such as telecommunications and others.

Mexico is whipped by drug violence, arms sales from the United States, and the steady increase of economic inequality. This creates a fertile field for organized crime, since it is the bribe given by monied elites to authorities that becomes the normal means of negotiation. Meanwhile, those most in need, who cannot find sufficient alternatives, acquire money by way of crime.

In this context, we called for a null vote (a blank or spoiled ballot or "none of the above"), and we reached a historic record of 2 million null votes in the last election. The principal objective of this movement was to place the political regime—its structure and its rules of the game, and its shallow or nonexistent democratic process—at the center of the debate.

The campaign to vote null and the protest camp of 2009 were small examples of a trend that would be magnified two years later in Spain and in the global Occupy movements. In fact, our camp was itself inspired by the *plantón*—mass protests after the 2006 federal elections in Mexico, in the form of urban occupations which sought to embody direct democracy in order to ensure electoral honesty. Our call for "Bridges to Dialogue" sought to open the political system and make room for a broader form of social control over all things public, beyond political parties and their captured political institutions. We wanted to change public discussion by emphasizing the lack of genuine democracy. Who really decided to allocate public resources to a suspension bridge to nowhere? How was it possible that private wealth could dominate so easily the basic decisions that affected the collective patrimony, everyone's quality of life, equal access to the city? Not only did we need to democratize the political system, but the city itself.

At the start of 2010 newly elected politicians took their positions.[15] We attempted once again to open dialogue and present the *PMUNM* to the new public officials. We were turned away with the argument that the project did not have legal grounds because the State had not been in charge of its generation![16] Once again we faced authorities resistant to changing the urban paradigm. But that was not the end of it.

In March of that year, the Jalisco State government announced the Via Express: an elevated expressway above Avenida Inglaterra, a long avenue that crosses the city, used at the time by a cargo train right-of-way with two car lanes on each side. The proposed highway would have toll booths every kilometer, would be constructed with private investment, and would cost 7 billion pesos (seven times the cost of the unrealized *PMUNM* of 1,500 km). We were terrified.

The disappointment of having lost the battle against the suspension bridge made us react slowly. We began the first meetings with a certain timidity, but already angry at what was happening. It did not take us long to find an earlier municipal project that proposed creating a pedestrian walkway on the same avenue where they now proposed to build the highway. We dusted off this project and alongside the *PMUNM* we began to promote an alternative to the Via Express: a linear citizen park—a new lung for the city.

Also at the start of 2010 we filed our petition with the World Carfree Network to become the seat of the 10th Towards Carfree Cities International Conference. We won, and in June we had to go to York, England to sign the contract. We took advantage of the trip by presenting a promotional video recently released by the State government of the Via Express with fabulous animations.[17] We showed it to the Carfree Conference and recorded the reactions of traffic planning experts. Our video rebuttal demolished the government's laughable propaganda. Before each argument shown on the State's video we inserted the severely critical response given by an expert, often mocking the Via Express as a project for the past century.[18] The video went viral in Guadalajara, with thousands of visits in a few days. It was even censored by the government under the argument that it violated copyright, but was reposted later after an exchange of arguments with You Tube. Soon it was being shared through hundreds of alternative channels. This detonated dozens of opinion editorials in the local media and in a short time, banners appeared along the length of Avenida Inglaterra where the highway was proposed, featuring phrases taken from our guerrilla video which had resonated in the neighborhood. The banners were put up by neighbors, who this time were actively reacting and showing their resistance.

We walked to a convenience store that had a poster and there discovered José Antero, a neighbor, and Doctor Alicia Jaik, a senior who quickly emerged as a neighborhood leader with her charisma and eloquence. She invited us to the neighborhood meetings where we presented the alternative project for a linear park. They loved meeting the authors of the viral video and immediately we rolled up our sleeves: every Saturday neighbors and organizations would go out to transform the area around the railroad right-of-way into a pedestrian walkway, with a community garden, games for children, tables, benches, and pedestrian signage; all constructed with recycled material and with no help from any official agencies.

During the following year we intervened in every way to stop the Via Express. At the same time, we began monitoring all the parties involved in the construction of the highway, from the responsible public officials and congresspeople that had to vote for the project, to the local and national construction companies set to benefit. We began to bring pinpoint pressure on each of those parties, using social networks, newspaper articles, new viral videos, and more street actions. Then we purchased a car without a motor to create a people's carfree monument of our own. We called for a massive bicycle ride on September 22, 2010, and on that day, just at the moment at which Critical Mass arrived at a particular intersection on Avenida Inglaterra, we welded the car to two tons of concrete, filled it with dirt, and planted a tree inside. We called it the *auto maceta* ("car pot" or "potted car"), a combat totem against the Via Express, and an invitation to think of the city as carfree, full of pots for plants.[19]

In October 2010, we carried out the "*La Jitomatiza*" (loosely translated as the "tomato launch"), an interesting action of symbolic violence to pressure legislators to reject the Via Express project and deny the concession license to the private enterprises that would be in charge of its construction. We went to Congress and we gave a tomato to each congressional representative, with the threat that next time it would be launched at them, if they failed to do their job and approved the project despite the counter arguments proving the Via Express concept was built on unfounded fantasies. *La Jitomatiza* generated much goodwill, and its provocative content left everyone with a strong impression!

A few days later, we were sought out by several business people of different sectors, some already active in the promotion of sustainable transit from years back, others just joining. They wanted to hold a press conference to protest the recent rejection by local mayors of the construction of Line 2 of the Bus Rapid Transit (BRT).[20] We decided to join forces, despite mistrust, agreeing that each organization would have a chance to speak. That is how it played out. Agreeing to this helped to engage the business sector in actively rejecting the Via Express, not so easy since some of them had already expressed their support and would need to recant. But they conceded after viewing the videos on the web. Within days we had sold them on the project for a linear park, including the proposal that instead of a cargo train, we could install an inner city passenger train and thus connect distant points of our city, which would clearly generate benefits for the real estate sector.

Little by little we convinced more business organizations, until the state governor announced in 2011 that he would do what business organizations told him to do regarding the Via Express. He did not know that we had already organized them to reject the expressway. Their definitive "no" was made public, and still the governor tried to pressure congressional representatives into approving the Via Express. But opposing pressure was so strong that they had no alternative but to reject the plan and thus sentence to death the Via Express. Our celebration lasted for days across the city. It was the first time that such a diverse coalition of citizens groups had been able to cohere around a single vision. The neighbors had been the pillar of this mobilization, which today is the clearest example of the new bottom-up democracy emerging in our city. Every Saturday, neighbors and activists continue to work on the green spaces of Avenida Inglaterra. We continue to collaborate on a broad alternative project, Metropolitan Guadalajara, looking ahead to the day when there will be sufficient political will to take the first steps.

Towards Carfree Cities, 2011

The great challenge of 2011, despite having stopped the Via Express, was to organize the 10th Towards Carfree Cities International Conference in September.[21] We didn't have funds to support it, so we were dependent on volunteers and everyone's free time. This posed significant organizational problems for a Conference of this magnitude, one that would challenge our city with more arguments and proposals to change direction.

Alongside the battle against the Via Express we continued promoting the *PMUNM* through a different civil disobedience campaign. We began creating our own *ciclovías* (bicycle lanes)[22] with our own resources and on the avenues that the languishing plan had designated. Evidently this was illegal, but our exasperation over the government's constant attempts to build car infrastructure, refusing to implement the *PMUNM* left us no alternative. Besides, it was extremely fun! For months we gathered to create signage and a system of symbols that made painting horizontal stripes more efficient. To a tricycle—a great example of Latin American engineering—we mounted a compressed air paint spray pistol to paint the line that would generate the first citizen's bicycle lane. It was a resounding success that concluded with the official acceptance by authorities of the citizen's *ciclovías*. There are even traffic fines for anyone who does not respect them. At this writing we are about to create the fourth citizen's *ciclovía* on one of the most important avenues of the city.

The Carfree Conference succeeded thanks to the generous participation of the private sector, each time more sympathetic to this citizen movement, as well as the collaboration of universities, opinion media and other organizations. The alliance against the Via Express allowed for sponsorships and the collaboration of many people. Today we have an interesting network where organizations, individuals, entrepreneurs, and academics gather periodically to work on topics of common interest that are threatening to further degrade the city.

The result of the Carfree Conference was the consolidated birth of new civil society organizations, each with particular emphases but directed in various ways at transforming the city. We also managed to draft the public manifesto "Guadalajara for Sustainable Transit,"[23] a live document that continues to be polished. It summarizes the demands of the movement and is now the basis for entering into dialogue with any authority, since it clearly distinguishes the vision of the city that we want from the one we do not want.

Enthusiasm and Trust, 2012

The success of our movement resides in the enthusiasm of the people who keep it alive, despite the unfavorable circumstances in Mexico for activism and citizen participation.[24] In Guadalajara there are more and more people joining an abundance of interventions—there are so many now that it is no longer possible to follow them all. Currently the citizenry is adopting public spaces in order to improve them. *Adopta un Bache* ("Adopt a Pothole") is a campaign for citizens to identify street repairs that the government has neglected. "Adopt a Sidewalk" and "Adopt a Null Politician" follow a similar logic to get commitments from local government to do what it is supposed to do.

These playful actions attract and sustain wide participation, because they are fun, generate enthusiasm, and gain sympathy from those who haven't yet joined. It is not possible to explain the success of our new "associationism" without this playful spirit, a spirit that crumbles the commonly held suspicion that anyone who participates in public activities is really seeking public office. This understanding is common in a country where 84% of citizens distrust one another. The distrust towards authorities nears 94%, and unions, police, and political parties are the most distrusted. In the face of this reality, it is difficult for people to think that those who act publicly do so for a common interest. This common interest is not counter to their personal interest, but actually deepens the meaning of "personal interest." We recognize that we are social beings and that without everyone's wellbeing, our own wellbeing is compromised.[24] This is the meaning of the dark desire that I mentioned at the beginning of this article and that surely will give people more to talk about in the coming years.

This movement in Guadalajara turned five years old in 2012 and at this point has already halted an expensive highway project; generated technical studies; and introduced the words mobility, city, and public space into the public debate. We join in denouncing the corruption and inefficiency of the political system, and propose to the city a culture of participation, inclusion, and respect. The most visible face of our accomplishments is a new social infrastructure.

None of this could be explained without Critical Mass, without the adventure of mounting a bicycle and setting off to pedal with a few hundred citizens, all lovers of this means of transportation, with the sole intention of having a good time, being happy and denouncing in a chorus of voices those things which are failing and need to be changed. The bicycle provides sufficient endorphines for brains to function, to dream, and to seek each other out. Critical Mass has given the pretext to meet, to create alliances, to organize amongst ourselves, and to discover a different city: one that belongs to us.

Notes

1 Throughout the article I will talk about "Critical Mass" in Guadalajara in two ways: on one hand, as an action of taking a bicycle and riding en masse in the streets, an inspiration from San Francisco's Critical Mass. In another sense, as a critical mass of organized individuals to achieve a common objective, beyond the demand for bicyclist mobility. To seek a harmonious, prosperous, and ecological city, which I summarize as a "sustainable city."

2 This is the other sense in which I will use the term Critical Mass throughout this text, while I may also refer to the bike rides en masse that take place nearly every day in the city and that have been a vital part of the movement that demands a sustainable city beyond the bicycle.

3 For now, I call it a bicycle movement to simplify, given that the *PMUMN* is laid out to facilitate and maximize the bicycling life of the city, but in reality the *PMUMN* provides input for a broader movement for a sustainable city.

4 *http://gdlenbici.org*

5 A photograph was taken every eight steps from which a marvelous video was later made, now available online. *http://urbanearth.ning.com/*

6 *http://citacomplot.blogspot.mx/*

7 *http://www.youtube.com/watch?v=M9s7J7Ei9fU* and *http://www.youtube.com/watch?v=gfEcCKdqrAU*

8 The first 10km of cycle paths had been built in 2008. Organized civil society groups followed this work to ensure good projects and avoid corruption.

9 *www.consejomovilidad.org*

10 Don Matute Remus is one of the historic urbanists of Guadalajara, famous for expanding its avenues and planning the principle city corridors, including an ortogonal axis for public transporation that was never completed. This same engineer opposed the public works that required the massive felling of trees.

11 Guadalajara went from being one of the most forested cities in the '40s to becoming a concrete plank with an average of 4m^2 of green areas per inhabitant and in many places only 2m^2.

12 Emilio González Márquez.

13 *http://www.youtube.com/watch?v=Qv0lGb5U0p4*

14 This platform united organizations with specific issues environment, transit, urban development,

Santiago River contamination, accountability for public monies, etc. They shared the same diagnosis: the government impedes civil society in its efforts to address social ills. Therefore, we had to create autonomous, recognized, and cross-linked institutions—a critical mass of participating citizens to socially control public resources and values.

15 At the executive level, the State government was the same, since Mexico changes Presidential administrations every six years, while municipal administrations change every 3 years.

16 Implicitly, the message sent was that the PMUNM had been signed by the State, in that time in hands of the Partido de Acción Nacional (PAN), and given that the new municipal administrations were from an opposing party, the Partido Revolucionario Institucional (PRI), they would not acknowledge the plan. Evidently, the citizens without representation by a party were of no interest.

17 Promotional video by the government of Jalisco for the Via Express: *http://www.youtube.com/watch?v=__uHSAz56_8*

18 Via Express video out in the world: *http://www.youtube.com/watch?v=9u3e9f0q7QY*

19 *http://www.youtube.com/watch?v=P7cj3eAOwWw*

20 Line 1 had generated a lot of heat—one political party took advantage of it to campaign against an opponent. Instead of continuing with more Bus Rapid Transit, the opposing party proposed light rail, but without presenting a project or a financing plan.

21 *www.carfree.mx* : In 2009, the second national urban cycling congress took place in Guadalajara, and a few groups had gained experience in generating an event of this type.

22 One: *http://www.youtube.com/watch?v=iFUbrme9V0M* and two: *http://www.youtube.com/watch?v=UmQw-1UL1MM*

23 *http://carfree.mx/mx/?p=1225*

24 Activists working on diverse topics have been assassinated throughout the country and currently Mexico is considered the country least favorable to reporters.

PHOTO: CHRIS CARLSSON

Guadalajara's Auto Maceta *in situ along Avenida Inglaterra, 2011.*

Nuevo León, Mexico

By Raquel Treviño and Gerardo Núñez

We are both students of the Autonomous University of Nuevo León, in Mexico, the third most important public university in the country. We are both urban cyclists, living in Monterrey, the second largest city in the country. But it also holds the infamous first place of the worst air quality among Mexican cities, and ranks at the top of the motorization rate. Our university has no bike infrastructure, but worst of all, approximately one third of our university land is dedicated to parking spots (which we find quite scandalous).

We watched how the bike movement started to form in our city, including the biking groups that have been formed here: *Pueblo Bicicletero, Biciérnagas, Biciregios, Zombies en Bici*... We decided to stop watching, and started to act. In April 2010, we created *"Tigre Bici,"* an independent student group which aims to not only build bike infrastructure, but to promote and improve the accessibility of all types of non-motorized mobility. We've started to talk with university authorities, with what we hope to be successful results. On January 23rd we organized our first Critical Mass ride (what we then thought would be our only) between two iconic University grounds: Colegio Civil, the first building the University built in the 19th century, (now the Cultural Centre) and the main campus. We had an amazing response, and wonderful help from the other biking groups of Monterrey. Overwhelmed, we decided to start monthly Critical Mass rides between the separate university grounds with a double objective: become visible to the other students and the population in general (and maybe inspire them get them on their bikes too), and to promote the project.

As we write these words, we are planning to do our second Critical Mass, now from the main campus to the Mederos campus (where the Economics, Political Sciences, Visual Arts and Music schools are located), which are 20 kilometres (12.5 miles) away from each other. And this image (see next page) is the flyer for the second Critical Mass. We are excited about it, and we hope that more and more people join the Critical Mass rides. And we hope to transform our city—as our fellows of Pueblo Bicicletero say—*"de una ciudad caníbal a una ciudad humana"* (from a cannibal city, to a humane city).

Tigre Bici

Nuevo León, Mexico

Positive Symbols And High Optimism In Budapest
By Justin Hyatt

The story of Critical Mass in Budapest is a curious one. Many a great thing has been accomplished, some of them in surprising ways, yet the storyline often diverges greatly from Critical Mass experiences elsewhere.

The year that saw the axles greased and the tire rubber screeching *en masse* was the phenomenal year of 2004. An unheard of Critical Mass ride took place that numbered 4,000 people. Fast forward a few years into the future, and 4,000 cyclists would be considered a mere trifle. But that propitious autumnal bike wonder in 2004 was the domino that kicked into action a veritable Hungarian cycle culture and the beginning of bicycle activism.

Every Spring and Fall season a new ride was organized, either to celebrate Earth Day on April 22 or strike up a chorus for modal shift on September 22 (World Carfree Day). And every ride for several consecutive years topped the last one.

4,000 cyclists turned into 10,000 the following spring. That was doubled again in the fall to 20,000. And we're still just getting started. Eventually all the major and some minor towns in Hungary put on their own rides. Towns whose names you would never be able to pronounce and places hardly a speck on the map achieved ridership to rival the giants.

> *This just in: We've had some big bike celebrations around the world today, in places like New York City, San Francisco, London, Paris and Orosháza...*

If numbers are a measure, the pinnacle of achievement in the history of Critical Mass Budapest to date was Earth Day in 2008 with 80,000 gleeful cyclists along for the ride. There has never been a larger ride that goes by the name of Critical Mass in the history of the world.

In 2009, appreciation for this feat came in the form of the European Mobility Week first place prize, which was awarded to Budapest by the Commissioner for Science and Research, as an acknowledgment both of the large rides as well as the progress made towards sustainable solutions in the city environment.

What Was The Recipe?

What brings people together like this in such big numbers? How was this achieved in Hungary of all places? Bike couriers from the company *Hajtás-*

Pajtás put their support behind organizing the rides. They did great work in rallying other cyclists and activists, putting out the publicity, going on radio and organizing flyering and stickering, from district to district. They formed the backbone of the rides.

It can be said the growth of Critical Mass and popularity of cycling went hand in hand with the rise in "coolness" of bicycles, and eventually everything connected to cycling—from cycling gear to fixies to the whole shebang.

Bicycles have now hit the mainstream. People gush that the Budapest cycling modal share doubles every year, and people routinely swear that, "This winter there were many more cyclists than last one." Winter is a good time to find out how many through and through converts are around.

In one area, however, the science of Critical Mass holds as valid for Budapest as it does for any other place: Whenever there are rides that people flock to, following the ride the number of everyday cyclists moves up the charts.

That has been the overt message of a number of Critical Mass rides—a battle cry for everyday pedal-powered self-propulsion. Such advice was hung from large banners in conspicuous places: "Cycle every weekday." And the masses heeded the call. While the effects of the ride might have been gradual, they have been no less than dramatic.

As previously alluded to, civic events, protests, activism, street parades and the like are usually attended by only a small handful of dedicated people in this small central European nation of ten million. That is not to say that activism and nonprofit organizations are not active in Hungary, they are, but in fairly small numbers, and usually connected to concrete projects. However, when it comes to large street manifestations, that has been largely reserved for revolutions or, occasionally, anti-government protests.

After the first few large rides in Budapest, people abroad started to notice. Bicycle activists from all over and organizations promoting sustainable transport began to talk about what was happening in Budapest. Chris Carlsson in San Francisco traded Critical Mass paraphernalia with me, and I held a workshop on the Budapest phenomenon at a World Carfree Network meeting in the Czech Republic. Newspaper articles and documentary films were also forthcoming.

Thus, I developed a way to describe what was happening and explain the background of the movement for audiences that had excitement written on their faces and who wanted to replicate such enviable successes in their home countries.

While holding firm to the notion that there must be something special to the spicy paprika that Hungarians eat, here are a few leading reasons:

First, it must be understood that these are rides that happen twice a year, not every month. There is therefore ample time to build up momentum and make a big splash of an event, something that would be a lot trickier were they held every month.

The rides are also registered ahead of time with the police and follow a given route, and thus hit a different note than the usual spontaneity and brazen independence of Critical Mass rides elsewhere.

The general consensus is that providing a legal basis for the movement has been an important compromise. This has allowed it to achieve much more than would have been the case had the recipe called for a loud, but limited, series of rides following a tiny trail of guerrilla cyclists.

People rightly point to the fact that the average Hungarian is fearful of breaking the law or engaging in civil disobedience. Since the rides have been legal and also maintained a strict neutrality regarding party politics, the doors have been opened widely to the masses. It is a family event, an activist event, and an occasion where the city's head mayor or Ambassador of the Netherlands might just show up (and have, in fact).

Thus, a key to its popularity could well be in the fact that the movement has gone to great lengths to stay away from party politics, otherwise so divisive in Hungary. When there were large anti-government protests and an internal political crisis in the fall of 2006, the ride was called off for that fall. And it has been noted that Critical Mass in Hungary has consistently drawn more folks than other events, either hued with political undertones or stretching the limits of cultural acceptability.

Critical Mass has therefore provided ordinary Budapest citizens with the opportunity to join a fun and dynamic movement that is free of the usual humdrum of everyday politics, and connect with others to take a stand for one very positive symbol: the bicycle.

Many also quickly recognized a powerful message that is inherent in the Critical Mass rides: Ride your bike—it is cheap, it is fun, and it doesn't pollute. Budapest has long been one of the most polluted cities in Europe. It is not a coincidence that one of the oldest organizations in Hungary concerned with the city of Budapest and sustainable transportation has the name "Clean Air Action Group."

As the snowball began to roll...

The bicycle infrastructure in Budapest is still sorely lacking in many respects, yet there have been significant advances. Many new paths have been built, both downtown as well as further out. Not all of the paths were brought to the level and standard to satisfy the wishes of cyclists and the ever more sophisticated eye of the Hungarian bicycle infrastructure specialist. Yet many have been built in the proper way, and a trend has been set.

Most importantly, the bicycle lobby has arrived, to the point where authorities now listen to and must consult with bicycle organizations (such as the Hungarian Cyclists' Club) before renovating or building a road. In the area of planning and policy, the change in atmosphere has also followed suit. Before the large rides, if you had asked the city authorities to dedicate a lane on a bridge in the summer months for cyclists to access the city's popular Margit Island, which is a large park, you would have been "laughed out of the room," in the words of János László, head of the Hungarian Cyclists' Club. Now the cyclist lobby has gained in stature, and such requests are frequently listened to, as this one in fact was.

At one point, the Ministry of Transportation even named a deputy minister for cycling affairs. This was a post that Ádám Bodor held from 2005 to 2008, while also serving as vice president of the European Cyclists' Federation.

Many large bicycle infrastructure projects have also been announced over the years, although change has been slow in coming—at least for the growing restless numbers of urban cyclists.

There is a smattering of new phenomena that will hopefully become standard features down the road. While contraflow bike lanes have been a priority of the Hungarian Cyclists' Club, three one-way streets to date have been cleared for two-way bike traffic. This is a breakthrough, as previous city traffic laws forbade this, yet the updated Traffic Law Regulations of 2010 made this possible for the first time. (This option must be declared individually for every street.)

There is now also a token blue bike box, installed on a rather quiet street. A graver issue is the near-universal scourge of bike paths built to share the sidewalk with pedestrians. While the bicycle lobby does its best to prevent such design flaws, this has only produced the desired results in some cases.

Several city districts have installed new bike parking (resembling the letter *P*, akin to the inverted *U* rack), in some cases an upgrade from a previous lower-quality rack, and in others, actually replacing a former car parking spot. These have generally become popular, although they are used rather often for short-term parking. Budapest sports not only fabulous architecture but also a whole gang of bike thieves, and thus most prefer to store their bikes overnight in their flat, courtyard, or bike garage, if available.

In the near future, the city is also expected to inaugurate a public bike system, along the lines of the *Velib* of Paris or the *Bici* of Barcelona. The Budapest system will be known as *BuBi* (from Budapest Bicikli) and is to consist of 74 docking stations and 1,011 bicycles in its initial layout.

Growing up

One sign of the maturing of a bicycle movement is that you can take a single inspiration and a straightforward goal, then watch it begin to develop and evolve. After a while, you take a step back and look around, and suddenly you notice that where there used to be one movement there are now hundreds.

Just as the Hungarian Cyclists' Club gained in prominence and clout, so also many other groups and initiatives sprang up. The Cyclists' Club itself helped foment the creation of regional working groups, and many towns throughout the country also have their own groups. They all organize on the local level, while maintaining contact with the head office.

Bike shops have appeared all over the city. Following the model that Jane Jacobs portrayed in *The Economy of Cities*, once cycling became a popular thing, duplication and substitution started, which meant that you might come across a bike shop that moved elsewhere, yet in the same space the new owner was also running a bike shop.

It seemed to me a sign of the times one evening as I took a stroll through the neighborhood I was living in, and was surprised to find a unicycle specialist shop that I had not noticed before. Without having done extensive research, my best guess is that there are not many other unicycle shops in Eastern Europe.

Even though the International Bicycle Film Festival has never come to Budapest, citizens have created their own bicycle film festival—also called *BuBi*. And since *Cycle Chic* came to Copenhagen, Budapest wanted one for their scene as well—and got it.

Apart from the two yearly larger rides, various occasions have prompted special rides. In 2006, leading up to parliamentary elections, a ride titled *Tour of the votes* hit all the major party headquarters to deliver a petition from the cycle movement. In 2009, the *Critical Diplomass* ride took place together with foreign diplomats in Budapest, at the bidding of the Czech Embassy.

Among the important projects that have been launched, one of the most successful was the *Bike to Work* campaign, which has been organized every year since 2007, and which rewards those who choose the bicycle as their form of transportation to get to work. This has also grown from year to year, with the last count of over 8,000 participating companies.

Ride-in was the name given to the campaign to help newcomers to cycling. These rides have helped those individuals feel more comfortable cycled who have not cycled in the city before or who do not yet feel comfortable enough to do it. They are led by experienced cyclists and follow a certain route, so that new cyclists are able to get a feel for trying out a number of different situations and terrain.

Recycle Mission Hungary has focused its efforts on making use of discarded bicycle parts and turning them into usable items, such as belts or key chains. They are also commissioned on occasion to create large bicycle artwork in the city.

Social Bike Business is a project of bringing bicycle repair and both bike and business savvy to the socially marginalized, empowering them to reach new opportunities via the bicycle. This was introduced by Hungarian Green Roots (ZOFI) with inspiration and background support from the U.S. based One Street. The latest activity involves setting up a mobile bicycle repair unit.

Bike Kitchen Budapest offers a DIY location for cyclists to fix their own bikes. This follows the trend of bicycle communities and fix-it-yourself groups sprouting up all over the place. At one time ZOFI ran an outreach program for female cyclists called, "Women teach women bike repair."

Further Signs of Maturity

One sign of maturity can also be seen in the gesture by Critical Mass Budapest fans in 2008 when New York City was experiencing a difficult period in their Critical Mass history. A special edition T-shirt was printed with the writing: "Critical Mass Budapest supports New York Critical Mass" and the proceeds of the T-shirt sales were funneled directly to Time'sUp! to support them in the struggle with the police crackdown of New York City rides.

In 2011, when a man drove his car through a mass of cyclists in a Critical Mass ride in Porto Alegre, Brazil (miraculously not killing anyone) Critical Mass Budapest activists sent a letter of sympathy and solidarity to cyclists in Brazil.

As the cycling culture in Budapest continues to evolve, it is important to note also that many things have yet to be improved—and among them is cycling etiquette. Pedestrian-cyclist conflicts have arisen in several parts of the city, since (new) cyclists occasionally slalom through crowds on the sidewalk. The response, happily, was a concerted "Don't do the sidewalk thing" campaign.

It has also taken some time to educate drivers as well as operators of the public transportation fleet. Bear in mind this is an assortment of road users who until recently have had the asphalt all to themselves. Some reported incidents among cyclists seem to indicate that the most acrimonious disputes that have arisen were in conjuction with taxi drivers.

The Bicycle as a Symbol of Optimism

One of the great traditions of rides is to engage in a bike lift at the end. This is where all of the able-bodied participants raise their bikes over their heads in a grand communal bonding session and to the eruption of, "Rah-rah we did it again."

While the Critical Mass rides in the past few years have certainly peaked in numbers—after reaching a glorious 80,000 we preferred to bask in the glory—the rides go on and important work continues to be done.

In a slightly bizarre yet auspicious footnote of Critical Mass Budapest, one fact underlines the optimism that comes with Critical Mass: in a country with plenty of rainy days, sunshine has always accompanied the rides. It might rain the day before or the day after, but to date nothing has come between the rider and his or her good mood. There have been a few close calls, but when it is time to unleash the first wave among the sea of impatient cyclists, the clouds move aside and the sun comes smiling through.

Budapest Critical Mass and Cycling Links:

http://criticalmass.hu—Critical Mass
http://kerekparosklub.hu—Hungarian Cyclists' Club
http://cyclechic.blog.hu—Hungarian Cyclechic
http://zofi.hn/projektek/szocbringa—Social Bike Business Budapest
http://www.bringakonyha.hu—Budapest Bike Kitchen
http://cyclingsolution.blogspot.com—A Budapest bike blog

Budapest Critical Mass 2008

We Have Changed Our City Forever
By Kükü and the Critical Mass Budapest Community

Critical Mass Budapest is a true civil success story with staggering and irreversible changes in the city itself and in the heart of its citizens. In less than five years a tiny subculture event blossomed into the largest civil movement in Hungary. Critical mass was reached years ago, the bomb exploded, activists have been replaced now by everyday people who are determined to choose their bike as the everyday tool of mobility. Let us tell you the secret behind this success, which is as simple as a wheel: jump on and roll...

The predecessor of Critical Mass Budapest was a regular ride organized by a group called Friends of Urban Cycling. It was much like the international Critical Mass, and ran for several years with 50-300 participants. At the same time the bike messenger community in Budapest often gathered for more hardcore rides, sometimes spontaneously or organized for special occasions.

However, the history of Critical Mass Budapest began only in 2004 when the Mayor moved Carfree Day to the weekend in order to avoid interruption of car traffic. At that point some of us decided to organize a Critical Mass ride on the original and internationally-recognized September 22 date as a protest. Although we didn't usually announce our rides to the police, at that time we did to be able to publicize the demonstration more freely and to make it easier for other residents of the city to join us. Three weeks before the ride, approximately 30 messengers and their friends gathered at a park where we divided the organizational tasks between us. The idea was to recruit not merely participants, but organizers. So we visited all the bike shops, pubs, cinemas, and universities around the city and left our leaflets that were printed partly at home and partly by a printing company as a gift, and tried to persuade someone at each place to spread the news."Critical Mass—The real Carfree Day," read the slogan on the leaflets. We invited everyone for a huge demonstration hoping for 500 participants (that was the highest number we could imagine).

Although at that time it was uncommon to see collections of cyclists in Budapest, we could see them arriving in groups of eight to ten as we approached Heroes' Square, the official starting point of the ride. At six o' clock, three to four thousand cyclists started off on the route we had planned in advance.

No journalists arrived at the event because we hadn't issued a press release. However, after hearing about the mass paralyzing traffic, press teams set off and eventually also got stuck in the traffic jams. In the evening news we declared our demand by phone: We want to live in a bicyclist-friendly city. We arrived back at Heroes' Square after dusk and the two thousand bikers who stayed there shouted and raised their bikes high above their heads, just as our logo depicts. Everyone felt that there was something important going on. The whole act was euphoric with all the flashing bicycle lights and the smiling, or even crying, faces.

It's no wonder everyone wanted to relive this experience. So we chose the subsequent Earth Day, in April 2005. This time, ten thousand bikers gathered and the number of participants has gradually grown each year. At present, there are typically 30,000 to 40,000 cyclists at Critical Mass rides.

Our events differ from the international ones in many respects. Instead of each month, we organize rides twice a year: one on the closest weekend to Earth Day in April, and one on Carfree Day, September 22. Because the ride might last for up to three hours, we recruit 300 volunteers to lead the crowd and close the junctions. From time to time, when the crowd becomes smaller, they let some cars through, so that the drivers in front do not quarrel with them to let them go. However, we focus most of our attention on letting the pedestrians through regularly. We always get 30 to 40 policemen as well, but they are completely passive. Nowadays, when Carfree Day falls on a weekday, Critical Mass does not have a fixed route, just starting and finishing points and the bikers can freely choose any route in between.

In the early days we did not have any definite goal, but as time went on we realized that we are one of the most progressive communities in town and it would be a giant mistake not to engage in outlining our needs and standing up for our wishes. With our small community behind us we started to collect demands online, and took our neat little wish list to the City Hall. As the demonstrations grew bigger and bigger, the town began building some new bicycle lanes and the two-wheel symbol suddenly appeared in political campaigns. But political support was not strong enough and only resulted in 30-40 kilometers of badly-designed and poorly-constructed bicycle roads, mostly at the expense of pedestrians. But we were too smart and enthusiastic to stop, so we reconsidered our goals and instead of politicians, we took aim at the people of Budapest. By this time a very strong net of cool activists started to take shape and we have slowly become the largest civil movement in Budapest, without any official organization, strict hierarchy, office, or expenses. Our blog has 1,500 visitors a day and 35,000 fans on Facebook.

The approximate $2,000 annual cost of organize the two rides is gathered from sales of Critical Mass T-shirts. We reject all sponsors and advertisers; the highest offer we had so far was $400,000 from a multinational corporation. The only stable partner of the demonstrations is the Dutch Embassy, who organizes extra bicycle events and lobbies for cyclists. All activists involved know that this whole mysterious thing is our common child and its success purely depends on the personal energy, time, and enthusiasm we spend putting into it. And it turns out we have friends everywhere. Some gave us free advertisements, others put our bills or stickers in their store windows. Journalists have formed almost a secret "Masonic Lodge" to organize media coverage on TV and radio, and in newspapers. We have representatives in all political parties. Unknown people have given us several thousand leaflets and our stickers (basically the only expenditure of the demonstrations) smile back at us from every second bicycle in the country.

Due to the increased media presence, and Critical Mass rides becoming an initiation ceremony to urban cycling for many, the number of cyclists on the streets doubles every year. As of today, 20-30% of Budapest's population use the bicycle occasionally, and 4-5% of them choose it for their daily commute. That's quite a triumph: when we began in 2004 urban cyclists were generally regarded as suicidal. People considered vehicular cycling dangerous, so the early pioneers had to defeat their fear of death first. The most important achievement of Critical Mass was the shattering of this fear.

As the number of cyclists grew, stereotypes began to wane. Bars and pubs were the first to brim with bikes. You would have to walk several blocks to find a suitable place to lock up. Universities and colleges came next, and soon workplaces had been conquered as well. The automatic bike traffic counter (made possible by donations of individual activists) located in the inner city of Budapest still registers a yearly increase of 100%, and there are certain spots in town where 15,000 cyclists pass every workday.

Unfortunately the city cannot keep up with the bike boom and is now facing a strange phenomenon: as cyclists have no dedicated space, they have simply begun to flood the streets and ride anywhere they can. In the beginning this led to numerous conflicts with motorists, but soon it brought a drastic drop in accidents, which fell to about 10% of their previous level; this in turn caused a further decline of the fear that inhibits people from riding bikes in traffic. There's something really unique going on in Budapest: the city is becoming bicycle-friendly despite the circumstances, without substantial investments. The coveted safety of urban cycling has been found with motorists—or their relatives and workmates—themselves becoming occasional riders. Cyclists are not extraterrestrials anymore, but regular everyday people. You can no longer try to identify a cyclist class, because people are now riding in suits as much as in workers' overalls.

Budapest has changed, Critical Mass Budapest has reached its goal.

This is a great honour for everyone who has taken part in it. We've moved past the never-ending growth as the agent of change. Now the everyday scene of enormous numbers of cyclists is the demonstration itself, spreading cycling like a virus to workplaces and schools. It is a pleasant feeling to work for such a good cause. The success is intoxicating but the best thing is to realize that critical mass has been reached. The unbelievable truth is that we have managed to change our city forever.

Budapest Critical Mass 2009

And Still We Ride

A Decade Of Critical Mass in Prague, Czech Republic

By Daniel Mourek

In 2011, we celebrated the 10th anniversary of our Critical Mass in Prague. In Czech, we call it *Cyklojízda*, which literally means "bike ride," as the Czech equivalent *kritická masa* has not caught on. Back in April 2001, Critical Mass was known to most of us only from websites or magazines, though some of us had personally experienced rides in the U.S., Canada, or Western Europe (such as rides like *VeloDemo* in Swiss cities).

Some background: in communist times, the main polluter of the air in Prague was industry. Old factories were built close to the city center during industrialization, but with property prices skyrocketing after the peaceful transfer to capitalism these factories began to shift to the periphery or to the outskirts of Prague. This was a relief for our air quality which had also been "enriched" by the coal smoke generated from heating Prague houses. This should all have been history. But with the Velvet Revolution and our quickly gained personal freedom, the automobile started to conquer the streets of Prague with the car mistakenly associated with freedom or defining social status. By the beginning of the millennium the number of cars tripled. The city with 1.2 million inhabitants has currently double the amount of cars per capita compared to Berlin or Copenhagen. And with increasing car numbers came again the problem air pollution. Now 70% of CO_2 emissions comes from car traffic, not to speak of road fatalities, deprivation of public spaces, and overpriced large infrastructure developments which were planned in the '60s and which are now being implemented.

The idea to start Critical Mass came from the Carbusters collective (later renamed the World Carfree Network) which moved to Prague from Lyon at the beginning of the new millennium. At that time several NGOs shared offices in the same building in the district of Strasnice. This building's garden and hallways later became a gathering place for workshops to prepare for the ride with activities such as silk screening, poster painting, bicycle decorating, and our biggest achievement—the bicycle sound system. The ride can be high adrenalin in heavy traffic or—in Prague the cycling community tends towards this development—more of a theme ride where people will get to know their city and social projects, and above all each other, better. After the early rides we would organize concerts with local bands or we would screen movies such as *We Are Traffic* or *And Still We Ride*. The idea of Critical Mass quickly spread among a rather tiny Prague cycling community. We had two dozen cyclists on that first ride, and I remember it quite vividly; I knew every one of them personally (it is not the case these days anymore...fortunately or unfortunately). We made banners with slogans like: *"Taky máte nohy/*We all have legs," (or, one needs legs to pedal and almost everyone has legs...) and *"Jezdím na mrkev/*I ride on carrots" (or, cars function on oil, bikes and their riders on food, and SOME on vegetable power!). Although in the '90s there were bicycle rides organized in Prague around the Reclaim the Streets movement, this was the first Critical Mass.

We decided to have *Cyklojízda*, our Critical Mass, every third Thursday of the month. (Do you want to know why not on Friday? Because lots of Czechs leave their homes from Spring to Fall on Thursday for their *datchas*, or summer houses, by car of course.) We start from the same place each month, at *Náměstí Jiřího z Poděbrad*, a square in the Vinohrady District. It was tricky to select a place that was both central and where a large crowd of cyclists could gather. We had to take in consideration things that may not be so important in other cities, such as the numerous tram lines (more than 30 in the city center) as well as buses. Our intention is not to block public transport *(Neblokujeme, my jsme doprava)* and it is still difficult to avoid it. Prague also has a medieval character with very narrow streets and large cobblestones that can be pretty hard on bicycles. Prague has a similar elevation to San Francisco, where the elevation differences between highest and lowest points can reach as much as 1,000 feet. Another unique element to *Cyklojízda* is that once everyone reaches the meeting point, we collectively agree on a route before setting off, rather than letting the route develop spontaneously. The combination of these conditions makes it sometimes tricky to collectively agree on a route that suits everybody.

In 2002 or 2003 we began to think about how to connect *Cyklojízda* with social groups, squatters, or independent cultural centers in order to give the rides more meaning beyond just the riding. We had a cold, Christmas ride for "baby Jesus" (the Czech version of Santa), a February Fashing ride with everyone dressing for a masquerade, a naked ride, and a Critical Mass "symphony" with pirate radio. In 2003 the *Cyklojízda* was already part of larger group of similar initiatives that were focusing on traffic issues and social changes in our town. We even wrote—after long quarrels and discussions - a manifesto with "rules" for *Cyklojízda* and what we aimed to achieve with it. We copied this together with some Andy Singer CARtoon characters and distributed the pamphlets throughout the city.

Reactions to *Cyklojízda* have changed over the course of the decade. Initial media coverage was mostly negative, accusing cyclists of blocking the free flow of traffic, but the message slowly began to change, and with more creativity coverage turned more in favor of *Cyklojízda*. Up until 2003 there was no police presence and or conflicts with police. The first arrest during a spring 2003 ride triggered a lot of sympathy among the cyclists of Prague for *Cyklojízda*. Cyclists got harassed by police during the ride and several riders were ticketed for ridiculous offenses like corking traffic that was at a standstill anyhow.

The first run-in with the police was rather funny. The police cornered the ride at a rather picturesque spot next to the Vltava riverbank. An argument started with them whether or not it is legal to ride in the city. The discussion got heated and the police arrested one of the cyclists on a ridiculous charge. The problem, though, was the bicycle. The cyclist refused to go with the police without his bike. The policemen looked rather helpless trying to fit the bike into a police car trunk (not a trunk like on a U.S. police car, remember, it is Europe, and much smaller). In the end we made a deal with the police that we would take the bike with us to the closest police station under the condition that we escort the police car. Imagine a police car surrounded by about hundred cyclists trying to move ahead! Our colleague was released after paying a fine. Since then the police have started to monitor *Cyklojízda* mostly by motorbike but otherwise do not harass the participants. The last fine we got was after the March 2004 ride. We burned an effigy of the pagan goddess of winter, Morana, in the form of a car. I remember another ride when we made a large campfire at the Vltava River and a policeman on a motorbike followed us all the way through a park. At the end we invited him for a beer (which he refused by saying he was on duty).

In 2003 a new civic platform of activists and artists which arose around *Cyklojízda* were also active in several other initiatives and NGOs. We decided to organize our first Carfree Day in September 2004 in the very center of Prague, in Wenceslas Square where most historic Czech events have occurred. This initiative supplemented some events such as a bicycle breakfast at the Czech National Bank. Carfree Day was totally organized by volunteers and *Cyklojízda* was also included, which had grown in numbers to hundreds of riders. But the artists brought a new perspective on how to make *Cyklojízda* more attractive with street performances at the beginning or at the end of the rides. Independent graphic designers created stickers and posters which added an attractive appeal to the whole movement. Workshops were organized prior to the rides focused on bike painting to prevent theft, Guardian Angels outfits for cyclists on dangerous spots, and other ideas.

Our long term goal with Carfree Day was to push the city administration to co-organize a large event that would lead to the permanent closure of an important and centrally-located square or street in the city center. Our event was monitored by police and "infiltrated" by undercover police officers on bicycles. At the end of the event a large mural depicting the polluted city was unfurled along the main highway which triggered a police reaction but no arrests were made. This may have been due to the fact that a young and already successful documentary filmmaker Martin Marecek had been recording the event. He was beginning work on a film, documenting *Cyklojízda* and the development of a new initiative called Auto*Mat. It was started to serve as a watchdog not only on cycling issues but advocating for smarter transportation issues in general, such as the downsizing of the Prague main highway which cuts through the historic city center, and a carfree area in Wenceslaus Square and the bank of the Smetana River. The name is a play on words: in Czech, *mat* means "checkmate" and the word *automat* reminds us not to behave like automatons or robots. *Automat* is one of the few Czech words which has become known internationally. Auto*Mat produced, among other things, the first Prague "Green Map."

With the birth of Auto*Mat, *Cyklojízda* caught momentum and started to grow in numbers thanks in large part to Honza Bouchal, aka Pup, one of Prague's leading bicycle activists. On January 6, 2006, he was hit by a car while riding home from work and died six days later in the hospital. One of the first ghost bikes in Prague was placed at the very dangerous intersection where he was killed. As of this writing we are still fighting the city council, police, and road authority to erect a monument that would commemorate our friend and colleague. The most famous Czech artists were approached and came up with memorable designs. The best project is a road depression in the shape of a concave street bump. It has never been accepted by Prague authorities for the fear that it would be too dangerous for drivers. Pup's death was a shock and big setback for the *Cyklojízda* movement and the Auto*Mat initiative of which he was a key organizer.

By 2006 we realized that the xerocracy and other ways we have promoted *Cyklojízda* have proven inadequate, and also unrealistic if we were to organize larger events in the future. Also that year we started a new model. There were still rides every month on the third Thursday, but in the spring and fall we organized a large *Cyklojízda* ride, one around Earth Day in April and one during world Carfree Day in September and as part of the European mobility week. A similar model is being used in Berlin with the *Sternfahrt* in June and the *Kreisfahrt* in September, and in Budapest and Vienna where there are big rides in April and September. Soon the numbers of participants of these rides exceeded 1,000 and we had to think of how to organize the crowds. Around 2007 Auto*Mat got involved in organizing the large spring and fall *Cyklojízda* rides. In 2009 Marecek completed his feature-length documentary *Auto*Mat*, which has since won several international awards and serves as a great witness of the Critical Mass movement in our city. Marecek's cinematographer could often be seen sitting in a trailer, filming the rides, towed by a particularly hardy cyclist. The movie is an unique documentary following five years of a pro-cycle, pro-pedestrian initiative which now counts hundreds of supporters and challenges the city on issues like humanizing the main Prague highway.

Today, after almost 120 rides, *Cyklojízda* still continues every month. The September 2011 ride grew into a large street festival we called *Zažij město jinak* ("Experience a different city") in which 12 various social initiatives were involved as part of Carfree Day with the motto: "Get to know your neighbor." We hit a record number of participants: 10,000! Other theme rides have sprung up in the city, including a commemoration ride for our friend Pup every January. In 2011 Critical Mass-style rides were also happening in other Czech cities and towns inspired by our example. Starting a second decade of *Cyklojízda* in Prague raises also the question how to continue. Upcoming years will hopefully prove that Critical Mass is still an alive and attractive model of how to mobilize an urban population around an important phenomena but certainly ways of communicating about this event will change or have already changed.

Although improvements in conditions for bicycling in Prague is one of our goals and we have already achieved some successes, our ultimate goal with *Cyklojízda* is to make our city more livable, with more alternative transportation, and less car dependent. The city of Prague is full of paradoxes: it supports heavily used public transport which is both affordable and efficient, but on the other hand it does not limit individual car use through such things as congestion taxes, low emission zones, or a consistent paid parking policy in the wider city center, or support more cycling. But, since the beginning of Critical Mass here, the bike share on modal split in the city grew from nothing at the beginning of millennium to 2.3% in 2010 and the goal is to reach 5-7% by 2015. Also, *BajkAzyl*, the first do-it-yourself bike workshop, bike rental, and café in the center of Prague has opened, along with workshops like *Bicykl* with *ReReRe* (Reduce, Reuse, Recycle), a free swap shop. The online portal for cyclists, *Prague By Bike*, has emerged, traffic engineers are designing and developing bike infrastructure, and politicians are trying to influence the transportation policy of the city. Young architects are even developing bicycle saunas.

Overall, through our *Cyklojízda*, a new generation of cycle and social change activists (within the DIY movement) has emerged in this rather conservative post-communist city, which I consider the largest achievement and personally feel proud of.

Links

http://www.worldcarfree.net
http://www.automatfilm.cz
http://www.cyklojizdy.cz
http://www.ReReRe.cz

Cyklojízda "cyklistky" in Prague, Czech Republic.

Critical Bike Ride and 30 Years of Mass Bicycle Demonstrations in Helsinki

By Eeva Luhtakallio, Otso Kivekäs, Olli Heikinheimo,

Angi Mauranen, Janne Nurminen

When the first Critical Mass rolled on the streets of San Francisco in 1992, Helsinki had already seen a number of similar mass bicycle demonstrations. The Helsinki Cyclists organized city rides as early as the 1980s. Already the early rides had the purpose of showing that the streets were not for cars alone. The form, organizers, and names of the rides have varied during the past decades, but the message has remained the same: to point out that bicycling is an important part of urban transport, and that cyclists should be better taken into account in traffic, urban planning, and legislation.

From Critical Mass Demonstrations to Critical Bike Rides

The Friends of the Earth (FoE) in Helsinki brought Critical Mass to Finland in the late 1990s. The first international-style Critical Mass ride took over the streets from cars and dedicated it to cyclists and pedestrians in 1997. In addition to Helsinki, demonstrations were organized in several other locations simultaneously. The routes of the rides were short back then: the participants joined together carrying banners both on bikes and by foot, and the gathering mainly took over one street and was more reminiscent of a street festival than a mass bicycle demonstration.

The police attempted to keep the Critical Mass demonstrations on the side of the road (ironically enough) so that they would not disturb the traffic flow. At some point Critical Mass joined forces with Street Party (later Reclaim the Streets) happenings, attracting activists interested in challenging the limited and primarily car-dominated uses of public space. The number of participants remained, however, rather limited.

From 2005 onward, Critical Mass became exclusively about cycling and FoE invited the Helsinki Cyclists to help organize the rides. The initial joint meeting resulted in the invention of a new name: Critical Bike Ride. Under this label cyclists still gather for monthly demonstration rides today. The Helsinki Cyclists promoted Critical Bike Ride to its fast increasing membership, but the practical organization was still in the hands of FoE Helsinki. The rides started gaining ever more popularity around 2010, as it occasionally gathered rather wide media interest, too. Critical Bike Ride became a local concept: a joyful event that was easy to join. As the number of riders grew, the ride has begun to really open people's eyes to the problems the Helsinki traffic environment creates for cyclists. Tensions, however, also intensify. There is a lot of encouraging support from bystanders, while some car drivers have started to feel the pressure and at times lose their patience with the swarms of bikes blocking their path.

Another change since the early days of the demonstrations is that the police have started to take the rides more seriously. With the number of riders constantly increasing, it has become a customary procedure for the police to close down lanes or entire streets to cars for the time of the ride, for the sake of the cyclists' safety. Nevertheless, each ride is a new negotiation with the city police, and oftentimes some pressure from the official representatives of the organizing associations is needed before the planned routes get police acceptance. Dynamics with the police are not straightforward: on the one hand, the organizers know just as well as the police that organizing the rides is an undeniable, lawful civic right, but on the other hand, some officers are far more reluctant than others to agree on the routes the cyclists present to them—always well in advance, as this is a policy required by the Helsinki police. The planning of each ride, then, has a moment of tension and anticipation when the announcement of the route has been made to the police, and the organizers wait for the response. There seems to be a strong car-traffic-supporting spirit within the police that views Critical Bike Ride as an unnecessary nuisance to smooth-flowing (car) traffic. During the summer months, however, the Helsinki police has a bicycle squad that also joins the rides every so often, and cooperation with this part of the police force tends to work out perfectly well—these officers know themselves what it is like to ride a bike in the Helsinki traffic.

The principle of Critical Bike Ride in Helsinki has been to ride especially on those parts of the road network where cyclists have been most harshly neglected, and where car traffic sets the rules. But even a good basic concept needs renewal of thoughts and practices—and new, enthusiastic people—to maintain the zeal.

FoE decided to start developing the bike ride concept further, and to getting new people involved in the fall of 2010. The idea was to form a new, open working group that would take charge of the organization and planning of the ride. The Helsinki Cyclists joined in with a stronger effort, as well as a bunch of bike activism rookies. After a few meetings following the monthly rides, a few dozen people began to form the basis of this new group, and finally took the organization in their own hands. Officially, the rides are still organized by the two associations, FoE and Helsinki Cyclists, but the informal action and planning group now takes care of the practical measures, promotion, and social media presence.

The new planning group also renewed some of the Critical Bike Ride practices. In previous years, the route of the ride stayed the same from month to month, but it was decided that this was one of the points people wanted to change. Hence, a different route is now planned for each event. The planning group also pondered how to support and promote the development of Helsinki cycling conditions in other ways. Alongside the monthly rides, a series of Bike Evenings have been organized, where, for instance, cyclist activists have met officials responsible for street planning and bicycle politics at the Helsinki City Urban Planning Agency.

The 2011 Critical Peak: A Bike Ride on the Western Freeway in Helsinki

The new organizing enthusiasm has resulted in bringing out record numbers of participants on the rides, and in increasing public attention. In 2011, the number of participants varied from nearly three hundred in May to about a hundred under pouring rain in August. But on Tuesday, September 13, 2011, there was no lack of cyclists, despite the rain falling on us (again): this was the grand event when 260 bicyclists headed west and took over the freeway that traverses the Western districts of central Helsinki. Opened in 1965, this road now saw cyclists for the first time. The police agreed to hold the car traffic in the end, after long negotiations and rather strong reluctance from their part to accept the idea of shutting down a freeway. Approaching the freeway ramp, many still found it hard to believe we were actually doing this. Cries of joy arose from the mass of cyclists when entering the freeway: the feeling of riding on the two and three lane freeway was of great freedom and happiness! It was inspiring to witness how many cyclists we could fit on a wide road like this, compared to the space that cars require.[1]

The reason to choose this route was to challenge Helsinki to think about why there are freeways in the middle of the city—and what would happen if the Western Freeway became the Western Boulevard instead! Architect Carlos Lamuela had created a plan in 2010 in which the freeway was turned into a regular street in the Helsinki area, providing space for 16,000 new inhabitants and 10,000 new workplaces, at the same time enriching the comfort of the current inhabitants. Also, under the plan, a continuous bicycle route from Helsinki to the neighboring city of Espoo could be built. Critical Bike Ride wanted to support this idea, and set out the message that a true city is a place with bikeable and walkable streets, with cafés providing outdoor terraces, shops, and services to stop by—not freeways with 50-60 mph speeds and exclusive access by cars.

The Critical Bike Ride that took over a freeway easily received widespread attention through the media. The following day, the Helsinki City Council received a motion demanding that the possibilities of a "Western Boulevard" should be examined through an official investigation. The motion was signed by 28 councilors from seven different parties. We are still eagerly waiting for the outcome!

New Directions

Even though many new people have come along in recent years, both to organize and to take part in the rides, there are also people at each ride who have been along since the very first rides in Helsinki. Reasons for participation are varied: some ride for the sake of bicycle activism, road conditions, and cycling infrastructure, and others see Critical Bike Ride as a means of fighting global warming and pollution, and promoting a sustainable lifestyle. Naturally, many relate to both groups. This diversity is a strong resource, creating, at times, vivid debates within the group, but also assuring that the rides remain open to a wide variety of cyclists.

As the number of participants has increased, winter rides have gained popularity as well. The theme for winter rides in Helsinki is self-explanatory: the winter maintenance of bike lanes in Helsinki is notoriously bad. So we organize "snowplow" rides: we ride in the snow, stop to shovel when necessary, and post videos online to gently encourage the city to get that snow off our lanes! Once, the ride was entitled "Operation Ice War,"[2] and the cyclists actually cleaned hundreds of meters of unplowed, icy bike lane right in the middle of the city in order to demonstrate how the city neglects winter maintenance of safe bike routes. As the conditions are often rather bad, quite few people ride regularly throughout the winter. The winter rides are a great occasion, firstly, for them to share the experience, and secondly, to set an example and show others that riding in the winter is very much possible, even if it takes a little bit of gear planning and courage at times. But above all, the winter rides are great fun: riding through the snow and seeing the surprised bystanders is rewarding, as is ending the ride in a warm bar with hot wine or chocolate, cheeks reddened and oxygen levels high![3]

In addition to Critical Bike Ride, new kinds of bicycle gatherings have also emerged in Helsinki during the past few years. In the summertime, there are bike events every other day now! An event collective called We love Helsinki organizes bicycle picnic fiestas, the Helsinki Night Bike Riders take over the streets in light summer nights, and the CycleInHel collective invites people to theme rides, like the winter Tweed run, showing that being chic and riding a bike can go together. All in all, the Helsinki bike activity scene is more and more diverse and fun—and it seems that the city is taking notice of this development as well.

In recent years, the City of Helsinki has committed to increasing the modal share target of bicycle commuters to 15% by 2020, and to instituting good practices for bicycle-friendly urban and street planning. In 2012, the city granted a half a million euro supplementary budget to the improvement of cycling infrastructure and promotion of cycling. This budget will help create a bicycle center in downtown Helsinki, promote bicycle commuting in Helsinki area enterprises, develop bicycle parking, and finally, produce a report on the development of bike lane winter maintenance!

Meanwhile, Critical Bike Ride continues to work for better cycling by moving cyclists toward a Helsinki where they are able to move faster, more safely, and more fluidly than today.

Notes

1   http://www.youtube.com/watch?v=y4GXivPT2WY from 4:22 onwards
2   http://www.youtube.com/watch?v=REU-Kk2illc
3   http://vimeo.com/37026656

Crowd assemble at the Ponce Main Square "Plaza Las Delicias" in front of the historic and emblematic (this bldg is a true symbol of the City of Ponce) Old Firehouse built in 1883 for an Agricultural and Industry Fair & Expo and later adopted as the headquarters for the City Volunteer Firemen Corp.

Ponce City Mayor Hon. María Melendez-Altieri riding with the people around the Ponce Main Square.

PHOTOS BY HERIBERTO RODRIGUEZ

Critical Mass Puerto Rican Style

By José R. Cepeda-Borrero & Sharon Clampitt-Dunlap, with Gary Gutierrez-Renta

Puerto Rico is a Spanish-speaking territory of the U.S. which consists of a group of islands located in the Caribbean Sea, 1,603 miles south-southeast of New York or 1,038 miles southeast from Miami. Its tepid climate and tropical breezes make it an ideal place for cycling any time of the year.

We learned about Critical Mass through the pages of *Bicycling Magazine* and Jeff Ferrell's book *Tearing Down the Streets: Adventures in Urban Anarchy*. Later, we discovered that a group had formed in San Juan, capital city of the Puerto Rican Commonwealth. We visited and rode with them in July 2006, where we learned that they had only just started riding as a Critical Mass in January that year. The San Juan Critical Mass traditionally met at the last metro rail station in the metropolitan neighborhood of Santurce and rode through main avenues, tourist areas, and some ethnically diverse communities around San Juan, concluding the ride at the same starting place.

Following the ride with the San Juan Critical Mass, we decided to start another Critical Mass in Ponce, a city of about 165,000 inhabitants on the southern coast of the main island. Our first Critical Mass ride started in September 2006 when a group of professors and students at Inter American University of Puerto Rico, Ponce Campus, invited Matthew Roth, a cycling activist from Transportation Alternatives in New York City, to speak about bicycle activism. That same day, we launched our maiden ride with Matthew and students and professors from the nearby Pontifical Catholic University of Puerto Rico Law School. Since then the Critical Mass in Ponce has been riding monthly without interruption. In the years since 2006 other Critical Mass rides have arisen in other towns around Puerto Rico. San Juan has given birth to a second Critical Mass which starts in Old San Juan, the old colonial walled city, and also the northern coastal town of Vega Baja has started their own Critical Mass.

In Ponce, we chose an urban park, Pedro Albizu Campos Memorial Park as the starting point for Critical Mass rides. Pedro Albizu was a well known political figure who promoted the political independence of Puerto Rico, and we considered the park and this historical figure emblematic, because we promote independence from the tyranny of the private car. From the memorial park we headed to the city's main square or Plaza Las Delicias. After circling the Plaza, we headed for another urban park, where the *Monumento a la Abolición* (Monument to Abolition of African Slavery) is located, and took pictures next to the monument of a slave freed from his chains. We adopted this monument as symbolic of the sense of freedom that cycling gives, liberation from the slavery of cars, and abolition of gasoline dependency. From that day on, every cyclist who rides with Critical Mass, or *La Masa* as we call it, has had his or her picture taken with the statue.

Occasionally we join with the riders in San Juan for special rides like December *Masarranda* which is a mix of *Masa* and *Parranda* (a kind of moving party where people sing local Christmas songs, eat and drink). Riders bring musical instruments like guitars and percussion instruments (such as *pleneras* [drums], *cencerros,* and *guiros*) to *La Masa*, and stop at different places during the ride to sing traditional Puerto Rican Christmas songs.[1]

Other times, some *maseros* from San Juan come to Ponce. For example in February we ride during the Ponce Carnival celebrations. One of our most celebrated events is the October ride known as the *Masa-ween,* where we invite the riders to customize their bikes. We had a local artist (world-renowned Puerto Rican painter and graphic artist Antonio Martorell) judge and hand out a prize for the best costume.[2]

We also organized a special *Masa* in honor of International Working Woman's Day in March. During this ride, the route takes the riders by the many monuments in honor of women in Ponce.

The "Velorution"

The Ponce Critical Mass has grown slowly but steadily, from sometimes just four riders, to an average of 25-40 riders. We topped out at over 80 riders, which is fairly large in our context. Our *La Masa* riders are casual urban and recreational riders, sometimes families and kids, from commuters to amateur mountain bikers and the occasional roadie. People from other countries have noticed the age, gender, and social class diversity in photographs we have posted in social media. There are lots of women in *La Masa*, and riders' ages span from 7-70 years old. Our riders are students and professors, public employees (including blue-collar sanitation workers among others), and even owners or managers of local businesses.

In addition to the traditional stop at the statue, another frequent stop is at an oceanside public art piece consisting of a group of sculptures and mosaics. This all but forgotten work of art (also by Antonio Martorell) was originally titled *La Ola Marina* (The Marine Wave). Not knowing its original name, the group began to call it *El Marullo* (The Tidal Wave) in pictures posted in the social media. Martorell has since adopted *La Masa*'s name for the work, and his piece has regained popularity, as people frequently ask how to get there. One rider wrote a poem about it which was published in a local newspaper, and an architect familiar with the piece is always willing to give *maseros* a narrated tour.

El Marullo is, in part, one of the favorite stops because of a nearby "oasis," a small local business where *maseros* mingle with the community and a variety of different beverages are available. When *La Masa* stops at the Abolition statue, many drop in a nearby bakery to buy fresh-baked bread and drinks. Lately, *La Masa*, fed by a younger group of college students— mainly from the downtown Pontifical Catholic University of Puerto Rico School of Architecture—ends up at the boardwalk, *La Guancha*, where a delightful selection of kiosks provides nourishment in the form of *empanadillas* (fried meat pies), hamburgers, and other goodies, as well as espresso coffee and an assortment of drinks. Frequenting small local businesses has become part of *La Masa* philosophy, where particularly accommodating businesses have earned the distinction of being a *bici-pana* (bike-buddy).

Critical Mass as the Beginning of Bicycle Activism in Puerto Rico

From *La Masa* in Ponce, a group of bicycling activists formed, most of them originally faculty members from the halls of Inter American University at Ponce. We adopted the name *Energía Roja y Negra* (Red & Black Energy) inspired by '70s environmental activists (Green Energy). Alluding to our city's colors, we chose red and black instead of green. Also red and black are classic colors for revolution and the anarchist movement, from which our group at Ponce has adopted as some of its core principles.

For example *Energía Roja y Negra* has never been registered with any governmental agency. We just exist, and when necessary, we claim space to promote the need for bicycle facilities and events. It is an amorphic group, much to the consternation of people who need to know who the "director" is, and whose "members" change according to specific needs. Anyone who rides in Ponce is a member, whether they know it or not.

Due to some of the group's relation to media as former journalists and publicists, radio, newspapers, and sometimes TV stations have covered us. We have been portrayed in regional and commonwealth-wide newspapers. We have also been invited to radio talk shows, and we were on *Univision*, broadcast across Puerto Rico.

We participated in public hearings on urbanism and transportation with the Puerto Rico Planning Commission and the local Chamber of Commerce. Additionally, universities invited some of our members to talk about bicycles as a means of transportation, and how they can make cities more livable.

From the beginning we sought out meetings with municipal authorities, and met with the past and current mayor to promote our ideas and to propose some specific initiatives to promote and facilitate cycling in Ponce, as well as other alternative transportation solutions. Some of them have been made a reality by the current administration.

Perhaps one our biggest successes, came as recently as February 14, 2012, when our city opened the Ponce collective transportation system. All the new buses have bicycle racks that transport up to two bikes; bicycle racks have also been installed throughout the city. Between 7-10 miles of exclusive riverside bike lanes are being developed along the river that crosses the city.

At the inaugural event for the bus system, Mayor María Melendez-Altieri invited Gary Gutiérrez, part of *Energía Roja y Negra* and one of the first Critical Mass riders, to offer a speech during the inauguration. Soon, Mayor Melendez's administration plans to open some mostly "shared" routes that will connect city neighborhoods, in addition to the planned dedicated bike lanes. In a recent action, the mayor even hired one of the *maseros*, architect Ricky Miranda, as the first city bicycle coordinator. Much of this attention to cyclists, and the success of *Energía Roja y Negra*'s efforts can be attributed to the initial and continuing awareness raised by *La Masa* rides.

Nowadays, other groups of activists have emerged around Puerto Rico especially in the San Juan Metro Area. With names like *bicijangueo* (bici-hangout) and PRFixed, they also promote bicycles from the perspective of new and younger generations. Also from the roadies' ranks came an initiative focused on safe sharing of roads by bicycles and cars. Their campaign is *Comparte la Carretera* (share the road) and was initiated by another colleague, Carmen Noemi, a music professor at Inter American University of Puerto Rico, San Juan Metro Campus.

Critical Mass as a Catalyst

In a place like Puerto Rico that is profoundly polarized between those who seek U.S. statehood for our country, and those who oppose statehood (mainly preferring the actual commonwealth—colonial—status quo) we manage to keep *La Masa* Ponce free of the "political party debate." That doesn't mean that *La Masa* hasn't been involved in other social initiatives. For example, last summer a group of students here in Ponce fought Walgreens and some developers who wanted to cut a lot of trees in a neighborhood to build a shopping center for the multinational chain drugstore. *La Masa* stopped by in support and some riders actually got involved in the campaign.

In 2008, at a Ponce City Mayor Candidates Debate, *Energía Roja y Negra* distributed a wish list to the candidates and the press. The wish list included our opposition to a then-proposed natural gas pipeline projected to run 70 kilometers from Peñuelas to the west of Ponce to Guayama in the east. *Energía Roja y Negra* proposed to build instead a bike lane that covers the entire 70 kilometers. The gas pipeline project was finally defeated by community opposition. But the press questioned the mayoral candidates about our proposals, and at the end all candidates included bicycle infrastructure in their plans for city development.

We have been able to open communications with local authorities to promote our ideas for a *rideable* town, and to seek improved mass transportation infrastructure. So far they are willing to give us the space to participate in city planning, so we do not find ourselves having to protest in support of our agenda.

The awareness created through *La Masa* rides has also led to the growth of other bicycle-related events. For example, the younger riders began to play *bici-polo* and already managed to have the San Juan mayor grant them an abandoned basketball court where they now have the first Island bike-polo court.

Alleycat races are being ridden with success and without any big public controversy. Even police authorities are very cooperative here in Puerto Rico with no major incident registered since all of this started in 2006.

In 2011, Ponce riders saw the organization of the Bogotá-inspired *Ciclo Días* ([Bi]cycle Days). For this event, the city closed several streets around town to form a circuit without motorized vehicles for several hours allowing the people to use it for riding their bicycles, or skates, or jogging for fun. Thus far, four editions of the event have attracted several thousand riders, including entire families from different cities and towns on the Island.

Ponce's Mayor Meléndez has attended and ridden in all four *Ciclo Días*. The event was so successful that other towns' mayors have replicated it with different names. San Juan calls it *Recreo Vía* (recreation-way), and Caguas, a city of about 150,000 inhabitants in the interior of the Island not far from San Juan, called the ride *Ciclo Ruta* ([Bi]cycle Route). But all these events offer similar conditions, and all have successfully attracted hundreds of cycling friends.

Throughout the year, there are at least a couple of bicycle events offering a 325-mile ride around the main island. *La Vuelta de los 9 Faros* (The Nine Lighthouses Ride) is one of the most popular. *La Vuelta* is promoted through magazines, including *Bicycling Magazine*, and the Internet, and attracts people from the U.S. mainland and other countries.

Slowly but steadily, Puerto Rico is becoming a bicycle-friendly place. The need still exists for safe routes and more facilities. But as in Amsterdam or Bogotá, it is a matter of time and continual awareness-raising which will change more peoples' minds about using the bicycle instead of a car for the daily commute.

From the halls of Inter American University at Ponce to the roads of our towns and cities, the Critical Mass inspired by the Far East's ways and born in San Francisco, has inspired us, and is alive and well in Puerto Rico where it's making a difference in the way we "make" communities.

¡Paz y Pedal!

Notes

1   You can see some clips of the *"Masarrandas"* at *http://www.youtube.com/watch?v=ZQWbyfb1T1E*
2   You can see clips of the 2008 *Masaween* at *https://picasaweb.google. com/104027946122407063207/albums/5263763616878948833?banner=para*

Budapest, Hungary Bike Lift at Critical Mass, 2009.

El Paseo Nocturno and Bicitekas

By Mónica Sánchez

From 1952 to 1966, Mexico City expanded through irregular settlements into a chaotic unplanned urbanization of enormous spatial and demographic magnitude. Since the 1950s, Mexico City approached the problem of urban sprawl by copying the U.S. model of connecting the city center to the suburbs by great highways. A road grid based on four to eight lane major avenues was also implemented, and rivers and water flows were buried in tunnels to create even more roadway corridors. From that moment to today, government authorities have continuously "solved" urbanization and traffic congestion by building more highways.[1]

By the late seventies, air pollution already dominated Mexico City, and environmental degradation was an urgent concern for city residents. In 1977, the *Índice Metropolitano de la Calidad del Aire*, or IMECA (Metropolitan Index for Air Quality) was established to publicly measure pollution and the consequent level of risk for human health, a risk that was soaring in that period. Outdoor activities—even school attendance—were prohibited on bad pollution days. By the 1980s, Mexico City had become a megalopolis. The unrestrained eagerness to reach modernity had led to excessive urbanization at the edges of the city, and with that growth, more congested roadways.

During this period, the bicycle never stopped being used as a means of transportation by lower-income populations. It remained an essential vehicle for many workers as gardeners, messengers, delivery men, bread and tamale vendors, knife sharpeners, etc. But, also, some people began using the bicycle as a more efficient means of transportation. Leisure bicyclists as well began making a presence in the megalopolis, most memorably, the *Bicigatos*. They were an open conglomeration of riders who would take off on a mass ride on Sunday mornings, travelling south on Insurgentes Avenue to the Ajusco foothills.

Nevertheless, these citizens were only a few, given that the majority of the population continued to see the automobile as a symbol of progress. Walking and cycling were not an aspiration for every citizen. Bicyclists had to confront traffic composed in its immense majority of automobiles and motorists that perceived themselves as the owners and sole permissible users of the streets. Therefore, any cyclist who dared enter traffic was seen as an annoyance, equal parts inconsiderate and crazy. This attack discouraged other people from embracing the bicycle as a means of transportation.

In 1986, Enrique Calderón Alzati and a couple of dozen enthusiastic bicycle advocates decided to form *el Movimiento Bicicletero* (the Bicycling Movement). An early member and president in 1992, Armando Roa described their mission to convert the city into a *pueblo bicicletero* (bicycle town). That historic phrase in Mexico, which is used to refer to a place as underdeveloped, was re-appropriated by the movement to erase its negative connotation, and to dignify the bicycle as a non-polluting, healthy, efficient, and economical means of transport.

The *Movimiento Bicicletero* was completely ignored by the government, but many people responded to the movement's call. They distributed information and carried out cycling protests in the *zocalo* (central plaza) of Mexico City to demand bicycle infrastructure. Thanks to their demands a temporary weekend-only cycling lane on Avenida Insurgentes—7 kilometers long and separated by orange traffic cones—was established in 1991. This initiative was cancelled as soon as the sponsoring politician's term ended. One of the main demands of this movement was to convert the recently cancelled train track route Mexico-Cuernavaca,[2] into a bicycling route, but it went nowhere.

By the end of the 1990s, no changes had taken place to improve conditions for cyclists, nor the environment. The road networks had expanded and city streets were even more saturated with automobiles. The system of urban mobility based on cars and streets was inefficient and slow. Road chaos, high population density, and elevated air pollution, had become the principle characteristics of Mexico City.

Over the next decades, a variety of bicycling groups, movements, and coalitions in Mexico City would arise to open space for bicyclists. Keeping in mind that social movements—like mass bike rides—are an accumulation of experiences, I focus here primarily on the actions of a group that called themselves the *Bicitekas*. Their long history as creative trailblazers—on bicycle—for citizen participation in public life runs parallel to the opening of political life in the city. Theirs is a case of riding the changing political landscape, as much as the cityscape itself.

A Serendipitous Encounter Leading to First Actions, 1997–1999

One day among many of commuting on the roadways, Guillermo Espinosa and Tom Dieusaert came face to face on the intersection of Orizaba and Álvaro Obregón in the neighborhood of the Colonia Roma. Surprised to encounter another cyclist in a suit, who had left the car behind, neither man could contain his joy at finding a peer with whom to share experiences. In 1998, they decided to go on a bike ride, invite some friends, and start from there. Without much clarity, they started to unite forces to confront the traffic problems besetting cyclists and citizens, generally, who used the public streets on a daily basis. Joined by Lenka Valles and Agustín Martínez, the group started to meet regularly. Considering that Mexico City is mostly flat, the riders started seeing opportunities for bicycling. Soon, others joined them. This was the start of *Bicitekas*.[3]

Bicitekas started as a loose organization without specific obligations. The group's initial meetings "were very free, basically we talked about bicycling, its history, our perspectives on why there wasn't more cycling in our city, and how to make that happen; we had a beer, listened to music. It was a very sweet phase because it was the seed of many things in growth today," says an early participant, Bernardo Baranda. Perhaps this is why many citizens found a space to participate. Each stage in the growth of *Bicitekas* has been shaped by the particular interests and capacities of its participants, as well as the interaction that took place between the organization, civil society, and government agencies. The core of the organization has always been held by about ten people (different people over time), but for 14 years now, all sorts of enthusiasts have showed up to contribute to the planning and organization of activities.

At the beginning, everyone who joined *Bicitekas* already used the bicycle as a daily means of transportation, and even had basic mechanical skills. Some were activists and journalists who knew how to use media – traditional and new—to get the word out about the need to change public policy. Others were urbanists and engineers who provided solid technical foundations for our proposals. From the confluence of these members, the bicycle stopped looking like a utopian fantasy, and took on the realistic dimension of an everyday transportation choice that could be offered to a broader range of citizens. *Bicitekas* took on the mission of spreading this message to decision-makers, and into the broader culture of Mexico City.

Bicitekas started a magazine, *Velo*, to promote daily urban bicycling. Tom contributed his journalistic experience, and Agustín his editorial design skills, to produce an early issue with an interview with Bernardo, who had recently returned from Holland where he got a master's degree in sustainable transport. The magazine was distributed freely in public spaces, in universities, and everywhere where there was a bicycle. However, lack of financing led to an early demise after just a few issues, but it was important because it made the issues public and new people joined our efforts.

There was also an initial effort to lobby for a dedicated bicycle lane in the Colonia Condesa. Unfortunately, the effort failed, as had similar efforts a decade earlier by the *Movimiento Bicicletero*; dismissed again as the concerns of a few crazy people. Soon after Areli Carreón, of the *Movimiento*

Bicicletero of the city of Cuernavaca contacted *Bicitekas*. Without having knowledge of the proposal of the *Movimiento Bicicletero* of the eighties in Mexico City, the Cuernavaca movement had also seen opportunity in using the old train routes as a bicycle way. Activists from the two cities began to work together.

Meanwhile, enjoyable, interesting rides were launched to show newcomers the benefits of bicycling as city transport. Attractive places to reach by bicycle were selected, and during the group ride, Guillermo our guide,offered descriptions and history of the types of period architecture along the way. This would be the precedent to *Bicitekas'* weekly mass bicycle ride.

El Paseo Nocturno and Beyond, 2000–2006

Meetings soon became arduous for a group that enjoyed riding their bikes, so the *Bicitekas* decided to engage in public actions that people could join immediately. After trying out several rides, in 2001 the *Bicitekas* decided to meet on Wednesdays after work, not only to chat, but to take a ride around the city. That's how *El Paseo Nocturno* (The Night Ride) was established. Up to the present, *El Paseo Nocturno* has been the best known activity of the organization and has drawn the most participants and supporters.

At the start there were only four or five members of the organization that would meet at 9 p.m. at the monument known as the *El Ángel de la Independencia* (Angel of Independence). Over the years, the number of Wednesday riders has been increasing. Not every person who goes to the ride has an interest in going beyond merely recreational use of the bike, but many people find this the first step to using the bicycle more often—especially once they acknowledge their abilities, improve them, and gain better knowledge about how to maneuver in traffic. New riders integrated not only to the ride, but also to *Bicitekas!*[4]

Guillermo, better known as "Memo," had such deep and obvious knowledge of the city on bicycle that he was acclaimed as the undisputed leader of these rides for many years. Over a decade, he helped shape the spirit and tone of the ride toward achieving more humane cities. Currently, *El Paseo Nocturno* has evolved, becoming more organic, horizontal, and self-organized with strong participation of attending citizens. The riders discuss needs, and rotate leadership to allow the ride to acquire its own dynamic, mostly without the intervention of those who began it.

El Paseo Nocturno has been the principal ongoing event giving rise to the culture of urban cycling in Mexico City. During the ride strong social bonds are made while rolling around the streets of the city. When the traffic and the heat have died down, chatting among citizens generates a positive experience. New political subjects are discussed on rolling objects, with the city as the backdrop. Most riders make a statement with their style, brightly adorned with their colors, new accessories, brilliant lights and reflectors, with the goal of making themselves visible to avoid accidents. Everyone is there, from the most audacious, sportiest, and trendiest; to the ideologists who sustain long conversations about bicycling on the ride. Riders at the front are usually those who know the city from end to end, and make the most of the bicycle's versatility to take unsuspected shortcuts, and reach parks, plazas, bridges, markets, fountains, and alleys that they would not have known about had they not been on the ride. Marc Augé says:

> On bicycle there are more changes and more exchanges. One glides surreptitiously through another geography, eminently and literally poetic, given that it offers the possibility of immediate contact between places that one generally only visits separately. It also presents itself as a fountain of spatial metaphors, of unexpected encounters and shortcuts that do not cease to arise, through the force of calves, the enlivened curiosity of new riders.[5]

There are also top-notch bike mechanics, who make the most of their knowledge by offering their technical help (especially as a chance to strike-up a conversation with a good looking rider). They are also the ones who help when someone gets a flat or a chain comes off. There are also intrepid gals that enjoy speed and downhills, and who leave the office wishing to clear their heads on a bike—*wanting* the air to mess up their hair. Then there are those who see in every sidewalk, fence, or pothole an obstacle to dominate, or those who never chat but sing their favorite songs at full volume. There are those who never stop talking. Another has installed a speaker in the cargo section of their bike, and always puts on music from the '60s and '70s, either to share or annoy! Parents come with their children, newbies who quickly tire, but never desist. And of course there are the ones who always come.

The guiding group enters into action: the guide (who designed the route and heads the group showing the way); the blockers or "corkers" (cyclists who cut off car circulation in the intersections when the group is very large, to avoid cars mixing into cyclist traffic), and the sweepers (cyclists who ride at the back making sure no one is left behind). Everyone assumes a role in this public space—they interrupt it, play, and have fun in it.

As the ride advances, there is both a symbolic and energetic unfolding produced by the physical action of pedaling that provides participants with a sense of well-being and undeniable freedom. Tiredness dissipates with the contagious enthusiasm to move forward and complete the route. Along the way, there may be an accident or mechanical problems that disrupt the rhythm, delay the ride. The ride falls flat on some occasions, but still manages to bring participants out of their routine. In general, *El Paseo Nocturno* not only leaves a good feeling, but also creates and extends the bonds of friendship that are nourished by experiences lived during the rides, problems solved, and fun shared. "In reality, they play since their true intention is, before anything else, to recover the pleasures of infancy and the complicities of childhood."[6] These bonds on many occasions go beyond the rides and into daily life.

Of course there may be some who leave the ride without feeling happy and never return. But even so, with a brief experience of *El Paseo Nocturno* they have learned how it feels to bicycle in Mexico City.

Around 2002, Chris Carlsson came to Mexico, met up with *Bicitekas*, and shared his experience of Critical Mass in San Francisco. Soon after there was a Critical Mass on a Friday; everyone dressed in suits and rode onto the *Periférico*, one of the most congested expressways of the city. A few attempts continued, but *Bicitekas* had its well-established weekly ride on Wednesdays, therefore, carrying out another ride the last Friday of every month didn't gain traction. Even though Critical Mass San Francisco was not a direct influence in the initiation of *El Paseo Nocturno*, we share the same spirit and ideals of opening public space to citizens. For the past 11 years, *El Paseo Nocturno* has taken place without interruption, and continues to grow steadily. In recent years, rides that take place on vacation days or holidays draw out as many as 500 cyclists, especially for a ride known as the *Rodada Hasta el Amanecer* (Ride Til Dawn Ride). Ride Til Dawn often kicks off the vacation period, or otherwise marks a calendar festivity, like New Year's Eve.

Bicitekas, Public Policy, and Bicycle Actions

Since those early years, *Bicitekas* not only kept the ride going, but continued its public policy work. The organization of the group began to change. In 2001, Xavier Treviño brought in new skills to incorporate the use of alternative media. The Internet became a great tool for the organization. An online forum and website of *Bicitekas* was created that gave cyclists in the city direct contact to each other, and opened links with organizations in other countries.[7] During this period, Roberto Cruz[8] and Leon Hamui also urged *Bicitekas* to establish itself as a Civil Association. *Bicitekas* gained more organizational credibility, and began acting on a greater breath of projects, even if for many it pursued a utopian mission.

Newspapers and other media also began showing greater interest in bicycling. Reporters came to inteview *Bicitekas* members, who promoted their proposals. Some politicians even saw an overlooked sector of the citizenry that formed part of a global movement in favor of the environment, and sought to publicly embrace *Bicitekas*. It was then that news broke of a new construction project for an elevated expressway over the *Periférico* (called the *Segundo Piso* or Second Deck) by the then Mayor of Mexico City Andrés Manuel López Obrador.[9] *Bicitekas* rejected this public work, which continued to promote the use of the automobile and with it, the pollution of the environment and degradation of public space.

The battle between different political forces surrounding the construction of the *Segundo Piso* captured the attention of the media and citizenry. Riding on a bicycle on this expressway was also prohibited. So, in 2003, *Bicitekas* led a protest ride to the highway in order to demonstrate that any roadway should be used by bicyclists. However, at the site there was a confrontation with transit police. Carlos García Robles, member of *Bicitekas*, organized riders to improvise a "die-in" with everyone dropping to the ground. This got a lot of coverage in the media and advanced the discussion about the construction of a cyclepath.

Bicitekas took advantage of the moment to insist on its years-old proposal to build a cyclepath on the railroad right-of-way between Mexico and Cuernavaca. Finally it was taken seriously and the organization was invited to participate in planning. *Bicitekas'* experts were sustainable transport professionals knowledgeable about building bicycle infrastructure, and who knew about the needs of cyclists. However, authorities ignored their input, and the cyclepath was inaugurated in 2004. Despite the negative experience with government, the *Ciclovía* was still celebrated enthusiastically by cyclists because it represented a first clear success in affecting public policy. That same year *Bicitekas* negotiated that bicycles be allowed aboard the Metro system trains on weekends.

The next years would be difficult for *Bicitekas*, mirroring in part the political climate in the city. Mexican presidential elections take place every six years, and they overwhelm the political agenda. The organization's activities dropped to an all time low, keeping to a minimum of meetings and communications. *El Paseo Nocturno* and the Internet forum continued, in part because they did not demand much. These remained as spaces for cyclists in Mexico City to vent bad experiences, and their general bad feelings around electoral confrontations. Despite disappointments in 2006 energy was harnessed for Mexico City's first World Naked Bike Ride on Avenida Reforma. *Bicitekas* also collaborated with other civil society organizations to produce a policy and strategy document titled *La Ciudad Que Queremos* (The City that We Want).

Yet, the situation would not improve after the July 2006 Presidential elections. López Obrador, presidential candidate of the left-PRD party, protested the election results as fraudulent, and called for an occupation of the main Avenida Reforma. The participants of the *El Paseo Nocturno* found their regular meeting space occupied! Even though the ride never stopped happening, frictions rose among riders over the political drama. It was a difficult time for citizens generally, but also for the cycling movement. Despite the low spirits, the fight for public space continued.

At the end of 2006, *Bicitekas* reevaluated its position. The group decided to take a more focused approach towards bicycling public policy. Throughout its first decade, *Bicitekas* had been run by volunteers in a horizontal manner. This choice reflected the freewheeling spirit that dominated the organization at the time, and personality of the *Bicitekas*. Moreover, it fit well with radical proposals and activism that required opposition to bureaucratic goverment. *El Paseo Nocturno* was born out of such horizontal organization. The change towards a more formal lobbying approach would distinguish *Bicitekas*, among other bicycling groups. As can be imagined, the shift did not go over well with every *Biciteka*. Organizational changes—over the last decade and a half—have sometimes taken a toll on relationships, while forging new ones, depending on political visions that depart or find resonance within the organization. But, these tensions were helpful, because they led to the creation of new cyclist groups in the city, while fine-tuning Biciteka's purpose.

In the last years, *Bicitekas* has been working on establishing a new administrative structure; one based on a commitment to civic participation, and democratic and horizontal decision making processes among its members and collaborators. Integrating diverse points of view can often make decision processes difficult, but we continue to do so in the spirit of enriching proposals and allowing synergies to emerge around sustainable mobility projects. There is no other way to maintain authenticity, freedom, and autonomy in the search for citizen well-being.

Since 2006, group bike rides multiply!

After elections, Mexico City had a new chief of goverment, once again from the left-PRD party, Marcelo Ebrard. The new mayor had previously agreed to promote the bicycle as a means of transport by endorsing the policy document "The City That We Want." *Bicitekas* established contact, and became directly involved in related government initiatives, advising, revising, and seeing that agreements be enforced, while also maintaining a critical view over bad decisions for bicyclists.

The first bicycling initiative adopted by the new Mayor was to implement *Lunes de Bicifuncionarios* (First Mondays for Bicycling Public Officers), which invited public officials of his administration to bike to work on the first Monday of every month. *Bicitekas* advised this project, and in support, members of the group accompanied Marcelo Ebrard on his first bike-to-work day. This event marked the beginning of a unique relationship between *Bicitekas* and Mexico City's government.[10]

The inauguration of *Lunes de Bicifuncionarios* would be followed by other new rides with widespread public engagement in Mexico City. By May 12, 2007, the Mexican capital inaugurated its first Sunday Streets closures and cyclethons. The latter was the first serious public policy promotion of cycling; also closely advised by *Bicitekas*. Then, in 2009, *Bicitekas* collaborated with *Muévete por tu Ciudad* (Move About Your City) and *Contacto Braile* in an innovative group bike ride called *Paseo a Ciegas* (Blind Ride). Riding on tandem bikes, people with visual disabilities were invited to experience the city on a bicycle, during the Sunday Streets closure of Avenida Paseo de la Reforma. In this manner, the rider was offered security in a humanized space, that is, in a space full of pedestrians and cyclists. The success of this project has led to further civic organizations joining in, and now has its own status as an autonomous organization.

Bicitekas continued to grow as a bicycling organization, with increased national and international ties, but it also stayed true to its activist origins.[11] Riding out in a group remains a critical instrument of protest. In one such action, the first Ghost Bikes were installed in 2009 to memorialize a rider's life lost in traffic. The *bicicletas blancas* (White Bicycles) also serve as an indication to other cyclists of a danger zone due to ill urban design, and draw attention from authorities. Around this time, new riders entering the roads encountered the cultural openings and public policy improvements that the bicycle movement was bringing. This boom in cyclists, alongside their participation in, and support for, advocacy spilled over into a boom of new bicycle organizations. Together, the expanding body of cyclists and their organizations, compose the present urban cycling movement.

In 2010, *Bicitekas* marched (and rolled) in solidarity with the *Frente Amplio Opositor contra la Construcción de la Supervía Poniente*, *Comuneros Unidos contra el Arco Sur*, and *Frente en Defensa de Wirikuta* all of which are specific organizations opposing big highway projects within the metropolitan area, and against urban projects that harm the environment.

In November 2010, *Bicitekas* as a member of *Bicired*, collaborated to organize a 24-hour ride around the lower house of Congress under the banner "*Urge $ para la Bici*" ($ Urgently Needed For The Bike). The action demanded allocation of a portion of the public budget towards bicycling promotion and infrastructure. More importantly, it succeeded in revealing to the public that the Metropolitan Fund was allocating 95% of its funds on public infrastructure for automobiles. Following this action, *Bicired*, *Colectivo Camina Haz Ciudad* (Collective Walk And Make Your City), and ITDP joined together in a campaign to demand that 5% of the transport budget go towards bikes and the pedestrian. Soon after, *Colectivo Camina Haz Ciudad*—whose proposals went hand in hand with *Bicitekas's*—joined in other projects together, including the drawing of a guerrilla bike lane (called a wikilane or *wikicarril*) made with resources and voluntary work by citizens, at the doors of the Federal Congress. The bike lane was erased by authorities less than 48 hours later. So, on November 6, 2011, the same organizations made a second wikilane 5 km in length. This work led for the first time ever to consideration of non-motorized mobility as a budget item in the Metropolitan Fund.

Bicitekas has also maintained its long tradition of solidarity with citizen struggles outside the realm of bicycling. In May 2011, we participated in the silent march called by the Movement for Peace to stop the violence generated by the "war on drugs." In October 2011, we were also present in the protest held by Huichol indigenous communities on the Wikiruta, against the predation of Canadian mining companies.

A New Space for Education and Workshops, 2010-Present!

Aware that the solution to traffic problems was not only about infrastructure, but also education, *Bicitekas* started collaborating with several educational institutions (schools and universities). With students, we carried out bike rides, and developed an urban cycling class called *Por mi Ciudad en Bici* (Through My City On a Bike). A university class began in July 2009 as a pilot program, and later continued as an ongoing class, and even a book project![12]

A year later, in August 2010, *Casa Biciteka* was inaugurated, and with it the first community bike workshop in Mexico City.[13] For the first time in 14 years, we have a physical space to develop work and open the door to new possibilities. *Casa Biciteka* allows us to host artists-in-residence, and provide free lodging for bicycle activists coming from out of town. We have already received cyclists from the U.S., Italy, Singapore, Tibet, Spain, Chile and Indonesia, all of whom have given different talks (formal and informal), services and/or workshops to share experiences and inspire young city dwellers. We've also had some rocking concerts!

Bicitekas is now a space allowing for new cultural forms by promoting the intersection between citizens, conversation, transit, enjoyment, and exercise of citizen rights to the city. After 14 years of dreaming and working, the members of *Bicitekas* have been able to put bicycling on the public agenda, and gestate and plan a different city. But I wonder if it would ever have been if possible, without its early members reminding each other that the joy of riding a bicycle together comes first.

In that spirit, I conclude with a welcome: *¡Casa Bicitekas es tú casa!* And, *¡El Paseo Nocturno* is your *paseo*!

Notes

1 Carrillo Barradas José Luis. (2004), "Ciudad de México: Una megalópolis emergente el capital vs la capital" *Red de cuadernos de investigación urbanistica*, Instituto Juan de Herrera (I.J.H.), Madrid

2 The city of Cuernavaca is located 85 km south of Mexico City in the neighboring state of Morelos.

3 In this article, a few names have been inserted as points of reference, but do not adequately reflect the critical group of people involved in each stage of this bicycling movement. Many different people have actively and poignantly made urban bicycling in Mexico City, and *Bicitekas* specifically, into what they are today. For a more detailed history about *Bicitekas*, as an organization, see Sánchez Mónica, (2011) "La interacción al interior de un sistema social: El caso de Bicietekas A.C." Tesis Universidad Intercontinental, México. Likewise, there are a wide variety of bicycling and citizen groups in Mexico City who have contributed tremendously towards creating the city that we want. By way of reference, some of these groups are mentioned in this text, and on the *Bicitekas* website under "Links (Otros Grupos)" and also under "Videos (Colaboraciones)".

4 The new Bicitekas included Boris *"Patateca"* Georgina, Arnold Ricalde, Ines Alveano, Thomas Bernal, Andrés Pérez, Javier Chavez, *Pachijavi*, etc.

5 Augé Marc. (2009), "The praise of the bicycle" Gedisa, Barcelona. (The quote was translated by the editors).

6. *Ibid*. p. 43

7 Thanks to the establishment of the online forum and the webpage, Armando Roa, the ex president of the *Movimiento Bicicletero* of the eighties, who at the time found himself living in San Luis Potosí, made contact with *Bicitekas* and on return to Mexico City met with the organization to share his knowledge and experience in the previous movement. The new media also facilitated harnessing support for proposals between cities, such as Arelí Carreón's proposal which in was again presented to authorities of Mexico City for creating a cycleway on the railroad right-of-way to Cuernavaca. The growing presence of *Bicitekas* caught the attention of León Hamui, who after having crisscrossed Europe on a bicycle, returned to Mexico intending to create more welcoming spaces for city bicycling. He was gathering citizen signatures for his own proposal, when he came upon *Bicitekas's* proposed project and immediately offered to collaborate.

8 A lawyer who traded his automobile for a bicycle.

9 The election of Manuel López Obrador of the PRD party, as chief of government (mayor) of Mexico City, was a continuum in the transition away from the one-party state under the PRI party that had dominated the Mexican political system for 71 years. Cuauhtémoc Cárdenas Solorzano also of the PRD party, was elected in 1997 as the first chief of government, after a series of reforms that for the first time gave Mexico City its own governmental city structure separate from the federal government. These were interesting times for citizens who found new spaces for political debate!

10 In April of 2007, *Bicitekas* presented the Mayor with the document "Promotion of the Use of Bicycles in Mexico City: A proposal for the Government of the Federal District 2007-2012" that described an integral strategy to increase bicycling in the city. In December of the same year, *Bicitekas* and ITDP México (Transport and Development Policy Institute in Mexico) carried out a study about the routes that cyclists naturally have used in the City and, based on this analysis, proposed a network of bicycle paths for sustainable urban mobility in Mexico City, delivering this study to the authorities.

11 In June 2008, *Bicitekas* organized the First Congress on Urban Cycling, with the support of the *Secretaría de Medio Ambiente* or *SMA* (Ministry of Environment) of Mexico City and the *Centro Cultural Español* or *CCE* (Spanish Cultural Center), with the goal of uniting the cycling groups in the country to discuss the topics of urban cycling, learn about national and international experiences, and increase the capacity of these groups. In this congress, *Bicitekas* promoted the creation of a *Red Nacional de Ciclismo Urbano* or *Bicired* (National Cycling Network) that would unite the organizations that promote urban cycling in different cities of the country, with the mandate of taking the Cycling Congress to these different cities. Since the first year, these Congresses have taken place in Guadalajara, Puebla, and Monterrey, the next one slated to be in the city of Oaxaca. *Bicitekas*, as member of Bicired, carried out the public action

Parque-ando (Park-ing) to celebrate the global Carfree Cities Day in 16 Mexican cities simultaneously. This activity consisted in using parking spaces as public parks, like the Park(ing) Day interventions in other countries, to use public curbside spaces for people instead of cars. In 2011, *Bicitekas* also became a member of the Alliance for Biking and Walking that gathers civic organizations from the U.S. and Canada that promote bicycling as a means of transport, making *Bicitekas* the first Mexican organization to join the group. *Bicitekas* worked for several years in the creation of Urban Cycling Manual of the City of Mexico, which was released on September 22, 2010, as part of celebrations for World Carfree Day.

12 After two years of research by Ruth Pérez, in April 2011, *Bicitekas* also published its first book *Por mi ciudad en Bicicleta* (Through My City On A Bike); a book that compiles interviews with city bicyclists to share their experiences with new cyclists, or with people who are undecided about riding a bike in the city.

13 It is located in the Centro de Artes Libres, A.C. on República de Nicaragua number 15 in the historic downtown of Mexico City.

Bilbao, Spain, Kritikona 2011.

Letter from Bilbao, Spain

By Bilboko Masa Kritikoa

Hello friends of the world!

I am the Bilbao Critical Mass, a tiny Critical Mass that has been growing little by little for years, because I'm not in a hurry. I don't need gasoline, but I want to go far, very far, and continue bicycling through Bilbao and well beyond.

I'm writing to tell you some things about myself and my friends. I want you to meet some really good-looking people that care for me in Bilbao. I encourage you to join us the last Friday of every month so we can enjoy a fantastic ride in good company.

I was born back in 1990, though they didn't give me this name. In that year Bilbao was a rapidly restructuring industrialized city where the car was king of the road. On the other hand it was, and continues to be, a place with great affection for bicycling as sport, with many sports cycling clubs, and many cyclists that ride miles and miles every Sunday on the lightest bikes at the fastest speeds. But very few people were using the bicycle as a means of everyday transportation. At that point, every daily rider knew each other since there were so few. One day six or eight of these sturdy folks decided to bring me into the world and began to ride together one day each month to demand their space in untamed traffic. So they rode together for eight months. My friends would leave little flyers on bicycles that they saw around greater Bilbao to inspire people to join our protest ride, and began to talk about starting an organization of urban cyclists. Nevertheless, there were very few people, and it was difficult to maintain the ride with so few. After those first months I was dissolving and left alone and without friends, hoping that at some point we could start riding together again.

One year later, in 1992, some people in San Francisco (the one in the U.S., not the neighborhood of the same name in Bilbao), began to get together to do the same thing on the other side of the world, but I didn't know about it, nor did my friends. Notice how people with the same problems on the other side of the world were doing the same thing that we did! And that began to reproduce itself around the world with the name Critical Mass, a beautiful name that, depending on who you ask, refers to cyclists in China, or chemical or nuclear reactions, but for everyone means the same thing: we come together to ride until there are more of us than there are cars.

A bit later, in 1994, some of these people that originally brought me into the world, got together with some ecologist friends and other bicyclists and started a nonprofit organization, *Biziz Bizi*, with a clear political spirit. They promoted the bicycle as an alternative to the car, started classes in city cycling, and celebrated the Day of the Bicycle and other campaigns for social awareness. They wanted to influence institutional decisions as much as possible so bicyclists would get more respect and that there would be more people cycling in the city, and less noise and pollution in the air. The beautiful name *Biziz Bizi*, is a play on words: *bizi* means "to live" in the Basque language. It's a small spelling change from *bici*, the Spanish word for bike—to live life, to live the bike, bike for life.

In the following years, I knew people were working for bicycles in Bilbao, but I was still shelved and without friends, though little by little I saw more people on bikes in the city.

Finally, in 2003, I was reborn in Bilbao, now with the name Critical Mass. Again it was the same people that had started *Biziz Bizi*. With the rush of pleasure that they had after organizing some meetings about bike touring in our Basque province, Bizkaia, they asked, "If they are doing it in Burgos, Gasteiz, Iruña, Zaragoza, Barcelona, Valencia, Valladolid… Why not in Bilbao? So a group of noisy and enthusiastic cyclists, playing drums, met on the last Friday of September 2003, in front of the regional government to start the first Critical Mass of Bilbao. Notice was given of my rebirth in a newsletter of the Association of Urban Cyclists to inspire people to come and join the celebration. Ever since I have been a monthly ride, usually with a small group of only 20 people—maybe it's because of the weather—but we still haven't stopped!

It was a great moment for me. To discover that I had many sisters in the most unexpected places of the world. Even without knowing each other, we were reacting to the same problems in very similar ways and with the same enjoyment… What a feeling to have hundreds of sisters and many friends! Nine years later I am still going, and on each ride I find more friends.

The gathering point continues to be the building of the Provincial Council of Bizkaia in Bilbao. I start from here because, though it has no power over traffic in Bilbao, it is the home of the people that build the highways throughout our region. In the year that I came back to life they issued the "Cycling Plan 2003-2016" so we thought it would be a good reminder during the following months to have a crowd of cyclists there. For sure it is still necessary to remind them, because they haven't carried out any of these plans.

In those first years, I had a gang of three or four friends who always came with me, who left flyers on bicycles they encountered throughout the month, and who tried to maintain the freedom and lack of hierarchy that characterizes Critical Mass across the world. Sometimes people came who were outside of the associative movement, but the core group continued to be animated by *Biziz Bizi*, my most intimate supporters.

This group rode happily together for various motives, e.g. demanding more bike lanes, seeking respect from motorists for cycling, and above all to have good fun. But I wanted more friends, I wanted a global gang! Many people lost their fear of cycling amidst aggressive cars with us, and I allowed them to feel comfortable. Many of my friends still followed the sentiment "Ride Daily, Celebrate Monthly"—we helped people take the daily step of dealing with cars and begin riding once a month during Critical Mass. But then many dared to make the bike what they really wanted it to be: a usual means of transportation.

I have had various eras, with debates between my friends about how to attract and excite more people to bring me wherever they want to go. I want to go to the favorite places of my new friends, where cars are accustomed to the bicycle being a transportation choice and we have to share the road, and pedestrians see us and envy us so much that they simply have to join us the next month. We had an era of thematic Critical Masses visiting monuments, gardens, and basque *pelota* courts in Bilbao. Nevertheless, it appeared much better to not bring pre-planned ideas, because I didn't want to be overly associated with a specific group. I want everybody to be involved in the decisions: where we go, what we do this Friday...

When I was a little girl, the first five years I stayed with practically the same group of friends, my closest family. If they didn't come, there was no Critical Mass. In 2008-09, more people began to come with great spirit to make it into an amusing ride, bringing with them wigs, bright flags, singing, and adapting the lyrics of different songs. "We are the greatest in the world / and we don't pollute it." "We are not from here, we are from Bilbao, so we bring our bikes wherever we go." I stopped having a gang made up exclusively of the *Biziz Bizi* folks. Still, the new friends kept looking at *Biziz Bizi*'s friends to start the Critical Mass.

In 2009, a group of twenty-five friends organized themselves, got all the bikes in a van, and went to the family reunion of all the world's Critical Masses, the Madrid *Criticona*, the first Spanish "Interplanetary" Critical Mass. That rush of happiness, what a pleasure to know my sisters across the state and beyond. The *Bicicletina* started there, which is how we decided to label the joy that arose, and has kept on rising, riding with so many people with the same goals, the same desire. In Bilbao I started to become more colorful, more noisy, more musical, and more numerous. At least 20 people would show up on rainy days and in winter, doubling or more in the spring and summer months.

In all this time, we always had enjoyable rides without problems. Some motorists were a little impatient when their progress was impeded, but beyond some beeping, there haven't been further consequences. Also there was a certain impatience when bicycles kept passing even after a light change, but some of my friends would stand and "cork" the traffic while explaining to drivers what we were doing. I rarely had any problem with local police either. A couple of times they stopped me, seeking those responsible, asking if we had a permit for our demonstration, and were quite surprised when they learned that I was not a demonstration, that nobody organized me, that there was no one in charge. They let me go on without any objection, sanction, or further delay, but they were quite bewildered.

Three years ago, a small group dedicated to me started producing a monthly bulletin, *kri-kri*, giving news of other Critical Masses in the world, how other cities have advanced the rhythm of cycling, how they've resolved conflicts, news of upcoming gatherings, some bicycle humor… 28 issues have already been distributed at the beginning of Critical Mass, and new people are invited to send their collaborations to the bulletin. My friends also distributed from time to time a small flyer with the basic things one should know about me. "Critical Mass is nothing more than a bunch of cyclists riding around together. Nobody is in charge. The only rule is to enjoy the experience and to stick together."

2011 was a very good year for me. I've continued growing strongly and I hope that soon I'll be able to become independent and leave to enjoy people from other groups, go to other places, listen to new music…

After the big *Criticonas* in Madrid, a tiny group of people were encouraged to celebrate a big party in my honor in Bilbao. What a thrill! I'm still smiling when I think about it, how important and happy it made me feel!

"How many bikes can fit in Bilbao?" we asked. La *KritikONA, Masa Kritika Mundiala*, was the name of my party. *KritikONA* mixes the word critical, from Critical Mass, with the critique of the system of transportation, with *ona* meaning "good" in Euskera (the Basque language), as well as being an expressive suffix meaning "big" in Spanish. It would be a big and beautiful Critical Mass.

More than half a year went into preparing the party, the ludic-festive program, inviting friends of my sisters from everywhere. They posted stickers, made calendars that would remind everyone about the date, and beautiful T-shirts as nice souvenirs. We arranged housing in *Kukutza*, an Occupied Social Center, for all the friends that were coming. And we staged a concert by the group that wrote a song in the name of all the Critical Masses—they premiered another new tune that day…

People came from Galicia, Asturias, Madrid, Barcelona, Valladolid, France, Italy, Germany, and many people from Bilbao—nearly 1000 people. We rode together for hours and hours through Bilbao, making waves on the Bridge of San Antón, at the entrance to the freeway, blocking traffic, reminding everyone that we are here, that we have come pedaling to stay, that we want to take our bikes on the train, without any incident on the road, because we aren't blocking traffic, we are traffic. It couldn't have been a more beautiful weekend. You can't imagine how many friends I've made in other places.

Only one thing makes me sad. In spite of so many years of work, it appears that the majority of people in Bilbao don't know who I am or that I am here, because I lack something. In a small circle of social organizations in Bilbao I am very well-known and I have many friends. I know many people who dream of coming to ride with me: the *mujeres* from the Assembly of Women, people from ecological and anti-racist organizations, folks from pirate radio stations, fixie riders and bike polo players, folks from Occupied Social Centers that gave us shelter during *la kritikONA* (and that were sadly evicted a few months later, and to whom I send a big hug). Nevertheless, it would please me to expand, to be independent, that people that pass us in their cars every month say, "Look, that is Critical Mass, celebrating and riding together every month," and in the following month they get out of their cars to join us and enjoy the ride. It would please me to appear in the newspapers, on TV, on radio. Why shouldn't we be in the news if we are almost a thousand people riding for hours and filling the city with bicycles during a weekend?

Nevertheless, I see the future with hope and a lot of encouragement. I see a future in which I will be totally autonomous and independent of any specific group. I will be durable, with more friends. *Bilbainos* will speak of me even if they have never come, and will say that they see, "such a great group, that next month I will inflate my bike tires and join those having a good time." Little by little, we help in this social transformation that we're all hoping and waiting for.

May I keep expanding. It's been two months since my latest little sister was born near here. In November they gave birth to Critical Mass Donosti, and already it has begun to happen the last Thursday of every month. Critical Mass keeps riding!

Happy 2012 kilometers on a bicycle wherever you are.

Building a Biking Community with Critical Mass Baton Rouge

By Moshe Cohen

Don't count out Baton Rouge, Louisiana because of neighboring New Orleans. Baton Rouge is part capital city, part oil town, part university town, and part small town. Its population is over 225,000, putting it at number 85 on the list of U.S. cities. Sprawl brings the Greater Baton Rouge metropolitan area to over 800,000. Critical Mass Baton Rouge meets the last Friday of every month at 5:30 p.m. in front of the Louisiana State University clocktower on the parade grounds.

New riders show up minutes before five thirty, giving them plenty of time to meet new friends as the mass slowly builds. BMXers do tricks on the oversized steps. Members of the LSU Cycling team race home to drop off their school stuff and switch rides. Local musicians amongst the ridership put on impromptu concerts. Mountain bikers with water packs and fingerless gloves show off the new coating of dirt they picked up at the local trails last weekend. Cruisers show up with reggae-blasting boomboxes in their baskets. Members of Baton Rouge Advocates for Safe Streets (BRASS) discuss the latest bike news. Local bike shop mechanics struggle to close shop so they can make it by six. Everyone waits until the last minute to get their bikes ready for Mass.

After the clocktower chimes, some local promoters make announcements. "If this is your first ride, say your name loudly on the count of three so that everyone around you will learn your name!" Someone gives communication tips to keep everyone safe during group rides: ride slow in the front; don't allow gaps for cars to try to squeeze into; call out information about upcoming turns and road debris. Then someone in a brightly-colored shirt with a BRASS logo steps up and tells the crowd about the current local bike-related issues. Lastly some key intersections along the route are listed and details about the obligatory after-party.

By design this ride is a positive party on wheels with cheering, waving, and smiling. This tricks new cyclists into learning routes and destinations across the city while arming them with the courage to take on the streets by themselves. More memorable rides have stuck to about 13 miles at a slow pace and have routes designed ahead of time to accommodate various pit stops. After-parties have included wine-and-cheese art shows, jamming to local bands at bike shops, dance parties at local businesses, and watching fire spinners at pool parties! The parade culture of Louisiana means that pedestrians, neighbors on their porches, and, yes, even drivers are more apt to smile, wave, and applaud than get angry. The few run-ins with law enforcement have resulted in cop cars holding intersections for riders and even high fives with officers!

Critical Mass Baton Rouge started small around 1999 and sustained a varying-sized ridership for several years, publicized by Baton Rouge Progressive Network (BRPN) in the early years of both movements. Many members had affiliations with LSU and in 2003 tried to hold Mass on the first Friday of the month because this made for more rides during the academic calendar. This did not work over the long term however, and rides on the last Friday were restored in 2005. Around this time "BuRPeN" biketivists introduced corking to the ride with quarter-sheet fliers that were also handed out to drivers. BRPN now hosts a community radio station and is still very closely tied to the bicycling community through BRASS.

The strong BMX community has supported Mass since these early years, keeping it clear that rides need to be moderately paced and relatively short. Starting in 2002, local ramp houses put on the Transitions Jam BMX festival, which served as one of the first after-parties for Critical Mass Baton Rouge around 2005. Because of this close relationship, new generations of BMXers make Mass a priority, and the ride is usually led by a swarm of young riders doing tricks in the middle of the street. As of 2010, one of the latest after-party locations is the new Baton Rouge Recreation Extreme Sports & Skate Park that also features a dirt BMX track and one of only twenty-four Velodromes in the nation!

Yeah, Bike!

When the current generation of Critical Mass Baton Rouge started up again in 2005, the campus newspaper was quick to write off the riders as hippies. Despite the mixed demographics, they only showed photos of sweaty white males. This stigma remained as the newly formed Environmental Conservation Organization at LSU promoted the ride. In particular, both groups struggled to be perceived as relevant by the more conservative culture of the state. Progressives often found it necessary to form close circles to help each other effect change. Because these types of groups did not exist in the mainstream, it was difficult for them to attract attention and grow.

Several progressive hubs emerged on campus for groups to share their projects and gain support. At the Hill Farm Community Organic Garden, rows of strawberries, tomatoes, and mustard greens were usually lined with bikes as well. Weekly community gardening days spurred ad hoc debates on how to spread the love of cycling. These set the precedent for the pre- and post-Mass discussions on how the ride could be improved and how a coherent message could be spread to more people. Despite the multitude of more minor messages that its members brought to the group, the main one was always: "Come ride with us!"

Unlike the mountain- and road-biking communities, urban cycling wasn't so popular in Baton Rouge, and so it wasn't so easy to spot new riders to attract to Mass each month. In fact there were so few that when this author passed another cyclist, he would shout in solidarity: "Yeah, bike!" This became a catch phrase amongst those at the garden, who would shout it in call-and-response when anyone else would arrive. It was an informal enough tool to cement this group of friends as they began to go on various biking adventures together.

It was also a useful way to signal to new friends that they were welcome to join the rides. The assorted underground progressive cultures appeared at a glance to be elitist and exclusionary, but this was more a defense mechanism from growing up in such a conservative culture than anything intentional. The general public could not, then, understand that Mass could be nothing more than an organized coincidence, a meeting of strangers. It was common to be asked, "Is this a bike gang? I'm already in a bike gang."

Someone carved a "YEAH BIKE" stencil into a drum head, and rides would begin with the spray painting of clothes, bags, and patches. These were doled out to anyone who wanted them, in an effort to prove that the movement was truly for the masses. Rides would end with stencil-making parties for new friends to create their own designs. These took on various themes reflecting recent group rides: special events like riding together to the annual St. Patrick's Day parade, for example, or trips to the downtown Red Stick Farmer's Market. Still, rides such as these were not planned in advance enough to attract anyone beyond friends of friends, and discussions turned to new ways to increase Mass ridership.

The Baton Rouge Bike Calendar

Inspired by the largely text-based, tri-folded, bi-monthly calendars that TimesUp! distributes at bike events in NYC, the Baton Rouge Bike Calendar was birthed. This hand-drawn half-sheet displayed the month-in-review dotted with silly pictures and ride names. The back listed each ride with date, time, meeting place, and whatever other information could fit in a line or two. These could be distributed at other progressive hubs throughout town and served as frequent reminders of Mass, the monthly main event where they were debuted. Despite, or likely because, these did not appear professional with hand-drawn artwork, bicyclists proudly displayed these on their refrigerators, eliciting more free advertising. Soon local artists were involved in contributing to and creating upcoming calendars.

Nicole moved to Baton Rouge on a Monday, found a calendar at a coffee shop on Tuesday, and by the end of the week had gone on both the Midnight Ride and Full Moon Ride. She discovered a new group of friends to help her learn the highlights of the city. Special events like Mardi Gras parades were featured on the calendar, as well, and would appear as "Bike to _____ together" on the back. The bicycling community was made up, after all, of artists, musicians, gardeners, roller derby girls, and people from many other walks of life.

Compiling this information over a month ahead of time sometimes proved to be difficult. As the advertising succeeded, Mass was getting bigger and the after-parties were growing more complicated to plan. A simultaneous solution arose: meeting a week before CM to talk about various bike-related current events, nominate rides to appear in the calendar, and figure out details of the big ride. This was an opportunity for new promoters to step up and become involved, as the meeting was held at a public venue. The location of the after-party was decided upon first, once ensuring that there was ample room for bike parking there. A route highlighting scenic long-cuts that paralleled major roadways was generally blended with one or two stretches of main thoroughfares that would give the ride more publicity amongst drivers.

To make sure all riders made it to the after-parties and to give them some security as they navigated new parts of the city, small copies of the route maps were handed out just before Mass. Taken from online maps, these featured major street names, the highlighted route, and some text blocks giving month, year, after-party into, etc. These were often stuffed into pockets without a glance by the very same people who led the group wherever they felt like it, but the promise of live music, art, or whatever else was planned usually made sure that at least those who wanted to got to the destination.

Before rides without after-parties planned ahead of time, regulars gathered to discuss possible routes and destinations. One particular Mass had two riders arguing whether to end up at a garden potluck party or a DIY hardcore show—both of which were too small for all riders to enjoy together anyway. The situation resolved itself as halfway through the ride, a group split off towards the garden, breaking down the numbers so that neither event became overcrowded.

Faces of Critical Mass Baton Rouge

The xerocracy at Critical Mass Baton Rouge encouraged others to get involved—including unsuspecting and otherwise quiet riders handing out safety tips, musicians and artists promoting their upcoming events, and graphic designers surprising everyone with funky bike art. Local musician and frequent rider Ben Herrington even wrote a song called "Critical Mass" performing it before several rides.

February 2009 saw the first full-page color calendar. The designer burst through the front door of an art show carrying a stack to distribute. Soon even the artists with work on the walls were talking about it. New-to-town Rosanne not only got her hands on one; she got her hands on a loaner bike because of the show. She is now one of the organizers of Velo Louisiane, a statewide bicycling festival organized with BRASS since 2010.

Over time the calendar grew to incorporate rides from several other biking groups in town like the Baton Rouge Area Mountain Bike Association and the Baton Rouge Bike Club. The cycling athletes of the latter group voiced their concerns about general safety of Mass, as it doesn't follow the same strict group riding rules as road bike races. "Why doesn't CM ride single file on busy roads?" Even some of the many bike shop folk spoke out publicly against Mass. This led to many great discussions about keeping people safe on the ride as well as getting out a coherent message to welcome new riders.

Often discussed was how to discourage negative behaviors to keep the rides fun and positive. In earlier years it had even been suggested that certain cyclists should hold elite status over others in order to reinforce the consistent message of inclusion. This idea was dismissed immediately. However it resurfaced in several forms, threatening to induce unwanted hierarchy. One month there were even specially designed spoke cards handed out to "frequent corkers."

A solution was found accidently. In the same spirit of "Yeah, bike" this author shouted somewhat obscenely throughout one ride: "Thank you, sexy corkers!" What started as a joke between some friends quickly became one of the standard interactions between riders and corkers at Critical Mass Baton Rouge. In just a few months it appeared on a T-shirt design. This message not only reinforces the appreciation for those who frequently pause to keep other safe but it hoisted the corker position into one of celebrity status. Soon everyone wanted the opportunity to be a corker.

A 22-year-old student at LSU named Mark Macmurdo said at the after-party of his first ever Critical Mass that it was the most fun he had ever had in Baton Rouge despite living here his entire life. He recounted his experiences: the hesitation he had as the ride gathered; the wide eyes with which he viewed roads that were new even to him; the new friends he met as he started to feel more comfortable; and the pride he felt when, on the return trip, he watched the entire Mass go by as a corker.

It turned out that Mark was an opinion columnist with the campus newspaper. He wrote a fantastic piece that was published the week of the next month's Mass. An excerpt of the 2009 article reads:

> When I first arrived at the University bell tower for the ride last month, my two friends and I disputed whether or not the event was "organized." Ultimately, I came to the conclusion the best way to describe the event is "disorganized organization." Critical Mass is not about protest—really, it's not about anything. There are no stated goals. There is no agenda. There is no message because there is no organization—it's little more than a time and a place. Instead, participants each give the event their own meaning. Some probably want to promote healthy activity in Baton Rouge. Some might be angry at our nation's addiction to oil. Others are just there to party.

Even after just one ride, he really understood some of the inner workings of the movement. It was powerful to read it—and to see others read it—in popular print. This is the kind of publicity that every Critical Mass needs.

Baton Rouge Advocates for Safe Streets

Despite its growing popularity, Critical Mass Baton Rouge was doing little to effect change citywide. Infrequently an article or letter to the editor would stir up controversy in the local newspaper, but there was no one to advance the cause in a legitimate setting.

BRASS spent the first few months of its inception in 2006 drawing up a constitution and applying for nonprofit status, but it earned one of its first successes by reaching out to Critical Mass. Brightside Drive is a neighborhood of mostly students located just a mile or so from campus. During its upgrade, the bike lanes were removed and were not slated to be re-painted. BRASS discovered this, brought a petition to Mass, and more importantly brought the signatures to the attention of the city.

One of Critical Mass's limitations is that it does not fall during normal business hours, and so its successes do not always reach the desk of government officials. Early on, BRASS worked to develop a relationship with city administrators. As a result it was invited to participate in the first semi-annual Mayor's Family Bike Day the morning after the 15th anniversary of the first Critical Mass ride in San Francisco. Critical Mass Baton Rouge riders celebrated the anniversary, screen-printed "One Less Car" T-shirts at the after-party, and even bestowed one upon Mayor Kip Holden the next morning. City officials got to see citizens on bicycles who weren't children or athletes firsthand—and all because BRASS invited Critical Mass!

BRASS picked up on the revelry of the monthly celebrations and started planning its own fun "Velo Velo" rides beginning in 2008. Each of these themed events begins with a short safety demonstration before a moderately paced ride and ends with the best Louisiana has to offer of local food and live music. Themes include histories of neighborhoods, education on local trees and birds, and celebratory tours of gardens and graveyards. Riders from 7 to 70 have had the opportunity to interact with each other afterwards in a much more official capacity than at a Critical Mass after-party. These have even given Mass some new route ideas, most enjoyably the tour of Baton Rouge cemeteries for the costumed October ride.

Word was spreading fast. BRASS was becoming a household name for Critical Mass Baton Rouge riders, who listened to current bike news at the start of each Mass, saw BRASS's name all over the calendar, and even went to events like the BRASS WORKS monthly maintenance workshops. The organization succeeded in getting new people cycling who weren't usual targets for Critical Mass by hosting rides on weekend mornings and afternoons that appealed to a different demographic. At the Mayor's event, BRASS began all the right relationships at the city level and was now invited to participate in upcoming bike-related planning. Surely this was never in the scope dreamed of by Critical Mass.

Over the next few years, BRASS worked together with the city as April was declared Bike Month, sharrows were painted on major streets while the number of miles of bike facilities in town tripled, and in 2009 Baton Rouge was declared a "bronze level bicycling-friendly city" by the League of American Bicyclists! The mayor even released a 30-second ad spot about bicycling to work that featured clips of Critical Mass.

Beyond

This is the legacy of Critical Mass Baton Rouge: all of the different bike-related projects that grow out of having some loosely affiliated community. Bicyclists are like blades of grass: the intertwining of roots creates a safer firmament on which to build. On its own, Critical Mass can only do so much to make the streets safer for cyclists throughout the month. Yet by bringing everyone together, new ideas can be incubated on what can be done to share the joys of bicycling with the rest of the world.

Critical Mass Baton Rouge helped to expand the thriving bicycling community past the genres of BMX, road racing, and mountain biking. It paved the way for other genres including fixed gears, bike polo, alley-cat messenger races, everyday commuting. The same spirit of Mass spilled over into neighboring Lafayette, Louisiana, which now has its own bike advocacy group and Critical Mass. Even more impressive, Mass gives these various groups the opportunity to blend, to intersect. Friendships made at Critical Mass Baton Rouge give individuals the opportunity to break out of their own genres and try on a new kind of bike.

For more about Critical Mass Baton Rouge:

http://criticalmass.wikia.com/wiki/Baton_Rouge,_LA — Critical Mass Baton Rouge general info.
http://www.brsafestreets.org/ — BRASS.
http://www.myspace.com/republicofwestflorida — Ben Herrington's song "Critical Mass."
http://www.lsureveille.com/opinion/murda-he-wrote-critical-mass-bike-ride-is-more-than-just-good-times-1.2041822 — Mark Macmurdo's full article on Critical Mass Baton Rouge.

San Francisco Critical Mass swirls down the famous Lombard Street curves, 2008.

PHOTO BY EDUARDO GREEN

Critical Mass in South Africa: Making Inroads Into a Land of Lycra

By Gail Jennings

Cape Town is a city with an international cycling reputation. Every March, the city hosts the world's largest individually timed cycle race: 35,000 entrants ride through 109 km of public roads closed to motorised traffic by local authorities. Entries open every September, and within a matter of weeks are sold out. Seeding rides are held throughout the year, road closures are advertised weeks in advance, and baggage limits are relaxed to allow bicycles on flights to and from Cape Town for the race weekend. The City of Cape Town invests approximately ZAR 1 million (approx. $115,000) in resources toward hosting the Cycle Tour event, with a return on investment of approximately ZAR 350 million (approx. $40 million), including the amount visitors spend on hotels, restaurants, and entertainment.

The *Cape Argus* Pick 'n Pay Cycle Tour, named after its major sponsors, is also the first event outside Europe to be included in the International Cycling Union's Golden Bike Series. Between December and early March, thousands of riders train for the race on congested, contested public roads —their "Argus time" is the benchmark by which their credibility is measured.

Yet despite its national and international pedigree as a cycling destination, utility or urban cycling is almost absent on Cape Town roads (and on South African roads in general). By the middle of March—the end of the "cycling season"— talk shows, SMS- and online-comment columns, and newspaper letter pages no longer buzz with driver-cyclist antagonism and accusations; motorists celebrate that they have "their" streets back. Bicycles are mothballed until the next racing season.

Except for those belonging to approximately 0.5% of Cape Town's population, most of whom have never entered a cycle race or participated in a cycle event. These cyclists use a bicycle as transport, and although their numbers have changed little over the past 25 years, there's evidence to suggest that their demographic has. Once the domain of school-going children, most bicycle commuters today are either the urban poor, living in outlying informal settlements and riding to save money on transit-fare, or the occasional middle-class, (mostly) car-owning activist.

What is evident, though, is that the number of occasions for the latter to take to the streets is steadily on the increase. The pace of activism— and urban cycling—is picking up, and even a cursory glance at Cape Town streets suggests that there are more bicycles and less Lycra.

Whether Critical Mass Cape Town was the chicken or the egg, we'll never know. Recent years have seen a perfect storm of social media, accessible discourses of climate change, new urbanism, and liveable cities, and an acceleration of interest in non-motorised transport opportunities brought about by the 2010 FIFA World Cup and COP17 (Durban was host to the UN Climate Change Conference in 2011). But there's no doubt that Cape Town 2012 is not Cape Town 2008, the year when Critical Mass began.

It was a dark and stormy night…

"There were four of us out one Thursday night in the middle of winter," says Gavin Rossouw, who founded Critical Mass in this sprawling, low-density Cape Town that's hostile to cyclists and still contests their right to the roads.

> We'd had a few drinks, it was getting on, and we weren't entirely sober. We started ranting about the lack of infrastructure and awareness for people riding bikes in Cape Town (and the greater South Africa), and as midnight turned—and after a few more cleansing ales—we decided that we needed to start a Critical Mass-type ride here at home.

They checked online and learned that Critical Mass usually happened on the last Friday of every month.

> Turns out that right now was the last Friday of the month," [he says] "so we sent messages to our friends and got them to meet us a few hours later for the grand unveiling of the Cape Town Critical Mass. After an all too brief nap we met in front of the Baxter Theatre in Rondebosch at 06:40. It was winter, it was dark, and it was kinda rainy. We rode into central Cape Town, and were later more commonly known as the "critical four" (there were four of us, and we were very critical).

The regular route is 16 km from the affluent southern suburbs into the central city, which in 2008 meant dodging informal mini-bus taxis (jitneys), lumbering buses oblivious to vulnerable road users, and impatient motorists, along a heavily congested main road; the same route is now able to bypass much of the main road and take in some of the city's new bicycle lanes. Installed with World Cup transport funding, these 3m-wide segregated bicycle lanes run parallel to the city's newly-built dedicated busway, designed for the MyCiTi integrated rapid transit system.

"The best thing about Critical Mass is that the people there aren't just your dyed-in-the-wool racer boys," says Rossouw, who is also one of the country's top marathon mountain bikers and in 2010 was South Africa's only participant in the 14-hour Solo MTB World Champs.

There're folks on dutch bikes, hipsters, bmx'ers and an assortment of like-minded people trying to escape their cars. It's sometimes the only ride where I get to chill out and chat to people who are bike enthusiasts. Most of the time we don't talk about bikes either, which is kinda cool.

Paul Edmunds, an internationally-exhibited visual artist with an aversion to bicycle gears, was there from the start, and agrees with Rossouw.

I like seeing riding buddies, and there does seem to be some safety afforded by larger numbers. Curiously I find motorists more tolerant of the CM group that they are for me as a single commuter. I think a few of the group—now numbering between 35-50—have begun to commute by bicycle, at least sporadically. I do harbour the hope that more people will realise just how impractical a tool a car is for most trips made in densely trafficked areas, especially over short distances. [Compared to Critical Mass in the U.S. and London] we are pretty tame. I think riding is more dangerous here: motorists are unaccustomed to large numbers of cyclists, and our rides regularly include inexperienced cyclists. I'm not sure I'd like us to get a reputation for being antagonistic and anarchic.

Gareth Pearson, one of the founders of Cape Town's first commuter advocacy group (2011), Cape Town Bicycle Commuter, is a fairly new participant in Critical Mass.

It has definitely introduced the idea of bicycle commuting to people who would otherwise be too intimidated to go it alone. It's been exciting to see so many other bike-minded people coming out of the cracks. Other "believers." We Capetonians love Critical Mass rides so much that we've started #moonlightmass, a night ride through the city at every full moon.

And it's not only Cape Town. Durbanite Brandon van Eeden witnessed Critical Mass in Times Square NYC around 10 years ago, after reading about it in punk fanzines a few years before that, saying:

A really amazing experience it was. Then last year I got my first bicycle since I was a teenager and noticed that more and more people in Durban were getting back on two wheels. I love being 'on the streets'. Every time I'm out I see something new and exciting that makes me feel much more alive. It's super addictive.

I noticed that Critical Mass had a good following in Cape Town so decided to start one here. I decided to do it in the evenings after work on a Friday as a really chilled sunset ride along the beach promenade. Nothing too hectic and nothing like the ride I saw in New York.

Word has spread and a lot of people now know about the ride, with varying numbers each month, the largest being 30 or so. We communicate using a

*Facebook group and send out event invites for each ride. In 2012 we hope
to print posters and flyers to put in bicycle stores and hand to people we see
out riding during the month.*

Van Eeden commutes to work by bike occasionally but only in the cooler months.

*The humidity is too high in summer and I work in a corporate environment
and have to maintain a "professional" image. I'm sure, though, that this ex-
pectation is slowly breaking down as people become more open to the idea of
bicycle transport. That's the idea of course about Critical Mass: to show that
you can dress normally and ride your bicycle. People are starting to see the
bicycle less as a sporting activity, and more as a possible commuter vehicle.
For freedom and escape.*

Like Cape Town, the Durban route has started to include city streets,
taking in the bicycle infrastructure built ahead of COP 17. The majority of
regular urban cyclists, however, tend to live in disadvantaged, low-income
peripheral areas where private car ownership is low and reliance on public
transport or informal minibus taxis is high. These are the areas beyond
the trendy, gentrifying central cities, in areas where bicycle infrastructure
is marginal but where the numbers of urban cyclists are high. These cyclists ride to save money, or to experience the freedom, flexibility, and independence that personal transport offers. Reducing their individual carbon
footprint, or making a point about urban quality and car dependency, is
scarcely on the agenda—a bicycle is a mode of transport, not a means of
making a mobile statement.

In addition, in a society in transition such as this, with a newly emerging middle class, bicycle transport carries with it the stigma of the past, a
reminder of former disadvantage and a lack of access to resources. Critical
Mass remains a largely white affair. Says a man who is a rare example of a
young black utility cyclist:

*I'm from the Eastern Cape—I have a bicycle there. But to come with a bicy-
cle... to Cape Town is a no, no... I think it's within us black people. For me, I'm
educated, but it's a matter of status. You know, I speak for black people—they
would say: "Why don't you have a car?" ... A friend of mine was like, "Wow,
shit, you can't be riding a bicycle." And she put that on Facebook... We need to
break the stigma that when you ride a bicycle you're poor.[1]*

There is nevertheless merit to the argument that fashionable activism
may raise the status of the commuter bicycle and facilitate its reappearance
as an aspirational mode of transport. The rising fuel price will play its part.
And, of course, there's nothing wrong with getting car-commuters onto

bikes, even if only a few of them, and even if only for a day a month.

"I'd like to think that Critical Mass has had a wide reaching influence of how people think about how they use their environment," concludes Rossouw.

> *But in reality I think Critical Mass has probably had only a small impact on some people, and that's about the best I could hope for.*

> *There have been a flurry of new bike paths since we started. Are they related? Probably not. But I'd like to think that we helped sway the thinking of at least one person and they then helped sway the thinking of someone else, who had something to do with the project. That would be cool.*

Notes

1   Interview by Stan Engelbrecht, *Bicycle Portraits*

Vigo Critical Mass, a Second Beginning

By Gael Sande Avendaño

Vigo is a small city near the sea in the northwest Spanish region called Galicia. During a windy winter day it is possible to hear the brave Atlantic Ocean crashing against the rocks on the dock.

> I remember the day that I decided to sell my car as one of my most reward-
> ing days. But honestly my car was dead for a few months before. It was two
> years ago during spring, when I started to think about the possibility of
> erasing it from our lives. Getting to work by car everyday was a mechanical
> action, similar to the one of taking a fork from the dish to your mouth while
> you're eating. You don't know what the direction of the fork will be, but you
> know the final destination of the food that's on it.

This was the story that a Critical Mass rider told me recently. He decided to sell his car just to be free, as a profound act of disobedience to a way of life accepted by most—a stinking tablespoon of cod liver oil that the doctor prescribed us when we were children.

Groucho Marx used to say that, "Politics is the art of looking for trouble, finding it, making a false diagnosis, and then applying the wrong remedies." In my life I have never found a better definition for a term. My ears hurt every time I turn on the radio and I hear one of our politicians talking about the world of cycling.

How could someone who moves every day in an official car (after winning an election campaign in part by private funding), be able to propose solutions for transportation that are so cheap they involve only an expenditure of 7 cents/km? How would they return the private money that funds their campaigns? In Spain we have believed for years that our politicians had the intention of building bike lanes, public bike services, or bike racks on public transportation to carry our bicycles when we feel tired—all empty words far from large population centers such as Madrid or Barcelona. For twenty years in little cities we have demanded improvements but we are stuck in the same spot. Only because of tremendous social pressure have there been small steps taken in the right direction. Politicians assume cycling is a weekend pleasure, but not a legitimate transportation choice for which it is worth building a strong and lasting infrastructure. The ideas emerge during every election campaign and get diluted like a sugar cube when politicians rise to power. In Spain urban cycling had been useful for selling "European convergence" or "green revolution" but actually shows the complete rigidity of our institutions.

An example of this is the construction of a cycleway between Vigo and Baiona, a town located 23 km away. The project bore the stamp of the regional government and consisted of the construction of two bike lanes to connect both population centers. The lane would run between the road and the sea with beautiful views all along the way. To build the bike path required recovering public land "stolen" (yes I said it, STOLEN) by people who, at some point in their lives, and in the face of passive public institutions, decided to extend their properties, incorporating public space from the road shoulder. When the government moved to reopen the public right of way to bicycles, people in cars counterdemonstrated, brandishing slogans against non-motorized vehicles. The political class began to notice the number of pro-car votes they could lose, and not how many pro-bike votes they could win. The project was abandoned and many cyclists are still risking their lives on a dangerous road. But wait a moment, didn't we say that governments are there to work for the common good, didn't they say during the elections that bicycles are a type of transport that must be promoted?

Like any self-respecting story, there are not only antagonists, there are social pressure groups and in our city they have a name: Vigo Critical Mass. Vigo Critical Mass was born in October 2004 in order to emulate similar events, with an eye on the mother of Critical Masses in San Francisco. The beginnings of Vigo Critical Mass was quite difficult. Initially the Masses were made on Sunday morning, a good day for lots of bicyclists, but a complicated day because of the decreased weekend traffic which reduced group cycling visibility. It was because of this and after three years of internal debate that we decided to change the day and time of the Mass to give it greater visibility within urban traffic by placing it on Friday evening at 8 p.m. In Vigo this is rush hour traffic. We wanted to show the world the validity of our model compared to private car transport. For this new event many posters were printed announcing the new time and day and they were distributed through the Internet. The date change was a success because now thousands of people saw a group of cyclists during rush hour claiming their space in traffic.

But we couldn't ignore the earlier work done by two important associations in the city: *Verdegaia*, a regional environmental association, and *A Golpe de Pedal*, a group responsible of the promotion of cycling in our city. The presence of these two associations behind Vigo Critical Mass, respecting the anti-hierarchical horizontal movement that characterizes all Critical Masses, is one of the pillars that give strength to it.

But the movement hadn't yet exploded. In Vigo bikes always have been seen on the streets. The number of people that were coming to Critical

Mass every month was not representative of the number of urban cyclists that we knew were in the city. It was clear that our efforts had not been enough. Many urban cyclists didn't know about the movement when they were asked about it. A final push was needed to make all Vigo cyclists aware of the last Friday of the month as a date to demand their space in traffic. This has been our work for these past two years. It has been difficult organizing a heterogenous group like Critical Mass, where the riders are a changing group of individuals who always have different concerns.

I remember that the point of no return came in February 2011. February 25, 2011, was one of saddest days of the Vigo Critical Mass. Only eleven intrepid cyclists ventured into city traffic that day. We could not lose one more second unless we wanted that event, to which we had dedicated so much spare time, to disappear. At a meeting in early March we agreed on a clear action. There was nothing to lose. If Critical Mass was only 11 cyclists it wouldn't make sense to keep the project going. After the initial excitement two years before, the number of cyclists had decreased gradually to the ridiculous figure of 11 in a city of three hundred thousand people. We knew for certain that there were at least 300 daily cyclists in the city. It was time to act. The objective was clear: in three months we had to quadruple the number of cyclists who normally came to the Mass. We wanted to become an effective pressure group in the city by May 27, 2011. We would do anything to reach it.

First we identified the root of the problem—the public simply didn't know about the monthly Critical Mass rides. I recall that meeting as tense, but a thrilling moment in my life. I remember the serious faces of my colleagues during the meeting. We were not fighting for ourselves, but for our children. We were fighting for our future. After seven years Vigo Critical Mass could disappear without leaving any trace. Have you ever believed in divine justice? If I'm honest I began to believe right after that meeting. Many ideas were raised during the meeting. Finally two ideas appeared that were going to completely change the path taken by Vigo Critical Mass.

"Create a Facebook group" was the first one. It seems obvious but we realized that the chat forums used to communicate among Critical Mass riders were too slow and could not be updated in real time. Also Facebook provided us a well-known way of communication where everybody could express themselves directly and immediately, even people that normally wouldn't come to a Critical Mass. We still honored the preexistent forums that had been working for years, such as the one of *A Golpe de Pedal* Association, as well as common discussion forums with the rest of the Galician Critical Mass rides.

However, the second idea that appeared at the meeting was something very easy that changed radically the situation of our Critical Mass. We decided to distribute "business cards" in Vigo's streets, similar to the ones you get at malls or shops, something fast and dynamic that could be delivered by hand to cyclists and pedestrians who asked us for information about Critical Mass. From this little idea at our meeting the new Vigo Critical Mass cards were born.

The new online and in-the-streets agitation was complemented by media coverage and distribution of posters in bicycle and outdoor sports shops to promote the event. Many press releases were sent and flyers were distributed around the city. The success was overwhelming. The seed for the rebirth of the Vigo Critical Mass had been planted and this time, it would thrive.

By fortunate coincidence, our campaign to rejuvenate Critical Mass occurred alongside the massive citizen demonstrations of May 15, 2011, in Spain. The May 15 movement of *indignados* ("the indignants") called for major reforms. Over six million Spaniards demonstrated all over the country demanding the recovery of popular sovereignty against a political class in crisis. We were unanimous in support of this movement. The May, 2011 Critical Mass ended at the Vigo *Indignados* Assembly, where we were showered with applause. That Critical Mass was really exciting—in three months we had reached our first objective, increasing the number of riders from 11 to 47. The most positive aspect was that there were 7- and 8-year-old kids that came with their parents.

Since then we had several new demonstrations related to the Critical Mass movement. The most important occurred on September 25, 2011, under the slogan *Móvete sen CO^2* ("Move without CO^2") which brought together more than 750 cyclists. We called for an improvement in safety and infrastructure for bicycles in the city. The week after this demonstration the advocacy organizations *Verdegaia* and *A Golpe de Pedal* tried to arrange an appointment with the city officials responsible for traffic in Vigo, a request that has not yet been answered.

Currently Vigo Critical Mass is the biggest Critical Mass in the northwest Iberian Peninsula. We gather the most cyclists and our community is one of the most active in terms of promotion and dissemination of information related to urban cycling on the Internet and in the mass media. Despite the silence that prevails about the use of the bicycle by political figures in Spain, Critical Masses continue to grow all over the country.

During a recent Critical Mass, one father told me that during the whole previous month his little daughter kept asking him, "How many days until I can ride my bike all over the city again?" She is only seven years old and she does not think in terms of activism, but she knew that she wanted to feel free. She knows that riding her bike makes her free. That was when I knew that all our efforts are worthwhile.

San Francisco Critical Mass, August 2008, at Ghirardelli Square

PHOTO BY ADAM AUFDENCAMP

Naples Critical Mass

By Luca Simeone, Roberto Coscione, Claudio Caccavale, Marì Muscarà,
Alfonso Borriello, Davide Chiarito, and Paolo Falanga

Naples Critical Mass was born in September 2005 with about 25-30 riders. The idea came from a group of friends after reading an Italian magazine article about San Francisco's Critical Mass. The group was part of an association involved in projects related to sustainable development, reclaiming social spaces, etc. At first, every rider already knew each other. After some Critical Masses, they got in contact on the Web with other people in Naples. Since 2008, Naples Critical Mass has become a strong movement with two monthly rides (first Saturday morning and third Friday evening) with a good number of people involved. Our ride is pretty much the same each month, taking over the main streets of the city center, but from time to time we like to go on unusual routes to other districts where bicycles are not so common. In the last two years we organized a bigger event on national level based on the Rome experience of *Ciemmona*: so we've already had two *Critichella* in our city, with about 300 people coming from Italy and Europe, and we're preparing for the third edition in 2012.

Naples Critical Mass is primarily organized by a local group of bicycle lovers monitoring the basic needs for a good experience: lending a bike to anyone who doesn't have one, being sure that Critical Mass happens regularly, etc. The core activists are about twenty persons whose average age is 30; some of them participated since the very beginning, but we also experienced a turnover in this group due to the normal course of life (job, other interests, etc.). Roughly the same people organize all the background work, but it is an ever growing movement. On the other hand, a lot of people don't take part in the background work but they are self-organized and regularly join Critical Mass. The people involved in Critical Mass are rather homogeneous, yet still different; ages range from 20 to over 50, but 20-30 is typical. Critical Mass riders are mostly university students, artists, creatives, employed or not. There are a lot attracted by word of mouth. Turnover is common, so we always have new faces around when we gather—also because we try to "collect" any cyclist we meet on our way—so it's easy to make new acquaintances. We hope that two kinds of people will get more involved in Critical Mass and urban cycling in general: those from the poorest and the richest neighborhoods. The first ones—especially the youngsters among them—because they often don't even see a bicycle, as they move only by scooter; and the second ones because they rely too much on the private car—maybe they see the bicycle as a toy, not as a means of transportation. So, as mobility conditions are getting worse and worse, and oil prices are rising, there is a little hope that they will rediscover the bicycle. There is some xerocracy among riders (we had much more at the beginning!) but the primary target is spreading "riding culture" among pedestrians and, above all, people in cars. So we ride without a pre-planned route singing some songs and carrying happiness and banners. Critical Mass in Naples is still too little: about 40 riders is a good number (with peaks of 50 and more) but the average is about 30... Obviously the number of participants grows with the coming of good weather, then slowly declines in winter.

Before Critical Mass there was not a "cycling scene" in Naples at all. Most of us live in the inner city or near it, many used go to the university every day by bicycle, so we could easily observe people throughout the city; well, we've never seen so many cyclists in the streets since Critical Mass started. The only real presence before Critical Mass was (and still is) the formal Cicloverdi Association (GreenCyclo, "environmentalist cyclists"), that is a local association federated with Italy's FIAB (the Italian National Cycle Network). Cicloverdi prefers country trips, artistic and historical visits and so on, but not really everyday bicycling (e.g. commuting). They did at least campaign and lobby for allowing bicycles on buses and local transportation, many of its members strongly support our initiatives, and we like very much to cooperate and exchange opinions with them about our city. So we can say that, in our case, there's an ever improving relationship with other cycling entities in the city and often their people take part in Critical Mass and other organized similar rides, too. The city of Naples has always seen the bicycle as a funny experiment, related more to sport and fitness than to daily mobility. Before Critical Mass and since the 1980s the use of the bicycle was promoted and disseminated by Cicloverdi. Then Critical Mass came four years ago with a lot of folks and its engaging and rallying urban rides. This injection of enthusiasm has certainly been good for bicycling. The inside/outside dynamic between Critical Mass and Cicloverdi leads to shared experiences and an interesting synergy of purpose that is doing well. We are building up a city of bikes by pedaling and pedaling!

That said, we proudly can declare that, hell yeah!, of course Critical Mass played a big role in expanding views about the bicycle and its potential in urban mobility! In a city dominated by car drivers and motorcyclists it should have been seen as a crazy thing, all these people shouting, laughing and enjoying a carfree road and distributing flyers to explain WHAT was going on and WHY. After some time, as we persistently remained in the streets, the Mass gained more and more visibility and new converts, likely because it was perceived as not only "cool," but also the "right thing to do." Now we are a well-recognized presence in our city, and often Critical Mass core activists dialogue with institutional representatives. We also opened a bicycle workshop in a self-managed social center that in the past had been the meeting point of many subcultural people and *antagonistas* (autonomous activists) and was slowly dying, so this brought it a new life. Generally speaking, as Critical Mass is well known in the city and also gave birth to satellite Critical Masses in the hinterland, we feel like it's been a big help for people becoming more respectful towards cyclists and more careful towards their own environment. There is a lively bicycle scene in Naples now.

There are two occupied spaces that are not part of Critical Mass but always give us their full support whenever we ask for it. One of these is L.O.S.K.A. (*Laboratorio Occupato Sociale di Kultura Antagonista*). It is the place where we currently run our bicycle workshop, which is networked with other activities in the place, such as Mass Radio, a webradio, the Popular School (a school for migrant people), and legal aid, all completely free activities that support our initiatives. Another one we are in touch with is *Radiolina*, a Web-based and former pirate radio. We do not take part in political party events, but we do support environmental issues when we know their origin is from informal political groups, associations, and mass social movements. In our city conflict is constant among the policymakers, partisan groups, and informal political groups: each individual or political group thinks that he/they could do better than those in power, whilst partisan political groups feel that the governed ones just want to create discomfort to society, similar to the Italian government.

Many people have begun to have a great interest in the bicycle world through Critical Mass, for example a friend of us started a webzine called *BiciZen*. He interviews many people using bicycles, like bike messengers and folding bike riders, there are travel diaries, useful advice for urban bikers or people approaching bicycling for the first time... really a lot of interesting things! Sometimes we stencil our bicycle logo on the street. Sometimes we stop in a square and shout, "This is Critical Mass Square!" Some friends during the Critical Mass event dress like Pulcinella, a famous character of Naples. L.O.S.K.A. is the place where we have the *CiclOfficina* named after Massimo Troisi, who was a famous Neapolitan actor. It is a free space where we collect and rebuild bicycles. Usually people come with their own bikes when they have problems and we try to repair or teach the owners how to repair them themselves. New bicycles are born here like tandems, tall bikes, and even a cargo bike that normally we use to bring the sound system during Critical Mass events. People like to have music while pedaling together! In

2011 there was also an art exhibition where an artist built Pulcinella with bicycle components. Last but not least, in our city Critical Mass people like to make many videos, in fact we even have a You Tube channel.

In conclusion, our final goal is to encourage the use of the bicycle for fun as well as everyday transportation. We noticed a great increase in people riding bicycles since we started doing Critical Mass. Surely there have been other factors contributing to this rise but surely the impact of Critical Mass is a main reason. It is pretty simple: if you are the only one cycling in the city you could feel a little bit stupid but if you see a lot of people going together and singing in the streets then you realize you're not alone.

Links
http://www.bicizen.it/
http://www.youtube.com/user/criticalmassnapoli?blend=1&ob=0

Naples Critical Mass

A Tumultuous Ride
New York City Critical Mass and the Wrath of the NYPD
by Matthew Roth

The first Critical Mass-style group rides in New York City started meeting at Astor Place at the intersection of the West and East Villages in 1993. The ride rarely attracted more than 50 to 100 people during the early years. Transportation Alternatives, one of the more established bicycle advocacy groups and an early promoter of Critical Mass, stopped after a couple years. While Critical Mass in San Francisco and other cities had exploded, with thousands regularly participating, New York City seemed a particularly hostile place for a ride and led to much gnashing of teeth among those who still believed it could be successful.

By 1999, Bill DiPaola, an organizer with Time'sUp!, an environmental and bicycle nonprofit was one of the few people who continued to believe New York City could have a functional Critical Mass. DiPaola met Chris Carlsson, one of the San Francisco founders of Critical Mass, in Seattle at the anti-WTO protests, where he asked him for advice on what to do to make the rides more successful.

"I told him how it wasn't working. I couldn't get enough people to come," said DiPaola. Carlsson asked DiPaola if he was having any fun on the rides. "It was horrible," DiPaola recalled telling him. Carlsson's advice was to make the rides fun. "And I knew that he was right," said DiPaola. "We talked a lot about fun."[1]

DiPaola imagined making the rides like a "moving circus," encouraging riders to dress up in costumes. As a musical party planner in his pre-activist days, he also decided the ride needed after-parties, which turned out to be one of the more successful draws for new people to participate.

Time'sUp! was also coordinating with More Gardens, which worked to save community gardens in New York City from being bulldozed and "redeveloped" into condos. In April 2000, they teamed up to throw a Critical Mass after-party in a community garden that was scheduled for closing. Participants at that month's More Gardens Critical Mass dressed as ladybugs and dragonflies and their favorite vegetables, imbuing the ride with a sense of mirth and whimsy. It was a great success.

The rides immediately grew from a handful of people to over 200 and stayed that way regularly for a couple years, with the exception of the Halloween event, when up to 500 would participate. Despite rising numbers and a more festive atmosphere, it was still hard to grow the ride.

I started volunteering regularly with Time'sUp in early 2001, a few months after my first Critical Mass. Among other rides that we publicized, we regularly promoted Critical Mass in the week leading up to the events. Thanks to a "liberated" Kinko's copy key, we made a healthy stack of fliers announcing the meet-up location and the after-party. We printed them on fluorescent paper and cut them into quarter-sized palm cards. The fliers were cute, with illustrations of cyclists riding atop overturned cars that sprouted flowers or, for the Halloween ride, ghouls and ghosts on bikes under titles like, "Wear a Spoooooky costume!"

Every Thursday night before the Critical Mass, a small group of Time'sUp! volunteers crisscrossed the East Village and the areas around New York University, taping (or "bike tagging") the quarter sheet fliers to bike seats, brake cables, spokes, and handlebars of bikes locked to street signs and parking meters.

While our propaganda had a measured effect, bringing in a few new riders here and there (often with their quarter sheet fliers in hand), *Bikesummer 2003* was a milestone for the growth of New York City Critical Mass. Bike clubs from all over the city joined us in organizing the annual month-long celebration of the bicycle. The June Critical Mass was the biggest we had seen at 800 people; by July it was double that!

At each successive ride, we saw the demographics grow more diverse. Bike messengers rode alongside bearded bicycle lifers with mirrors on their helmets; crusty squatters with milk-crate bike baskets pedaled next to spandex-clad weekend warriors on carbon frames; parents hauled their kids in trailers next to BMX groups popping wheelies; frat boys from Jersey rode their full-suspension mountain bikes while trying to hit on roller-skating girls in striped stockings; and fashionably-dressed city commuters on upright bikes chatted up college students out for their first ride in a city.

There were still a lot of environmentalists and bicycle advocates on these Critical Mass rides—the early adopters who viewed cycling in a city as a political statement—but we were no longer the majority. Regular participants like me started to recognize fewer people as the overall numbers swelled. Local newspapers and magazines began to list Critical Mass as a must-do event,[2] and we even occasionally met international tourists who rented bikes while on their vacation to ride with us.

Massive Growth

By July 2004, New York City Critical Mass grew to more than 4,000 participants. Just as we had done in March that year, we poured out of Union Square down Broadway. I was on my sound trike, pumping loud music and generally making people happy. When I crossed Canal Street at the front of the ride, I radioed some Time'sUp! friends on a walkie-talkie who were riding at the back of the Critical Mass. They hadn't cleared Union Square. The back of the ride was twenty blocks north of me. We were over a mile long!

Two blocks south of Canal, cyclists at the front of the ride turned west on White Street. We had come up a small incline after Canal and I gained a vantage point, where I stopped the tricycle and looked behind me. The crowd of cyclists stretched as far as I could see up Broadway. It was amazing.

Eventually, the ride snaked its way to West Street, the perimeter street on Manhattan's west side. For several months, we had been taking advantage of the ride's size to take over West Street (nicknamed the Westside Highway). West Street south of 57th Street had stoplights, though it was still wide and functioned like a highway, with drivers routinely hitting 50-60 miles per hour. Riding a bike on this portion of road was a triumphant feeling. It felt like we were being very bold, somewhat naughty. I loved it.

That night, as we headed south on West Street, I was again near the front of the ride, given the tendency of cyclists to stay behind my speaker, enjoying the loud music. A young man on a BMX bike beside me suddenly hopped up on the frame, balancing one foot on the handlebar crossbar, the other foot on the seat and surfed his bike as far as his momentum would take him.

This same guy was the first person I heard that night say the fateful words, "Let's take the FDR!" Fateful because the New York Police Department would frequently cite our riding on the FDR Freeway, Manhattan's Eastside perimeter road (a true freeway, without stoplights) as the final insult to order and decency on the streets they controlled the other 30 days of the month.

The July 2004 ride was beautiful, but it was the very last Critical Mass in New York City where riders weren't arrested, ticketed, rounded up in plastic netting pens, and otherwise harassed by the NYPD. That night was the last time I can remember Critical Mass being fun.

Why Critical Mass Matters in the City

Critical Mass created safety in numbers, a bubble of solidarity, moving in space, formed momentarily in time by the mutual consent of like-minded cyclists. Its simplicity was its power. For at least three hours a month, you could be reasonably sure you were safe from bodily harm, and you might even come away with camaraderie and new friends. When the other 740 hours of the month were potentially life-threatening or life-mangling, these three hours on the last Friday were a personal, visceral liberation.

But the rides weren't necessarily benign and giddy. At the edge of the bubble, you had to contend with pissed off drivers who felt the indignity of their traffic jam exacerbated by this strange parliament of hoot owls on bikes who ignored red lights and corked oncoming traffic. At the edges of the bubble, the menace was palpable and often terrifying. Yelling could turn to threats of violence with a car. Threats of violence occasionally turned into actual violence, when drivers rammed their vehicles into the owls blocking their way.

Christopher Ryan, an artist and filmmaker who first started riding in Critical Mass in late 2002, described the rides as an antidote to traditional protests, where people marched in circles and carried placards.

> I felt Critical Mass was more an illustration of an alternative, rather than just a reaction to the endless stream of crap that we were bombarded with. You were constantly asked, 'What are you protesting against?' Your answer was, 'Nothing.' That was just so awesome to see people—they would blink 3 or 4 times and you could tell their brain was turning upside down and they were trying to digest that.

> The second question was always, 'Hey who's sponsoring this?' Like Gatorade was having stealth advertising? When you say, 'No one,' then that was just sort of the one-two punch. Now I don't know what the fuck is going on. I enjoyed that.

Mike Green, a production technician in television and the founder of *Bike Blog NYC*, emphasized the fun that you could have if you got people out to ride. "If you could just get people to ride their bikes, you could talk about politics later. For the most part you could just have fun and ride your bike in the city. It was door opening, mind opening—that was the coolest part of it."

For many, Critical Mass was a revelation that encouraged them to ride more often. Surveys showed that one of the most significant barriers to riding in New York City was feeling unsafe. If you rode a bike in the days before Critical Mass, you had to squeeze into the margins, compelled to sidle through the narrow gaps between car lanes, at the mercy of doors that might swing open at any point and crunch your soft flesh and bone.

Leah Rorvig, a volunteer with Time'sUp! who helped develop our press operation, described the first time she went on a Critical Mass ride in early 2004, a particularly rainy and wet event:

> I had barely even been comfortable cycling in New York at this point. Then we rode around in the rain for two hours, chanting and screaming our heads off. It was pure exhilarating fun and joy, but with no drugs and with no alcohol. It was a mobile bike party of freedom. That pretty much had me hooked from there.

Critical Mass also took you back to your childhood, riding bikes with friends, finding liberty in short bursts as you explored new parts of your town. Ben Shepard, a professor, author, and regular Time'sUp! volunteer, described it as an extension of that childhood wonder:

> *I've ridden my bike my whole life. The bike was always a space for imagination. I remember as a kid riding home from a Star Trek movie and riding my bike and thinking about the movie and fantasizing about the world and running almost directly into a car and having to lift my bike directly up in the air, ride sideways somehow and pull away from the car. Riding a bike was always a way of imagining another world.*

Despite the nostalgia and connection of bike riding to the innocence of youth, trying to ride in a big bad city could be scary. Shepard reflected on that dichotomy. "On a bike you're always free to move however you need to move—for me it really is poetry," he said. "But it's also a dialectic of death. There is also always the fear. You shouldn't have to feel like you're taking your life in your hands when you're riding a bike."

For Brandon Neubauer, another Time'sUp! volunteer and one of the central organizers for us leading up to the Republican National Convention (RNC) protests in August 2004, riding his bicycle was nearly akin to weekly worship.

"It's that whole vibe of it being like church to us. It was a key part of the rhythm of each month," he said. "Because I was looking forward to it every month, it deserved a high level of respect and thankfulness that it even existed. I just knew that every month I had this thing to look forward to. It activated a special part of your brain."

Neubauer added:

> *Riding your bike in general is about your own agency. You are the agent of your locomotion and that makes it very unique in its own right. But then to do it in a group of people, it takes advantage of the very unique qualities of a bicycle and urban community. In New York, because the control of public space is so much a part of what the police do and it is the capital of capitalism, it was really powerful to turn that whole thing on its head and turn it into a progressive, hard-lefty space.*

New Yorkers have to fight for every inch of their domain and the most visible piece of shared space is the street. In a city with some of the most expensive real estate in the world, where even the "unused" air above a building has value that developers have monetized and sold to each other, the fight for the 120 feet or so between building lines has always been epic. New York City's legendary traffic was so bad they had to come up with a new word to describe it: gridlock. It is a city where parking is such a contested commodity that novels have been written about obsessive space squatters: *Tepper Isn't Going Out*. Filmmakers love to show a panning shot of a sea of heads on Fifth Avenue as shorthand for everything city.

Yet, public space is rarely acknowledged as being a shared asset. Ask any New Yorker what they consider to be public space, they will likely indicate Central Park. I doubt they will talk about the street, though streets cover more than a third of the land area. Shepard argued that interaction in public space was a fundamental piece of our conception of democracy.

> For me it's the simple idea that de Tocqueville talks about in Democracy in America. Democracy is contingent on public space intermediating between the market and the government. There has to be this idea of a civil society, a place where people get together and talk, build ideas, share ideas, deliberate about problems.

Unfortunately for all of us involved in Critical Mass in New York City, its nadir in the summer of 2004 also marked the transition of the ride from a nurturing and enjoyable public space to a place where we constantly feared arrest and police intimidation.

Republican National Convention Protests

On August 27, 2004, we knew Critical Mass would be enormous. That weekend, the Republicans were descending on New York City for their quadrennial nominating party, the RNC. Every progressive activist worth their salt was hot on their tails, planning enormous marches and demonstrations. United for Peace and Justice, an umbrella organization formed in opposition to the Iraq War, had a parade permit for 250,000 people. Many activists had been planning for at least a year. The Republicans themselves had budgeted for the most expensive convention up to that point in history, at more than $91 million. After four years of President George W. Bush, the standard bearers of conservatism were coming to one of the more liberal cities in the country, a city decidedly opposed to nearly every part of the conservative agenda.

The press also wrote extensively about the intricate security plans the NYPD had in place, including the mobilization of more than 10,000 officers. Police were closing off much of Midtown Manhattan around Madison Square Garden in a series of checkpoints and barricades. The police vowed to preserve order and maintain peace, despite the huge throngs of protesters expected to arrive in town. NYPD officers had infiltrated planning meetings of peace activists for the past year, spying on puppeteers, street theater activists, and church groups in cities around the U.S., Canada, and Europe.

The city was being locked down in preparation for something bad (in addition to the Republicans, I mean) and they were sparing no expense in preparation, or in propaganda. For at least a month, Mayor Michael Bloomberg, the NYPD, and the media had been fanning the flames, with commentary and stories about "Anarchists Hot for Mayhem"[3] and many references to possible terrorist plots, no small matter for a city with a raw memory of the much-invoked 9-11. Many New Yorkers were getting out of the city.

Homeland Security had given special designation to the event, placing the U.S. Secret Service in charge of coordination. Department of Homeland Security head Tom Ridge announced that they had credible threats that Al Qaeda was planning to "carry out a large-scale attack in the United States in an effort to disrupt our democratic process."

At Time'sUp! we were also planning for the influx of people and we wanted to connect them with a fun way to see the city. Over the course of the week leading up to the RNC, we organized a slate of rides we called the Bike National Convention, or BNC. The events included a Paul Revere ride in Revolutionary War garb, tricornes, and papier-maché horse heads on bike handlebars; a Radical Community Tour of the Lower East Side; and two Bike Bloc rides meant to coincide with the larger protest days.

While we expected the Critical Mass to be huge, none of us was prepared for the massive crowd that gathered at Union Square that Friday night. The official police estimate of the crowd was 5,000, a number that I still think is low.[4] We overflowed the staging area in the north end of the park and blocked a lane even before we started.

Within an hour of riding, we had separated into several groups, with some of my friends on walkie-talkies telling me they were passing through on streets I had not traveled that night. The group I was in made it to the after-party at Saint Mark's Church some time around 9 p.m., where I locked up my bike and milled around the info tables that were set up. Ten minutes after I had finished the ride, I went looking for beer at a nearby bodega on 2nd Avenue. As I walked away from the mass of people still finishing their ride, I saw a phalanx of cops in riot gear marching down the street from the north, hemming people in from that direction. Another group of cops were approaching from the west. More were closing in on the other points of egress.

The police swarmed, arresting any who had not cleared the road, lashing their wrists in plastic tourniquets, the oversized zip ties too many of us would get to know very well the next six days. The same thing was happening at various locations throughout the city, with officers unfurling plastic net fences that they wrapped around cyclists. Their total catch for the evening was 264.

The arrests were very violent, with police dropping cyclists to the ground, putting them in submission holds, pinning them under their own bikes. Shepard was at St. Mark's Church, where the after-party had been planned, and he witnessed much of the turmoil.

"I think they felt like they were showed up," he said. "I'll never forget the end of the ride at St. Mark's Church. The police were literally going into the street and grabbing cyclists and knocking cyclists off of their bikes and arresting them. There was a fury in the streets, fury about a bike ride!"

He added, "I think that's when the other shoe dropped for Critical Mass in New York City. That's when the innocence of the prior five years of the ride ended. It stopped feeling innocent and it started feeling like a fight."

A Sunday Ride Through the City

The media had been frothing all week in anticipation of conflict and they pounced on the story of the first arrests. Immediately we were the top story of the late news and the again for the morning cycle on Saturday, offering the perfect storyline of protestors trying to shut down the city by ignoring red lights. Never mind that we had done the exact same thing the month before and the month before that. There were too many cameras and too many cops for it to be just another Critical Mass. We were global. I got an email the next morning from a friend on a medical mission for Doctor's Without Borders in Darfur, Sudan, telling me he heard about the arrests on BBC World News and wondered if I had been among those incarcerated. While I told him no, my turn was right around the corner.

The Time'sUp! Bike Bloc met Sunday, August 29th, a half hour before the big United For Peace and Justice march. The day was gorgeous, in the mid 80s. There were approximately 200 riders who met at Union Square Park, where I discussed the ride and told them about Time'sUp! There was no prepared route, but we figured we would ride up near Madison Square Garden and observe the main march, then determine further riding from there.

We left Union Square heading west on 17th Street. There were police officers everywhere but many seemed in good spirits, waving us through lights. As we passed through midtown riding north on 6th Avenue, a group of people on scooters came rushing up from behind us. They were dressed in T-shirts and shorts, a couple of them in team jerseys. I yelled out for people to make room and let them pass, but they had other intentions. One of the men on the scooters rode up and swerved suddenly at me, growling. At the next intersection the scooters lined up across 6th Avenue, blocking our way. They weren't out on a casual ride at all. They were cops in plainclothes.

We panicked and, riding much faster, passed 37th Street before seeing a group of squad cars block the way to the north. A number of people doubled back and the front of the ride went west on 37th. The plainclothes scooter cops continued to trail us as we flew down 37th trying to get away. As the front of the ride crossed 7th Avenue, the trap closed on us. Squad cars and SUVs screeched to a halt in the middle of the street. Some of people darted through the line of cops as they unrolled an orange plastic net across 37th Street. I was already past the netting and could have escaped without arrest, but I dismounted my bike instead. An officer rushed up and detained me.

Of the 80 cyclists who were arrested that day, I may have been the only one to voluntarily submit. It wasn't an act of planned civil disobedience, I felt like I would be abandoning a bunch of people behind me who had never gone on a Time'sUp! ride and who weren't expecting to be arrested on their visit to New York City. I was one of the organizers and I had given the introductory speech at Union Square a half hour earlier, telling everyone assembled that we would have a fun ride and we would have an enviable perspective of the demonstrations, given our mobility.

I can't say I would make the same decision today. Considering the conditions I was held in over the ensuing 24 hours—from the filth and razor-wire fencing at Pier 57 to the interminable hours at 1 Center Street shackled to a bench in a waiting cell, or marching in a daisy chain to get fingerprinted—it was not fun. But the transformation of my life personally and professionally can be traced back to that moment on 37th Street and 7th Avenue a few minutes after noon on August 29, 2004.

People Jail, Bike Jail

When I got out of jail the next day, 24 hours after I was arrested, I was charged with five violations, from failure to properly stop at a light, to several different kinds of "disorderly conduct." I was told my bike would be held as evidence until my case worked its way through the legal system, which would likely be months. The same was true of the nearly 350 cyclists who had been arrested over the previous three days, including at Critical Mass.

I reached out to Norman Siegel, a prominent civil rights attorney and former head of the New York City Civil Liberties Union and told him we had a spreadsheet with 230 names of people who were told they might or might not get their bikes back for half a year. He made a quick phone call to the Manhattan District Attorney's office and threatened litigation on our behalf, arguing that holding our bikes as "evidence" of a crime was preposterous and amounted to nothing more than punishment. The District Attorney agreed and convinced the NYPD to relent. A few days later, the first wave of us headed out to a warehouse in Queens to retrieve our bikes.

As we got closer to the September Critical Mass, the media once again set upon us in a frenzy, playing up the arrests from the month before. Several of us were up before dawn to do interviews at Union Square with the morning news. That evening more than a thousand people showed up for the ride, despite trepidation that mass arrests would ensue. The police handed out fliers saying it was illegal to ride in a group on the streets without first obtaining a permit. Several police officers in Community Affairs windbreakers tried to engage riders and ask them for a route or for the leader of the ride, but came away with nothing.

We rode warily around the city, flanked by a phalanx of scooter cops and with a caravan of SUVs in the middle of the ride. Cops filmed us from the SUVs. We were worried we were about to be swept up in orange netting and arrested en masse. Still, the ride made it uptown and through Times Square for the traditional bike lift. Proceeding down Broadway though, the cops made a move, trapping a handful of cyclists and arresting eight. A number of other riders on a crosstown street realized they were being penned in, so they jumped off their bikes and locked them up to whatever they could find nearby, including scaffolding. They then walked away on foot.

When they returned to unlock their bikes thirty minutes later, they came upon the darndest scene: an NYPD Emergency Service Unit truck was nearby and officers were summarily cutting bike locks with a huge power saw. The cops cut through $100 boron-reinforced hexagonal-link bike locks in minutes and stacked the bikes in a pile, before putting them on an old MTA bus. Despite pleas from the owners of several bikes to let them use their keys to unlock their bikes, the officers went on and threatened anyone who got too close with arrest. The police took 40 bikes that night, five times more than the number of arrests.

Lawsuits Abound

Siegel urged several bike-less riders to consider a lawsuit against the NYPD for taking property without due process. A few days later we had gathered a good number of the people who had their property taken and picked five of them to be plaintiffs in a federal lawsuit, Bray v. The City of New York, which sought to obtain a preliminary injunction to prevent the NYPD from taking property without due process.

Very shortly after we served the City, they countersued, seeking injunctive relief from the courts to prevent Critical Mass riders from assembling and riding in a group without first obtaining a permit. I started organizing around the Bray case, helping Siegel's legal team prepare supporting documents. Because I was rather clean-cut, owned a suit, and didn't fit the stereotype of an anarchist or a hippie bike activist, and because I had a long history of participating in rides, Siegel requested I write an affidavit that established the historical account of New York City Critical Mass.

On October 28, 2004, the day before Critical Mass, Federal Court Judge William Pauley convened an unusual meeting with us in his chambers. DiPaola, Neubauer, and I were requested to attend, along with our legal team. We arrived at the Federal Couthouse in southern Manhattan and met several very high ranking NYPD officers standing in a circle. They eyed us with no small degree of scorn. Eventually we filed into a room and sat at a long table opposite some of the most powerful and intimidating men in the NYPD.

First was Chief Bruce Smolka, the Borough Commander for Manhattan South of 59th Street, a bulldog of a man who was notorious for leading the Street Crimes Unit. Four of the members of his unit had killed Amadou Diallo, an unarmed immigrant, in a hail of 41 bullets. Next to Smolka was David Cohen, the Deputy Commissioner for Intelligence, a position that had been created after September 11, 2001 to deal with terrorism (and bikes, apparently). Cohen was a deputy director of operations at the CIA before moving to the NYPD. Next to him was Lt. Daniel Albano, a very large man who I had first met the month before when he showed up at the Time'sUp! space and tried to convince me to give him the route for the ride.

The meeting perfectly captured the culture clash between the loose organization of Critical Mass and the rigid hierarchy of the NYPD. Judge Pauley was hoping to broker a deal between us to resolve our differences and mitigate the need to continue the lawsuit, but it was clear within a few minutes that the NYPD was only interested in establishing the details of a route. Cohen spoke first, demanding we tell him what the route was going to be on the ride the next night. When I explained that Critical Mass didn't have a route, that people rode where they wanted to without a pre-established direction.

"We see you guys out there with your radios," said Cohen. He said he knew we were the leaders and he asked that we cooperate with them. He seemed genuinely flummoxed that we couldn't agree to this simple demand.

We tried to explain that the walkie-talkies were merely for communicating with each other along the way, to know when the ride had broken up so we could try to encourage people to slow down or stop. To them, this was a clear indication that we were leading the ride. I tried to explain from personal experience that on various occasions I had been near the front of the ride and had tried to get people to turn on a particular street, only to see the mass of cyclists ride right by, ignoring my entreaties.

Exasperated after 30 minutes talking in circles about the ride, Cohen leaned over the table and looked me in the eyes, "Just tell us if you're going north or south out of Union Square. You don't have to say anything else."

In the end, the meeting didn't achieve what the cops wanted. Perhaps the only benefit that I saw was the opportunity we had to highlight an inflammatory Op-Ed that NYPD Commissioner Raymond Kelly had published in the *New York Daily News* that morning. The headline was "Extremists Have Hijacked the Ride," and in the article Kelly asserted that anarchists with ill intent had taken over the ride since August and were trying to inflict mayhem on New York City.[5]

The offensive headline and the timing of the story probably worked in our favor. Later that day, Judge Pauley issued his preliminary ruling, wherein he partially upheld the cyclists' injunction by prohibiting the NYPD from taking bikes without due process. He also denied the city's counterclaim. He chastised the NYPD for only bringing their case after they had been sued by us, noting they had years before the RNC ride to make a claim and two more months after, if it was really such a pressing issue.

Judge Pauley argued that the material concerns of the NYPD had to do with state laws regarding parade permits and minutia of traffic rules, so his ruling on the issue would be an overstep of fairness and comity standards with respect to state jurisdiction. In a very memorable line in his decision, he wrote, "This Court declines the City's invitation to wander into a Serbonian bog before a state court has had an opportunity to illumine the path."

If You Can't Beat Them, Sue Them

While there were over 30 arrests on the October ride, a huge group of riders dressed in Halloween costumes still managed to mass up and travel throughout the city. Many people ended at the Time'sUp! space on Houston, where we had a dance party and two DJs playing. Some time around midnight, I went home and caught up on a month's worth of sleep deprivation. When I woke in the morning, I turned on my phone to find several messages explaining that all hell had broken loose a half hour after I left.

The party was packed inside and there were so many bikes outside that we took up the first lane of traffic on Houston Street. Somebody found sawhorse barricades and put them out on Houston near Mulberry Street. At some point a Lieutenant from the nearby precinct, Carolyn Fanale, arrived on the scene dressed in a Washington Redskins jersey and entered the space unannounced. According to people in the party, she started knocking beers out of people's hands and treated people roughly. She then left the space and started writing tickets for open containers outside, now with her badge clearly visible.

When she tried to push her way back into the space, people inside barricaded the door. Fanale and a couple of other cops tried to force the issue, but they couldn't. The people inside even began to chant, "We don't consent to a search! We don't consent to a search!" Sometime during this tussle, an "officer in distress" signal went out and Houston Street in front of the Time'sUp! space suddenly looked like a disaster zone, with dozens of police vehicles blocking the entire road, red and blue lighting up the night. Videotape of the evening shows one officer toting a large shotgun.

During the scuffle, Fanale subdued a woman who was videotaping the scene at the door, wrenching the camera from her hands and tweaking her wrist. Adding insult to injury, the woman was then charged with assault. Fanale claimed she was was assaulted, though charges were never filed. DiPaola woke Siegel and asked him to come down to help negotiate.

When Siegel arrived after 2 a.m., the people inside the space were still blockading the door and officers swarmed all around. Siegel was able to negotiate the release of the people inside the party without further arrests.

Amazingly, police officers with the Emergency Services Unit powered up their saws and cut bicycle locks and took bikes that were hanging on an iron fence alongside the Puck Building. Just a day after a federal judge had ordered the department not to take bicycles, the police did it anyway. Needless to say, Pauley was not pleased with this and in December, he denied their request for permanent injunctive relief.

We were obviously thrilled with the outcome, but the feeling would not last long.

On March 22, 2005, I got a call from DiPaola at Time'sUp! and he said I needed to get down to the space. When I arrived, he handed me an envelope that contained a lawsuit filed by the City of New York, the NYPD, and the New York City Parks Department against Time'sUp as a group and Bill, Leah, Brandon, and me personally, as well as "all those acting in concert" with us. The lawsuit picked up where Judge Pauley left off and tried to get a New York State Court judge to enjoin us and anyone else from riding in a group ride like Critical Mass without obtaining a permit. In a fun new wrinkle, the lawsuit also sought to prevent us—or by extension any group of at least 50 people--from meeting on Parks Department jurisdiction, such as Union Square, without first obtaining a permit. The final and most ludicrous facet of the lawsuit tried to enjoin the four of us, Time'sUp! as an organization, or anyone else from "advertising" Critical Mass rides in any capacity.

The four of us were named because we were the most visible volunteers in Time'sUp! and we had been regularly quoted in the news. They even referred to us in the court document by our titles as they were attributed to us in news stories, so that I was "Matthew Roth, Media and Legal Liaison for Time'sUp!"

There was also a bit of vengeance involved. We had consistently and vocally stood up to the NYPD in the media and in the courtroom. Four volunteers had been leading a press operation in their spare time and after work that went toe-to-toe with a massively financed and well-staffed press team at 1 Police Plaza. That had to rankle them.

On the merits of the lawsuit, it seemed to us on first blush that we were going to win. I wasn't going to face criminal charges, nor would I have to pay money, but I would undoubtedly lose another year of time fighting the case. Fortunately, Siegel and his team of lawyers were happy to defend us *probono*. The assembly and parading parts of the lawsuit seemed like they were winnable based on the precedent in the Pauley decision. The third charge, even to my untrained, non-legal reading, seemed ludicrous. The city actually wanted to keep us from promoting a bike ride?

New York State Judge Michael Stallman didn't use such frank language in February 2006, when he ruled in our favor on all three accounts, but he was quite emphatic in his dismissal of their claims. In a 25-page decision that is still as much a joy to read today as it was back then, Stallman, a Republican appointee who we initially worried might be politically opposed to a ride like Critical Mass, rebuked every one of the NYPD arguments, from the assertion that everyone riding with us constituted a class of people that could be considered "in concert" with us, to the claim that we were sponsors of the ride.

He understood, better than the NYPD probably ever has, that the lack of hierarchy and leadership on the rides is a core issue. "The taxonomy of Critical Mass rides presents a conundrum that permeates all issues in this litigation," he wrote. He also dismantled the NYPD's assertion that Critical Mass constituted a parade or procession that required a permit. Critical Mass, he wrote, did not "seem to conform to the ordinarily understood sense of a march, motorcade, or a promenade."

He did, however, leave one door open to the police, which they would later pursue, when he suggested, "For many reasons, it would be sensible for Plaintiffs [NYPD] to develop and promulgate criteria for what constitutes a parade or procession, as a function of its size." The NYPD would do just that. On February 25, 2007, they simply re-wrote the parade rules to state that any group over 50 had to obtain a permit. Though they were challenged by the Five Borough Bicycle Club, the case was eventually dismissed in 2010, and the rules stand to this day.

No Longer a Fun Ride With Friends

In light of repeated defeats in the courts from 2004 through 2006, the NYPD took it out on us on the streets. Critical Mass became a battle-ground of arrests, tickets, and harassment. Most months dozens of people were arrested for riding their bikes; some months the total was as high as 50. Every month the cops showed up with hundreds of scooters; they positioned mobile tactical command vehicles nearby; they deployed several helicopters; they handed out fliers saying it was illegal to ride in a group without a parade permit; and in March 2005, they literally wrapped the entire northern part of Union Square in orange netting and refused to let riders leave unless they walked single file out of one corner.

As a result of regular monthly arrests, riders began to organize them-selves to fight their charges and educate the newest batch of arrestees. The FreeWheels Bicycle Defense Fund was a nonprofit founded by a group of arrested cyclists. For 18 months, FreeWheels volunteers waited at Central Booking or local precincts after every Critical Mass to greet new arrestees and give them information about how they could fight their charges.

Video evidence also became critical for fighting charges. From as early as the RNC Critical Mass, video had been essential for contradicting NYPD claims in court and in the press. I-Witness Video collective members helped catalog footage for numerous arrests and helped people fight their charges. In one case from the RNC arrests, I-Witness Video was able to get charges dropped after they showed the NYPD had edited their version of videotape to remove evidence that backed up the case of the arrestee.

So many people were taking videos on Critical Mass rides that Time's Up! began holding meetings after every ride to log tape and comb through foot-age to see if anything important turned up. On many occasions, TV and print journalists started showing up at the space on Houston Street to get footage of the rides.

The most visible case of video evidence refuting an NYPD lie occured on the July 25, 2008 Critical Mass. Christopher Long was riding down 7th Avenue in Times Square when one of two officers standing in the middle of the street body-slammed him, sending him flying from his bike to the sidewalk. The officer, a rookie named Patrick Pogan, the son of an NYPD officer and who had only been on the job for two weeks, affirmed in his ar-rest report that Long had been swerving between lanes, obstructing traffic, and that Long deliberately tried to knock him down.

Fortunately for Long, an Indian tourist who was filming the ride from the sidewalk in Times Square recorded the event. The video, which Time's Up!, the Glass Bead Collective, and I-Witness Video uploaded to

YouTube, clearly shows a different picture. In the video, Pogan is in the middle of the street and as Long rides by, the officer lunges into him, body-checking him and then arresting him. Within days the video went viral, with nearly a million views. Pogan was stripped of his badge and gun, and not long after he was fired. The charges against Long were dropped, while the Manhattan District Attorney filed assault and falsifying arrest documents charges against Pogan. In the end, Pogan was found guilty of the felony charge of falsifying the arrest reports, though he got off without doing any time.

A Different Kind of Commissioner

Ironically, as the NYPD under Kelly continued its crackdown over the years, a different agency in the city was about to spark a remarkable transformation of the streets. On April 27, 2007, Mayor Michael Bloomberg appointed Janette Sadik-Khan as Commissioner of the New York City Department of Transportation (NYCDOT). The hope was that Sadik-Khan would take bicycling, transit, pedestrian safety, and public space issues seriously. No one could have anticipated how far she would move the needle in a few short years.

One of her first moves was to hire a number of transit, bicycle, and public space advocates to be special advisers and deputy commissioners, shaking up the ranks of the agency. Some of the bicycle advocates I worked with at the time joked that she was either very serious about changing the car-first culture at the NYCDOT, or she was defanging the bicycle advocacy movement all by herself. Almost as soon as she was sworn in, it was obviously the former.

Street by street, Sadik-Khan removed space from cars and turned it over to pedestrians and cyclists. The first physically separated bike lane was installed on 9th Avenue in Chelsea, which required the removal of a traffic lane and moving the parking lane off the curb and into what would have been the left-most travel lane under the old configuration. Following the success of this lane, the NYCDOT added physically separated lime-green lanes all over the city.

The most dramatic public space transition of all was the trial closure of Broadway through Times Square, the same spot where so many Critical Mass rides had stopped as cyclists raised their bikes above their heads and imagined a different city. In place of cars, the NYCDOT and Times Square Alliance set out lawn chairs. Overnight one of the busiest and most congested parts of the city became an asphalt beach, as tourists swarmed the chairs to relax and take pictures. Despite outrage by the tabloid press, locals and workers even embraced the changes, eating lunch on the chairs and enjoying the new space. The trial closure was a great success and traffic was not adversely affected, so the NYCDOT made the transition permanent.

Sadik-Khan's tenure hasn't been without conflict. Adding over 250 miles of bike lanes in a few short years has led to consternation and backlash from community groups upset at losing parking spaces. But polls show a majority of New Yorkers support the changes.

The Future New York City Critical Mass

In many ways the NYPD crusade to crush Critical Mass has been a success. The January 2012 ride had five participants. The NYPD still showed up in force and tailed the five riders the whole time they rode with a phalanx of scooter cops and unmarked sedans. It is still unclear why the NYPD hasn't relented. They have been immune to the criticism that they wasted millions of dollars policing a bike ride. As long as Raymond Kelly is the boss, there will be no reckoning.

Ryan hypothesizes that it is a power issue:

> They needed to prove that they could control a bunch of cyclists. They are supposed to be the big bad guys who are the last line of defense from pure chaos—and they can't handle a bunch of people with blinky lights? ... They just had to make sure that people did not think that they could [gather and ride together because] it's a powerful tool for change and revolution. Other times I think it's just that it's a good training exercise.

Neubauer lamented the change. "It's so hard to go from where we were, which was so glorious and big and this overwhelming force to this stupid little cat and mouse game that is arbitrary and made up. It's disheartening," he said. "It's so sad to me. They attacked because the police know it was subversive. They can't have a space like that open up."

No matter the NYPD's motivations or how long they continue their crackdown, the current state of cycling in New York City is a far happier story. Cycling has radically expanded and with the flourishing bicycle infrastructure, more and more people are riding. The City's own bicycle data show the number of bike riders started to climb significantly after 2000, the same year Critical Mass became more popular. That growth has been exponential since 2007, when Sadik-Khan took over.

There are plans to increase the number and quality of the bike lanes and New York City will be the first U.S. city to implement a large-scale public bicycle sharing program, similar to those in Paris, France and Barcelona, Spain. City planners throughout the world point to New York City as a best practice example of the radical transformation of the urban realm. Sadik-Khan is a luminary in sustainable transportation circles who speaks at events all over the world.

Even the traditional Critical Mass meeting place on the north side of Union Square Park is nothing like it was in the past. The ratty asphalt has been replaced with expensive pavers. Trees in planters line the edge of the plaza. On 17th Street at the north end of the square, two vehicle lanes have been removed, traffic is only allowed in one direction, and there is a big green bi-directional bike lane that connects Union Square to Central Park 45 blocks north.

Even the cops acknowledge the change, though perhaps ruefully. According to Barbara Ross, a regular Time'sUp! volunteer who has been on Critical Mass rides since the late 1990s, some of the cops who she sees every month recognize her and engage in conversation, just like in the days before the protest. A familiar officer recently exclaimed in disbelief, "Why do you keep coming out? You guys got what you wanted!"

In many ways, the officer was right. No one participating in Critical Mass rides in New York City wanted to be arrested and locked up for riding a bicycle through the streets in a group; no one wanted to spend months navigating the judicial system fighting trumped-up charges for 1st Amendment-protected activity only to have the complaints inevitably dismissed by an impatient judge; no one wanted the stress of being the target of one of the world's largest martial forces as it mobilized thousands of its soldiers to monitor and harass a bike ride; and no one wanted to see the demise of an authentic and magical mobile community space that had opened up in the heart of a regimented and rigid physical urban center.

But we all wanted to feel safe riding our bicycles, free from the unceasing fear of maiming or death. We wanted to know that our simple choice of transportation was not aberrant, or only for the brave. We wanted the space to ride without constant fear of doors swinging open or the daily harassment of drivers who refused to acknowledge our right to the road. We wanted to feel dignified, healthful, and happy as we explored our hulking metropolis, the sun in our eyes and the wind on our cheeks.

Slowly, joyfully, this is starting to happen.

Notes

1 Interviews were conducted by author with Bill DiPaola, Christopher Ryan, Mike Green, Leah Rorvig, Ben Shepard, and Brandon Neubauer.

2 "Best Disruption of Traffic in New York" according to the Village Voice in 2003 *http://www.villagevoice.com/bestof/2003/award/best-disruption-of-traffic-494343/* "Best Socially Aware Tourist Attraction," New York Press *http://www.nypress.com/article-8188-manhattan-living.html*)

3 *New York Daily News http://www.nydailynews.com/archives/news/anarchists-hot-mayhem-police-guard-violent-tactics-article-1.601189*

4 *New York Times. http://www.nytimes.com/2004/08/28/nyregion/preparing-for-convention-protesters-100-cyclists-are-arrested-thousands-ride.html*

5 "Extremists Have Hijacked the Ride." Police Commissioner Raymond W. Kelly. *The New York Daily News*, October 28, 2004

PHOTO BY JONATHAN McINTOSH

Protester at 2004 Republican National Convention in New York City.

Critical Mass
New York City

Portland's Critical Mass: Policed to Death?

By Joe Biel

Critical Mass, the monthly leaderless bicycle ride celebrated in cities around the world, ostensibly ceased to exist in Portland in 2007. But the speculation and conjecture about Portland's Critical Mass continued to bounce around years later. One commonly adopted meme became that Portland had moved beyond the need for Critical Mass. The reality, of course, is far more complicated. Four years ago I began tracking down the people who were present at the beginning and retracing what happened to Portland's Critical Mass for work on the documentary film, *Aftermass: Bicycling in a Post-Critical Mass Portland*. I wanted to know what it meant that Portland, one of the best North American cities for cycling, has virtually no Critical Mass. Was it no longer relevant, did its activity not appeal to a cycling"mainstream," or did a police crackdown succeed at stopping it?

Bicycle pavement markings began to appear all over town in 2005 and difficult connections like bridges were finally redeveloped to accommodate cyclists. It became necessary to risk your life only once or twice on your bike commute to work. In 2006 the League of American Bicyclists awarded Platinum status to the city and *Bicycling* magazine named it the best place to ride a bike in the U.S. Most important, the number of riders was skyrocketing and people were citing their interest in getting around on a bicycle as a reason they were moving to Portland. Mayoral candidates began campaigning on their commitment to bicycling. Tom Potter's slogan was, "Incumbent or Re-cumbent." The recumbent won. The mainstream advocacy organization, the Bicycle Transportation Alliance, had a celebration citing accomplishment of their goals. People began saying that Portland had arrived.

But after the 2007 departure of Critical Mass, street level activism began to disappear and advocates became too comfortable, friendly, and at ease with city government. Bicycle improvements stagnated. Despite political will behind him, Sam Adams, our "bicycle-friendly" mayor, was not receiving public support when needed and began to backpedal when he came under fire for catering to cyclists as a "special interest group."

As bicycle funding increased, people turned out in droves to testify at City Hall about the money being spent on cycling projects. *The Oregonian*, our conservative daily newspaper, fueled the fire and challenged the city's embrace of bicycling. Despite the fact that a bicycle commuter pays for their road usage, necessary build-outs, and even leaves some of their tax money to be spent on car-centric projects, pundits still claim that people who ride bicycles are getting a free ride and not paying their way.

Transportation bicycling in Portland had gotten its first boost in 1971 when Don Stathos's "Bicycle Bill" wrote into law that 1% of highway funding must be spent on pedestrian and bicycle projects. But it took until 1993 and a lawsuit from the Bicycle Transportation Alliance to actually make that happen. Still, everyday cycling did not take off immediately, many potential cyclists finding the unsafe streets a daunting impediment.

Critical Mass started in Portland in 1993 and helped many people find their road legs to become daily cyclists. Group bike rides like Critical Mass create that feeling of safety as well as statistically making the participants truly safer. Public health researcher Peter Jacobsen has proven that as more bicyclists are seen on the streets, motorists become familiar with how to behave around bicyclists and the rate of serious crashes decreases—including all motor vehicle crashes.[1]

Additionally, Transportation Commissioner Charlie Hales said,

> Critical Mass was important. It was out in the street making the point that bikes were a valid means of transportation. There were a lot of people who did not agree with that proposition. There's a time in politics where it's helpful to have someone else wave the big stick. The Bicycle Transportation Alliance and Critical Mass were hugely influential [in 1993].

Most riders described a nervous feeling unique to Critical Mass and absent in other bike rides in Portland. Yet there was often no distinction in the way Critical Mass behaved, nor in how many participants it had. Portland's bicycle coordinator Roger Geller even admitted in a letter to the Police Department that Portland Bureau of Transportation bicycle rides would move through stop signs as a group much the same as Critical Mass. During its decline, Critical Mass was attracting far fewer participants vis-à-vis police officers while many other rides were much larger. Where was this tension coming from?

In December 1994, after a year and a half of peculiar tickets being issued for nonexistent violations at Critical Mass rides, Fred Nemo helped organize 17 people into a class action suit in federal court. A year later they were awarded $50,000 and some documents that began to explain the origin of police harassment. Instead of referring to the group as "Critical Mass," in these documents the police always dubbed them the "Anarchist Bicycle Rally," which seemed to indicate bad intelligence on the part of the police. No one else had called it that.

These documents were shocking, but also nothing new. Beginning in 1993, the Portland Police Department had been spying on Critical Mass through their Criminal Intelligence Division (CID). CID had been around since at least the 1950s and was originally dubbed "The Red Squad." Denying its existence back then, the Red Squad spied on communists and undermined the political activities of its citizens. Similar in fashion to the tactics of the FBI's COINTELPRO in the 1970s, the Red Squad set out to discredit radical politics and protect the status quo. Over time it went through several rebrandings but its function remained similar. Michael Munk, a professor of history and author of *The Portland Red Guide*, says the Red Squad (CID)—and its current form Criminal Intelligence Unit (CIU)—never significantly changed its goals or function since sixty years ago when it interrogated members of the Industrial Workers of the World and whose bodies were later found in the river.

Potter, the police chief in 1993 and mayor in 2005, tried to explain in a 2010 interview that CID is supposed to work on things like bomb threats, Ku Klux Klan assassination plans, or violence brewing within the city. When shown that CID was spying on transportation bicyclists he responded that it was a waste of time and denied having had knowledge that it was happening. The current Portland Police acting Traffic Captain Eric Schober frames this use of CID as appropriate, saying blandly, "CID's job is to make other officers aware of problems that could happen." But in 1993, CID was only three officers in a police force of over 1,000 and had a tiny budget. That they found it reasonable to use scarce resources to spy on Critical Mass seemed suspicious. Critical Mass hadn't even happened yet—they were still a dozen people meeting at a downtown cafe to discuss the climate of transportation bicycling in the city of Portland.

• • •

In July of 1993, two months before CID began spying on Critical Mass, the "X Ray Riot" unfolded several blocks from where Critical Mass would meet, resulting from the police interrupting a punk rock show and a later series of escalating protests directed at George Bush, Sr. and the local authorities.

A local activist, Douglas Squirrel, attended the subsequent meetings of both Critical Mass and B.E.I.R.U.T. (Boisterous Extremists for Insurrection against Republicans and other Unprincipled Thugs), the group who had organized the George HW Bush protests in summer 1993. Squirrel's presence seemed to be sufficient evidence for the police department to claim that Critical Mass was organized by B.E.I.R.U.T. and thus that it was an anarchist organization. When the first ride attracted over 150 participants, the police hung back and watched from a block or two away. In their after-action report, the officers on duty sound almost afraid, like they expected something more than joyful bicyclists riding in a group. Before the ride, police intelligence claimed, "The purpose of the Rally is to have approximately 50 to 100 bike riders impede the flow of traffic on West Burnside and SW Broadway during rush hour traffic," while the Critical Mass meeting notes that I obtained from the very same police file paint an entirely different picture. "There is a definite school of thought that is agreed to by the participants that this event is to be structured as non-confrontational as possible and that we actually try and educate people."

In September 1993, the first ride took place. Advertised from the beginning as a self-empowerment ritual, Critical Mass put forward language like: "Tired of being run off the road by cars? Of riding alone, afraid, intimidated? Come ride your bike or board for a sustainable, environmental future!" Critical Mass began to draw people from various types of cycling. Despite this, police enforcement behavior appears to have been inconsistent and irrational over the next year, starkly contrasting with the friendly demeanor that these officers typically displayed. After many tickets were issued and then successfully contested and dropped, the clash culminated in November 1994 with the police surrounding the riders, ordering them to disperse from a public park, and immediately ticketing the riders and issuing park exclusion orders.

Actually, that month the Critical Mass ridership had become wise to the presence of a police spy within their group and had discreetly changed their meeting spot at the last minute. The police force waited at the usual spot for the group to congregate and begin their ride. When the ride was spotted near Pioneer Square the officers rode the mile to meet with them as the ride was concluding. Frustrated, they delivered the exclusion orders and citations.

No actual law had been broken. The group was not demonstrating in a public park as the exclusion order claimed. With the ride concluded, participants were merely enjoying a public place as individuals. It got uglier for the police when it was revealed that officers were restraining people who were trying to comply with the police order to disperse. The resulting federal court case demonstrated Squirrel's effective ability to cross-examine a police officer, and gained the aforementioned $50,000 in damages for the participants. The ensuing public release of documents confirmed the presence of an illegal spy and the police insistence on referring to the ride as the Anarchist Bicycle Rally.

Squirrel used his portion of the money to purchase lights for future Critical Mass participants who showed up without them. The biggest reward, however, was that police harassment and heavy-handed enforcement at Critical Mass rides ground to a halt for a few months.

Still, the documents provide little clue as to why the police became so obsessed with spying on and spending so much overtime pay on enforcement during the rides. Looking at other CID cases where spying is involved sheds a little more light. In police work, a sole source of information without corroboration is a dangerous and a slippery slope. Additionally, once a spying unit has infiltrated an organization, pressure mounts to prove that the spying is justified. Such justifications require turning standard traffic violations into trumped-up charges like "disturbing the peace" or "disorderly conduct."

Traffic lights and stop signs were treated as yields by Critical Mass riders. They explained the purpose of this was for safety and keeping the ride together. But the police explained that this was done to block traffic for longer periods of time and cause disturbances, an explanation that the media repeated until it stuck. This in turn attracted cyclists who believed that this behavior is what the ride was designed for. As ridership grew, so did incidents. Some people thought the front of the ride should go through a red light—even if the tail of the ride was a mile behind. Without leaders or rules, these things could happen and slowly annoy longtime participants until they stopped showing up. Likewise, parents, children, old-timers, and anyone who couldn't afford the standard $290 traffic ticket stopped coming.

Geller reported in an internal email to the city:

> Motorists, when they see a large group of cyclists at a stop sign, will themselves stop and allow the cyclists to proceed. Something in human nature allows this type of polite interaction. However at the Critical Mass ride, cyclists were required to come to a complete stop at stop signs. This obviously delayed their crossing of the street and delayed the motorists who stopped and somewhat defeated their purpose in stopping.

Some participants believe that the aggressive new riders were actually moles and agent-provocateurs—undercover police or hired agents who came to the movement for the purpose of disrupting it. They figure when spying proved ineffective at stopping the rides, the police shifted tactics.

When I first began reviewing the police documents, it struck me as a mistake that within the Critical Mass files were accounts of anti-fur protests, something called the "Fuck Authority Coffeehouse," Buy Nothing Day rallies, and George Bush, Sr. protests. But the police believed that all these events were conducted by the same group of people. They saw political struggles as more interconnected than even the Critical Mass participants seemed to.

• • •

As a result of finding the police had been spying on him, Squirrel prosecuted the police department for opening a file on him—and won. After a long period of the city stalling and stonewalling, the trial finally took place from December 18-19, 1995. During the trial, Squirrel learned that the police had been spying on him and his friends since 1990, when B.E.I.R.U.T. posted a flyer about an upcoming Bush visit.

Officer Greg Kurath—who also happened to be the officer communicating CID's Critical Mass intelligence reports to the police department—came out to testify in defense of police spying. Kurath cited how spying had been helpful in catching the 130-pound massage therapist for the heinous crime of blocking the sidewalk and insisted that the spying was necessary because he suspected something more was going on and that the group might have been using a public park for some kind of unspecified "criminal activity."

Kurath's defense would have held up if the group was meeting in front of the police station, but meeting in a public park is not a crime. Even if police suspect someone might be up to criminal activity, it did not—at that time—give them the right to spy. The 2001 PATRIOT Act changed that, simplifying spying laws across the board to "protect against domestic terrorism." But police had always been able to investigate anyone conspiring to commit a crime, even misdemeanors like blocking the sidewalk. Despite this, a 2001 federal court concluded, "If the...investigation cannot begin until the group is well on its way toward the commission of terrorist acts, the investigation may come too late to prevent the acts or identify the perpetrators." But if crimes could always be investigated, why were the new measures necessary? Was local law enforcement actually fighting social change? Perhaps, as J. Edgar Hoover believed, it wasn't crimes that needed investigating, it was political ideas.

In March 2001, Commissioner Hales publicly rode with Critical Mass and observed firsthand the police misbehavior. In a 2010 interview, Hales admitted that he had attended the ride discreetly for a few months before attending publicly. "What I was concerned about was the fact that the police thought this was a big deal at all," he said. "Hey! These are just some people riding bikes. If someone gets hurt they'll call 9-1-1. Why don't we leave these folks alone?"

In a 2011 interview, Acting Traffic Captain Eric Schober said, "Our stance is completely different now, today, than it was twelve years ago. I remember those days. I remember the victims (sic)—people getting their cars bashed in, dented. The whole group would take up three lanes of traffic and block traffic on purpose." But the police's own after-action reports don't mention these or other incidents of cyclists causing property damage during the rides. And when verbal conflicts occurred, it seemed to result from the belief of police or motorists that bikes didn't belong on the road in the first place. When I inquired about the lack of property destruction in the police reports, Schober responded, "There may be other documents that you don't know about."

Through the framing of what their intelligence reports were telling them, the police understood these gleeful faces committing traffic offenses to be part of an anarchist conspiracy to intimidate and antagonize citizens and motorists. In their after-action reports, police make a distinction between "person" and "bicyclist" and discuss the proximity of bicycles to women and children. They even claimed the bicycle could be used as a weapon.

Commissioner Hales commented, "The police bureau was invested, I think, in the old idea that streets are for cars and bikes need to be somewhere else."

In August 2002, *Bikesummer*, an annual traveling bicycle culture festival, descended on Portland and the city-sponsored Critical Mass ride was attended by approximately 1,500 riders. The police response was severe and heavy-handed. One gentleman, suspected of being a leader, had his hands and feet handcuffed together and was carried away by the handcuffs as they cut into his flesh. One person was arrested for videotaping an arrest. Another was arrested for asking questions of arresting officers. The police response was probably inflated due to large protests the same month for a visiting President George W. Bush. Both incidents were kept in the same file.

Angry letters stacked up in the mayor's office about the police's brutality. The police's response to the ride incensed citizens, who began to see bicycling as a political issue. When the U.S. invaded Iraq in 2003, weekly bicycle protests further confused the police department's intelligence reports and hurt the relationship that the city had been developing with monthly Critical Mass rides, which had begun to include sit-down meetings between city officials, Critical Mass participants, and the police.

As things began heating up, Geller made public appearances at Critical Mass and wrote public reports to city officials about what he saw there:

> While we've all read both directly and secondhand reports from citizens about these monthly rides, the August [2003] ride almost universally elicited smiles, waves, and cheers from people it passed...A motorist stopped without having a stop sign to allow the group of cyclists, who did have a stop sign, to pass. Again, all cyclists came to a complete stop as they came to the stop line, looked both ways, saw the motorist not moving, and then tentatively proceeded through the intersection. Observing this, an officer in a squad car got on the loudspeaker and advised the cyclists that they "had to allow the motorist to proceed," which would have been fine had the motorist any intention of proceeding. She didn't. She was trying to be polite and helpful and allow the cyclists to pass as a group...During the course of the

ride I saw several motorists violate traffic laws right in front of police offi-
cers, for the same types of offenses for which cyclists are commonly cited: not
coming to a complete stop at stop signs and running red lights. No tickets in
those cases I observed...When the ride began to head across the Hawthorne
Bridge and the bicycle officers dropped off from the ride, many riders wished
them well and thanked them for their presence.

But in the police after-action report for the same ride, between blacked out pages, the conclusion was, "Critical Mass rides need to be monitored. When criminal acts or traffic violations occur, action needs to be taken. The consequence for the rider's actions is the most effective tool to date."
In a 2005 interview, Geller said:

I really like Critical Mass. On the Critical Mass rides I've been on, the
reception from the public has always been very positive. People on the side-
walks will clap, laugh, and cheer for the cyclists going by. Everybody loves
a parade. I look at Critical Mass as a very pro-bike statement and I think
we've got to a point within the city where the rides are running well.

While Hales' and Geller's personal appearances at the ride had tamed law enforcement for a period, the city's amicable relationship with the ride didn't last. In January 2005, Mayor Potter joined Critical Mass on a friend-ly ride that elicited smiles all around. But because the police union had an old and fractured relationship with their former chief, the police response to the ride the following month was harsh and produced a new set of angry letters to City Hall.

By the end of 2006, police attention had returned, meetings with police re-sumed, and officers were outnumbering participants on an ongoing basis. At-tendance dropped to an average of fifteen riders per month. The main reason cited by former participants for the drop-off was that the ride was no longer fun. Law enforcement had targeted the ride and developed strict enforcement policies that exceeded the standards generally imposed on traffic. Increased enforcement and officers expecting trouble created a self-fulfilling prophecy.

At a party, a traffic commander admitted to a ride participant that the police's goal in the second round of meetings was to shut down Critical Mass. Critical Mass's notoriety would attract new participants who would quickly learn of the tense situation with police and either never be seen again or join the embittered struggle to change the conversation about Critical Mass. Jonathan Maus, journalist proprietor of *BikePortland.org* re-ferred to this phenomenon as the "lightning rod of controversy." The police had more resolve and Critical Mass slowly faded away from Portland.

A Parallel Story in Santa Barbara, California

On the evening of February 29, 2008, Critical Mass rolled through Santa Barbara—a city with only 4% bicycle commuting despite its tropical temperatures and conducive terrain. The ride drew about 30 people and snaked its way back and forth across town. Wearing red clown noses and riding in circles can annoy some motorists, though most were left hardly inconvenienced.

But there were still complaints. Detective Jaycee Hunter was dispatched to the scene, driving an unmarked police car—due to being assigned to anti-gang surveillance. Hunter, who considered himself an authority on Critical Mass, wrote in his report that it was a wonder Homeland Security was not called out.

> I have had extensive training and experience with this anarchist bicycle group. I had received training of their terrorist-type behaviors with law enforcement and am aware that I must be extremely conscious of officer safety due to their radical, aggressive/violent attitudes toward law enforcement officers. In the process of the ride, they will intentionally and maliciously commit numerous traffic violations, often endangering their lives and the lives of other citizens.

It's fortunate that things did not get more out of control, given this perspective. When Detective Hunter pulled up behind some stragglers at a red light, Michael Howard Miller and some other riders jumped a curb. Hunter pursued Miller and pulled his Taser out on the fly. The other riders doubled back to see what was going on and Hunter describes it thusly, "I was in extreme danger. I was surrounded by a rapidly approaching, militant, anarchist group who were behaving in the exact manner that I was trained they would behave."

Carleigh Michelle O'Donnell emerged from the crowd and began asking Hunter questions. Hunter describes the encounter as, "She attempted to engage me in discussion as a distraction technique so the group could creep closer to him and snatch away [Miller]." He waved off the crowd with his Taser and called for backup, eventually arresting three riders, including John Patrick Flannery.

Flannery's first Critical Mass ride in Santa Barbara happened to be this one. There were no major incidents during the ride until it ended up in Rainbow Park and he heard someone say "Oh my god, they got him." Flannery evaluated the scene: The officer was sitting with his knee on Miller's neck and pointing a laser-guided taser at people's chests, like a scene out of a *Terminator* movie.

Flannery, 47, a former communications company operator who had lost a leg several years before after being hit by a drunk driver, was on the sidewalk during Miller's arrest. Flannery was ordered to cross the street but possessing only one leg, he determined it would be too difficult to comply. He cited his handicapped status and the officer arrested him for interfering with a police officer. Noting that his $4,000 custom-built carbon fiber bicycle was beginning to fall over, Flannery reached over to steady it. That action got him a further charge of resisting arrest. But most peculiarly, he was also charged with being a member of a global terrorist and anarchist network.

A study by Research And Development (RAND) Corporation found that local law enforcement agencies define "terrorism" much more broadly than did their federal counterparts, often applying the label to environmentalist, animal rights, and union activities that affect large, powerful employers who often work closely with police.

In a meeting at City Hall the following month, the cyclists told their story. For a cop to pull a Taser for running a red light, they said, seemed extreme. Hunter appeared out of nowhere, swerving the car to a cinematic *Adam-12* stop too close for their comfort, and turning on the lights simultaneously as he jumped out of the unmarked car. They feared he was planning on crashing into them. Riders jumped the curb as to not be run over. There was next to no warning. The group argued that inconveniencing motorists does not equate to being run over by a car—an ongoing problem for cyclists in Santa Barbara and across the globe.

Hunter failed to appear at the meeting. A year later in court, when Flannery informed the officers that the entire incident was filmed by TV news, all of his charges were dismissed. Due to prior court appearances, Miller got sentenced for sixty days in jail for jumping the curb as the officer drove up. O'Donnell received ten days for requesting Hunter's badge number and information about Miller's arrest. She was charged with interfering with a police officer. The Judge threw out everyone's charges of global terrorism.

Flannery does not plan a countersuit against the police department because he fears having, as he says, "a target painted on his back. It's a small town."

How Do We Know When We've Arrived?

Early on the morning of March 22, 2011, Portland Police Sergeant Joe Santos was riding his bicycle to work when a motorist drove past him at a distance of a few inches. When both arrived simultaneously at a traffic light, Sergeant Santos rode to the right of the car. When the light turned green, the car aggressively swerved into Santos' portion of the lane. Santos recovered, switching to riding on the left side of the car, slapping it as he passed. The car next swerved at him on the left, pushing him into the oncoming traffic lane.

At the next intersection, the car went into reverse and attempted to back into Santos on his bike. Jumping off the bicycle, Santos ran to the sidewalk. The bicycle was struck and the car sped away. The police officer called in the license plate to 9-1-1 and the driver was arrested on second degree assault. The officer eventually dropped the charges, preferring to sit down with the motorist and resolve the matter outside of court.

In an interview in August 2011, Santos said:

> *It seemed like this guy had it out for me and wanted to run me off the road. But the nature of me being a cop and the [officers on the scene] knowing me, I had instant credibility. I think a lot of officers are just like the general community: they view cyclists as aggressive and rogue and probably the problem half of the time. I think that's a mischaracterization. When a cyclist isn't doing something wrong, most people don't even notice. But when they see someone run a red light, that sticks. And cops are no different than the general public.*

In Portland and across the globe, one thing that cannot be solved by markings on pavement or enforcement of the rules is a culture shift. Portland's culture shift may be a little faster and further along than Santa Barbara's or many places in the U.S., but coming quickly behind that shift is a reaction and feeling that the old way of doing things is being threatened. And while the people threatened are increasingly marginal and in the minority, they do occasionally tend to find themselves in positions of power—the police department, reporting for a major news organization, city planning, traffic engineering, or working in the mayor's office. And as shown in these examples, perception forms your opinion and can make all real-world facts irrelevant.

The month before Officer Santos was targeted on his bicycle, in Porto Alegre, Brazil, a Critical Mass turned bloody. A man accelerated his Volkswagen Golf through the pack of 100, injuring 30 cyclists, many of them severely.

The driver, Ricardo Jose Neis, 47, an official of the Brazilian central bank, checked himself into a private psychiatric clinic immediately after the event but was later transferred to prison, as his act seemed deliberate. Each video of the ride shows a far-from-aggressive pack of cyclists, including the elderly, many women, children, and even a dog on a trailer. A young boy can be seen clearly in the videos of the incident just feet from the front of the car as it tears through the group of cyclists like dominos.

While Neis faces seventeen accounts of attempted murder, he is a powerful banker with a powerful lawyer and it is likely that his attempts at insanity pleas will prevent the discussion from getting too close to discussing his powerful stature and how it shields him from justice. Later, in a pre-trial interview with the press, Neis said, "I was panicking. I was scared. I was afraid...I ask myself often: Did I evaluate the situation correctly at the time? I really think so." A year later he is still awaiting trial and sentencing. And while his defense arguments have publicly changed several times, he has no remorse for his actions.

Jacobsen's "safety in numbers" study proves the safest thing we can do is put more bicyclists onto the streets. More people must also join together to challenge old ideas like, "The street is for cars."

Forty years since the Oregon Bicycle Bill, it is happening. In Portland, the World Naked Bike Ride, a free, grassroots event originally organized to draw attention to the vulnerability of cyclists, was described to me as attracting "a mere 4,000" people on a cold night in 2011 because the previous year it drew over 10,000 participants. The Bridge Pedal, a for-profit bicycle ride across each of Portland's many bridges attracted over 19,000 participants the same year. Those visible groups create a public pressure campaign that allows advocates to ask for more from governments. The more vocal everyone is in cities across the world, the more this cultural shift can move forward unimpeded, leaving the dinosaurs in the dust.

Notes

1   "Safety in numbers: more walkers and bicyclists, safer walking and bicycling" *Injury Prevention*, PL Jacobsen. *http://injuryprevention.bmj.com/content/9/3/205.abstract*

London Critical Mass

By Des Kay

Central London Critical Mass attracts cyclists from all corners of the metropolis. For eighteen years we have been gathering on the South Bank of the Thames under Waterloo Bridge. An informal coalition known as Cyclists Have A Right to Move (CHARM) ushered in London's own Critical Mass in early 1994. What started with a handful back then has progressed to between a few hundred and thousands of cyclists, sound systems, decorated bikes, skateboarders, wheelchairers, roller skaters, and pedestrians. One of the original CHARMers—Chris Eardley — explained the thinking behind the protest:

> *"First and foremost, it's a chance for cyclists to get together and have a good time. A couple of hours a month of slowing the traffic up is really just our way of pointing out to people what a hideous bloody mess the roads are in the rest of the time. The whole thing lasts for about 2 hours usually, so obviously some people drift away during that time. . . Others stick around and have a bit of a party afterwards—we usually try and finish up somewhere like Trafalgar Square or Hyde Park. The police are very cooperative nowadays."*

Over the years there have been a few focused rides tinged with politics or environmentalism, climate change, or poor road planning, for example, or visits to mourn a precious cyclist's life, mown down on London's busy streets. Before the ride starts, printed documents circulate among the riders. More often than not, it's a great social event with riders and observers having fun, a few regulars but a constant flux of new riders coming and going over the years.

Callum Wilson made some observations after the September 1995 ride, capturing the quirky experiences that often comprised a Critical Mass ride in London at the time.

> *One guy had a sign that said "I love taxi drivers—I love you Mr. Taxi driver." The chap reckoned that taxi drivers are too used to being called wankers! At one point the whole Mass stopped to let a guy dressed head to toe in black PVC cross the road. Mr. black PVC said to a biker, "You guys are weird." An observer on the sidewalk called out "I would have come today, but I had both my wheels nicked." Someone was shouting at all sports cars, "big car small willy!"*

Six months later, in March 1996, Wilson recorded more memories:

> *There was a Scandinavian chap who had a covered recumbent bike that he had cycled all the way from Harwich. It looked like the front section of*

a WWII fighter plane! He was warm and dry—unlike the rest of us. We had an odd bunch of motorbike cops that time. One of them was really pro-Critical Mass and helped riders by telling an irate driver that "cyclists may protest in London if they wish to!"

This "happy coincidence of bicycle anarchy and chaos in their most joyful forms," had a few police outriders on motor bikes in the early days who were mostly friendly and helpful, and would do all the corking necessary to assist us on our way. The same cannot be said for Metropolitan Sergeant #86, who at every opportunity would race up behind some of our more boisterous massers and quote yet another bit of the law.

Once I was cycling well ahead of the mass towards Piccadilly Circus (on a one way road) in the empty street. I was enjoying the space by cycling big wide circles waiting for everyone else to catch up. Met 86 came flying up and said, "This is one way street." Eh? On another occasion, a lady was blocking a taxi from blasting its way through the Mass. A few moments later, officer 86 arrived to say, "You don't have any lights..." The cheeky reply: "Someone nicked them—it's not safe to leave our bikes anywhere in London—go and find who nicked them rather than hassling me."

The only incident that I saw was when a taxi tried the old trick of ramming cyclists to get through instead of waiting 5 minutes. The driver got quite upset—especially when one chap lifted his leather jacket out of the open window and tried to bargain with, "Wait here and get your jacket back..." Some youngsters then started kicking the taxi (not very hard, i.e. noise rather than damage) which was a little out of order. It's no use getting into trouble, it just brings our reputation down.

The largest London Mass was in the middle of 2008 to oppose police controlling the event. They wanted to bind us to all sorts of bureaucracy, such as sending them a route map (!) and a list of organisers (!). A month earlier we were handed letters purporting that our London Friday night get-together was unlawful. They eventually cottoned on to the joys of joining us on bicycles, and their support and cooperation continued until the legality was questioned.

I spearheaded the London Critical Mass court case to stop the Metropolitan Police from making it illegal. It was taken to the highest courts in the land via Friends of the Earth Rights and Justice Centre and we initially won, then lost on appeal, and finally on October 20, 2008, the case went to the House of Lords where it was heard by five Law Lords. Their decision was that, "the appeal is allowed and Critical Mass is a commonly or customarily held procession without organisers and therefore does not need to inform the police of each ride." Once that precedent was set, no mass bike ride in the country has had any interference. The police must believe that after 18 years, we're grown up enough to go out on our own.

I wrote a letter commenting on the outcome, excerpted here:

> *I'm delighted that the House of Lords yesterday unanimously upheld my appeal.[1] This case has now been running for nearly three years since Inspector Gomm first handed out his flyers telling us that the Mass was unlawful and that we needed to give advance notice and decide in advance what route we were going to take. I'm glad to say that isn't the case and we no longer have to fear the threat of arrest.*
>
> *The London Mass is exempted from the requirements of the Public Order Act and so there is no need to give advance notice. That should give cyclists a lot of comfort. In particular, anyone who is interested in self-stewarding the ride will now feel considerably more comfortable. However, the House of Lords had lots of very positive things to say generally and there is much that is useful in the judgment for other people wishing to set up Critical Mass Cycle Rides elsewhere in the country.*

Since we won, the situation has become much better. Also, our sound systems used to be shut down by police in the vicinity of Parliament but that too no longer seems to be much of a problem. So, on the whole the London Critical Mass itself seems to have improved in the last few years. At 18, London Critical Mass has matured towards a more relaxed and laid-back kind of affair.

We haven't lost that radical edge, but we now are more aware of the power we have to command the roads we choose to cycle along. Our corking skills are almost innate now and with no police in tow and regular stops while the cyclists have an opportunity to mass up, we enjoy a splendid social get-together catching up with old friends and making new ones. There are opportunities to discuss whatever is on the agenda and our common interest to ride together. Critical Mass liberates the streets that are usually dominated by motorists, while interacting with Friday night social gatherings scattered over our route.

The initial coming together at our meeting point under Waterloo Bridge on the south bank of the Thames between the National Theatre and the British Film Institute (which has splendid watering and ablution facilities) is just as important as the ride itself. As the numbers build, the social interactions increase, punctuated by the odd cheer and ringing of mass bells and hooters, the arrival of a sound system, demonstrations of new led displays, wireless music connected to low wattage speaker arrays, the latest bike technology for some to gawp at, watching the displays build up by the flamboyant few...

Students gather outside the classroom to start their weekend pushing pedals together. Old friends who don't see each other in between the rides catch up. Someone gives out cake, some drink Film Institute brews. The excitement builds with anticipation and suddenly for no specific reason people are riding the slope that leads to the big roundabout at the end of the bridge dominated by the IMAX Roundhouse where we are able watch others emerge and re- orientate into cycling mode, ready for the adventure that lies ahead.

Of course there are many different personal reasons that attract the riders. London Critical Mass has included the cyclist commuter who wants to wind down after a week in front of a computer, the 40-ton trucker who wants to try out his new hybrid, the foreign student who misses her hometown Critical Mass, or the theatrical extrovert dressed in flamboyant costume with matching cycle. The radicals, the anarchists who revel in the power of stopping traffic, the parents with their kiddy seats, the young people who were in those same seats when they first came so long ago. Bicycles like the penny farthing, the tallbike, the laid-back low-down recumbent. The good, the bad and the ugly—they never look that bad when they are on a bicycle.

Young and old ride together which lifts the spirit. The younger carry the energy and excitement and the older, longer-term riders are the anchors that help with continuity. Doug, one of our elders, now at the edge of his eighth decade, has contributed a great deal, including adding to our website, filming numerous videos, and helping prepare this essay.

Ian, who has spurred us on, towing his excellent home-built sound-system trailers, recalls the influence Critical Mass has had on his life:

> I used to love cycling as a kid but by 2002 I no longer had a bike and had forgotten the joys of riding. Then someone lent me some wheels and persuaded me to come down to the Mayday Critical Mass in London. I had a great time and found it hugely inspiring. Ever since then I have been a keen cyclist and cycling advocate. I don't often go on the Mass any more but it is something I like to support because it got me back into cycling and I hope it will continue to do the same for others. It also got me into designing and building mobile sound systems.

We have a thousand different agendas yet drift through London's streets much like a flock of birds not knowing when or where the next turn will be until the collective will moves the Mass, unexpectedly perpendicular to wherever we thought we were heading, sometimes causing the front runners to come chasing back and submit to the collective will.

Most overt hostility comes from drivers, particularly taxi drivers. Occasionally drivers try to deliberately ram our corkers out of their way and with no police around there is little that can be done about it, other than to protest loudly and increasingly take photos or videos. We no longer have police accompanying the ride but when they did some of them also seemed to be fairly hostile.

There is some limited hostility from some other cycling groups but that doesn't seem to deter them from joining in with Critical Mass when they want to make a point. Some other groups do not seem to believe in anything resembling direct action. London Critical Mass has a fairly strict non-hierarchical set-up, anarchic if you like, and for that reason cooperation with some other groups can sometimes be tricky, unless they too are non-hierarchical.

While mostly we have arbitrary routes on the day, decided by a group of front riders, our ride is sometimes joined by other political groups which we allow to lead from the front, providing no riders object. So there are times when, through the sheer willpower of a few riders, we manage to stumble upon a demonstration where we can show our solidarity, or a protest camp where we can all gather round as temporary participants. Or we protest about dangerous roads and intersections or visit somewhere where a cyclist has been killed. For the most part, this doesn't seem to create conflict. I believe the collective heart beats to the same rhythm—saving the world, supporting the oppressed. Most of the time we ride through the Capital's streets being oppressed by drivers who believe they own the road. Perhaps this gives us more vigor to fight for just causes. Our combined power gives us strength to join other protests and Occupy movements and realize the potential we all possess to make a difference when acting together.

The idea of mass rides, whether for leisure or protest, developed from Critical Mass. We realize that a small number of riders can make a significant impact by spreading across a main artery to slow down traffic, making a important statement about safety for cyclists and pedestrians. Any ride which is not taking place on the last Friday of the month is described as, "A Critical Mass Style Ride," which has little or nothing to do with our regular ride.

Critical Mass has empowered people to become stronger and braver on London's terrifyingly unfriendly roads and strengthened their resolve to use the power of mass cycle action to influence decision-making. The politicians and road planners are beginning to take notice and there are currently regular protest rides to make London's streets safer for cyclists.

Sixteen cyclists were killed on London's roads during 2011, so we still have some way to go in changing London's transport priorities to safeguard our journeys. London Critical Mass continues.

Note

1   *http://www.publications.parliament.uk/pa/ld200708/ldjudgmt/jd081126/metro-1.htm*

Protesting for bicycle access to bridge crossing the Bosphorous from Europe to Asia in Istanbul, Turkey, 2010.

The Johnny Appleseed of Critical Mass

By Jason Meggs

"Critical Mass changed my life!" he shouted, a gentle guy with a big heart and a huge smile, wiggling and wheeling a long-horned cruiser alongside my ride, chatting congenially with a breathless, toothy grin. His cheeks were rosy in the late summer's eve dusk, and we were carried along in a throng of bikes still moving massively after a lovely ride which had surely crested 20 miles and lasted more than two hours.

I, the interviewer paused to contemplate as the bikes flowed on. Silence in motion, a street transformed: gentle clicking of gears, jingling of bells, peace in the streets so rare—the giddy hush of a street liberated from motor traffic—giggles in the distance, waves and bike lifts, corkers diligently holding the line so we could pass, and every so often a dog in a basket or a "tunebike" setting the pace and the mood, pause for but a moment to take it all in before replying; the tape recorder came back to my luscious lips and I cajoled, "Do tell!"

> Really! No, REALLY! I'm not joking: it changed everything about my life. I used to have a car, and since finding Critical Mass I realized, I don't need it anymore! I gave it up, I sold it, and it's great! Now I get almost everywhere by bike, and don't miss the car at all. It's literally like a whole new world opened up—I got new friends.

He leaned closer, and swung a big arm all around to show. "I mean really, I got a whole new community."

"Critical Mass!" I confirmed. "Friendship in motion. Magic on wheels."

> Yeah yeah, but it changed more than that. I began to see the whole world differently. I started to FEEL the whole world differently. I started to realize that there were so many things I thought I needed, that I was struggling to have, but then I started to see I really didn't need them, they were really just things that didn't serve me. So I just started giving them up, one thing after another, but instead of getting more empty, actually my life was getting more full. The new things I was finding were more rewarding—I stopped buying so many things. I started living more in the moment. Now I feel better than ever and wouldn't dream of going back. It may sound like a cliché, but it's true!

He looked me in the eye and threw back his head, letting out a gusty "WAAAAHOOOO!" then peeled away and rolled off into the throng which stretched now as far as the eye could see front and rear— bicyclists as confetti, a milicyclist snaking serpent of joy.

A few more moments of jingling, chattering crowd noise, and my radio voice kicks in again.

"There you have it folks! A whole new you awaits and just like you it's FREE! So come on down to Critical Mass!" <<click>> Off went the tape recorder. One more interview "in the can" and ready for the regularly rowdy three hours of Friday night call-in chaos on Bicycle Liberation Radio.[1]

That lovely little testimonial moment happened well before San Francisco's 10th Anniversary Ride. Critical Mass had already gone global. It had seen its first major explosions in the press, and power struggles in the streets. It was just one of many interviews on one of hundreds of rides; but that night on the air, recounting the interview sparked my own reflections, the ways Critical Mass changed my own life and others around me. After twenty years of Critical Mass, through thick and thin, it's a bit mind-boggling.

Critical Mass made me a video activist and filmmaker; it sent me to jail and then to law school, and again to graduate school for healthy cities. It provided us the space to build a vibrant bicycle culture, and to feel free and alive in cities that otherwise felt hostile, caustic, and alien. It inspired art and was a central space to connect and organize with cyclists from around the Bay Area. It was a way to bring new cyclists into the fold, giving them a relaxed and joyful way to tour the city without danger and without obstructions. It made new cyclists!—perhaps the biggest challenge we've faced as bicycle activists. Over the years I took so many different people to experience the ride: my brothers, my father, and my mother came on Critical Masses whenever they visited, and eventually we began to see public officials, including elected representatives and even Caltrans employees, riding with us. Even my love life revolved around it, and yet one could say it was the love of my life. I knew no other place to be so happily human in public, no other place where people came together and lived beyond the walls and above the prison gang mentality: drive to work, work to drive.

Granted, I was one of those wild and wooly characters willing to dedicate my life to protecting our freespace. But I'm far from alone. The time was ripe: it was the era of globalization, the tail end of a major recession and another war for oil. Across Right and Left there was a sense of losing traditional ways; of losing individual power; of becoming more and more mechanized, dehumanized, and oppressed by the ever-growing structures of social, economic and physical imprisonment—even as materialistic indicators of wealth might suggest we'd all become kings and queens, each with our own private chariot.

Cycling as an adult had almost always been a solitary experience for me before Critcal Mass. I was the only one I knew who cycled to my high school of 2,000 students. When I found my first Critical Mass I was absolutely ecstatic, incredulous that we could fill the road, feel happy and carefree rather than pummeled in public, relegated to the gutter. Absolutely unable to wait a whole month to get my fix of road-rompin'-revelry, I helped start our own ride in Berkeley in the middle of the month, the first one on International Women's Day, March 8, 1993. In two months I was starting a ride in Manhattan, and two months later was cast into jail for a week for being a "leader" of 100 cyclists who took over that much-contested Bayshore Freeway during the July 1993 Berkeley ride—the first of over twenty arrests and over a hundred traffic charges (just for me, let alone thousands of others around the world)! Many more rides followed in the Bay Area, often on the first or third Friday, even on the "leap Friday" but along with San Francisco, only Berkeley Critical Mass survived year after year, putting up uncompromising resistance to the many efforts to shut us down. In Berkeley the ride dovetailed nicely with the bicycle activist "guerrilla theatre" that had sprung up around a campaign to stop the widening of already massive Interstate 80 along the bay shore.

Berkeley Critical Mass Begins

Those early rides were legendary—moment to moment ecstatic joy and street threatre. The combination of bike activists and freeway fighters with anarcho-environmentalists on wheels was a combination that couldn't be beat. Like a newscaster once said of Critical Mass, back then we were DRUNK WITH POWER. A circle of bikes in an intersection felt like a spontaneous amphitheatre. One could sing, shout, dance, and bounce as if the world were our trampoline. It was addictive! People wore costumes and sculptures.

"What happens when the planet is choked with cars?" went the call.

"We all DIEeeeeeeeeeeeeeeeeeeeeeeeee!"

Flopping to the street like so many bodies overcome by pollution, main street Shattuck Avenue filled with collapsed cyclists while others acting as emergency responders rushing around rescuscitating us with bike pumps and front tires bouncing on our chests—whole-bike CPR—the street was our spontaneous playground.

After each ride I'd want to share the amazement, document it. I'd pour out pages of details, blow-by-blow, in manic beat-poet phraseology about all the wildness and wonder. Those records were on old Macintosh 3.5" disks, swept away in the mists of techno-time like the dot-com boom to come.

Such was the spirit of the early Berkeley rides. I finished our first ride in the late night riding between lumbering cars singing "Rawhide" and miming a lasso, as if to capture and tag them moto-dawgies. They just seemed so slow and clumsy. Meanwhile, a hint of what was to come: one solitary cop, the infamous "Jones #5" was looking quite stressed, apoplectic even, watching in horror and mouthing darkly into his shoulder radio. The next ride was swamped with overwhelming police presence. Like every ride to come in the U.S., the joy quickly came into conflict with authorities. Although the first ride was a joyride with harmless intent, the second faced repression, which polarized the situation and set us on a track for eight years of needless conflict.

After the police came, a touch of class war was felt. On Berkeley's second ride, a girl was pushed by an aggressive sports car driver in the hills; when he continued to scream at her, she reached out and snapped off the hood antenna on his fancy red sports car. On one ride, just as my eyes were glazing over from watching the mesmerizing circus of bikes swirling not only around a McDonald's and through the "Drive-Thru" but even into the door and through the entire building, I was snapped awake by the unexpected flutter of flags dropping to the ground. McDonald's' own flag went riding off draped over a cyclist, clutched in the raised fist of a punk kid. In another incident, a punk kid, taking advantage of the Temporary Autonomous Zone, rode out of a chain supermarket carrying bottles of wine, shot off fireworks, and spray painted messages to cars on the streets before the police finally bloodied him up leaving a scar on his face for life.

By our fifth ride, when 100 cyclists took over, Berkeley Lieutenant Lopes helpfully declared to the world we were "nothing more than self-proclaimed anarchists and local activists who had new tactics." The absurdity of this statement, and the Cold War mania that still gripped Berkeley and certainly its police, led to the publication of the zine *The Bicycle Terrorist: Lampooning the Status Quo Projection of Cyclist Banditry*. Ironically it would be eight years of police repression until the events of 9/11 convinced the police, who were embarrassed by the extreme and escalating repression that year, to call it off.

The tumultuous beginning mellowed over time, but in the years that followed the legendary rowdiness of a Berkeley ride kept it relatively small—usually under 100 people, but still enough to feel massive, make an impression, fill one or two city blocks, and remain intimate and creative. Despite the ever present blue meanies (except when it rained, then they went to get burgers until we taunted them through the window with our snorkel masks, forcing them to drag themselves out to chase us again), we kept it upbeat and evolving.

Thanks to handmade "Bikes at Work" trailers we discovered we could carry an entire living room couch, which became our regular mascot, picking up passersby and carrying them on a spontaneous joyride. The sight of people rolling by on a couch pulled by bike almost never failed to bring a bright smile to waiting motorists. On one ride after an anti-globalization protest, activists brought their giant inflatable octopus. Thanks to techno-geeks we began to load up utility trailers with speakers—sometimes broadcasting from pirate radio—and fortified by installing fragile equipment and wires inside the large speaker housing. Although police still tried to kick, rip, and beat them apart on more than one occasion, or repeatedly confiscate them, more than ten years later they still roam the streets.

After 9/11, four lawsuits, and a directive from City Council for the police to talk to us, we were finally free. Although there was fear that the escalating police violence would be even worse after 9/11, the latest leader of the bike officer squadron that plagued us called me up and said, "We have too much on our hands right now...I have family in New York, too... we're not gonna be there this time. We trust you all to go out, do what you do, and have a good, safe ride."

We finally got to prove what I'd been saying all along: the problems came from police and motorists. The police aided and abetted motorists who attacked us. The next twelve years were remarkably problem-free.

Action and Reaction: Defending the Incomprehensible Critical Mass

"What is it about you guys, how do you do it?" asked an old-time lefty politico. "I mean you go out and block the whole street and get away with it, month after month; it's hip, it's happening, and yet somehow you refuse to get a permit. You are so cool!"

Many Critical Mass purists didn't want anything to do with battling the conventional media: "Just ignore them!" A wonderful notion emerged, that no reporter be spoken with who hadn't experienced the ride.

In the first frenzied, manic year of Critical Mass, as the ride grew to be so big you couldn't see either end of it, a photo captured the magic: a corporate businessman stood watching, dazed after a long day at work, suit and tie, briefcase in hand. As he realized the magnitude of the procession going past, he smiled and his jaw dropped! In this day of bankers having us by the balls, nice to think the ball we have on the ball bearing (which was invented for the bicycle, naturally), can melt a dour demeanor and inspire a smile.

Why did the police set upon us like we were an insurrection, knocking over smiling people with flowers in their baskets and "Thanks for waiting" signs in so many cities across the U.S.?

If we follow the money, and its influence, consider this: if that executive with the briefcase were in certain industries, he'd look out across the field of shimmering bike helmets happily trailing into the distance and do a density calculation: ten blocks in view. One hundred cyclists per block, minimum. Each one potentially realizing that needing a car and all that goes with it is a mirage. The $6,000 per person per year dedicated to his industry is in jeopardy. Millions being reallocated. Once this catches on, he's in ruins! Damn straight: with that view, they tried to beat us off our bikes and back into the boxes.

At one point there was a wave of criticism that Critical Mass blocked emergency vehicles. Although we'd learned the hard way that parting the waters for a police car was a recipe for injustice, the fact is that in a true emergency we were far more efficient than cars at letting an emergency vehicle through. The onset of video activism was able to prove this conclusively. On one ride it seemed deliberate, maybe five fire trucks cut through the ride at different times, and each one rolled through as if the street were empty. In a flash the bikes can get to the side of the road. Have lives been saved because of Critical Mass? Quite possibly! (As a high school student on an Art Department field trip to museums in NYC, I saw an ambulance stuck in traffic, siren wailing, unable to move. Years later I saw the same thing on Interstate 80 in Berkeley.)

This got me thinking: how else can we quantify the benefits of Critical Mass? Training in Environmental Health Science introduced me to study design, and a world of literature on air pollution, noise pollution, and the health benefits of not only exercise, but of being social, all things which Critical Mass does. Being at the interface between street happenings and wonky government process, I realized Critical Mass could even be considered a public health intervention. Jokingly, I'd tell people at the Air District that it should be considered a Transportation Control Measure for reducing air pollution. The more people who cycle and walk, the safer we all are—says the landmark findings of Peter Jacobsen and others, known as "Safety in Numbers."[2] The effect Jacobsen documented appeared true in cities around the globe, and held true not just at the city level but at the level of individual streets, and intersections, whether through adaptations in culture, infrastructure, or both.

It would be easy to view the value of Critical Mass simply in terms of the benefits for cycling: in particular, creating new cyclists, creating a culture of cycling, giving visibility and credence to cyclists in politics. Critical Mass purists would surely counter, "It's not about bikes!" But increasing cycling is essential and imperative to a healthier, happier world. More cycling is akin to oxygen, literally and figuratively. As a society, as a world, we die without more cycling.

Key to increasing cycling is simply getting people to try. Large rides create that space. I developed a Beginner Bicyclist Survival Course and began urging new cyclists to join Critical Mass, where they could ride in a supportive environment, relatively safe from cars, and see the city with a minimum of trouble. Carried away by the energy of the crowd, the hours go unnoticed. At the end the realization: "I just saw the whole city! I can do this!"

For those who have been on the front line of this movement, particularly anyone who had illusions that we really are all equals, it is a weighty thing to realize that we live in a country that violently suppresses bicycling, that the car comes before life itself. On every level, a new class of heroes has been created: from the transport and land use planning that kills and maims by the millions, to the stark repression of Critical Mass in so many U.S. cities and the resultant traumas people have suffered, the PTSD we've seen and the dreams that have been crushed while fighting for this dream. Because like so many battles for justice throughout history, for a ride to survive requires the determined efforts and risk of many people. These are veterans in the truest sense, certainly not recognized as such by the state but essential to our collective future.

Perhaps there's some justice for me at least: I managed to escape to bicycle-friendly Europe for a time. As I'm writing this I'm on a train between Dresden and Austria, watching the river unfold like a snaking urban cyclehappening. (Sun Tzu would surely agree, bikes are like water through obstacles.) On this trip I've been in Berlin, will be in Graz, and am passing through Prague before returning to my home base in Bologna, Italy. Lucky me, I'm on a tour for work, bridging two bicycle projects and a meeting of the European Cycling Federation. Tracing back the cause and effect sequence, Critical Mass accounts for my being in Italy now on a bicycle study. Totally new to Bologna and not knowing any Italian, my first friends were Critical Massers, who helped me get a bike together at the CiclOfficina, much like the Bike Libraries I started in Berkeley/Oakland. And once a year for the *Ciemmona* thousands congregate on Rome for a three-day Critical Mass weekend. What a way to see the world!

There are curious dichotomies that emerge in the Critical Mass world. Not wanting to take power over another, yet being so powerful. Not wanting to be a leader, yet taking initiative and influencing outcomes for thousands. And in a sense, not being professional (being "quintessentially anti-professional"), yet inspiring so many. What is the relationship of Critical Mass to politics? We wisely kept it pure: no leaders, no political platform. Yet the result is a free speech stage on wheels, where anything can happen, and certainly there is some political and cultural self-selection. In the early days the song of "no leaders" could feel very shrill, as we weren't believed—nobody understood. The media and police in particular were constantly in conflict with this idea, a forefront of the cultural change brought on by Critical Mass. As a military-type strategy, police target leaders, as a rule—even recently in Germany the Berlin ride was surrounded by police and a first time rider, from Poland, was interrogated again and again with: "Who is the leader?"

Being as there were key organizers and individuals who had influence or took prominent initiative, in fact over time, I realized we DID have leaders, and I was absolutely one of them. However, true to the philosophy (anarchist if you like), there was no hierarchy and no compulsory behavior. Leaders of Critical Mass were motivators and artists of spontaneous cohesion, not commanders. In the end not having leaders meant the ride couldn't be co-opted (although people tried) and so it remained politically alive and inclusive. Of course the secondary benefit was we were safer from being sent to jail for conspiracy or pressed into liability for the ride. (I once tried to organize a special ride through official channels and was told to pay $20,000 for insurance.)

Having no political platform certainly didn't mean the ride was apolitical. In court once we even claimed First Amendment (freedom of speech) rights and said each bicycle was like a political banner, declaring the issue. Transport policy was so polarized, and once Critical Mass arose nobody could ignore the issue of bicycles any more. Lack of political dogma allowed the space, and allowed individuals to thrive, feel free, and feel ownership. There was always a political undercurrrent and certainly in liberal San Francisco many took for granted that leftist assumptions were predominant.

How did this help the ride and influence culture? The power of the mass to lift spirits and transform a situation can't be understated! Whenever there was a labor struggle going on, the ride was urged to visit. When a lonely and stressed group of picketers sees an army of support flash-flooding up the street, it's a game changer, it's a world-saver. Euphoria! Validation! Support! Resounding cheers and glowing gratitude! We'd slowly pass by slapping high fives like we'd all won. Even if most of us arriving on bikes didn't know the issue, now we had an inkling. Even if the strikers didn't know about Critical Mass, now they loved us.

Tying Critical Mass to a specific platform could be a mistake, however, because the "purity" of the ride was compromised, and the police had a reason to attack. If we look at the nightmares that took place in New York City and Portland, where good rides were going strong and doing amazing things, there is a pattern. In both cases, the rides saw severe police repression after they came into conflict with Republican President Bush, the junior.[3] From a long view it was as if the nastiest of the Feds said, "zero tolerance, kill this now," and they did. Even as we publicly declared "no platform" and laughed at the mainstream media hysteria about "anarchist scofflaws," "thousands of whooping cyclists snarling traffic" and "guerilla warfare on wheels," mainstream politics weaved through Critical Mass history, sometimes catastrophically.

Now after 20 years, a veteran, a wizzened ol' maaan (but kept young by the youthful spirit of Critical Mass!), I would certainly agree that the monthly rides were and are not enough. Critical Mass supported us, brought us together, made many things possible, been a catalyst (as the bicycle itself often has been, such as for the liberation of women). We gave ourselves a place to ride. We got a taste of the world we wanted to share. And we did it once a month—a treat, a respite. How many of us could have sustained ourselves without that breath of fresh air on a regular basis, given the horrors, the outright repression, and constant discouragement we faced on so many levels?

My Critical Mass experience pushed me into law by necessity, taught me much about the government I thought was too corrupt to ever open space for daily urban cycling, and most of all gave me a venue for my passion for a new Bicycle Age. Critical Mass was "training wheels" for bike advocates, even as it can be for new bicyclists, simply learning to ride.

For a long time I've wanted to apply professional methods to evaluating Critical Mass's effects. I suspect a survey would show many people agree it has changed their lives. Informal surveys always have. New cyclists, fresher air, and quieter streets mean big benefits for society as a whole. All those new cyclists means reduced overall mortality, and probably also reduced morbidity (death and disease). It means a stronger and more resilient local economy: less social isolation, more peace in the streets. The benefits are broad and deep.

Any city that dares to actually make good on its lip service to reduce driving and improve public health will embrace, nurture, and cherish its Critical Mass events, wherever it is so lucky for them to appear.

Note

1   Free Radio Berkeley, 104.1 FM broadcast for six straight years as pirate radio, documenting the Critical Mass movement around the Bay Area.
2   P.L. Jacobsen, "Safety in numbers; more walker and bicyclists, safer walking and bicycling." *Injury Prevention. http://injuryprevention.bmj.com/content/9/3/205.abstract*
3   See articles in this volume by Matthew Roth on NYC, and Joe Biel on Portland.

"Kiss-In" in Portland, Oregon, 2008.

Inventing an Autonomina
By Tatiana Achcar

Transportation by bike always seemed like an obvious choice to me. Cheap, clean, healthy, enjoyable, and a way to make it through my day-to-day travels. I started riding a bike when I was already grown up, since my parents never even dreamed of adopting such a lifestyle for our family. In Brazil, bikes were always thought of as something kids or poor people would use. I think that's why there's a gap between my childhood and adulthood where cycling practically seemed not to exist. I imagine the same thing has happened in the lives of plenty of other Brazilians who now ride a bicycle as a conscious choice. On the first bike trip I took through the center of the country, a truck driver, from way up on his enormous truck, shouted rather loudly as he passed our group: "Buy a car!" That phrase, somewhere between a joke and an expression of disgust, made me think that that man simply couldn't imagine how we were enjoying ourselves tremendously in the process of transporting ourselves with our own bodies.

I was caught up in the sense of freedom on two wheels and my bicycle took over larger and larger parts of my life. But I have to admit that the daily struggles of being a cyclist in São Paulo were depressing. I felt very insecure, like an alien, and I didn't know how to behave in traffic or how to ride safely. A bike activist friend, Eduardo Green, took me along and I discovered the *Bicicletada* and joined the group, rather small at the time. I didn't understand exactly what it was: A ride? A protest? With what purpose and what destination? There was a spirit of resistance there and the slogan *menos carro, mais bicicleta* ("less cars, more bikes"), shouted along the huge avenues, was proof of that. Through this crowd I also discovered some anarchist collectives that I found mind-opening, like *Espaço Impróprio* and CrimethInc. São Paulo had become too small for me. I needed to carve out a sense of autonomy and see the world. By undertaking a journey, I recalibrated my life forever. I packed my bags, gave up my apartment, and left. Thus began an intense and unforgettable series of firsts.

I set out for the United States. What could the most car-filled country on the planet teach me about cycling, citizenship, and sustainability? It was June 2008 and Portland, with its great infrastructure, safety, and relaxed and festive climate for cyclists, was hosting the worldwide conference Towards Carfree Cities. My first night in the city was also the first time in my life that I rode naked, alongside thousands of other cyclists who were demonstrating how fragile (and beautiful) we are on two wheels. I confronted the northern cold and the embarrassment of being naked, and celebrated with the pedestrians who greeted us out on the streets. When the police passed by the naked mass, I was sure I would be arrested. (I wasn't.) The Pedalpalooza festival was also shaking things up in the city with over 200 events—art shows, film festivals, workshops, and playful theme rides. Where else could I kiss my boyfriend as a protest in the center of the street right in the middle of rush hour? Our messages were "liplock not gridlock," "less parking space, more sucking face," and "cyclists taste better." The police turned up again and tried to shut down the party—unsuccessfully. However, the conversation we struck up with them was a lesson in civility for me, accustomed as I was to the brutality of Brazilian police.

Over the course of fifteen days of festivities, I learned to fix my bike, went to watch the Sprockettes female bike dancers, tried out exotic tall bikes, cheered for a gladiator trying to keep his balance on a unicycle, zoomed down the zoo hill in the regular Sunday Zoo Bomb ride, played like a child, and made friends. A whole world of exchanges and of solidarity began to reveal itself. Sara Stout, a visual artist, bike mechanic, and gardener, was a generous hostess, and showed me how her passion for bikes gives rise to beautiful sculptures and murals. Roger Noehren, a founding member of the City Bikes Co-op, took me to plenty of shops until we found a used bike that he transformed into my most faithful companion, Velvet.

Dense, nervous, and multicultural, San Francisco gave a shock to my safe, naïve experience as a cyclist in Portland. Mountains to conquer, complicated traffic (cars, buses, cable cars) train tracks to dodge, bike messengers and hurried commuters piled up at the stop lights on Market Street. There's a competition for space and for coexistence between cars, pedestrians, and cyclists on the streets and this is a good fight, but it's not the only one. There's a dynamic of resistance in San Francisco that takes in many other causes: immigrants' rights, gay rights, womens' rights and street-dwellers' rights, free speech, Reclaim the Streets, growing food in the city, the Really Really Free market, the right to eat organic food. Resistance is on every corner—on poles, in murals, marches, discussion groups, soirées, community radio stations, even in the flowerbed of a community garden. It's a motivating force that permeates the entire city and which, I'm sure, only revealed itself to me because I was riding a bicycle. As a cyclist I was also part of a minority, even if I felt like part of a majority compared to the situation in Brazil. In Brazil, political darkness and police brutality crush direct and democratic struggles and make it difficult to turn oneself into a citizen. In the United States, the minority is more conscious and active in exercising its rights and more creative and respected in its demands.

In this sense, the most relevant demonstration that I became a part of was clearly the enormous San Francisco Critical Mass. Just as in my first *Bicicletada* in São Paulo, I couldn't understand exactly what was going on in that enormous mobile meeting, without leader or destination. I needed two or three months to start to entrust myself to the Mass and to flow with it. We were many people, united by the desire to occupy the streets, to celebrate our gathering, to claim our right to share this space and to make it a common and peaceful space for everyone. There was boom boxes, music, pamphlets, posters, laughter, shouts, fantasies, games, and new friendship. There was also conflict and a lot of dialogue and negotiation. It seems like every cause coexisted and gained power within the Mass, so in the end nobody goes through it unaffected. A tremendous feeling filled my heart; "Another world is possible," I thought, and I was creating a part of it.

With map in hand and with the help of generous and committed friends—Chris Carlsson, LisaRuth Elliott, Mona Caron, Jon Winston, Karen Franklin, Victoria Perenyi, Marina Lazzara—I got to know spaces of autonomy and empowerment: DIY bike shops, food co-ops, farmers markets, traveling bike parties, and, finally, the community gardens, a cause I was really motivated to work for. Everyone was willing to help you do things with your own hands. Building and repairing your own bike, growing your own food in the city or meeting the farmer who feeds you—all this taught me that it is possible to do things directly, without involving a middleman. I was used to paying for all these services, along with the majority of Brazilians who've gone to school and have a better financial situation (and who, curiously, are too busy gazing at their own navels). But by visiting these places and getting to know the volunteers, I learned that, in order to create another world, we have to give of ourselves and get our hands dirty.

As soon as I arrived in New Zealand, I began following this philosophy. To my grateful surprise, there was a free, public bicycle assembly stand at the Auckland airport. "Wow," I thought, "if this trip starts like this, what comes next?" I hadn't ridden even a mile when I realized the traffic follows the British custom of driving on the left-hand side. I quickly stopped to switch the rearview mirror to the other side of my handlebar and rode on. The roads in New Zealand are not particularly bike-friendly, so I was riding on the shoulder. New Zealand is a predominantly rural country with long distances separating the cities. There are no buses most places and the population is accustomed to driving everywhere in their cars. Bicycles are forced to share the roads side-by-side with high-speed traffic most of the time. Empty bottles and cans littered the roadsides, apparently discarded by passing motorists, a danger signal for cyclists. There are scenic cycle routes in some touristic areas, but no significant bicycling life in most major towns. The exception I discovered was Wellington, a charming city on the South Island, where a spirit of resistance was percolating. I visited a radical social center that had a flourishing urban garden and a DIY community bike shop. The folks there were very friendly and set me up with a used wheel and showed me how to true it and get it ready for my journey. (The two other projects underway when I visited were a tallbike-building workshop and a film project on collective living.)

Resistance is fertile and has no borders, but it's clear that it's born within one's own community. So, after a year traveling through three continents, I came back to Brazil, the place that I've chosen as my home. My time abroad helped define my existence as a cyclist with new skills and new knowledge. It was a turning point in my life, but arriving back in São Paulo was like coming back to square one and riding in a complete desert of infrastructure and education about non-automotive transportation. The city seemed like a war zone, and I wondered, "Where can we find the love here to create the revolution?" Clash! But I was determined to resist, despite the traffic, the pollution, the shock and discomfort of my friends and family, who warned me against cycling, saying: "It's dangerous, girl!" I see that now I influence people with my choices and attitudes. And I'm not alone. The mass of people using active and conscious means of transportation in Brazilian cities is growing in the face of the crazy congestion, traffic accidents and deaths, the high level of air pollution, the environmental damage, and the enormous public health costs. We are men and women who are adopting the bicycle as a lifestyle choice and who are starting to exercise not just our bodies and minds but also our rights of citizenship.

"Critical Mass " Meets Italian Cycle Touring*

by Marco Pierfranceschi

I (re)discovered and fell in love with the bicycle when I was twenty, at the end of the eighties. Living in Rome, I soon joined a local pro-cycling environmentalist association committed to spreading awareness and usage of the human-powered two-wheel vehicle. Mainly, we were busy organizing, on a purely voluntary basis, cycling tours for our members.

Through the years the association grew in scope and size, and joined the Italian Federation of Bicycle Friends (FIAB), sharing its goals and activities. After having been the chairman of the local association for some time, I also was involved in the workings of the national FIAB Committee.

In the meantime, the first Critical Mass group was forming in Rome—and their whole approach was far different from what I was used to. After a little while, FIAB asked me to explore ways to cooperate with Critical Mass, and in the process I ended up rapidly understanding their philosophy, and finding it mostly reasonable as well. However, I was unable to achieve the goal of opening a dialogue between the two worlds, as each one claimed to be the only right way.

As I was getting more and more acquainted with the Critical Mass approach, I began to find myself disagreeing with the more bureaucratic, slow, and ineffective FIAB style. In time, this motivated me to resign from the FIAB local group chairmanship and to leave altogether soon afterwards.

Thanks to the Internet, through the now defunct *Roma Pedala* blog, I nonetheless managed to keep in touch with many cyclists. As I witnessed the increasing ranks of people dissatisfied with their previous groups and associations, I was driven to conceive and carry out something really new.

Rethinking a Reliable Mechanism

It is now time to clarify the old system that I was trying to revolutionize.

Since the beginning of our activities in FIAB, everybody was convinced that only meticulous scheduling could ensure the satisfaction of people taking part in our bike rides. However, this requires the existence of an organizing board that takes lawful responsibility for the event and the implied risks, both for the cyclists joining it as well as for possible damages caused to others. Such responsibility lies firstly on the guide of the specific

---

* Or, how I found myself inventing a new way to share cycle tours with friends, and how this idea has turned into a very lively and populated experiential workshop: the *CicloAppuntamenti*, an online forum.

287

ride, but goes all the way up to the association chairman.

This is what is called "presumption of competence" in legal jargon (in the U.S., it's a persistent question of "liability"). In practice the guide has to take care of all those joining the event, and the association chairman is supposed to ensure that its guides are able to carry this burden with little effort. This implies that all guides have to be prepared and instructed accordingly.

Also, each bike ride has to be tested and documented, while people willing to take part have to be registered, often individually by phone, their membership status checked; all this is usually left to the guide who has proposed the specific event.

Since most associations guarantee that nobody taking part in a cycling tour will be left behind, a second partner is needed, charged with checking the tail end of the group while in motion. This end-of-the-line partner has to master some mechanical know-how as well, in case of punctures or other small technical issues that threaten to delay some of the riders.

Last but not least, all rides are planned well in advance, so that the guide will have to wait some months to actually carry it out. This often means the guide is not as strongly-motivated and willing when the event finally takes place—as the participants can easily see!

In time, as groups joining the cycling tours tended to grow in size, this became increasingly difficult to manage for most voluntary guides, and caused them to significantly limit the number of trips each of them was willing to schedule.

This implied the existence of an unsolvable dilemma for the FIAB association: we could not lessen the liability burden implied by our activities, and we could not increase the number of events and the amount of people taking part in them, since our voluntary guides could not be expected to do more. That was a dead end.

A Different Way of Thinking

Since Italian laws attribute specific liabilities related to events promoted by registered organizations, the only way out is to get rid of any rigid organizational structure. Collective events like cycling rides then become the effect of simple cooperative action among peers, without any need for such things as "presumption of competence."

Once the actual goal is clear, i.e. people want to meet and cycle together, I began to look at any set of formal rules supposedly conceived to regulate the event as useless obstacles to full freedom of interaction among participants.

What we really needed was simply an efficient and easy way to enable individuals to suggest to others, and personally join, specific cycling tours, so that everybody would share responsibility for the ride, assuming that the sum of the single cyclist's experience and judgment could be a better framework than any set of predetermined rules.

This approach stems directly from my experience with Critical Mass, where the group is formed spontaneously and "goes where those who happen to be in front choose to go." In other words, the organized groups of old had to be turned into small Critical Masses devoted to touring by bicycle.

The concept was put into practice via an online forum. Forums like this are quite commonplace nowadays, as they allow people to freely discuss any specific issue among large numbers of participants. In the present case, however, the debating and relational potential of this, the *CicloAppuntamenti Forum,* is focused on the bicycle rides, an instrumental purpose rare in Italian online fora.

A forum advantage, when compared to blogs or other Internet tools, is its strong peer character, as anybody (not only the site administrators) can independently suggest trips to others. The typical proposal will simply read, "I will have a ride in [this or that area], with [this or that technical features], on [day X]... Anyone can join at his/her own risk."

All those interested will post on the forum itself, confirming their willingness to join, possibly requesting further information, or even suggesting small modifications to the initial plans. In this context no one has "organizing" responsibilities, as the proponent simply declares that he/she is planning to have a ride, while those who manage the forum do not have any obligation to ensure that people posting possess any know-how.

The bike trip is then a simple gathering of cyclists that happen to be interested in the same route at the same time. No booking is actually necessary: even people who did not post (or even register) on the forum can simply decide to be at the starting place and go with the others.

After the trip, those who were there can comment on the forum in the same discussion where it was suggested, possibly adding pictures and tales of the experience. The site administrators will then simply move old discussions to a specific part of the forum, devoted to past tours. Anybody can go back to this section, and maybe take note of previous tours to propose something similar him/herself. Such a forum helps to avoid delays and long preparation time spans, so that everything is swift and spontaneous, while everybody can jump at opportunities as they present themselves. Another positive aspect of this forum is the relative absence of confrontation or aggression, due to the fact that most of the participants know each other personally thanks to the bicycle excursions they've already enjoyed together.

Some Reactions to the Change

The forum was opened in 2007 by a small group of cyclists, all annoyed with their associations for various reasons. Today (in February 2012) it boasts more than 1,200 registered users. It is based in Rome, but its scope covers the whole Lazio region, and sometimes even a larger area.

The number of proposed rides has been gradually increasing, up to 15-16 distinct proposals on the busiest weekends. In four years, it has accumulated a total of more than 1,800 proposed trips.

Specific sections were created to classify the rides based on difficulty level, type of bicycle, length in days; a specific section even contains routes that the proponents post because they plan to go exploring for the first time. Some special sections discuss other bicycle-centric issues, even if they are rather less crowded.

This full freedom has brought along a rich variety of suggested trips, from city breaks to great mountain climbs, from picnic trips to exotic long-distance tours (North Africa, Montenegro). The group size has grown as well, and today averages between 15 and 30 people.

Some people have actually experienced some difficulties adapting to this new paradigm. Many friends who have taken part from the beginning were strongly ingrained in the "organizational" logic of their previous groups, and initially suffered for the relative uncertainty of the new context. At first some were tempted to introduce further regulations, as the benefits of being "disorganized" were still unclear. Personally I have always declined such requests, since I was convinced that there was no better mechanism than the simple, free-for-all described above.

As time passed, mostly everybody started to realize that fully unprogrammed rides could be more successful than those planned to the last detail. There is actually in many of us a strong cultural mindset that values the affiliation to strictly-regulated organizations, as this is often psychologically instilled since birth. However, an effort to disregard it, and reach a higher degree of freedom for ourselves, is always worthwhile.

This relatively "risky" activity, without official memberships, rules to abide or organizations to join, end up attracting people who tend to be self-sufficient and independently-minded. Groups thus lose any hierarchical structure, and the divide between the guide(s) and participants vanishes.

This has made proposing a trip a far easier, less time-consuming job, allowing all to enjoy the ride in the same way. Association guides normally have not planned more than three events per year, but the more keen cyclists are now proposing rides through the *CicloAppuntamenti Forum* on a weekly basis.

Ideas and trips of all kinds are welcome on the forum, with no restrictions whatsoever. Since there is no need to forcibly and preemptively agree among participants on strategies and guidelines, all explicit or implicit arguments that were unavoidable in more structured organizations are gone. Forum administrators (about a dozen people at the moment) carry out maintenance duties collectively on a "first come, first act" basis.

Recently, with the widespread adoption of GPS technologies in annotating and sharing cycling routes, things have gotten even easier and better, and more diversified arrangements are possible. Anyone who has a GPS device knowing the present route can act as a temporary replacement for the tour guide, or can lead a subgroup with a specific level of expertise on a partially alternative route—easier or more challenging as the case may be.

Nobody is formally on duty to guarantee technical support in case of mechanical problems, as happens in structured association rides. But of course all people who can contribute in this context volunteer. This avoids the typical asymmetric customer-supplier mindset.

A lot of people taking part in "organized" rides come to expect this typical kind of logic almost as if it were some kind of business arrangement; as there are some rules mentioning it and maybe they have paid a small amount to join the event. This turns a fully a spontaneous offer of help into a obligation for which there need not be any gratitude. Getting rid of this kind of hierarchical perception also paves the way to better personal relationships.

The appearance and development of the *CicloAppuntamenti Forum* has not significantly altered how existing associations (in the Rome area) operate, even though a lot of mixing among people from the two sides has been going on. A preliminary analysis would suggest that many do not find themselves at ease with the "enforced freedom" approach as they feel the need for organized and structured belonging.

Many people need to feel protected and cared for when undertaking a "risky" business like bicycle riding. They need to perceive some authority telling them what to do, and need to know there is always someone around skilled enough to solve their mechanical troubles. It is also true that some people need to be part of a structured and successful team, wearing the social colors as an uniform, and are much less less motivated to join an informal group.

In some instances, however, the success of the *CicloAppuntamenti Forum* has encouraged some associations to revise their policies, for example the rigid long-term scheduling, allowing for some events to be held on shorter notice. Besides, not all the FIAB local groups follow rules as strict as the one in Rome does, so the urgency to export our vision does not appear to exist everywhere in the rest of the country.

Our forum has been growing constantly for four years now, and it seems to have still further potential. Of course, as older contributors slow down their posting, newcomers come to the fore to replace them. As it stands today, *CicloAppuntamenti* is an open stage where new ideas and developments are tested spontaneously and without impediments. Every bicycle ride reproduces a "creative chaos," where everyone actively takes part in the experience. The spontaneous, horizontal self-management style we learned from Critical Mass has freed our more formal rides from the bureaucratic constraints that were once impeding us. Recreational cycling, too, can be a liberating experience, especially when it escapes the dominating logic of organizations, unnecessary rules, and insurance.

Good Times and Plastic Smiles in Dubai, Mapping the Invisibles in France
Critical Mass As a Tool for Oblique Environmental Justice
By Daisy Gowda and Uma Sherwood

Heading to Dubai, two ladies set off from the UK on bicycles in March 2011. Over the 5 months and 15 countries they traveled, regardless of language or regime, Critical Mass rides were a means to meet collaborators and celebrate the bicycle. The bicycle became not only a vehicle and a home, but a vital tool in a variety of audacious transformative stunts. The 10,000 km journey of green hills, deserts, and mountains was sandwiched between two distinctly significant and unusual, though not obviously successful Critical Mass rides.

Calais: The Bicycle As An Urban Predatory Police-Tailing Tool

In the very first evening of our trip, we roll off the clunking metal ramp of the boat which had ferried us from Britain. Our introduction to the continent, we cycle into the sleeping French town of Calais.

At any given time, there are between 200 and 2,000 *sans-papiers* in Calais, representing a rich tapestry of stories and lives lived. They are Sudanese, Kurdish, and Pashtun; Somali, Palestinian, and Zimbabwean. Because asylum in Britain can only be claimed from UK soil, undocumented claimants must make dangerous, covert journeys into the country, often under lorries, hidden in containers, or small boats. Calais serves as a holding point for migrants preparing to make the journey across the channel, and UK Border Security puts pressure on the local French police (CRS) to disperse migrants from the area. The *sans-papiers* are routinely beaten, tear-gassed, detained, and evicted; their shelters destroyed, sleeping bags, and cooking materials confiscated. "We prefer to monitor sporting events," one CRS officer confides.

The work of NoBorders activists in Calais is brave and vital. If a pink-skinned "international" is there, particularly with a camera, the brutalities which are daily carried out by the police onto the migrants are reduced drastically.

Dawn Raid Bike Chase

It's morning, 6.45 a.m. Dawn. Pale pink strips of sun are slanting into a street of Calais. Two vans marked "CRS" are pulling up at Africa House where many of the migrants reside, with empty spaces for arrestees. Activists sound the alarm and the multitude of shadows grab their few key possessions, sprinting across the courtyard and darting onto precariously high roofs. Whistles and shouts of, "Police! Police!" echo. Until then the huge concrete structures had been silent with slumber. Within seconds of the scattered frenzy of flight, the place is quiet again—but tense and alert. Dozens of ears strain from dark corners and high rooftops.

After this first morning raid on a migrant squat, a swarm of six activists on bicycles decides to pursue the riot-cop van. The chase goes on for several kilometres, a self-explanatory but surprising, sweaty spectacle for the Calaisiens. A bizarrely-inverted police chase, in and through Calais, drawing on previously-dormant predatory instincts in the cyclists. As we track the van in the main street, at speed, the police in front lean out of the window of the van and launch (in front of a gaggle of astonished locals) a cloud of pepper spray behind them for us to cycle into. The toxic cloud catches two riders in the face. They give up the chase, coughing and unable to see.

We arrive at the migrants' homes, noisily enough for them to escape the pepper-spraying, beatings, and arrests which are customary. No arrests are made on this morning.

A call out to cyclists: an ongoing mass game of cop-predating-surveillance by bike in Calais would be a wonderful thing.

"Legal" and "Illegal" Humans

The presence of refugees and migrants seems to offend the deepest sensibilities of those with desirable passports. On some level they are a jarring reminder of the fragility of an illusion central to global capitalism—that the spoils of wealth are less a product of ingenuity and perseverance than wars, cheap labour, and extraction. Walls all across the earth protect "legal" humans from the "illegal" ones, "desirables" from "undesirables"—dividing forests, farms, and olive groves—imposing themselves on the undulating landscapes of an indifferent earth.

In de-politicized neoliberal economies, the exclusion of people from land is drained of its ideological significance. Concerns of undocumented peoples are placated with reference to abstract notions of human rights, rather than a fundamentally political economic issue of access to resources and autonomy over their use.

Bicycles and Borders

Viewed from a bicycle traversing vast expanses of land, borders come to seem arbitrary. Speckled across landscapes like service stations, stray dogs and butterflies float freely across while people and papers are intensely scrutinized. Moving at a steady cycling pace though 15 countries to arrive in Dubai, the artifice of borders is jarring. Clearly of no correspondence to the contours of cultures, the border between Turkey and Iran bulldozes through the Kurdish area—where locals have their own Kurdish language and identity. As the bike is wheeled along the immigration queue, across a line into another nation, drastically different laws and behaviour codes suddenly apply. Mandatory headscarfs are donned, for flapping across the arid Iranian terrain. Though in Iran the first rule we will learn is that rules are there to be broken and bent, we panic and rummage through our panniers for any soon-to-be-illegal alcohol.

Any illusion of racial equality also bursts like a bubble when a Western passport gets you waved through borders with relative ease. The Emirati immigration officer, when we inquire, obligingly rattle off the list of nationalities, arranged from "strong" to "weak" passports. The "weak" passports coincide with the nationalities of the migrant labour, often exploited.

Living, Breathing, Toolkit of Resistance

Moving east, the privilege of the maroon booklet containing your name and photograph become glaringly obvious. The journey we are undertaking, inspired by the DIY ethic and "people power" that characterise the Critical Mass phenomenon, hits a wall of contradiction when we are reminded at borders that—though everyone can ride a bike and defy petrol-traffic-norms—we are very few with "strong" passports to have the privilege of movement.

Acknowledging this inequality of passports, it seems all the more reason to tailor our itinerary along sites of struggle, both social and environmental. It seems all the more reason to work with these movements and carry the stories with us, to other groups, across other borders, involved in audacious projects of resistance. Tales and tactics for celebratory resistance, transported by bike along with our camping mats and tool kits.

Calais Critical Mass

Back to Calais and No Borders. The day after the police chase, we call for a Critical Mass, the first in Calais. Some years ago, it was the monthly Critical Mass rides in the UK that, like fireworks, stimulated our involvement with creative forms of protest. It blew our minds time and time again, how these loud and inviting swarms of cyclists can defy the neat polarity of audience and participant, protest and spectacle.

In Calais, witnessing the police raids and the tired and unseeing general public who walk by, it strikes one as a textbook example of environmental injustice. The rates in Calais for unemployment and alcoholism are among the highest in France. It's a recurring pattern: communities which are already economically- or ethnically-marginalised are laden with the burden of the impacts of dirty industry or of a dysfunctional and cruel immigration infrastructure.

We hope Critical Mass might be an event the Calais public could engage with, spectate, and digest. An enticing change to the tired and angry struggle of everyday Calais life.

Simply a Critical Mass was called for—no explicit relation to the issue of *sans-papiers*. However, locals and journalists and migrants are, predictably, among the bike swarm too. Soon the Mass ends up touring the usually segregated and unseen migrants' squats and "jungles." We cycle around the abandoned factories and warehouses, often on the outskirts of town. The cycle swarm stops to meet and speak to some of the migrants at their reclaimed temporary homes. In the town centre, the eclectic swarm of cyclists celebratory and loud, fliers about migrant solidarity are cheerfully received by the locals. In topic and in geography, Critical Mass serve as an oblique way of giving access and visibility to front line struggles.

Dubai: The Bicycle as Common Ground between the Good Times and Slave Labour

A Critical Mass culture is badly needed in Dubai. Scratch the surface of the "Good Times and Plastic Smiles," shiny new cars, and shiny new buildings, and you find an aggressively paranoid regime built on slave labour, tightly conditioning hyper-capitalist behaviour. As we arrive by ferry from Iran, we witness non-wealthy Iranians being turned back on the boat. "They are clearly not proper tourists," the border guard quips to us. "They have not come to spend money, like a tourist does."

In a country where bloggers requesting moderate reform disappear into desert prisons, one has to be a bit careful about how one's actions might be construed. A Critical Mass, with no leader, no itinerary and no agenda, is perfect for such a climate. It is inherently joyous and political in equal proportion, but obliquely so. A Critical Mass stands alone as an event—it requires no justification or agenda in order to exist. Despite needing no overt political drive, something as simple as the route it happens to engage on, or the visibility it lends to the participants, can inject the Critical Mass with transformative potential. As do the finest of direct actions, it can act as a knife driven through the sheen of the everyday and pry it open, so for just a moment new spaces are revealed, and new forms of thinking can emerge. Events occur that no one, in the objective light of day, ever thought possible. Direct action allows new spaces to open, for new visions to occur. Its power lies both in its ability to create a story without the usual narrative structures, and in giving authorship of this story to the participants and ultimately to the public. Also, no organisers—and so, in theory, no heads to roll.

In Dubai, new SUVs tear up and down the brand new roads. As in every metropolitan city, there are cyclists. In Dubai they come in two very distinct types. Specialist European cycle club riders sport carbon fibre frames, Lycra, and gadgets galore. We try to get our bikes fixed—they are apologetic but genuinely don't know how to fix "old-fashioned" bikes. The other type of cyclist is the Indian/Pakistani/Bangladeshi gardener, who will never have a car and can't afford public transport. The use of a bicycle is perhaps solely what unites these two poles of society.

Dubai's Labour Camps

Planning the Dubai Critical Mass serves as an opportune excuse to distribute flyers in Dubai's labour camps—strictly off limits to the public—the dark underbelly of Dubai. Without the slave class Dubai would not be full of shiny new buildings and plastic smiles. The dizzyingly tall towers and the sparkling malls are all built from the—very inexpensive—sweat and blood of the migrant workers.

Cycling, we swoop around the industrial block a few times. 52 degrees celsius makes for sweaty cycling. Spotting what we are looking for, we accost the group of men at the gate. The workers are warm and welcoming. Standing in the courtyard, the block of flats extends 3 floors up. Six pairs of sandals are piled up at the front of the doors of each bedroom.

In Dubai every contained space is air-conditioned—even the the bus stops. The only exceptions to this AC bubble over the desert town are the labourers' quarters and their transport. The green workers uniforms are stretched out drying on the balconies all the way up the buildings. Flags of sorts line each camp, bearing the colours of its company. Dwelling inside are Malians, Pakistanis, Bangladeshis. All men. Though surprised to see us, they are pleased to show us around and talk candidly about their salaries and working conditions. I assumed one man was fresh off the boat, to work for such a small salary, in such trying conditions. "No, 17 years so far," says Amir.

"What are you here for?"

"To hand out flyers for Critical Mass. Printed in Hindi, Arabic, English, and Urdu. It's a cycle ride. For everyone. A celebration of cycling and to make cyclists feel more safe on Dubai roads. Would you like to join us?"

"Yes, certainly I'd like to. I'll try to make it. I work 6 days a week, 8 am to 8 p.m. on a construction site and it's 2 hours drive from here. But I'll try to make it."

A security guard rudely interrupts. We are escorted out rapidly. Clearly the general public is not supposed to walk past the "No Entry" sign.

We acquire hi-viz vests and hard hats (doubling as cycling helmets) to distribute, so as to ensure Critical Mass would be beyond reproach, legally. Construction hats were the most economical option, over cycling helmets. The fortunate side effect of this bargain is that our Critical Mass features pink, brown, white, and black people seemingly all dressed as the otherwise invisible construction workers.

John, European and resident in Dubai for 7 years, a prospective participant for Critical Mass suggests:

> It would be best to get plenty of local support, i.e. from Emiratis. Because a lot of people here are expats, they are a little less inclined to do things that could be perceived as critical to their hosts as, by and large, they are grateful for the opportunity to work here. So if there were a few Emiratis involved too, people wouldn't feel bad.

Critical Mass and Teething Issues

So on this day in August a nervous and very eclectic set of cyclists gather at 6 p.m. under the date palm tree mapped on the flyers and Internet. The anticipated visibility of bikes is exciting. But equally exciting is the visibility in the city of workers, beyond mere sweating shadows crawling up and down scaffolding in the desert heat. No destination is planned, except that we will break fast together for Ramadan with dates and milk.

Collected are an unlikely posse of cycling Lycra, office shirts, salwar kameeze—everyone on empty stomachs. We set off cycling, the Dubai Critical Mass stumbling with all the classic teething issues. We lose some stragglers and subsume a gang of gardeners on bikes. We break the fast on Juma beach, the daylight fades. The mosque calls to prayer. The Dubai Critical Mass Facebook page calls for the next Critical Mass assembly…

"We could get quite a big crowd for a future event," assures Ben, a European working in Dubai. A tad apologetic for the small turn-out, he explains,

> The whole concept of Critical Mass is a new one for most in Dubai. The roads are not cycle friendly and even the road laws are biased against cyclists. This time round it's August and 40 degrees celsius. Plus it's Ramadan, which means people can't even drink water in public before sunset, making it even less conducive to cycling.

Indeed, small turnout and a shambolic cycle parade, the first Dubai Critical Mass might, from the outside, have looked like a flop. But it felt like a massive landmark, a suitably oblique way of bringing people together publicly, radiating references and imagery relating to some of the most taboo topics in Dubai.

A Cautionary Tale

A seed of celebratory and transformative action was sown with the Critical Mass in Dubai. Dubai the counter example, a cautionary tale. Built in a desert and built on slave-labour. Dubai, 1.5km-long shopping malls and artificial palm islands stretching into the sea. Dubai, as rootless and unnatural as the indoor-grown hydroponic food it consumes. Surprisingly, the humble bicycle might well be a critical tool for right there, in the strange dystopian future that is Dubai. The smallness of actions such as Critical Mass might be dismissed and dwarfed against the backdrop of towering environmental and social brutalities in Dubai. But it is precisely these small actions that might momentarily allow a glimpse of a new vision, a new space with this bubble of capitalism and consumerism taken to their logical extremes.

Links for more stories and information:

http://calaismigrantsolidarity.wordpress.com/
http://www.100daystopalestine.org/2011/08/08/undocumented-seeds-undocumented-people-undocu-mented-stories/

International Solidarity
The Bicycle As Creative Response
By Robbie Gillett

"You did what?"
         "We cycled to Palestine."
"Blimey, how long did that take?"
"About 4 months."
"What, did you do it for charity or something?"
"Well, not exactly for charity. It was to support Palestinians who are living under a military Occupation."
"Right."

When we take part in Critical Mass rides, we remind ourselves not only how we can re-imagine our urban landscapes away from the dominance of the motor car, but also how we can use our bikes as a form of collective action. Over recent years, many mobilisations and protests such as the anti-capitalists demos against the G20 in London in April 2009, have had a Critical Mass contingent as part of the plans. The concept of longer distance solidarity rides has also been used in Europe and elsewhere with groups such as Bicycology riding from Southern England to Gleneagles in Scotland for the G8 counter-summit in 2005.

After a few months of planning and preparation in March 2011, a group of 20 cyclists set off from London to make a 7,000 km journey across Europe and the Middle East within a loose target of 100 days. Having stopped in several communities along the way, the "PEDAL—100 Days to Palestine" riders arrived in the West Bank in July 2011.

With the tradition of Critical Mass in place, there were two immediate inspirations for our cycle project to Palestine. The first was a project within the environmental direct action movement, in which many of us have played an active role over the last few years. In May 2010, a solidarity bike caravan was organised between two communities resisting carbon-heavy infrastructure: an open cast coal mine in Merthy Tydfill, Wales and a high-pressure gas pipeline funded by Shell in Rossport, Ireland. Both places are confronting developments that not only threaten the health and safety of local people— but that also push us further towards the edge of climate catastrophe.

The second inspiration occurred at the same time as this Merthyr-to-Mayo ride. On May 31, 2010, a Turkish aid ship, the *Mavi Marmara*, was en route to Gaza to provide humanitarian aid and construction materials for people besieged by the Israeli-Egyptian blockade. Whilst still in international waters, Israeli commandoes boarded the ship and killed nine people on board. In the subsequent days, thousands took to the streets in protest in cities all over the world.

The confluence of these two events provided the catalyst for PEDAL.

The bicycle was not simply our mode of transport. If resistance is art, then the bike was our form! We saw the ride as a creative response to the Palestinian Civil Society's 2005 joint call for a programme of Boycotts, Divestments and Sanctions against Israeli companies and institutions complicit in ongoing human rights abuses in the West Bank and Gaza. We saw the ride as a creative response to this call out. Just as we might distribute a flyer, poster our streets, blockade an arms factory, or organise a mass boycott—so too could we use the bicycle as a spectacle through which to talk about the realities of Palestinian life under Occupation—and how can we oppose it.

Along our journey, PEDAL visited several communities with three overall specific themes in mind:

+ To respond to and promote the call out for Boycotts, Divestments and Sanctions.
+ To promote environmental justice and to "Big up the Bike." Many of our crew also came from a DIY food-growing background, so we wanted to link the issues of food sovereignty with people across Europe and in Palestine fighting for access to land, seeds, and water.
+ To share stories of resistance from the UK to Palestine.

In several places we organised Critical Mass rides in order to meet people, find out more about various sites of contention within different communities, and to listen to the stories of people who lived there.

In **London**, PEDAL assembled a Critical Mass via the Israeli embassy and Ahava cosmetics store in Covent Garden (where Dead Sea mud from the Occupied Territories is sold as a beauty product). We also visited a mural in Cable Street, site of a famous street battle in 1936 where a contingent of British fascists were beaten off the streets by a successful counter-mobilisation in what was then a predominantly Jewish neighbourhood.

In **Calais, France**, PEDAL worked with migrant communities to fix bikes in Africa House—a large, abandoned car garage (now demolished) where the *Sans Papiers* sheltered as they prepared to cross the Channel into England. We used our bikes to monitor police patrols, who regularly stop, harass, and arrest non-Europeans for lacking the correct paperwork. We also held a Critical Mass bike ride around Calais and distributed flyers about the plight of migrant communities passing through their town.

In **Brussels**, PEDAL met up with local activists and held an anti-militarist Critical Mass in which we visited several office headquarters of arms industry organsations such the European Defence Agency. Critical Mass helped us connect the dots in the the murky world of the military-industrial-research complex that is heavily represented in the European capital. We also learned how Israeli defence companies are being awarded European grant money for researching security technologies which are often tried and tested on Palestinian people first before being exported to world markets.

Stopping in **Ljubljana, Slovenia,** PEDAL held a bike maintenance workshop in the *Metalkova*, a squatted military barracks and held a seed swap. We also held workshops with local activists about the situation in Palestine. A new Boycott, Divestment and Sanctions group has formed there since we left.

There has been a strong Critical Mass community in **Istanbul, Turkey** for many years now. PEDAL was fortunate enough to attend an annual mass bike demonstration across one of the large bridges that links Europe and Asia across the Bosphorous Strait. Cyclists are currently prohibited from using the bridge and local groups are campaigning for a cycle lane to be installed.

Upon our arrival in the **West Bank, Palestine**, we were honoured to be invited by the Popular Committee of Bil'in village to hold a bike-themed

demo at their weekly protest against the illegal apartheid Wall. It was humbling to see local community organisers who have endured tear gas, rubber bullets, live ammunition, imprisonment, and the death of family members over many years borrow our bikes as we demonstrated with them against the illegal settlements on the other side of the Wall. We also held a chaotic bike maintenance session at Aida Refugee camp in Bethlehem with lots of children bringing out their battered and punctured bikes to get them fixed up.

Looking back on this, we can see how the Critical Mass demo format can be used in a variety of ways: as a Reclaim-the-Streets/carnival-style protest in London; to confront the arms industry in Brussels; to advocate better cycling provisions in Istanbul; and to create a visual spectacle summarising our whole journey in Palestine.

As many long-distance bike riders will understand, the process of cycling across borders for extended periods of time provides a personal opportunity to reflect: not only on the communities we visited but also what was motivating us to make the journey in the first place. Some of us come from Jewish backgrounds, and were keen to further understand the relevance of an international Jewish anti-Zionist network which we could do by meeting up with dissenting Israeli groups like Anarchists Against the Wall and Boycott from Within. Others amongst us had been motivated into action by the ravages of Western imperialism in Iraq, the legacy of British colonialism in the wider Middle East, or by Palestinian friends who had arrived in the UK to study and who have shared their grief with us over the last few years. As we progressed on our bikes we found some space to think about these criss-crossing identities, motivations, and geopolitical forces.

Now that the trip is over, PEDAL members continue to organise back in the UK, and with Palestinians and dissenting Israeli groups abroad. One of the ongoing projects is to expose the greenwash behind a new cycle path between Jerusalem and Tel Aviv. The path has been sponsored by the Jewish National Fund—a key Zionist organisation playing an active part in the ethnic cleansing of Palestinians from their land. The cycle route will link different recreational parks, including Ben Shemen Forest. Some of these forested parks were planted over the top of former Palestinian villages, in attempt to erase the heritage and memory of the people who were pushed from their homes. As bike lovers, we find it disturbing that environmental values and practices such as tree planting, green spaces, and cycling are being used to mask serious human rights abuses and breaches of international law.

From the far corners of Europe to the heart of the Middle East, we ride for fun and we ride for pleasure. But as with Critical Mass, we can also ride to create alternative visions and to fight for social justice. When oppressed peoples call for solidarity, the bicycle can form part of our creative response. Critical Mass has played an important part in developing our own awareness of this collective power. Long may it last!

For more information and a map of the route and communities see:
http://www.100daystoPalestine.org

The campaign against the cycle path between Jerusalem and Tel Aviv:
http://www.StoptheJNF.org

Take a Bike to Ecotopia
(Take a Car to Hell)
by Alissa Staroub

Imagine you go on a Critical Mass in your local town, you ride a route around the city center and then the bike tour just continues. All the cyclists just keep going to the next town, form a Critical Mass there shouting, "Two wheels are enough!" and "System Change not Climate Change!" and then move on to the north or to the south ... whatever has been decided. With all the other cyclists you camp on a field somewhere along the way and continue the next morning. You won't come home for the next few months, maybe years, because you finally broke free from your daily routine, or whatever prevents you from going on the journey, and now are reclaiming the streets for non-polluting cyclists everywhere in the world.

Now imagine it's true. There is a version of an almost never ending Critical Mass—or at least some kind of ride that goes through different countries and lasts for few months. It is called Ecotopia Biketour and I would like take you on a ride through its history.

The Ecotopia Biketour started two years before the ride known as Critical Mass began in September 1992 in San Francisco. Certainly some of the Ecotopia Biketour participants joined Critical Mass once the phenomenon started to appear in Europe. One could say that the Ecotopia Biketour is a European thing. Where else could you cross so many borders in a few months by bike? So far the Ecotopia Biketour has not left Europe because it's hard to cycle across the Ocean, but there are chances it could extend to Africa or Asia. It all depends on how far you want to go.

In the beginning was "Ecotopia"

"Ecotopia" could be best described as an annual international gathering of people who come together to discuss social and environmental issues, camping together temporarily in an environmentally-friendly way in varying locations in Europe. It is visited by environmental youth groups, families, activists, and hippies. At the first Ecotopia in 1989, a group of people randomly met in a chai tent and discovered that they had a similar plan for the following year: all were planning to go to the UNSAID Festival in Bergen, Norway—that focuses on things left unsaid about climate justice—before they would meet again at the second Ecotopia in Hungary. They promised each other that they would travel from Norway to Hungary by bike. They organized the first and biggest (in terms of participants) Ecotopia Biketour ever. It was called "Take a bike to Ecotopia (take a car to hell)." Despite its theme it was not really a 100% bike tour yet as it was followed by the Dutch flying kitchen activist collective *Rampenplan* bus which catered three meals a day to the 125 cyclists on the tour.

This first Ecotopia Biketour remains the most organized. In later years it mutated quite a bit. The number of participants decreased. In addition to no longer having a bus to cater for the cyclists anymore, in 1991 people on the Ecotopia Biketour started to camp in fields and farms along their way from Scheveningen in the Netherlands to Ecotopia at Tudulinna in Estonia and not in pre-booked gymnasiums like on the very first tour.

A slow metamorphosis happened to it as well. When the Biketour finished at the Ecotopia in 2008 in Sarikum Nature Reserve in the Sinop province in Turkey it had become a real activist DIY community. Its participants wild-camped in the middle of nowhere, financed all their necessities from a common cashbox, and performed both spontaneous and pre-organized direct actions such as helping local environmental NGOs lodge a complaint in the municipality against illegal transformation of forests into ski resorts, organizing Critical Masses, or—in the case of the 2004 Ecotopia Biketour—an art performance which dragged a motorless car on ropes across the city to be demolished with hammers and swords.

Ecotopia Biketour Without Ecotopia

In 2009, an event turned the life of the Ecotopia Biketour upside down: Ecotopia would not take place. The organizing NGO had decided to discontinue the annual summer camp. Despite Ecotopia not taking place that year, the Biketour still happened, but when Ecotopia returned again in 2010, the ride didn't use the gathering as its destination. In 2009, the Ecotopia Biketour turned more activist than ever before, and for the first time volunteers organized funding from the EU program Youth in Action to enable a tour coordinator to continuously work on the project.

From the beginning of July until the end of August 2009, between 20 and 35 people from mostly European countries traveled by bike from Belgrade via Skopje to the Mnogo u Malom camp near Jagnjedovec, Croatia. On their way they cycled through Albania, Montenegro and Bosnia and Herzegovina.

The tour stopped at places with pending environmental issues, good or bad. During the journey, the participants reported through the Web and through local media on the issues they encountered. The aim was, on one hand, to raise general environmental awareness among citizens and local policymakers. On the other hand, the Ecotopia Biketour wanted to bring the environmental issues of the Balkans to a more international audience, to add to the pressure on the delegations of the Climate Conference in Copenhagen to come up with a more ambitious climate agreement. COP15, although one of the biggest international meetings in the history of diplomacy, was a disaster in the end, since only an ideological-political minimum consensus was arrived at that was non-binding under international law. But the Biketour remained an untamed and idealist environmental project.

The Exact Opposite of an All-Inclusive Flight

In the months before the actual Biketour starts, sometime in autumn someone on the endless email list of volunteers writes something like "Heya! What about the next Ecotopia Biketour? Where is it taking place and when? I´d be up 4 doing sth. Who´s with me?"

All email-hell breaks loose then. People from all corners of Europe write proposals, contacts, ideas, then an organizing meeting is planned at someone's place somewhere. The people who meet there write an application to receive EU Youth in Action program funding and discuss the theme of next Ecotopia Biketour. Which issues are problematic and why? What do we want to change or raise attention to? The organizers always agree at least to the following common values: a sustainable way of traveling is preferable, cars are crowding out bicycles from the roads, the international community should strive towards a more environmentally sustainable way of living with no hierarchy, no borders, no oppression, rather with sustainability, community, and peace instead. This is why the Ecotopia Biketour is organized as it is organized. It's total chaos but it works.

Sometime after the winter meeting someone sets up the Ecotopia Biketour Wiki online where the question is: So where are we going after all? The people who respond to this question with ideas might not even participate in the end. The route is made to include permaculture festivals, environmental gatherings, actions planned by NGOs, available sleeping and shower places like squats or organic farms, and other events like Critical Masses to join. Maps are composed, and local coordinators take on the task of being informed about routes and locations in specific sections of the tour. Part of the funding is used to buy two huge bicycle trailers, a rocket stove and other kitchen equipment, a first aid kit, bike repair tools, and SIM-cards.

In early summer the almost never ending Critical Mass just starts. It could be best described as a Critical **Mess** though sometimes ... constantly changing sleeping places, varied group composition and food quality, changing tasks over the course of the day like just getting by bike to a certain place or paint huge banners for the next spontaneous direct action.

Yet, when joining the Ecotopia Biketour you can count on some things to remain the same. For instance the daily morning circle where all decisions are made in consensus, all tasks being equally divided between the participants and, of course, the common cashbox where everyone contributes an amount they think is appropriate for them.

You will likely first hear of the Ecotopia Biketour by word of mouth. Someone tells you that there is some kind of do-it-yourself environmental activist bike tour across Europe and you think, "That sounds great!" and check it out on the Internet. On the Wiki you can see the exact route. It's no problem to join the Biketour when it is already in progress. Most participants will do so and leave at some other point before the final destination. All you have to do is let the coordinators know that you are coming, put your belongings in a bicycle bag—don't forget your tent and a sleeping bag!—grab your bike, and hop on a train.

You will be surprised when meeting members of the Ecotopia Biketour for the first time. They are easily recognizable, but different age groups are represented, totally different occupations, nationalities, philosophies, and political views. All have two common interests: cycling and environmentalism. The common language is English, bikes are loaded with luggage; people might be barefoot, sunburned, with dreadlocks or leaves in their hair. To their T-shirts and bikes they will attach colorful banners with "Ecotopia Biketour" or "Climate justice!" written on it.

At first you see a group of three or five cyclists and you wonder: "Is the Ecotopia Biketour that small?" But when all participants come together to set up the sleeping place, to cook dinner, form a circle to talk about the past and coming day, and sit around the fire you will realize that the participants didn't cycle in a big group altogether but split up in small teams instead. Later you will see how convenient this is.

So How Does It Feel to Go on an Ecotopia Bike Tour?

The first action I performed joining the Ecotopia Biketour was dumpster diving at a Dutch discount supermarket to get some more ingredients for the common dinner. In rich countries up to 30% of the food produced and imported ends up unconsumed in a dumpster. Most of it is still very enjoyable; sometimes the eat-by date hasn't arrived yet. Mass consumption, overproduction, and a really bad pricing policy that aims to produce more at cheaper costs creates a very environmentally unfriendly thing. So I learned to perceive dumpster diving for food as a political action.

The cyclists with banners on their bikes and the leaves in their hair who picked me up introduced me to the whole Ecotopia bike tour community.

We reached an organic goat farm in the afternoon of my first day. Twenty people arrived bit by bit to the garden where we were camping. Later on some of us would sleep smoothly on soft hay bales in the neighboring barn. Cyclists exchanged stories from their ride and collected firewood to feed the rocket stove which would heat our delicious vegan curry dinner. At dawn we all sat in a circle around the fire and I experienced real consensus decision making for the first time.

One of the participants volunteered to moderate the circle. Everyone was asked to suggest discussion topics: the cycling route for tomorrow, welcoming new members, the feeling during the past days, the direct action that was planned for tomorrow when we would reach a bigger city in the afternoon, etc. A decision was only taken if all members of the group agreed. Sometime in the future this method would lead us to have endless discussions on whether a Critical Mass that we planned should cause a traffic jam or not.

On the way from Holland to Belgium and then Germany we met up with various local environmental NGOs, participated in a demonstration in Brussels, some of us gave many interviews to local media, we attended a permaculture festival, organized a Critical Mass in Gent and joined one in Cologne, cycled through the heaviest rain that I have ever seen, some of us lost our shoes and decided that we didn't need new ones for the moment, some of us slept in a tree house one night.

My head is stuffed with pictures of all the nice people that we met who shared our interest in cycling and environmentalism. One of them is the man who brought all his self-constructed crazy bicycles with huge wheels and double seats to the Climate Action Camp in Germany that we attended on the way. He gave us his bikes so we could cycle along with several hundred people to protest against the exploitation of a newly-opened open-pit coal mine.

Magic Time Gaps Between Environmental Actions

Between all these events there are these magic gaps, where you lie on your back next to the other participants on a deserted peach plantation and talk about the future of the planet or about your personal past. When sitting around the fire in the evening there is still space to think about the question of how an inclusive and sustainable lifestyle is possible and what it means to take action for the environment. How do we promote environmental action? How to do this best together, in the most convincing way?

Definitely getting on your bike is a first step. And if you can form a Critical Mass it's even better. In more than ten years of existence the Ecotopia Biketour has definitely contributed to the strengthening of an international network bringing together countless participants from different countries who have taken environmental action together. Maybe one day you will decide that your ride reclaiming the streets for bikes and climate justice should never stop—or at least not stop for a few months of your life. If you want to find out how it feels to spend the summer doing a long Critical Mass, the DIY activist community will be welcoming you—as usual somewhere in Europe. There is still much room for creativity in helping to shape the Ecotopia Biketours to come…

2012 Ecotopia Biketour

In 2012 the Ecotopia Biketour cycled through southern Europe, starting on a journey "towards degrowth"—challenging the damaging growth mentality of capitalism which overlooks real social and environmental values. Visit *www.ecotopiabiketour.net* to learn more about an eco-mobile do-it-yourself activist community going strong for more than 20 years.

Starting point: Barcelona in early July

Goal: Venice, in time for *Conference on Degrowth*, late September

In between: visiting bike workshops, ecological agriculture projects, action camps, intentional communities and ecovillages

The Occupation Will Be Pedal Powered
by Elly Blue

Occupy Wall Street began as a rally and encampment in the heart of New York City's financial district on Sept 17, 2011. It was an undefinable, leaderless, evolving happening that took many forms, from encampment to march to dance party to rallying cry. It was someone's idea that hit the mark and went viral; it was something different to every participant (and to every opponent). The Occupy movement spread immediately to other cities, always recognizable by its rallying cry of "We are the 99%" but always in a form adapted by local needs and styles, from the throng of well-to-do students in Harvard Yard to the handful of respected small business owners in tiny, industrial Oregon City, Oregon.

From the start, there were bicycles. Occupy is not a bicycle movement, but rather a popular movement, and bicycle transportation has played a role analogous to the complicated one it plays in the general populace—ordinary and disruptive, useful and jubilant, contentious and obvious, a tool of the uprising as well as of its suppression.

The Legacy of Critical Mass

At the first Occupy rally in Portland, which filled the waterfront before marching to set up the city's first encampment across the street from City Hall, every railing and fence was stacked two or three deep with locked bicycles. A bike was surely the best way to travel downtown that day even if it wasn't your usual mode of transportation—parking for cars is expensive and few lots are near the rally's starting point. But for participants in the giant, amorphous marches that took over downtown all that week, the crowd was so tightly packed as to make bicycling through it impossible, and few bikes rode in the march. The crowd was too thick, the pace was too slow, and law enforcement too ready to write tickets.

But for the police, it was the ideal vehicle. Bicycle-mounted officers could get ahead of the marchers, anticipating their route and guiding them down certain streets and away from others. Using their bikes as a barricade, they could keep marchers in the street or on the sidewalk. And they could exercise their well-trained charm offensive, holding off a line of marchers with a friendly smile and a firm direction.

Portland didn't always have such a well-trained bicycle-mounted police force. In February 2005, I participated in my first Critical Mass ride in Portland, which was policed by officers on motorcycles, who revved closely past bike riders at high speeds and then cut them off, impeding the ride to issue infractions for often-imaginary traffic crimes. "You're just a bunch of college students," one of them sneered at me, "holding up real people from getting home from work." Several participants complained to the mayor after this experience. I was one of them, and shortly afterward found myself participating in monthly diplomatic meetings between Critical Mass participants, city representatives, and traffic police leaders. We could see no reason why Critical Mass rides required policing, but we settled for trading motorcycle officers for ones mounted on bicycles. The police grumbled, but stuck to the policy. And it's no wonder why.

At first it seemed like a win for us. The bike police were friendly and approachable, they looked us in the eye and joked with us and went after the occasional driver who sped too closely past us or committed their own infractions. It seemed like perhaps the tables had turned. Many of the officers were inexperienced riders and struggled with hills and with keeping their bikes upright when the group slowed to a crawl in order to stay together at a traffic light. We waited for them, encouraged them, gave them pointers.

The police learned quickly, and as they did the tenor of the ride changed. Officers began mingling at the beginning of the ride, passing out xeroxed fliers with cheerful memos exhorting us to obey the law. "Stay in the right lane!" officers would say impatiently as we rode, and the whole black and yellow troupe in their bulletproof vests would form a pace line to squeeze the ride into a second single-file line, right in the door zone. "Now we're turning right!" an officer would suggest, and the line of officers would see to it that this route was followed. The officers on the street and their commanders in the ongoing monthly meetings were as unfailingly polite as they were firm. The mayor, who was having political problems of his own, was silent.

The promise of Critical Mass had taken a surprising turn—anyone at all can, indeed, be a leader, if they can get the ride to follow. We followed for a few months, and though breakaway groups coordinated smaller outlier rides, these were coordinated on private email lists and most people still only heard about the police-led rides. Critical Mass stopped being any fun and by the end of 2007 people simply stopped showing up.

Years later I ran into one of the police leaders we had negotiated with and he said, "Our goal was to put a stop to Critical Mass." One day I watched several dozen officers ride by down a quiet residential street—they had come to Portland for a training in bicycle-mounted policing—and realized that Critical Mass was a valuable training ground for the police, if there ever were a mass uprising.

Fast forward to that first Occupy rally in Portland. The bicycle police were different individuals, but their training was eerily familiar. I watched as they mingled with the outskirts of the crowd, chatting and smiling and posing for photos with wide-eyed little kids. When it was time to move, they were confident on their bicycles and responded with practiced ease to the shifting demands of directing and controlling a large crowd that was, on foot, not able to respond quickly or notice that they were being herded by the friendly men and women on black Treks. We'd trained them well.

#occupybicycles!

In other cities where Critical Mass is still a regular event, kept alive both despite and because of aggressive motorized police enforcement, bikes became part of the Occupy movement right from the start. Nearly every report I read from another city's occupation included some passing mention of bicycles. In the photos and videos, there were always bikes.

Take New York City, where scrappy environmental organization Times-Up! quickly began running support for the Occupy movement. During its long history of successfully outmaneuvering police on the streets and in the courtroom, TimesUp! had learned the benefits of pervasive use of bicycle-mounted video cameras to document every moment of every ride. Thanks to Critical Mass, Occupiers already knew that a bicycle was the best way to get quickly through a crowd or a barricade or away from a police line, even while transporting something heavy, like food for hundreds of demonstrators or a mobile sound system. Logistical support for the encampment was "easier to do on a bicycle," one Occupy organizer told the Village Voice.

TimesUp! has kept Critical Mass alive for two decades, during which time it has ranged from freewheeling to embattled, sometimes tiny, sometimes huge, always with a hard New York edge of defiance. Unlike Portland, these New Yorkers weren't easily fooled by police, and the police seemed disinclined to attempt any "soft" diplomatic tactics when strategically flinging open the door of an unmarked SUV would do just as well.

The last Friday of September 2011, was less than two weeks after the Occupy encampment settled into Zuccotti Park, and Critical Mass took to the streets with renewed vigor and numbers. Most existing Occupy movements marched that night, and from Chicago and Denver as well as New York City, reports came in of successful interventions by two-wheeled marchers. In these cities, when the foot marchers became cut off or surrounded by police, the pedalers swooped in, barricading and surrounding the riot police, creating new openings for the crowd to surge through and preventing the beatings and arrests that were already starting to become the norm whenever the police and Occupy met. On two wheels, marchers could fill an entire street or instantly break apart, melting into the urban landscape to regroup later wherever they were needed. Later, when police and cyclists were in a standoff, the foot marchers got word via cell phone and crowded over to successfully break up the detente; this time it was the police who dispersed.

Late that night, the celebratory spirit of Critical Mass showed through as a bicycle-mounted sound system was pedaled to the vicinity of the Wall Street protest and a thumping, costumed sidewalk dance party ensued that lasting into the wee hours of the morning, rolling a few blocks each time police scrutiny became uncomfortable.

Bike Check! Bike Check!

In Portland, bicycles did finally come to the aid of the Occupy movement. "We need to bring Critical Mass back!" Dan Kaufman told me on the phone one day as excitement about the movement was building. He had been using his giant gold cargo tricycle, known as the "disco trike," to bring supplies to the Occupy encampment and occasionally to carry a mobile sound system along on marches. A few days later the Bike Swarm was born, the disco trike blaring in its midst. When the two dozen riders swooped, whooping, through a tense protest, shouting enthusiastic messages of support, the police line gave way.

Here is how they describe themselves:

> *We are the Occu-riders, the cavalry. We fill the streets with our wheels and our voices. We are a peaceful, convivial band of riders, reminding our fellow demonstrators to stay nonviolent, excited, and diligent. As busy bees, we can fly through downtown and protect the march with our buzzing mobility. We circle sites of civil disobedience, bring messages to and fro, and draw the interest of other Portlanders—including the agents of the empire. When not in flight, we use our bikes to form a protective honeycomb around those on foot. We ride swiftly and stand strong. We are a team. We are a tactic. How can you swarm?*

On November 17, 2011, Occupy movements all along the West Coast had a day of port blockades. I joined them with my camera, half trepidacious collaborator, half journalist. Two dozen bike swarmers met at a Portland light rail station before dawn in below freezing temperatures. We rode to the end of the line and then five miles further down an icy highway to join the protesters who were blockading several port entrances.

The spirit of joy and good-natured determination was clear among the bike swarmers from the start. Also familiar were the organizing principles. "You're in charge of this operation?" I asked Katharine Ball, who is largely given credit for founding the Bike Swarm and maintaining its energy. "Not in charge, I just help make it happen," she said.

The bike swarmers weren't the only ones taking tactics from the Critical Mass playbook. About two miles into the ride, while it was still dark, we came to our first bike lane. A group of police officers on motorcycles were waiting for us there. Lights and sirens went on immediately as we rounded the bend, and two of the riders who had not immediately fallen into single file were pulled over and issued citations for riding outside the bike lane. A hundred feet further and the sirens went on again; two more tickets were written for improper lighting, and a polite, if factually incorrect, lecture was thrown in about the legality of riding on the sidewalk. "Let's go, we can't let them stall us," said Kaufman. "Time to ride super legal." The riders who had been stopped agreed to meet us at the port, and the rest of us rode off single file. The police operation was familiar, well-practiced, and effective.

The first two terminals we came to had already been shut down; we were greeted by cheers and calls of, "Thank you, Bike Swarm!" Ball climbed up on a concrete barrier and yelled, "Bike check!" and "Bike check!" responded the swarmers. Other Occupiers, not on bikes, went about their own business around us. Across a wide parking lot, a more traditional "mic check" style public assembly was being held, each speaker's phrases amplified by repetition of the crowd. Ball announced that we would divide into two groups, one to stay and one to move on. I followed the second group, single file and watchful, to the next terminal, where the day's shipping operations had not yet been shut down. There, the Bike Swarm added their numbers to the picket line, holding their bikes in front of them as part of the material blockade.

Another contingent of bike swarmers arrived after it got light. They proved what I had been starting to expect: the primary function of Bike Swarm is to raise morale. This new group, dressed in hot pink, twirling matching batons, hoops, and streamers, turned the grim, cold blockade into a dance party, much to the approval of the volunteer medics who had been urging everyone to keep moving to stay warm.

Occupy continued throughout the winter. On January 25, Kaufman participated in Portland's edition of that day's Egyptian solidarity actions. He had stopped playing music—it had been Bob Marley, and essential in calming a tense situation—and had begun filming the march when police officers grabbed the camera from his hands, cuffed him, issued him a citation for "unlawful operation of sound equipment," and impounded the trike along with his equipment. The local media went wild for the story, and the #freediscotrike hashtag spread across Twitter. Kaufman released his video of the encounter, and the story made the front page of national political blog

Daily Kos on the same day that th Bike Swarm threatened to ride on City Hall if the disco trike was not released. The mayor intervened, and the next day the trike was freed, resulting in yet another news cycle for the story and sealing the Bike Swarm's role in the movement's history.

Back to the Future

Much as the Occupy movement has its roots in the culture of radical protest, the Bike Swarm's evolutionary ties to Critical Mass are clear, both in Portland and in Los Angeles, where a similar tactic is used. As much a celebration as it is a demonstration, both are organized in a similarly leaderless fashion, both with intrepid resourcefulness, friendly inclusive spirit, and natural, organic flow. The Bike Swarm brings speed and agility of physical movement and decision-making that the Occupy movement sometimes lacks.

But Bike Swarm also calls on new influences and new strategies. Katharine Ball told *BikePortland* that her inspiration for Bike Swarm came from Europe, where she learned of the tactic at the climate talks in Copenhagen in 2009. Perhaps the European influence is what gives the Bike Swarm its tactical edge—rather than a giant, semi-ruly parade, easy to lead but also easy to police, the Bike Swarm rides with forethought but without a predictable structure or path, and always in relation to and in support of an event or cause beyond its own very existence. Critical Mass is generally an end in itself; the Bike Swarm is a means to whatever its participants make of it.

By the same token, participation in Critical Mass is what made the Occupy movement immediately comprehensible to me, and perhaps many others. The idea of a leaderless organization, a protest that was also a celebration, a movement where people could work together despite each one having a distinct and perhaps conflicting reason for being there—and ultimately the effective, concrete demonstration of an alternate vision for society—would it have made sense without the experience of riding freely through downtown streets on the last Friday of the month?

Even among bicycle activists there is often talk of the need to move beyond Critical Mass. The Bike Swarm, along with other uses of bikes in the Occupy movement, has done that. By a different name, they take the same concept to the next level while proving critics wrong and evading the public relations snarls that beset the original. The bicycle movement, where it meets Occupy, has moved forward and risen above, bringing all the joy and energy and baggage and friction, and in ways far cooler than I could have imagined.

CM@20: Revolution in the Street

By Iain A. Boal

One summer day in the late '60s I drove with a friend across London to Camden Lock. Our destination was the Dialectics of Liberation Congress at the Roundhouse, an event that marked the full flowering—for better and worse—of the '60s counterculture in Britain. The congress described itself as, "a unique gathering to demystify human violence in all its forms, the social systems from which it emanates, and to explore new forms of action." As a very young medical student energized by the radical psychiatry movement, I was there to get a look at R.D. Laing—his *Divided Self* revealed the nuclear family as one of the main forms of human violence—but also to listen to Allen Ginsberg. My friend Hugh and I were both avid readers of the City Lights Pocket Poets.

Despite its billing as a countercultural event I can't remember any of my acquaintances that day showing up on a bicycle. I certainly did not. London, after all, was not Amsterdam. There was nothing to compare with the "White Plans" presented by the political wing of the Provo movement to the Amsterdam city council in 1965, most notoriously the "White Bicycle Plan" initiated by Luud Schimmelpenninck, which proposed the distribution of 20,000 bikes by the municipality, free for anybody to use. The vehicle I did arrive in was an open 1940s MG (Morris Garages) with leaking gaskets and a blown manifold that I soon abandoned in favor of a Morris Minor, the car of choice among Anglican curates and country midwives. I liked the MG for many of the same reasons I took pleasure in the Raleigh roadster bicycle that, in a familiar teenage rite of passage, I had recently cast aside— it was fun, stylish, open to the elements, and it took me places.

It never occurred to me then that the similarities between the Raleigh bicycle and the MG were literally built-in. Historically the "light car"—of which the wire-wheeled MG was a classic example—evolved out of the bicycle. Indeed they very often emerged from the same workshops. Young Bill Morris, who eventually rivalled Henry Ford as a global auto manufacturer, had begun as bicycle mechanic in the 1890s. If anyone had cared to ask, I would probably have said that I considered both the Raleigh and the MG as "liberation technologies," but preferred the car because it was mobility for grown-ups. Not so different, it turns out, from Hou Mingxin, a Cherokee driver and resident of Beijing, who in 2010—a year of explosive growth in road construction and automobilism across China—told the *Financial Times*, "I like the speed, I like the freedom, I can't imagine not having a car."[1]

"Speed" and "freedom of the road" were, if truth be told, values dear to many pioneering cyclists, eagerly adopted by the overlapping motoring fraternity, and shared by both communities in the face of resistance by pedestrians and other slower-moving denizens of the late Victorian street.

I would have been quite mystified if anyone had suggested that the very idea of a normal progression from bicycle to car (in London and San Francisco, if not in Amsterdam or the *jhoggies* of Delhi) was a pertinent topic for the Dialectics of Liberation Congress, specifically its relation to "human violence [and] the social systems from which it emanates..."

I thought of all this at a recent anniversary gathering in London convened by veterans of the counterculture. "Dialektikon 2012" involved the re-enacting of several key speeches delivered at the original Congress—by Stokely Carmichael, Herbert Marcuse, R.D. Laing, and Paul Goodman. It was, however, the remarks of Gregory Bateson that left the deepest impression. The audience (at the re-enactment, that is) was palpably taken aback by the uncanny resonance of Bateson's warning about environmental catastrophe. He had clearly grasped the twofold character of the crisis, by linking capital and nature together in a single nexus. He spoke concretely of the imminence of a likely five degree celsius rise in global temperature and the inundation of coastal civilization. More importantly he did so in relation to commodity culture and the logic of endless accumulation within capitalist society. Several in the audience expressed shock at Bateson's "prescience"—as if there was something uncanny about his foresight, or that he was somehow ahead of his time. A comforting illusion. The reality is that the greenhouse effect was public knowledge by the 1960s. (It was first theorized as long ago as the 1890s by the Swedish physical chemist Svante Arrhenius.) In that sense we have indeed "lost" at least forty years in the struggle for a habitable world.

Four decades on, the response by the global powers to the prospects of mass extinction and a biblical cataclysm that will make Noah's flood look like a minor plumbing problem has a zombie-like quality. They have no Plan B. At the COP15 climate talks in 2009, capitalism was tacitly acknowledged by its managers to be unreformable, and it was confirmed in Cancun a year later. On offer is a ghoulash of projected techno-fixes and the commodification of the atmosphere in the bifurcated form of a perverse trade in pollution licenses and a dysfunctional market in carbon.

In the patchwork of so-called "green solutions," bicycles have caught the attention of neoliberal city planners and politicians as one remedy for air pollution and congested roads. But the result is for the most part half-baked, even dangerous, gesturing—for example, "bike lanes" guaranteed to put obedient cyclists in the path of car doors and storm grates. Experienced riders are well aware that they are often more at risk in dedicated cycle lanes than taking their chances in traffic.

In the run up to the 2012 London Olympics, bicycles have been touted by the authorities as a means of relieving entirely predictable gridlock during the weeks of the games. Not however to the point of being allowed on the special routes across the capital which will be privatized and reserved for limousines ferrying the "Olympic Family" of athletes, officials and sponsors. Trespassing cyclists, it has been announced, will be fined $300.

There has been considerable hoopla over the capital's new bike scheme. Since the summer of 2010, a fleet of clunky, theft-resistant rental bikes have become a familiar sight on the streets of Central London. Erratic visitors and occasional local riders pay for the privilege of advertising the scheme's corporate sponsor as they ride around the city. Mini-billboards, integrated with the rear mudguard, display the cerulean blue livery of Barclays Bank. The bikes are free for the first half hour, then the tariff rises steeply, reaching $80 for 24 hours, with a $250 fee for late returns. London's municipal bike scheme (dubbed "Boris bikes," for Boris Johnson, the current mayor) is to neoliberalism what Amsterdam's White Bike Plan is to anarchism.

Boris bikers, in addition to the possibility of an expensive ride, are often the object of hostility not only from motorists but also a growing tribe of commuting cyclists who reveal themselves—by their spine angle, posture, and aggressivity—to be locked in the very logic of the automobilism they affect to oppose. The antagonism between this breed of cyclist and car drivers may be genuine but they share an ethos as remote from the spirit of the Provos as the Boris bike. What the speeding commuter on two wheels also shares with the motorist moving at 20 miles an hour is a structural antagonism to pedestrians. Structural, that is, because "cyclist" and "car driver" describe in this scenario not an identity but a condition—namely, the condition of moving at speed with respect to pedestrians. (With different momenta, to be sure—a fact which has important implications "in the event of an accident," as they say.) There is nothing essential, nothing congenital about being a "cyclist" or a "driver"; they may of course become internalized or projected outwards as identities, but they are historical and contingent. It should be remembered that when the very first bicycles made their appearance on the streets of Europe in the second decade of the 19th century, they were regarded as an illegitimate and dangerous nuisance by city dwellers who mobilized successfully to have them banned by municipal ordinance, just as the early motor cars were likewise perceived as illegitimate and dangerous intruders into urban space.

Motorists first had to challenge customary understandings about sharing that space, as well as the rhythms and modes of movement in and through it. Once the motor car's right to a place in the streets was established, the restrictive speed limits on such vehicles (as low as four miles an hour) had to be abolished before traffic and highway engineers could get to work remaking the modern city in the motorist's image. And then paving the planet. Hegemony was established when all other users (and uses) of the street—human and animal—were marginalized, banned, or subordinated to the imperatives of automobilism, and the carnage on the roads accepted as normal.

Yet our brief glimpse into this history points to the tangled complexities, and complicities, of the cyclist's relationship to the motorist, and of both to their machinery and to other users of urban space. It shows, for one thing, that there are no "liberation technologies" as such. The bicycle is no exception, any more than the computer is, even if the one has titanium components and a fixed wheel and the other can be shrunk from a Cold War behemoth of soul murder and alienation into a handy, smart, personalized tool. Just ask the rickshaw-puller working sixteen hours a day and sleeping on his "fixie" or the data-entry neo-slave bound to their PC with a full bladder and digital palsy.

Of all modernity's artifacts, the motor car retains, despite its clear enslavements, the reputation as a "liberation technology" *par excellence*. We have noted how the domination of contemporary life by car culture, which was more or less complete—at least in the global North—by the middle of the 20th century, first required a revolution in the street. To underestimate that revolution, and the profound changes in the tempo and patterns of daily life and in forms of human settlement and sociability, is just one further measure of its triumph.

It has been the great achievement of Critical Mass to make visible some major ramifications of that revolution. Without the *mass*, without the celebrants coming together as one collective body (sort of), in motion, in the street, the *critique* would not only be blind to the true depth and taken-for-grantedness of the spatial order, but would not have had the power to offend. The intensity and the occasional violence of the responses to these peaceable human-powered processions has revealed, like nothing else, how thoroughly automobilism structures daily life, and has penetrated the psyche of modern subjects. By challenging the traffic norms and exposing the arbitrary nature of arrangements in modern cities, Critical Mass has the effect of rendering the domination of the motor car a less than natural thing. It is, in other words, a form of ideology critique—at least, that is, for the duration of a ride which acts as a kind of rolling consciousness-raiser for all who happen to be in the vicinity. In the same way, the San Francisco freeway revolt of the 1960s afforded the first serious challenge to the power of the highway engineer, because it made room to reimagine the city beyond the agenda of Bechtel, General Motors, and Chevron.

Nevertheless, the twenty first century is poised to witness the culminating triumph of the highway engineer and the traffic bureaucrat. The furious buildout of the road network in China, the criminalization of the cargo rickshaws in India, the sacrifice of street life on the altar of circulation—this juggernaut rolls on, even as the social and environmental catastrophe of automobilism becomes undeniable.

It is therefore the urgent and historic task of the Critical Mass network worldwide to mobilize consciously against the clearances and destruction of life not yet dominated by the logic of commodities in circulation. That is, to prevent the completion of the (counter)revolution begun a hundred years ago by the agents of "motordom," as they dubbed themselves.

This is no Friday night exercise. It will mean more than rolling occupations of the street every month. There is pride in reflecting, on the twentieth anniversary of Critical Mass, that the home of the movement can draw upon deep reservoirs of antinomian energy. They will surely be needed in the common project of building an ample life in common, South and North, beyond the wasteland. Above all, by linking the movement in the streets to the movement in the squares.

Notes

1   "China embraces freedom of the road," April 23, 2010, *http://www.ft.com/frontpage*

This essay draws on The Green Machine *(London: Notting Hill Editions, 2012).*